A DICTIONARY OF
RELIGIOUS
& SPIRITUAL
Quotations

A DICTIONARY OF
RELIGIOUS & SPIRITUAL
Quotations

Compiled by
GEOFFREY PARRINDER

SIMON & SCHUSTER

New York   London   Toronto   Sydney   Tokyo   Singapore

First published 1989
by Routledge
11 New Fetter Lane, London EC4P 4EE

and in the USA by
Academic Reference Division
Simon & Schuster
15 Columbus Circle
New York, NY 10023

Library of Congress Cataloging-in-Publication Data

Parrinder, Geoffrey.
A dictionary of religious and spiritual quotations / compiled by
Geoffrey Parrinder.
p.   cm.
ISBN 0-13-210121-1
1. Religion—Quotations, maxims, etc.   2. Spiritual life—
Quotations, maxims, etc.   I. Title.
PN6084.R3P37   1990
200—dc20   90-33251
                                                       CIP

CONTENTS

PREFACE

Religious literature is the most extensive in the world, going back over more than three millenia. It would be impossible to include all important statements in a book of 3,000 quotations, even if it were limited to the Judeo-Christian tradition. *The Oxford Dictionary of Quotations* has over 2,000 references from the Bible alone, including the Psalms from the Book of Common Prayer.

This dictionary aims at being comprehensive and selective, ancient and modern. In these days there is a wider knowledge of many religions, east and west, than ever before and it would be parochial to ignore the great religious literatures of Asia, though reference depends upon translations and availability. But free use has been made of the Koran and other Islamic writings, Zoroastrian Gathas, Hindu Vedas, Upanishads and Bhagavad Gita, Sikh Adi Granth, Buddhist Dhammapada and Nikayas, and Chinese Tao Te Ching and Confucian Analects.

It will be seen that the material has not been arranged alphabetically, by author or subject, but under 177 topic headings arranged under 18 section headings, with illustrations from major traditions and later writers. Here the Bible presents a peculiar problem. Its contributions, if fully used, would far outweigh all the rest, because of its familiarity and diversity. So the solution adopted has been to select under nearly every heading only one quotation from the Hebrew Bible (Old Testament) and one from the New Testament. That many other appropriate biblical texts might have been included is obvious, but they would have swamped the book and destroyed its balance. There are plenty of Bible concordances and reference books available if there is need to track down a half-remembered verse, but under the topics listed here simply specimen texts are given. Quotations are from the Authorized (King James) Version, as familiar, memorable and the best English, with occasional use of the Revised Version (RV) or Revised Standard Version (RSV).

Frequent quotation is made from the Jewish Mishnah, the basis of the Talmud, and from the Koran whose breadth of interest is noteworthy, and then there are many quotations from Christian and other writers, old and new.

English literature has been widely drawn on and the most quoted author, Shakespeare, if not narrowly religious, is profound and memorable. Religion, as the first topic reveals, can be defined in many and even contradictory ways and here the broadest definitions are followed, the ideas and ideals which guide life.

Many modern writers are included, theologians and anthropologists, novelists and poets, believers and sceptics. Even in our own time there is such a vast array of religious reference that no volume could hope to be all-inclusive.

This book is not a source for every needed religious verse or saying. Many popular lines will be found, but others have been elbowed out for lack of space. On the other hand, the aim is to be useful, both to the general reader checking and browsing through religious statements, and to specialist writers or speakers seeking a collection of views on one topic or another. With such a wide range through the religious literature of the world this book may be claimed as unique.

In addition to the list of topics under the heading of Contents, further guidance may be obtained from the Subject Index. This provides keywords to help in tracing a reference or, as often in such works, to suggest other words and themes and encourage wider reading.

References to publications have been provided throughout and dates usually refer to the first appearance in the original language. In ancient texts precision is hard to come by and often reference is to the nearest century, or even three or five centuries. Suggestions have been made, though they may sometimes be debatable, to indicate the general period of the writing. Dates have been given as CE, Common Era (or AD), and BCE, Before the Common Era (or BC).

The most frequently quoted sources have not been dated but here are some general indications. The Hebrew Bible ranges through the first millenium BCE, and the Christian New Testament mostly in the first century CE. The Mishnah is post-biblical, leading up to the Talmuds of 400–500 CE. The Koran (Qur'ān) was committed to writing in the seventh century CE.

Estimates for the composition (and much later writing) of the Hindu classical texts vary greatly: the Vedas perhaps around the first millenium BCE; Brahmanas, Upanishads and Laws of Manu between 800 and 300; the epic Mahabharata which includes the Bhagavad Gita about 400–100, and the Ramayana epic somewhat later; the Sankhya-karika and Yajnavalkya lawbook about the fourth century CE, and the Pancha-tantra tales later.

The enlightened Buddhist emperor Ashoka, with his pillar and rock inscriptions, provided dating for his reign, 269–32 BCE, and sayings of the Buddha must have been uttered before these dates though they were doubtless recorded and enlarged later. The Nikayas, 'collections', Digha, Samyutta and Majjhima, may have been written down from the third century BCE. The Mahavastu and Ashta-Sahasrika perhaps come from the turn of the eras. The mystical Buddhist poet Shanti-deva lived in the seventh century CE.

Similarly the Sutras of the Indian Jain religion, Acharanga, Kalpa, Kritanga and Uttara-dhyayana, have been dated from the third century BCE. Tamil

Quatrains come from about the sixth century CE, Jinabhadra in the seventh and Hemachandra in the twelfth centuries.

Opinions have differed vastly over the dates of the Gathas of Zoroaster or Zarathushtra, from the sixth to the sixteenth centuries BCE, but now there seems to be agreement for about the times of the early Vedas. Later Zoroastrian liturgical and philosophical texts, Denkart, Bundahishn, Menok i Khrat and Shikand Gumani Vazar have been placed from the sixth to ninth centuries CE.

Chinese texts are, at first sight, more straightforward. Confucius is said to have lived from 551 to 479 BCE, but not even all the brief Analects can be safely attributed to him, and even less of the Classics for which tradition gave him credit. The Lao Tzu or Tao Te Ching was perhaps produced by an 'anonymous Quietist' about 240 BCE, and other Confucian and Taoist works may be dated within a century or two. The Japanese Kojiki and Nihongi were written down early in the eighth century CE.

Sikh texts are much later, coming from the known dates of the ten Gurus beginning with the first of them, Guru Nanak, 1469–1539 CE.

Definite or approximate dates are suggested in the text for Greek and Latin authors, except for the most quoted: Plato lived from 420 to 347 BCE, and Aristotle from 384 to 322 BCE.

Modern works are usually fairly easily dated. The Book of Common Prayer in its familiar form comes from 1662 and its Articles of Religion from 1571. Shakespearean scholars differ over the times of publication of his writings, but the plays must have been composed between 1580 and his death in 1616.

This dictionary is a book to browse in, as well as a source for particular references and subjects. I wish the reader as much joy in its perusal as there has been in its compilation.

GEOFFREY PARRINDER

INTRODUCTION

1 WHAT IS RELIGION?

1 Pure religion and undefiled before God and the Father is this. To visit the fatherless and widows in their affliction, and to keep oneself unspotted from the world.
Epistle of James, 1, 27

2 Religion . . . means the voluntary subjection of oneself to God.
The Catholic Encyclopedia, XII (1913)

3 Verily *the* religion in the sight of God is Islam [submission]; and those to whom the Book has been given did not differ until after the knowledge had come to them, out of jealousy among themselves.
Koran, 3, 17

4 The Good Religion is Innate Wisdom, reason; and the forms and virtues of Innate Wisdom . . . are begotten of the Good Mind and the Bounteous Spirit.
Denkart, 117 (9th century)

5 Of all Religions this is the best Religion, To utter the Holy name with adoration, and to do good deeds.
Hymns of Guru Arjan Dev, *Astapada*, 3 (16th century)

6 Nor is religion manifold, because there are various sects and heresies in the world. When I mention religion, I mean the Christian religion; and not only the Christian religion, but the Protestant religion, and not only the Protestant religion but the Church of England.
Henry Fielding, *Tom Jones*, iii, 3 (1748)

7 My country is the world, and my religion is to do good.
Tom Paine, *The Rights of Man*, ii, 5 (1792)

8 The true meaning of religion is thus not simply morality, but morality touched by emotion.
Matthew Arnold, *Literature and Dogma* (1873)

9 Religion is so great a thing that it is right that those who will not take the trouble to seek it, if it be obscure, should be deprived of it.
Blaise Pascal, *Pensées* (1670)

10 Religion either makes men wise and virtuous, or it makes them set up false pretences to both.
William Hazlitt, *The Round Table* (1817)

11 Even the weakest disputant is made so conceited by what he calls religion, as to think himself wiser than the wisest who thinks differently from him.
Walter Savage Landor, *Imaginary Conversations* (1824–9)

12 *Religion*, n. A daughter of Hope and Fear, explaining to Ignorance the nature of the Unknowable.
Ambrose Bierce, *The Devil's Dictionary* (1911)

13 The old religionist cries out for his God. The new religionist cries out for some god to be his.
G.K. Chesterton, *All Things Considered* (1908)

14 There is only one religion, though there are a hundred versions of it.
George Bernard Shaw, *Arms and the Man* (1894)

15 One's religion is whatever he is most interested in.
J.M. Barrie, *The Twelve-Pound Look* (1910)

16 One man finds in religion his literature and his science, another finds in it his joy and his duty.
Joseph Joubert, *Pensées* (1842)

17 Religion is the sob of the oppressed creature, the heart of a heartless world, and the soul of soulless conditions. It is the Opium of the People.
Karl Marx, *Critique of Hegel's Philosophy of Right* (1844)

18 Throughout this treatise the term Religion will be used to express that state of complete harmony peculiar to human life.
Auguste Comte, *Système de politique positive* (1851)

19 Religion is what the individual does with his own solitariness.
A.N. Whitehead, *Religion in the Making* (1926)

20 Religion is not a thing alien to us. It has to be evolved out of us. It is always within us: with some consciously so; with others, quite unconsciously. But it is always there.
M.K. Gandhi, quoted by C.F. Andrews, *Mahatma Gandhi's Ideas* (1929)

21 So long as religion is only faith and outward form, and the religious function is not experienced in our own souls, nothing of any importance has happened.
C.G. Jung, *Psychology and Alchemy* (1953)

22 In the peasant's world there is no room for reason, religion, and history. There is no room for religion, because to them everything participates in divinity.
Carlo Levi, *Christ Stopped at Eboli* (1947)

23 Religion in so far as it is a source of consolation is a hindrance to true faith.
Simone Weil, *Notebooks*, i (1956)

24 Religion is unbelief. It is a concern, indeed we must say that it is the one great concern of godless man . . . It is the attempted replacement of a divine work by a human manufacture.
Karl Barth, *Church Dogmatics*, I, xvii (1936)

25 We are moving towards a completely religionless time; people as they are now simply cannot be religious any more.
Dietrich Bonhoeffer, *Letters and Papers from Prison* (1953)

26 It seems best to fall back at once on this essential source, and simply to claim, as a minimum definition of Religion, the belief in Spiritual Beings.
Edward B. Tylor, *Primitive Culture* (1871)

27 A religion is a unified system of beliefs, and practices relative to sacred things, that is to say, things set apart and forbidden – beliefs and practices which unite, into one single moral community called a church, all those who adhere to them.
Emile Durkheim, *The Elementary Forms of the Religious Life* (1915)

28 If religion is essentially of the inner life, it follows that it can be truly grasped only from within. But beyond a doubt, this can be better done by one in whose inward consciousness an experience of religion plays a part. There is but too much danger that the other [non-believer] will talk of religion as a blind man might of colours, or one totally devoid of ear, of a beautiful musical composition.
Wilhelm Schmidt, *The Origin and Growth of Religion* (1931)

29 We, as heirs to the somewhat chaotic developments, commonly employ the term religion in four quite distinct senses . . . First, there is the sense of a personal piety . . . Secondly and thirdly, there is the usage which refers to an overt system, whether of beliefs, practices, values, or whatever . . . Finally, there is 'religion' as a generic summation, 'religion in general' . . . My own suggestion is that the word, and the concepts, should be dropped — at least in all but the first, personalist, sense.
Wilfred Cantwell Smith, *The Meaning and End of Religion* (1964)

2 THE ORIGINS OF RELIGION
See also 9. ANIMISM, 10. TOTEMISM

1 There is nothing more ancient in the world than language. The history of man begins, not with rude flints, rock temples or

pyramids, but with language.

The second stage is represented by myths as the first attempt at translating the phenomena of nature into thought.

The third stage is that of religion or the recognition of moral powers, and in the end of One Moral Power behind and above all nature.

Max Müller, *Science of Mythology* (1897)

2 With all due diffidence, then, I would suggest that a tardy recognition of the inherent falsehood and barrenness of magic set the more thoughtful part of mankind to cast about for a truer theory of nature and a more fruitful method of turning her resources to account . . . In this, or some such way as this, the deeper minds may be conceived to have made the great transition from magic to religion.

J.G. Frazer, *The Golden Bough* (1890)

3 In a general way a society has all that is necessary to arouse the sensation of the divine in minds, merely by the power that it has over them, for to its members it is what a god is to his worshippers.

Emile Durkheim, *The Elementary Forms of the Religious Life* (1913)

4 When we consider all the data brought forward in our earlier chapters to show the existence of monotheism among men with the oldest and most primitive cultures, we cannot for a moment doubt that if we go back still further than these cultures, to the common religion of primeval humanity, we shall find man's faith, obedience and worship entirely directed towards the one great dominant figure of the Supreme Being.

Wilhelm Schmidt, *The Origin and Growth of Religion* (1931)

5 The origin of religion . . . the belief in spiritual beings appears among all low races with whom we have attained to thoroughly intimate acquaintance.

Edward B. Tylor, *Primitive Culture* (1871)

6 Using the phrase ancestor-worship in its broadest sense as comprehending all worship of the dead, be they of the same blood or not, we reach the conclusion that ancestor-worship is the root of every religion.

Herbert Spencer, *The Principles of Sociology* (1882)

7 The theorist who believes in ancestor-worship as the key of all the creeds will see in Jehovah a developed ancestral ghost, or a kind of fetish-god, attached to a stone — perhaps an ancient sepulchral stele of some desert sheikh. The exclusive admirer of the hypothesis of Totemism will find evidence for his belief in worship of the golden calf and the bulls. The partisan of nature-worship will insist on Jehovah's connection with storm, thunder, and the fire of Sinai.

Andrew Lang, *The Making of Religion* (1898)

8 All evolutionary schemes of religion, without exception, in the determination of the primordium and the serial stages of alleged development, proceed upon a purely arbitrary and uncontrolled basis.

Frederick Schleiter, *Religion and Culture* (1919)

9 The idea of ghosts inevitably — Spencer's favourite word — develops into that of Gods, the ghosts of remote ancestors or of superior persons becoming divinities . . . It is a fine example of the introspectionist psychologist's, or 'if I were a horse', fallacy . . . If Spencer were living in primitive conditions, those would, he assumed, have been the steps by which he would have reached the beliefs which primitives hold.

E.E. Evans-Pritchard, *Theories of Primitive Religion* (1965)

10 I want to state the conclusion that the beginnings of religion, ethics, society, and art meet in the Oedipus complex.

Sigmund Freud, *Totem and Taboo* (1913)

11 Western scholarship spent almost a century in working out a number of hypothetical reconstructions of the 'origin and development' of primitive religions. Sooner or later all these labors became obsolete, and today they are relevant only for the history of the Western mind.

Mircea Eliade, *Australian Religions* (1973)

12 Notwithstanding their radical differences, these ideologies have two things in common: 1. their obsession with the *origin* and the *beginnings* of religions; 2. their taking for granted that the beginning was something 'simple and pure'. Of course, the evolutionists and the romantic-decadentists understood quite differently this primordial simplicity. For the evolutionists, 'simple' meant *elementary*, that is, something very

near animal behavior. For the romantic-decadentists, the primitive simplicity was either a form of spiritual plenitude and perfection (Lang, Schmidt) or the naive simplicity of the Noble Savage before his corruption and degeneration brought on by civilization (Rousseau, Enlightenment).
Mircea Eliade, *Australian Religions* (1973)

13 The test of a religion or philosophy is the number of things it can explain.
R.W. Emerson, *Journals* (1836)

14 Religion is the reaction of human nature to its search for God.
A.N. Whitehead, *Science and the Modern World* (1925)

I
RELIGIOUS FORMS

3 NON-SCRIPTURAL RELIGIONS

1 All men by nature were but vain who had no perception of God.
Wisdom, 13, 1

2 When the Gentiles, which have not the Law, do by nature the things contained in the Law, these, having not the Law, are a law unto themselves.
Romans, 2, 14

3 We raised up in every community a messenger, with the message: Serve God and avoid idolatry. Some of them there were whom God guided, and some there were upon whom error was justly laid.
Koran, 16, 38

4 Savage religion is something not so much thought out as danced out.
R.R. Marett, *The Threshold of Religion* (1909)

5 Pre-logical, applied to primitive mentality, means simply that it does not go out of its way, as we do, to avoid contradiction. It does not have always present the same logical requirements. What to our eyes is impossible or absurd it often accepts without seeing any difficulty involved.
Lucien Lévy-Bruhl, *Primitive Mentality* (1923)

6 The reality in which primitives move is itself mystical. Not a being, not an object, not a natural phenomenon in their collective representations is what it appears to us.
Lucien Lévy-Bruhl, *How Natives Think* (1926)

7 It is a remarkable fact that none of the anthropologists whose theories about primitive religion have been most influential had ever been near a primitive people. It is as though a chemist had never thought it necessary to enter a laboratory. They had consequently to rely for their information on what European explorers, missionaries, administrators, and traders told them.
E.E. Evans-Pritchard, *Theories of Primitive Religion* (1965)

8 The 'evolutionist' scholars (Spencer, Frazer, Hartland, and others) were convinced of the impossibility of a genuinely high religious conception among the Australian aborigines, for they were convinced of the aborigines' mental and spiritual inferiority.
Mircea Eliade, *Australian Religions* (1973)

9 Among the Brobdignacians when a man meets his mother-in-law, the two abuse each other and each retires with a black eye . . .
In old Caledonia when a native accidentally finds a whisky bottle by the road-side he empties it at one gulp after which he proceeds immediately to look for another.
Bronislaw Malinowski, *Crime and Custom in Savage Society* (1926)

10 The Samoan background which makes growing up so easy, so simple a matter, is the general casualness of the whole society . . . Neither poverty nor great disasters threaten the people to make them hold their lives dearly and tremble for continued existence. No implacable gods, swift to anger and strong to punish, disturb the even tenor of their days.
Margaret Mead, *Coming of Age in Samoa* (1928)

11 The ancient Samoans, then, quite contrary to Mead's assertions, were a highly religious people with a system of religion . . . [including] belief in a pantheon of spirits and gods, culminating in the supreme creator god, Tagaloa.
Derek Freeman, *Margaret Mead and Samoa, The Making and Unmaking of an Anthropological Myth* (1983)

12 There still lingers the idea that mental stress and mental illness are the prerogative of 'over-civilised' societies: that the simple savage may have Ancylostomiasis but cannot have Anxiety: that he may, in his innocence, believe his neighbour to be making bad magic against him, but he still sleeps like a top. Nothing could be further from the truth.
Margaret J. Field, *Search for Security* (1960)

13 Nothing justifies the supposition that, during the hundreds of thousands of years that preceded the earliest Stone Age, humanity did not have a religious life as intense and as various as in the succeeding periods.
Mircea Eliade, *Shamanism, Archaic Techniques of Ecstasy* (1964)

14 Victorian and Edwardian scholars were intensely interested in religions of rude peoples, largely, I suppose, because they faced a crisis in their own . . . Laymen may not be aware that most of what has been written in the past, and with some assurance, and is still trotted out in colleges and universities, about animism, totemism, magic, &c., has been shown to be erroneous or at least dubious.
E.E. Evans-Pritchard, *Theories of Primitive Religion* (1965)

---

4 HISTORICAL RELIGIONS

---

1 I am the God of thy father, the God of Abraham, the God of Isaac, and the God of Jacob.
Exodus, 3, 6

2 God, who at sundry times and in divers manners, spake in time past unto the fathers by the prophets, hath in these last days spoken unto us by his Son.
Hebrews, 1, 1–2

3 He is the reason [Logos], in which every race of men did share. Thus those who lived with reason are Christians even if they were counted godless, as of the Greeks, Socrates, Heraclitus, and others like them.
Justin Martyr, *Apology*, i, 5 (2nd century)

4 We have believed in God and what has been sent down to us, and what has been sent down to Abraham and Ishmael and Isaac and Jacob and the Patriarchs, and what has been given to Moses and Jesus, and what has been given to the prophets from their Lord, making no distinction between any of them.
Koran, 2, 130

5 The best possession of Zarathustra Spitama has been revealed: It is that the Wise Lord has granted, through the Right, eternal bliss to him and to all those who have observed and practised the words and deeds of his good religion.
Gathas, *Yasna*, 53, 1

6 I proclaimed this Yoga to Vivasvant, it is eternal. Vivasvant told it to Manu, Manu spoke it to Ikshvaku. Thus in line of succession the royal seers knew it . . . and this same ancient Yoga is proclaimed to you by Me today.
Bhagavad Gita, 4, 1–3

7 It is now ninety-one aeons ago, brethren, since Vipassi, the Exalted One, Arahant, Buddha Supreme, arose in the world. It is now thirty-one aeons ago, brethren, since Sikhi, the Exalted One, Arahant, Buddha Supreme, arose in the world . . . It is in this auspicious aeon, brethren, that now I, an Arahant, Buddha Supreme, have arisen in the world.
Mahapadana Suttanta, 2 (4th–1st centuries BCE)

8 The Master said, I have transmitted what was taught to me, without making up anything of my own. I have been faithful to and loved the Ancients.
Confucius, *Analects*, 7, 1

9 Tao gave them birth; the power of Tao reared them, shaped them according to their kinds, perfected them, giving to each its strength.
Therefore of the ten thousand things there is not one that does not worship Tao and do homage to its power.
Tao Te Ching, LI

10 Says Kabir, I have told them
and so have Brahma and Mahesh —
Ram's Name is the essence of Reality;
such is my teaching for all!
Sākhī, 3, 26 in Charlotte Vaudeville, *Kabīr*
(1974)

11 The Vedas proclaim him, So do the readers
        of the Puranas;
the learned speak of him in many
        discourses;
Brahma and Indra speak of him,
Shivas speak of him, Siddhas speak of him,
The Buddhas he has created, proclaim him.
Hymns of Guru Nanak (Adi Granth), *amul
gun* (16th century)

5 MONOTHEISM
See also 20. GOD

1 Hear, O Israel: The LORD our God is one
LORD.
Deuteronomy, 6, 4

2 Well, Master, thou hast said the truth: for
there is one God, and there is none other but
he.
Mark, 12, 32

3 They were commanded simply to serve God,
making him the exclusive object of religion,
as monotheists.
Koran, 98, 4

4 This God is one. He is not two nor more
than two, but one. None of the things
existing in the universe to which the term
one is applied is like unto his unity.
Moses Maimonides, *Mishneh Torah*
(1170–80)

5 That which is One the sages speak of in
various terms; they call it Fire, Death, Wind.
Rig Veda, 1, 164, 46

6 This is a natural attribute of Buddhas that
only one Buddha at a time appears in the
world. For what reason? Because of the
greatness of the qualities of the all-knowing
Buddhas. Of other things also which are
great in the world, there is in each case one
only to be found. There is one great earth
only, one great ocean, one great
world-mountain. Wherever any of these
arise, there is no room for a second.
Milinda's Questions, 239 (1st century
BCE–1st century CE)

7 To make the World God, is to make all; and
therefore this Kind of Monotheism of the
Heathen is as rank Atheism as their
Polytheism was proved to be before.
Henry More. *An Explanation of the Grand
Mystery of Godliness* (1660)

8 What we find among uncivilized peoples is
not monotheism in its historically legitimate
sense, but the idea of a Supreme Being, and
the erroneous identification, the misleading
assimilation, of this idea to true
monotheism can give rise only to
misunderstandings.
Raffaele Pettazzoni, *Essays on the History
of Religions* (1954)

9 A theistic religion need not be either
monotheistic or polytheistic. It may be both.
It is a question of the level, or situation, of
thought rather than of exclusive types of
thought. On one level Nuer religion may be
regarded as monotheistic, at another level as
polytheistic, and it can also be regarded at
other levels as totemistic or fetishistic.
E.E. Evans-Pritchard, *Nuer Religion* (1956)

10 When the missionary speaks of God as
ndina, he means that all other gods are
non-existent. The native understands that
He is the only effective, reliable god; the
others may be effective at times, but are not
to be depended upon.
A.M. Hocart, *Man*, 'Mana' (1914)

11 The latter form of faith, the belief in One
God, is properly called monotheism,
whereas the term of henotheism would best
express the faith in a single god.
Max Müller, *Semitic Monotheism* (1860)

12 If Christianity claims to be a monotheism, it
becomes unavoidable to assume the
opposites as being contained in God.
C.G. Jung, *Psychology and Religion* (1958)

13 The One remains, the many change and
        pass;
Heaven's light forever shines, Earth's
        shadows fly;
Life, like a dome of many-coloured glass,
Stains the white radiance of Eternity.
Percy Bysshe Shelley, *Adonais* (1821)

14 The One who, himself without colour, by
        the manifold application of his
        power
Distributes many colours in his hidden
        purpose,

And into whom, its end and its beginning,
    the whole world dissolves —
He is God.
Shvetashvatara Upanishad, 4, 1

6 POLYTHEISM
See also 21. GODS

1 All the gods of the nations are idols: but the
LORD made the heavens.
Psalm, 96, 5

2 Though there be that are called gods,
whether in heaven or in earth, (as there be
gods many, and lords many) But to us there
is but one God the Father, of whom are all
things, and we in him; and one Lord Jesus
Christ.
1 Corinthians, 8, 5–6

3 It is not for the prophet nor for those who
have believed to pray for pardon for the
polytheists, even though they be near of kin.
Koran, 9, 114

4 How many gods are there? . . . As many as
    are mentioned in the Hymn to All
    the Gods, namely, three hundred
    and three, and three thousand and
    three . . .
Which is the one god?
Breath, said he. They call him Brahman,
    That.
Brihad-aranyaka Upanishad, 3, 9

5 An exchanged Polytheism in worshipping of
Saints, Images, and the Host.
Samuel Purchas, *Purchas his Pilgrimage*
(1613)

6 How various, how loose, and how uncertain
were the religious sentiments of Polytheists.
They were abandoned, almost without
control, to the natural workings of a
superstitious fancy.
Edward Gibbon, *The History of the Decline
and Fall of the Roman Empire,* 15 (1776)

7 Among all nations, through the darkest
polytheism glimmer some faint sparks of
monotheism.
Immanuel Kant, *Critique of Pure Reason,* II,
iii (1781)

8 Polytheism Proper has always gone with
great progress in material civilization and
with very remarkable advance in mental
culture.
John Oman, *The Natural and the
Supernatural* (1931)

9 Practical polytheism has . . . shown itself
well satisfied with a universe composed of
many original principles, provided we be
allowed to believe that the divine principle
remains supreme, and that others are
subordinate.
William James, *The Varieties of Religious
Experience* (1902)

10 It would be useful to devise a term which
would denote religions that have a supreme
God and also worship other gods.
Geoffrey Parrinder, *Religion in an African
City* (1953)

11 For the purpose of a descriptive label, we
would like to suggest such a startling thing
as 'Diffused Monotheism' . . . in which the
good Deity delegates certain portions of His
authority to certain divine functionaries
who work as they are commissioned by
Him.
E. Bolaji Idowu, *Olódùmarè, God in
Yoruba Belief* (1962)

12 If we say that in spite of the many different
spirits Spirit is one and that Nuer religion is
in this sense monotheistic we have to add
that it is also modalistic. Spirit, though one,
is differently thought of with regard to
different effects and relations.
E.E. Evans-Pritchard, *Nuer Religion* (1956)

13 Neither the religions called 'primitive' nor
those classed as polytheistic are ignorant of
the idea of a God who is the Creator,
omniscient and all-powerful.
Mircea Eliade, *Myths, Dreams and
Mysteries* (1960)

7 DUALISM — TWIN GODS

1 Now at the beginning the twin spirits have
declared their nature, the better and the evil,
in thought and word and deed . . . And
when these two spirits came together, in the
beginning they established life and non-life.
Gathas, *Yasna,* 30

2 The reason and occasion for the wise
activity of the Creator which is exemplified

in the creative act is the existence of an
Adversary.
Shikand Gumani Vazar, 8, 39–40 (9th
century)

3 Though the fundamental dualist tenet that a
good God could not be responsible for evil
was never disputed, there did exist in
Sassanian times a sect which sought to
derive the two principles of good and evil
themselves from a common non-moral and
androgynous father who was Infinite Time.
This heterodox sect is conventionally called
'Zervanite' because *Zurvān* is the Pahlavī
name for the Genius of Time.
R.C. Zaehner, *The Teachings of the Magi*
(1956)

4 In affirming that evil had an independent
existence and is co-eternal with God, the
Manicheans provided a ready answer to the
problem of theodicy.
Samuel N.C. Lieu, *Manichaeism* (1985)

5 He is the great and highest good and it is he
who made all the lesser goods, but both the
Creator and the created things are all good.
Whence then is evil?
Augustine of Hippo, *Confessions*, VII, v, 7
(5th century)

6 The nearest approach in Judaism to such a
dualistic notion is found in the Lurianic
kabbalah, with its concept of the 'other side'
(*sitra achra*), the dark and the demonic
realm which is said to be the result of God's
'self-contraction'.
David J. Goldberg and John D. Rayner, *The
Jewish People* (1987)

7 I would be inclined to denominate those
who implicitly acquiesce in the primitive
duality as given in Consciousness, the
Natural Realists or Natural Dualists.
William Hamilton, *Metaphysics* (1836)

8 The combined essences of heaven and earth
became the Yin and Yang, the concentrated
essences of the Yin and Yang became the
four seasons.
Huai-nan Tzu, 3, 1 (2nd century BCE)

9 The Great Ultimate through movement
generates the Yang. When its activity
reaches its limit, it becomes tranquil.
Through tranquillity the Great Ultimate
generates the Yin. When tranquillity reaches
its limit, activity begins again.
Chou Tun-yi, 1, 2 (11th century)

10 Of old, Heaven and Earth were not yet
separated, and the In and Yo not yet
divided. They formed a chaotic mass like an
egg, which was of obscurely defined limits,
and contained germs. The purer and clearer
part was thinly diffused and formed
Heaven, while the heavier and grosser
element settled down and became Earth.
Nihongi, 1, 1 (720)

11 Clement of Rome taught that God rules the
world with a right and a left hand, the right
being Christ, the left Satan. Clement's view
is clearly *monotheistic*, as it unites the
opposites in one God.
  Later Christianity, however, is dualistic,
inasmuch as it splits off one half of the
opposites, personified in Satan, and he is
eternal in his state of damnation.
C.G. Jung, *Psychology and Religion* (1958)

12 Thou shalt have one God only; who
Would be at the expense of two?
Arthur Hugh Clough, *The Latest Decalogue*
(1862)

8 PANTHEISM — MONISM
See also 29. IMMANENCE

1 'Pantheism', when translated into English,
of course, means 'all-God-ism.'
R.C. Zaehner, *Mysticism Sacred and
Profane* (1957)

2 Those experiences which are usually termed
pantheistic, the experience which tells you
that you are all and that all is you . . . It
would be far more accurate to describe this
experience as 'pan-en-hen-ism',
'all-in-one-ism', for that is what in fact the
experience tells us.
R.C. Zaehner, *Mysticism Sacred and
Profane* (1957)

3 We are parts of him, his offspring, as the
Greek poet, a pantheist quoted by the
Apostle, observes: And the reason is,
because a religious theist, and an impious
pantheist, both profess to believe in the
omnipresence of God.
William Warburton, *The Works of
Alexander Pope* (1751)

4 A Greek papyrus has preserved a magical
prayer based on Hermetic theology, in

which occur the words: 'Enter thou into my spirit and my thoughts my whole life long, for thou art I and I am thou.'
S. Angus, *The Mystery Religions and Christianity* (1925)

5 Verily, in the beginning this world was Brahman. It knew only itself: 'I am Brahman!' Therefore it became the All . . . Whoever thus knows 'I am Brahman!' becomes this All; even the gods have not power to prevent his becoming thus, for he becomes their self.
Brihad-aranyaka Upanishad, 1, 4, 10

6 These rivers, my dear, flow, the eastern toward the east, the western toward the west. They go just from the ocean to the ocean. They become the ocean itself. As there they know not 'I am this one,' 'I am that one' — even so, indeed, my dear, all creatures here, though they have come forth from Being, know not 'We have come forth from Being.' Whatever they are in this world, whether tiger, or lion, or wolf, or boar, or worm, or fly, or gnat, or mosquito, that they become.
    That which is the finest essence — this whole world has that as its soul. That is Reality. That is Soul. That art thou.
Chandogya Upanishad, 6, 10

7 OM! — This syllable is this whole world. Its further explanation is:
The past, the present, the future —
Everything is just the word OM.
Mandukya Upanishad, 1, 1

8 As therefore the individual soul and the highest Self differ in name only, it being a settled matter that perfect knowledge has for its object the absolute oneness of the two; it is senseless to insist (as some do) on a plurality of Selfs, and to maintain that the individual soul is different from the highest Self.
Shankara, *Commentary on the Vedanta Sutras,* 1, 4, 22 (9th century)

9 Our view implies a denial of difference in so far as the individual 'I' is of the nature of the Self; and it implies an acknowledgement of difference in so far as it allows the highest Self to differ from the individual soul in the same way as the latter differs from its body.
Ramanuja, *Commentary on the Vedanta Sutras,* 4, 1, 3 (11th century)

10 By deep meditations, let him recognize the subtle nature of the supreme Soul, and its presence in all organisms, both the highest and the lowest.
The Laws of Manu, 6, 65

11 If the Element of the Buddha did not exist (in everyone), there could be no disgust with suffering.
Ratna-gotra-vibhaga, 1, 40 (1st–5th centuries)

12 I am he whom I love, and he whom I love
          is I,
We are two spirits dwelling in one body,
If thou seest me, thou seest him,
And if thou seest him, thou seest us both.
Husayn al-Hallaj (d. 922), trans. R.A. Nicholson, *The Legacy of Islam* (1939)

13 I have put duality away, I have seen that the
          two worlds are one:
One I seek, One I know, One I see, One I
          call.
He is the first, he is the last.
He is the outward, he is the inward.
Jalalu'l-Din Rumi (1207–73), trans. R.A. Nicholson, *Divani Shamsi Tabriz* (1898)

14 All things that are, are in God, and must be conceived through God, and therefore God is the cause of the things which are in Himself. This is the first point. Further, no substance can be granted outside God, that is, nothing which is outside God exists in itself; which was the second point. Therefore God is the immanent, but not the transcendent, cause of all things.
Baruch Spinoza, *Ethics,* 1, 18 (1677)

15 It was a worship of all the separate, mysterious, living souls he approached: 'souls' of grass, trees, stones, animals, birds, fish; 'souls' of planetary bodies and of the bodies of men and women; the 'souls', even, of all manner of inanimate little things.
J.C. Powys, *Wolf Solent* (1929)

16 God is present in nature, but nature is not God; there is a nature in God, but it is not God himself.
Henri-Frédéric Amiel, *Fragments d'un journal intime* (1884)

17 I felt the sentiment of Being spread
O'er all that moves, and all that seemeth
          still,
O'er all, that, lost beyond the reach of
          thought

And human knowledge, to the human eye
Invisible, yet liveth to the heart.
William Wordsworth, *The Prelude*, 2,
401–5 (1850)

18 It is eternity now. I am in the midst of it. It is
about me in the sunshine; I am in it, as the
butterfly floats in the light-laden air.
Nothing has to come: it is now. Now is
eternity; now is the immortal life.
Richard Jefferies, *The Story of my Heart*
(1883)

19 I was now a Not-self, simultaneously
perceiving and being the Not-self of the
things around me. To this newborn
Not-self, the behaviour, the appearance, the
very thought of the self it had momentarily
ceased to be, and of other selves, its
one-time fellows, seemed not indeed
distasteful . . . but enormously irrelevant.
Aldous Huxley, *The Doors of Perception*
(1954)

20 The sense of the divine as non-personal may
indeed reflect an aspect of the same infinite
reality that is encountered as personal in
theistic religious experience.
John Hick, *God and the Universe of Faiths*
(1973)

21 As early as in St Paul and St John we read
that to create, to fulfil and to purify the
world is, for God, to unify it by uniting it
organically with himself. How does he unify
it? By partially immersing himself in things,
by becoming 'element', and then, from this
point of vantage in the heart of matter,
assuming the control and leadership of what
we now call evolution . . . This is indeed a
superior form of 'pantheism', without trace
of the poison of adulteration or
annihilation.
Pierre Teilhard de Chardin, *The
Phenomenon of Man* (1959)

9 ANIMISM — MANA

1 I propose here, under the name of Animism,
to investigate the deep-lying doctrine of
Spiritual Beings, which embodies the very
essence of Spiritualistic as opposed to
Materialistic philosophy. Animism is not a
new technical term, though now seldom
used. From its special relation to the
doctrine of the soul, it will be seen to have a
peculiar appropriateness to the view here
taken of the mode in which theological ideas
have been developed among mankind.
Edward B. Tylor, *Primitive Culture* (1871)

2 It is Animism in the loose sense of some
writers, or, as I propose to call it,
Animatism.
R.R. Marett, in *Folk-Lore* (1900)

3 Animism is, in any case, in its developed and
most typical forms, found not in primitive
societies but in such relatively advanced
societies as those of China, Egypt, and the
classical Mediterranean.
E.E. Evans-Pritchard, *Theories of Primitive
Religion* (1965)

4 The Melanesian mind is entirely possessed
by the belief in a supernatural power or
influence, called almost universally *mana*.
This is what works to effect everything
which is beyond the ordinary power of men,
outside the common processes of nature; it
is present in the atmosphere of life, attaches
itself to persons and things, and is
manifested by results which can only be
ascribed to its operation. When one has got
it he can use it and direct it, but its force
may break forth at some new point; the
presence of it is ascertained by proof.
R.H. Codrington, *The Melanesians*
(1891)

5 The idea of *mana*, though it is to be found in
religions outside the Melanesian area, is not
a universal idea, and therefore can hardly be
taken to represent the first phase of all
religions.
Mircea Eliade, *Patterns in Comparative
Religion* (1958)

6 I will only draw passing attention again to
the appalling fog of confusion, which lasted
for many years and is not yet entirely
dispersed, about the (mainly Polynesian)
concept of *mana* . . . Recent research seems
to have established that it should be
understood as an efficaciousness (with the
allied meaning of truth) of spiritual power
derived from gods or ghosts, usually
through persons, especially chiefs — a grace
or virtue which enables persons to ensure
success in human undertakings.
E.E. Evans-Pritchard, *Theories of Primitive
Religion* (1965)

10 TOTEMISM

1 To these are added his badge, called, in the Algonquin tongue, a totem, and which is in the nature of an armorial bearing.
Alexander Henry, *Travels and Adventures in Canada and the Indian Territories 1760–1776* (1809)

2 Here are to be seen (and will continue to be seen for ages to come) the totems and arms of the different tribes.
George Catlin, *Illustrations of the Manners, Customs and Condition of the North American Indians, 1841* (1844)

3 Among totem peoples . . . the sacred animal is forbidden food, it is akin to the men who acknowledge its sanctity.
W. Robertson Smith, *The Religion of the Semites* (1889)

4 The sex totem seems to be still more sacred than the clan totem; for men who do not object to other people killing their clan totem will fiercely defend their sex totem.
J.G. Frazer, *Totemism* (1887)

5 Every individual of the tribes with which we are dealing is born into some totem — that is, he, or she belongs to a group of persons each one of whom bears the name of, and is especially associated with, some natural object. The latter is usually an animal or plant.
Baldwin Spencer and F.J. Gillen, *The Native Tribes of Central Australia* (1899)

6 There are then several forms of totemism in Australia, namely, individual, sex, moiety, section, sub-section, matrilineal social clan, patrilineal social clan, localized cult clan and dream-totemism. A number of these may be found in one tribe, that is, one person may have several kinds of totem.
A.P. Elkin, 'Studies in Australian Totemism' in *Oceania* (1933)

7 Who knows what 'totemism' is, if it is all this at once? Can a thing which can be divided up into an almost limitless variety of ways have any ultimate existence? It seems that we are once again being presented with the case of the Emperor's clothes.
Claude Lévi-Strauss, *Totemism* (1963)

8 One day the expelled brothers joined forces, slew and ate the father, and thus put an end to the father horde . . . They accomplished their identification with him by devouring him and each acquired a part of his strength. The totem feast, which is perhaps mankind's first celebration, would be the repetition and commemoration of this memorable, criminal act with which so many things began, social organization, moral restrictions and religion.
Sigmund Freud, *Totem and Taboo* (1913)

9 Freud tells us a just-so story which only a genius could have ventured to compose, for no evidence was, or could be, adduced in support of it . . . In the vast literature on totemism throughout the world, there is only one instance, among the Australian aboriginals, of a people ceremonially eating their totems, and the significance of that instance, even if its veracity be accepted, is dubious and disputed.
E.E. Evans-Pritchard, *Theories of Primitive Religion* (1965)

10 The god of the clan, the totemic principle, can therefore be nothing else than the clan itself, personified and represented to the imagination under the visible form of the animal or vegetable which serves as a totem.
Emile Durkheim, *The Elementary Forms of the Religious Life* (1915)

11 It is also a just-so story. Totemism could have arisen through gregariousness, but there is no evidence that it did.
E.E. Evans-Pritchard, *Theories of Primitive Religion* (1965)

12 Totemism is an artificial unity, existing solely in the mind of the anthropologist, to which nothing specifically corresponds in reality.
Claude Lévi-Strauss, *Totemism* (1963)

13 Totemism is like hysteria, in that once we are persuaded to doubt that it is possible arbitrarily to isolate certain phenomena and to group them together as diagnostic signs of an illness, or of an objective institution, the symptoms themselves vanish or appear refractory to any unifying interpretation.
Claude Lévi-Strauss, *Totemism* (1963)

14 If one can show (as has been done in recent decades) that the religious lives of the most primitive peoples are in fact complex, that they cannot be reduced to 'animism', 'totemism', or even ancestor-worship, that they include visions of Supreme Beings with

all the powers of an omnipotent Creator-God, then these evolutionist hypotheses which deny the primitive any approach to 'superior hierophanies' are nullified.
Mircea Eliade, *Patterns in Comparative Religion* (1958)

---

11 TABOO

1 Of their flesh shall ye not eat, and their carcase shall ye not touch; they are unclean to you.
Leviticus, 11, 8

2 There is nothing unclean of itself: but to him that esteemeth any thing to be unclean, to him it is unclean. But if thy brother be grieved with thy meat, now walkest thou not charitably. Destroy not him with thy meat, for whom Christ died.
Romans, 14, 14–15

3 He hath only forbidden you (what is found) dead, blood, the flesh of swine, and that over which any other name than that of Allah has been invoked. But if anyone is compelled without his own desire or deliberate transgression, no guilt rests upon him; verily Allah is forgiving, compassionate.
Koran, 2, 168

4 Garlic, leeks and onions, mushrooms and (all plants) springing from impure (substances), are unfit to be eaten by twice-born men . . . There is no sin in eating meat, in (drinking) spirituous liquor, and in carnal intercourse, for that is the natural way of created beings, but abstention brings great rewards.
The Laws of Manu, 5, 5 and 56

5 Some slay animals for sacrificial purposes, some kill them for the sake of their skin, some kill them for the sake of their flesh, some kill them for the sake of their blood . . . A wise man should not act sinfully towards animals, nor cause others to act so, nor allow others to act so.
Acharanga Sutra, 1, 1, 6 (4th–1st centuries BCE)

6 Monks, one should not knowingly make use of meat killed on purpose for one. Whoever should make use of it, there is an offence of wrong-doing.
Vinaya Pitaka, 1, 238 (4th–1st centuries BCE)

7 Not one of them would sit down, or eat a bit of any thing . . . On expressing my surprize at this, they were all *taboo*, as they said; which word has a very comprehensive meaning; but, in general, signifies that a thing is forbidden.
James Cook, *A Voyage to the Pacific Ocean in 1776–1780* (1784)

8 One of the great instruments used by both king and priests for maintaining their power and their revenue, was the system of 'tabu' or 'taboo'.
Manley Hopkins, *Hawaii* (1862)

9 Holy things are not free to man, because they pertain to the gods; uncleanness is shunned, according to the view taken in the higher Semitic religions, because it is hateful to the god.
W. Robertson Smith, *The Religion of the Semites* (1889)

10 For Robertson Smith taboo is the very vehicle of primitiveness . . . though the highly complex India caste system and the sophisticated, highly consistent though manifold, attitudes corresponding to it have been maintained for at least forty centuries.
Franz Steiner, *Taboo* (1956)

11 Without stretching ideas we can speak of a taboo conscience and a taboo sense of guilt after the violation of a taboo. Taboo conscience is probably the oldest form in which we meet the phenomenon of conscience.
Sigmund Freud, *Totem and Taboo* (1913)

12 As Freud's readers soon discover, the plausibility of the theories may be ideologically important, but it is not relevant proof.
Franz Steiner, *Taboo* (1956)

13 The mention of her neighbours is evidently taboo, since . . . she is in a state of affront with nine-tenths of them.
Mary Russell Mitford, *Our Village* (1826)

14 To labour hardest as a Bishop is to incur certain taboo.
Reginald G. Wilberforce, *Life of the Right Rev. Samuel Wilberforce* (1853)

12 MAGIC
See also 61. SHAMANS

1 The king commanded to call the magicians, and the astrologers, and the sorcerers.
Daniel, 2, 2

2 To him they had regard, because that of long time he had bewitched them with sorceries.
Acts, 8, 11

3 A person who refrains from practising divination is assigned a place in Heaven which even the ministering angels are unable to penetrate.
Mishnah, *Nedarim*, 32

4 When they see a sign, they seek to make fun, And say, This is nothing but magic manifest.
Koran, 37, 14–15

5 If this be magic, let it be an art Lawful as eating.
William Shakespeare, *The Winter's Tale*, V, iii, 110–11 (*c.* 1609–10)

6 I have often admired the mystical way of Pythagoras, and the secret magic of numbers.
Thomas Browne, *Religio Medici*, i, 12 (1643)

7 For in and out, above, about, below, 'Tis nothing but a Magic Shadow-show.
Edward Fitzgerald, *The Rubáiyát of Omar Khayyám*, 46 (1859)

8 The Lord abides in the heart of all beings, causing all beings to turn around, fixed in a machine, by his magic power.
Bhagavad Gita, 18, 61

9 If my analysis of the magician's logic is correct, its two great principles turn out to be merely two different misapplications of the association of ideas. Homoeopathic magic is founded on the association of ideas by similarity: contagious magic is founded on the association of ideas by contiguity.
J.G. Frazer, *The Golden Bough* (1890)

10 Magic is a spurious system of natural law, as well as a fallacious guide of conduct; it is a false science as well as an abortive art.
J.G. Frazer, *The Gold Bough* (1890)

11 The apparent futility of Frazer's analogy between science and magic is due to the fact that he sees both as modes of thinking . . . If he had compared a magical rite in its entirety with a scientific performance in its entirety instead of comparing what he supposes to go on in the brain of a magician with what he supposes to go on in the brain of a scientist, he would have seen the essential difference between science and magic.
E.E. Evans-Pritchard, 'The Intellectualist (English) Interpretation of Magic' in *Bulletin of the Faculty of Arts*, Cairo (1933)

12 While one anthropological theory is that magic and religion give men confidence, comfort and a sense of security, it could equally well be argued that they give men fears and anxieties from which they would otherwise be free.
A.R. Radcliffe-Brown, *Structure and Function in Primitive Society* (1952)

13 Magic does not dominate the spiritual life of 'primitive' societies everywhere by any means; it is, on the contrary, in the more developed societies that it becomes so prevalent.
Mircea Eliade, *Patterns in Comparative Religion* (1958)

14 Classical Anthropology distinguishes between religion and magic by saying that religion involves a deity whom man implores, magic involves forces which man commands.
Margaret J. Field, *Search for Security* (1960)

15 Bad magics for killing or harming others can be obtained only from bad medicine-men . . . Good medicine . . . is practised by respected men.
Margaret J. Field, *Search for Security* (1960)

16 Magic desires to obtain its effects without entering into relation, and practises its tricks in the void. But sacrifice and prayer are set 'before the Face . . .'
Martin Buber, *I and Thou* (1937)

13 WITCHCRAFT

1 Thou shalt not suffer a witch to live.
Exodus, 22, 18

2 Now the works of the flesh are manifest,

which are these . . . idolatry, witchcraft, hatred.
Galatians, 5, 20

3 The chief of the sorceresses told me that if a man meets witches, let him say . . . O witches, so long as He was gracious to me and I was careful, I did not come into your midst; and now that I have come into your midst, become bald for me and I will be careful.
Mishnah, *Pesachim*, 110.

4 I take refuge with the Lord of the Daybreak . . . from the evil of the darkening when it comes on, and from the evil of the blowers among knots.
Koran, 113, 1–4

5 Saul inquired of his servants, and learned from them that a witch still lived at the village of Endor . . . The sacred writer has not described her appearance, so we are free to picture her according to our fancy. She may have been young and fair, with raven locks and lustrous eyes, or she may have been a wizened, toothless hag, with meeting nose and chin, blear eyes and grizzled hair, bent double with age and infirmity.
J.G. Frazer, *Folk-lore in the Old Testament* (1918)

6 It has indeed lately come to our ears, not without afflicting us with bitter sorrow, that . . . many persons of both sexes, unmindful of their own salvation and straying from the Catholic Faith, have abandoned themselves to devils, incubi and succubi, and by their incantations, spells, conjurations, and other accursed charms and crafts, enormities and horrid offences, have slain infants yet in the mother's womb, as also the offspring of cattle, (and) have blasted the produce of the earth.
Bull of Innocent VIII, *Summis desiderantes* (1484)

7 Certain wicked women, perverted by Satan and seduced by the illusions and phantasms of devils, do actually, as they believe and profess, ride in the night-time on certain beasts with Diana, a goddess of the pagans, or with Herodias and an innumerable multitude of women.
Heinrich Kramer and James Sprenger, *Malleus Maleficarum*, II, i, 3 (1486)

8 It is a certain rule Witches deny their Baptism when they make Covenant with the

Devil, water being the sole element thereof, and when they are heaved into the water it refuseth to receive them but suffers them to float.
James VI and I, *Daemonologie* (1597)

9 *First witch*: When shall we three meet again In thunder, lightning, or in rain?
William Shakespeare, *Macbeth*, I, i, 1–2

10 S. Augustine saith well, that he is too much a fool and a blockhead, that supposeth those things to be done indeed, and corporally, which are by such persons fantastically imagined.
Reginald Scot, *The Discoverie of Witchcraft* (1594)

11 As for Witches, I think not that their witchcraft is any real power.
Thomas Hobbes, *Leviathan* (1651)

12 I cannot forbear thinking that there is such an Intercourse and Commerce with Evil Spirits, as that which we express by the Name of Witchcraft.
Joseph Addison, *The Spectator*, 117, 2 (1711)

13 To deny the possibility, nay, actual existence, of witchcraft and sorcery, is . . . to contradict the revealed word of God.
William Blackstone, *Commentaries on the Laws of England* (1769)

14 The witch laws, with the executions and judicials thereupon, and the witches' confessions, have beguiled almost the whole world.
Reginald Scot, *The Discoverie of Witchcraft* (1594)

15 While the episcopal blessing was thus enthusiastically given to the questioning spirit of science, it is not surprising that in the later years of the Century, the reaction of educated minds to charges of witchcraft was very different from what it had been a short time before . . . In 1736, greatly to the indignation of many simple folk, Parliament repealed the already obsolete law that condemned a witch to die.
G.M. Trevelyan, *English Social History* (1944)

16 When dealing with the records of the medieval witches, we are dealing with the remains of a pagan religion which survived,

in England at least, till the eighteenth century.
Margaret Murray, 'Witchcraft' in *The Encyclopaedia Britannica*, 14th edn (1929)

17 Miss Murray has over-stated her case . . . It is difficult to believe that an organized secret society of the kind she describes ever existed.
E.O. James, *The Concept of Deity* (1950)

18 A witch performs no rite, utters no spell, and possesses no medicines. An act of witchcraft is a psychic act.
E.E. Evans-Pritchard. *Witchcraft, Oracles and Magic among the Azande* (1937)

19 The witch animals of Japan are creatures believed to be capable of assuming a discarnate and invisible form, and in such guise of penetrating inside the human body and inflicting upon it a variety of painful torments.
Carmen Blacker, *The Catalpa Bow* (1975)

20 Witches, in contemporary West African belief, are associated with a secret religious cult of their own. No such cult in fact exists . . . The fact that a witch has been demonstrably asleep on her mat throughout the night she is supposed to have spent in feasting, and the fact that the corpse of her victim, supposedly slain by witchcraft, has clearly suffered no cannibalistic ravages, are covered by African dogma. It is the spirit of the witch that leaves her sleeping body and flies to the meeting place. It is not the victim's material body but his vital *kra* [soul] which is eaten by the witches.
Margaret J. Field, *Search for Security* (1960)

21 There is much loose discussion about witchcraft. We must distinguish between bad magic (or sorcery) and witchcraft. Many African peoples distinguish clearly between the two and for ethnological purposes we must do the same . . . Witchcraft is an imaginary offence because it is impossible. A witch cannot do what he is supposed to do and has in fact no real existence.
E.E. Evans-Pritchard, in *Africa* (1935)

22 We cannot lightly discount the fact that diviners, witch-doctors, and ministers of ordeals were frequently bribed to give a favourable or unfavourable decision, and that if they happened to be honest men it

was an even chance whether an innocent man was punished or a guilty one escaped.
C.K. Meek, *Law and Authority in a Nigerian Tribe* (1937)

23 The aggression invited by witchcraft beliefs is as harmful as anything a society can produce in the way of 'disruptive' practices; the relief offered by witch-hunting and witch-punishing is no more than temporary and their capacity to allay anxieties no more than illusory: for if witchcraft beliefs resolve certain fears and tensions, they also produce others . . . We may liken witchcraft beliefs to a safety valve: but let us be clear that the engine which needs it has been badly constructed; nor is the safety valve itself safe.
S.F. Nadel, *Nupe Religion* (1954)

---

14 SUPERSTITION

---

1 They have walked after the imagination of their own heart, and after Baalim, which their fathers taught them.
Jeremiah, 9, 14

2 I perceive that in all things ye are too superstitious.
Acts, 17, 22

3 O ye unbelievers, I serve not what ye serve, and ye are not servers of what I serve.
Koran 109, 1–3

4 There is a superstition in avoiding superstition.
Francis Bacon, *Essays*, 'Of Superstition' (1625)

5 Opposing one species of superstition to another, set them a quarrelling; while we ourselves, during their fury and contention, happily make our escape into the calm, though obscure, regions of philosophy.
David Hume, *The Natural History of Religion* (1757)

6 Superstition is the religion of feeble minds.
Edmund Burke, *Reflections on the Revolution in France* (1790)

7 Superstition sets the whole world in flames; philosophy quenches them.
Voltaire, *Dictionnaire philosophique*, 'Superstition' (1764)

8 It would be a gain to the country were it

vastly more superstitious, more bigoted, more gloomy, more fierce in its religion than at present it shows itself to be.
John Henry Newman, *Apologia pro Vita sua* (1864)

9 To become a popular religion, it is only necessary for a superstition to enslave a philosophy.
William Ralph Inge, *Outspoken Essays* (1922)

10 No philosopher was at hand to tell him that there is no strong sentiment without some terror, as there is no real religion without a little fetishism.
Joseph Conrad, *Victory* (1915)

---

15 ATHEISM AND IRRELIGION

---

1 The fool hath said in his heart, There is no God.
Psalms, 14 and 53

2 Having no hope, and without God in the world.
Ephesians, 2, 12

3 There are some of them who listen to thee over whose hearts we have placed veils lest they understand it, and in their ears heaviness, and if they see any sign they do not believe in it; so that when they come to dispute with thee, those who have disbelieved say: 'This is nothing but old-world tales.'
Koran, 6, 25

4 They say the world is without truth, without religious basis, without a God. It does not originate in regular causation, but is moved by desire alone.
Bhagavad Gita, 16, 8

5 According to the 'worldly' doctrine . . . There is no other world than this; there is no heaven and no hell; the realm of Shiva and like regions are invented by stupid impostors of other schools of thought.
Shankara, *Sarva-siddhanta-samgraha*, 8 (9th century)

6 Believing that it denied souls and God(s), and that it adjured reliance on mysterious forces and supernatural powers, Buddhism was viewed by many of its Western interpreters as an essentially ethical religion,

akin to modern Humanism or ethical culture . . . [but] anthropological studies of living Buddhism have shown that Buddhists differ very little from people in general.
M.E. Spiro, *Buddhism and Society* (1970)

7 The western misunderstanding of Buddhism as atheistic explains the statement (in English) of a Sinhalese estate clerk that Buddhism is 'not a religion but a practice.'
Richard F. Gombrich, *Precept and Practice* (1971)

8 No one who in early life has adopted this doctrine of the non-existence of gods has ever persisted to old age constant to that conviction.
Plato, *Laws*, 10, 888

9 Men who cast providence out of human life, and who do not believe that God takes care of the affairs of the world, nor that the Universe is governed and continued in being by that blessed and immortal nature, but say that the world is carried along of its own accord, without a ruler and guardian.
Josephus, *Antiquities*, x, xi, 7 (1st century)

10 An irreligious man is not one who denies the gods of the majority, but one who applies to the gods the opinions of the majority. For what most men say about the gods are not ideas derived from sensation, but false opinions, according to which the greatest evils come to the wicked, and the greatest blessings come to the good from the gods.
Epicurus, *Letter to Menoeceus*, 123 (3rd century BCE)

11 I count religion but a childish toy
And hold there is no sin but ignorance
Christopher Marlowe, *The Jew of Malta* (1592)

12 God never wrought miracle to convince atheism, because his ordinary works convince it.
Francis Bacon, *Essays*, 'Atheism' (1625)

13 He [Charles II] said once to myself, he was no atheist, but he could not think God would make a man miserable only for taking a little pleasure out of the way.
Gilbert Burnet, *The History of My Own Times* (1724)

14 No Religion is better than an Unnatural One.
William Penn, *Some Fruits of Solitude* (1693)

15 Whenever a man talks loudly against religion, — always suspect that it is not his reason, but his passions which have got the better of his creed.
Laurence Sterne, *Tristram Shandy*, ii, 17 (1760)

16 By night an atheist half believes a God.
Edward Young, *Night Thoughts* (1742)

17 God is dead; but considering the state the species Man is in, there will perhaps be caves, for ages yet, in which his shadow will be shown.
Friedrich Nietzsche, *Joyous Wisdom*, III (1910)

18 She, stirred somewhat beyond her wont, and taking as her text the three words which have been used so often as the inspiring trumpet-calls of men — the words *God, Immortality, Duty* — pronounced, with terrible earnestness, how inconceivable was the *first*, how unbelievable, the *second*, and yet how peremptory and absolute the third.
F.W.H. Myers, 'George Eliot', *Century Magazine* (1881)

19 'There is no God', the wicked saith,
  'And truly it's a blessing,
For what he might have done with us
  It's better only guessing.'
Arthur Hugh Clough, *Dipsychus*, vi (1865)

20 Man has never been the same since God
    died.
He has taken it very hard. Why, you'd think
    it was only yesterday,
The way he takes it.
Not that he says much, but he laughs much
    louder than he used to,
And he can't bear to be left alone even for a
    minute, and he can't
Sit still.
Edna St Vincent Millay, *Conversation at Midnight* (1937)

21 When I was an atheist I had to try to persuade myself that most of the human race have always been wrong about the question that mattered to them most; when I became a Christian I was able to take a more liberal view.
C.S. Lewis, *Mere Christianity* (1952)

22 If primitive religion could be explained away as an intellectual aberration, as a mirage induced by emotional stress, or by its social function, it was implied that the higher religions could be discredited and disposed of in the same way.
E.E. Evans-Pritchard, *Theories of Primitive Religion* (1965)

23 The great questions of whether we are going to survive as a human race. Why aren't the churches in the forefront of these discussions? Sometimes I wonder if they aren't full of atheists — people who almost deny that there really is a living God. They seem to be in the business of running some sort of club.
Donald Reeves, in *Priestland's Progress* (1981)

24 The faith of a Catholic is not better or stronger than the faith of a Protestant, but a person's unconscious is gripped by the Catholic form no matter how weak his faith may be. That is why, once he slips out of this form, he may easily fall into a fanatical atheism, of a kind that is particularly to be met with in Latin Countries.
C.G. Jung, *Psychology and Religion* (1958)

25 'Atheists are atheists usually for mean reasons', Voss was saying. 'The meanest of these is that they themselves are so lacking in magnificence that they cannot conceive the idea of a Divine Power . . . *Atheismus* is self-murder.'
Patrick White, *Voss* (1957)

---

16 AGNOSTICISM AND HUMANISM
See also 110. DOUBT

---

1 As I passed by, and beheld your devotions, I found an altar with this inscription, TO THE UNKNOWN GOD [*agnōstō theō*]
Acts, 17, 23

2 I took thought, and invented what I conceived to be the appropriate title of 'agnostic'.
Thomas Henry Huxley, *Collected Essays* (1893)

3 Agnostic was the name demanded by Professor Huxley for those who disclaimed atheism, and believed with him in an 'unknown and unknowable' God; or in other words that the ultimate origin of all things must be some cause unknown and unknowable.
The Spectator, 11 June 1876

4 The agnostic doctrines, he once said to me, were to appearance like the finest flour, from which you might expect the most excellent bread; but when you came to feed on it, you found it was powdered glass, and you had been eating the deadliest poison.
James A. Froude, *Carlyle,* II (1884)

5 A sort of know-nothingism or Agnosticism, or belief in an unknown and unknowable God.
R.H. Hutton, *Essays* (1871)

6 A man who has passed from orthodoxy to the loosest Arminianism, and thence to Arianism, and thence to direct Humanism.
S.T. Coleridge, *Literary Remains* (1834)

7 'Humanism' is perhaps too 'whole-hearted' for the use of philosophers, who are a bloodless breed; but, save for that objection, one might back it, for it expresses the essence of the new way of thought, which is, that it is impossible to strip the human element out from even our most abstract theorizing.
William James, *Collected Essays and Reviews* (1920)

8 He [Sartre] calls his existentialism humanism. But if he calls it humanism, that means he has an idea of what man essentially is.
Paul Tillich, *The Theology of Culture* (1959)

9   Belief,
As Unbelief before, shakes us by fits . . .
Just when we are safest, there's a
           sunset-touch,
A fancy from a flower-bell, some one's
           death,
A chorus-ending from Euripides, —
And that's enough for fifty hopes and fears
As old and new at once as Nature's self,
To rap and knock and enter in our soul,
Take hands and dance there, a fantastic
           ring,
Round the ancient idol, on his base
           again, —
The grand Perhaps!
Robert Browning, *Bishop Blougram's Apology* (1855)

10 Non-existent there was not, existent there
           was not then.
There was not atmospheric space, nor the
           vault beyond.
What stirred, where, and in whose control?

Was there water, a deep abyss? . . .
This creation, whence it came into being,
Whether it was established, or whether
           not —
Only he who is its overseer in highest
           heaven
Only he knows — or perhaps he does not
           know!
Rig Veda, 10, 129, 1 and 7

11 In spite of a few agnostics . . . we have every reason to believe that the doctrine of rebirth in other worlds and in this was often spoken of in the Upanisads and taken as an accepted fact by the Buddha.
Surendranath Dasgupta, *A History of Indian Philosophy,* I, V (1922)

12 Buddhism differs from agnosticism in that it asserts an innate transcendental faculty in man which by elimination of all elements of 'defilement' (*āsavas*) may contemplate Reality and attain perfect knowledge and enlightenment — Nirvana.
Christmas Humphreys (ed.), *A Buddhist Students' Manual* (1956)

13 The list of undetermined questions that are to be put aside by the disciple has been the reason for calling Buddhism agnostic. It is not agnostic except on these points, and even on these points it was never held that Buddha did not know the answers. They are useless for the disciple's purpose, but are never called unknowable.
Edward J. Thomas, *Early Buddhist Scriptures* (1935)

14 The agnostics were criticized in the Buddhist sources as 'eel-wrigglers' because they wriggled out of every question that was put to them and refused to give any firm answer.
Trevor Ling, *The Buddha* (1973)

15 The Way that can be told of is not an
           Unvarying Way;
The names that can be named are not
           unvarying names.
It was from the Nameless that Heaven and
           Earth sprang;
The named is but the mother that rears the
           ten thousand creatures.
Tao Te Ching, I

16 While ancient apologetics was confronted with a humanism that was pagan in substance, the distinctive factor in modern

apologetics is its confrontation with a humanism that is Christian in substance.
Paul Tillich, *On the Boundary* (1967)

17 DOGMATISM
See also 93. CHURCH

1 Thou shalt not bow down thyself to them, nor serve them: for I the LORD thy God am a jealous God.
Exodus, 20, 5

2 Neither is there salvation in any other: for there is none other name under heaven given among men, whereby we must be saved.
Acts, 4, 12

3 Verily those who have disbelieved of the People of the Book and the Polytheists are in the fire of Gehenna to abide therein — they are the worst of Creation.
Koran, 98, 5

4 Those who, murmuring against it, do not follow my doctrine, deluded in all knowledge, you must know that they are lost, the fools.
Bhagavad Gita, 3, 32

5 There is no path in the sky, there is no recluse outside of us, mankind delights in worldliness; the Buddhas are free from worldliness.
Dhammapada, 254

6 By means of one sole vehicle, to wit, the Buddha-vehicle, do I teach creatures the law; there is no second vehicle, nor a third.
Lotus of the True Law, 2, 36 (1st century)

7 Pilgrimages, penances, compassion and almsgiving
Bring a little merit, the size of sesame seed.
Hymns of Guru Nanak, 21 (16th century)

8 The sacrificers and the sorcerer princes . . .
Shall be tortured by their own soul and their own conscience.
Gathas, *Yasna*, 46, 11

9 No salvation outside the church
Cyprian, *De Catholicae Ecclesiae Unitate*, 6 (3rd century). See also Augustine of Hippo, *De Baptismo*, IV, xvii see 94, 9

10 Whosoever will be saved: before all things it is necessary that he hold the Catholick

Faith. Which Faith except every one do keep whole and undefiled: without doubt he shall perish everlastingly.
Athanasian Creed, *Quicunque vult* (5th century)

11 The Athanasian Creed is the most splendid ecclesiastical lyric ever poured forth by the genius of man.
Benjamin Disraeli, Endymion, 54 (1880)

12 From the age of fifteen, dogma has been the fundamental principle of my religion: I know no other religion; I cannot enter into the idea of any other sort of religion; religion, as a mere sentiment, is to me a dream and a mockery.
John Henry Newman, *Apologia pro Vita sua* (1864)

13 However strong and confident may be my conviction that my own approach to the mystery is a right one, I ought to be aware that my field of spiritual vision is so narrow that I cannot know that there is no virtue in other approaches.
Arnold Toynbee, *An Historian's Approach to Religion* (1956)

14 Profound ignorance makes a man dogmatic. The man who knows nothing thinks he is teaching others what he has just learned himself; the man who knows a great deal cannot imagine that what he is saying is not common knowledge, and speaks more indifferently.
Jean de La Bruyère, *Caractères* (1688)

15 It is in the uncompromisingness with which dogma is held and not in the dogma or want of dogma that the danger lies.
Samuel Butler, *The Way of All Flesh* (1903)

16 There are two kinds of people in the world: the conscious dogmatists and the unconscious dogmatists. I have always found myself that the unconscious dogmatists were by far the most dogmatic.
G.K. Chesterton, *Generally Speaking* (1928)

18 SYNCRETISM — MINGLING

1 When I bow myself in the house of Rimmon, the LORD pardon thy servant in this thing.
2 Kings, 5, 18

2 In him we live, and move, and have our
being; as certain also of your own poets
have said, For we are also his offspring.
Acts, 17, 28

3 Each has a direction to which he turns; so
strive to be foremost in good deeds.
Koran, 2, 143

4 Whatever being shows wide powers, or
majesty or vigour, be sure that in every case
that is sprung from a fraction of my glory.
Bhagavad Gita, 10, 41

5 The Gita does not know that pantheism and
deism and theism cannot well be jumbled up
into one as a consistent philosophic creed.
**Surendranath Dasgupta, A History of
Indian Philosophy, II, XIV (1932)**

6 Sikhism attempts to effect a synthesis of the
two streams of religious consciousness.
Essentially it lies in the authentic pattern of
the way of life of Indian humanity,
enlivened by the perennial themes of Hindu
philosophy. But it has shown great
sensitiveness to the essential truths
enshrined in the other streams. In this it is
primarily indebted to Islam.
**Sohan Singh, Sikhism, 'Sikhism among
World Religions' (1969)**

7 It is unlikely that Sikhism will reject its own
sectarian marks; it will argue that a Sikh
should remain a Sikh and a Muslim a Muslim
. . . It is strongly opposed to any tendencies
to hop from one religion to another.
**W. Owen Cole and Piara Singh Sambhi,
The Sikhs (1978)**

8 Instead of reacting against Buddhism,
Shinto raised its prestige by identifying itself
more closely than ever with the interests of
the central government, co-operating with
Buddhism in that respect. The identity of
the Sun-goddess with the Buddha Lochana
was formally proclaimed in connection with
the foundation of the Central Cathedral.
**Masaharu Anesaki, History of Japanese
Religion (1930)**

9 The Baha'i Faith upholds the unity of God,
recognizes the unity of His Prophets, and
inculcates the principle of the oneness and
wholeness of the entire human race. It
proclaims the necessity and inevitablity of
the unification of mankind.
**Shoghi Effendi, Guidance for Today and
Tomorrow (1953)**

10 Though never officially canonized, both
Barlaam and Josaphat were numbered by
popular acclamation in the roll of saints
recognized by the Roman Catholic Church,
their day being November 27 . . . Despite
the composite, indeed disparate elements of
which the Christian legend of Barlaam and
Ioasaph is composed, it manages to retain a
surprisingly large element of the authentic
teachings of Gautama Buddha.
**David M. Lang, The Wisdom of Balahvar
(1957)**

11 Christianity is sociologically speaking,
certainly one religion; it is the ancient
paganism, or to be more precise the
complex Hebrew-Helleno-Greco-Latino-
Celtico-Gothico-Modern religion *converted*
to Christ more or less successfully.
**Raymond Panikkar, 'The Relation of
Christians to their non-Christian
Surroundings' in Christian Revelation and
World Religions (1967)**

12 I am a sort of collector of religions: and the
curious thing is that I find I can believe in
them all.
George Bernard Shaw, Major Barbara (1907)

13 I never could understand how a man could
be of two religions at once.
**John Henry Newman, Apologia pro Vita
sua (1864)**

14 *Calixtin.2.* An adherent of the opinions of
George Calixtus (1586–1656), a Lutheran
divine and professor . . . noted for his
moderate and conciliatory views and
writings on controversial points; a syncretist.
Oxford English Dictionary (1933)

15 Independency being a meer complication
and Syncretismus, or rather a Sink and
Common Sewer of all Errours.
**Clement Walker, The Third Part of the
History of Independency (1651)**

16 Syncretism, under every possible form —
ethical, political, social, and theological,
was the favourite policy of the Roman
emperors.
Fraser's Magazine, XLVII (1853)

17 The process of syncretism, by which various
god-names and god-natures are mingled, so
as to unite the creeds of different nomes and
provinces.
**Andrew Lang, Myth, Ritual and Religion
(1887)**

19 RELATIONS BETWEEN RELIGION
See also 99. UNITY AND ECUMENISM

1 From the rising of the sun even unto the going down of the same my name is great among the Gentiles; and in every place incense is offered unto my name and a pure offering.
Malachi, 1, 11 (RV)

2 Many shall come from the east and west, and shall sit down with Abraham, and Isaac, and Jacob, in the kingdom of heaven.
Matthew, 8, 11

3 Those who have believed, the Jews, the Christians and the Baptizers, whoever has believed in God and the Last Day, and has acted uprightly, have their reward with their Lord; fear rests not upon them, nor do they grieve.
Koran, 2, 59

4 Even those who are devoted to other gods, and sacrifice to them full of faith, are really worshipping me, though not in the prescribed fashion.
Bhagavad Gita, 9, 23

5 My Lord is both the Muslim Allah and the Hindu Gosain, and thus I have settled the dispute between the Hindu and the Muslim.
Guru Arjan, *Rag Bhairon,* 1136 (16th century)

6 The lamps are different, but the Light is the same: it comes from beyond.
O thou who art the kernel of Existence, the disagreement between Moslem, Zoroastrian and Jew depends on the standpoint.
Jalalu'l-Din Rumi, *Mathnawi,* III, 1259 (13th century)

7 My heart is capable of every form,
A cloister for the monk, a fane for idols,
A pasture for gazelles, the pilgrim's Ka'ba,
The Tables of the Torah, the Koran.
Love is the faith I hold: wherever turn
His camels, still the one true faith is mine.
Ibn al-Arabi, trans. R.A. Nicholson,
Tarjumanu 'l-Ashwaq (1911)

8 The area in which our investigation will take place makes nonsense of that conventional distinction hitherto observed by most western writers on Japanese religion, the separation of Shinto from Buddhism.
Carmen Blacker, *The Catalpa Bow* (1975)

9 Toleration has been the prevailing attitude of Buddhism and Taoism towards Confucianism . . . The three are complementary rather than antagonistic to each other, and together they make a fuller provision for human needs than any one of them does separately. Consequently no clear line of demarcation popularly exists between them. For general purposes we may say that the shrines of each are open to all and availed of by all.
W.E. Soothill, *The Three Religions of China* (1929)

10 Modern exponents of Hinduism should make it explicit that such statements as 'All religions are true' are made only on their own authority, and do not represent the orthodox Hindu tradition.
K.S. Murty, *Revelation and Reason in Advaita Vedānta* (1959)

11 A man is born upon the bank of Indus and there is none to tell of Christ, nor none to read, nor none to write; and all his volitions and his deeds are good as far as human reason sees, sinless in life or in discourse. He dies unbaptized and without faith; where is that justice which condemns him?
Dante Alighieri, *Paradiso,* XIX, 70–6 (1320)

12 The Religions of all Nations are derived from each Nation's different reception of the Poetic Genius, which is every where call'd the Spirit of Prophecy.
William Blake, *All Religions are One* (1788)

13 'The Jews, the Mohammedans, the Confucians, the Buddhists — what of them?' He put to himself the question he had feared to face. 'Can these hundreds of millions of men be deprived of that highest blessing without which life has no meaning?' He pondered a moment, but immediately corrected himself. 'But what am I questioning?' he said to himself. 'I am questioning the relation to Divinity of all the different religions of mankind.'
Leo Tolstoy, *Anna Karenina,* VIII (1877)

14 One religion is as true as another.
Robert Burton, *The Anatomy of Melancholy,* 4, 2, 1 (1621)

15 The Humble, Meek, Merciful, Just, Pious, and Devout Souls, are everywhere of one Religion; and when Death has taken off the Mask, they will know one another, tho' the

divers Liveries they wear here makes them Strangers.
William Penn, *Some Fruits of Solitude* (1693)

16 I found no narrowness respecting sects and opinions, but believed that sincere, upright-hearted people in every society, who truly love God, were accepted of Him.
John Woolman, *Journal* (1774)

17 If you are a Christian you do not have to believe that all the other religions are simply wrong all through. If you are an atheist you do have to believe that the main point in all the religions of the whole world is simply one huge mistake.
C.S. Lewis, *Mere Christianity* (1952)

18 When the deepest foundations of all the religions of the world have been laid free and restored, who knows but that those very foundations may serve once more like the catacombs, or like the crypts beneath our old cathedrals, as a place of refuge for those who, to whatever creed they belong, long for something better, purer, older and truer . . . Though leaving behind much of what is worshipped or preached in Hindu temples, in Buddhist viharas, in Mohammedan mosques, in Jewish synagogues, and Christian churches, each believer may bring down with him into that quiet crypt what he values most — his own pearl of great price.
Max Müller, *Lectures on the Origin and Growth of Religion* (1878)

19 I have to be a Hindu, a Buddhist, a Jain, a Parsee, a Sikh, a Muslim, and a Jew, as well as a Christian, if I am to know the Truth and to find the point of reconciliation in all religion.
Bede Griffiths, *Return to the Centre* (1976)

20 The great religions have as yet no common vocabulary or theological way of speaking and this makes it necessary to take a stand within the framework of one religious tradition.
William Johnston, *The Inner Eye of Love* (1978)

21 By the word of God — that is to say by Jesus Christ — Isaiah and Plato, Zoroaster, Buddha, and Confucius, uttered and wrote such truths as they declared. There is only one Divine Light, and every man in his own measure is enlightened by it.
William Temple, *Readings in St John's Gospel* (1945)

22 The Church has never declared that the Judeo-Christian tradition was alone in possessing revealed Scriptures, sacraments and supernatural knowledge of God. It has never declared that there was no affinity at all between Christianity and the mystical traditions of countries other than Israel.
Simone Weil, *Letter to a Priest* (1953)

23 The Catholic Church rejects nothing which is true and holy in these religions . . . In Hinduism, men probe the mystery of God and express it with a rich fund of myths and a penetrating philosophy . . . In the various forms of Buddhism the basic inadequacy of this changing world is recognised and men are taught with confident application how they can achieve a state of complete liberation . . . The Church also regards with esteem the Muslims who worship the one, subsistent, merciful and almighty God . . . They venerate Jesus as a prophet . . . Given the great spiritual heritage common to Christians and Jews, it is the wish of this sacred Council to foster and recommend a mutual knowledge and esteem.
Second Vatican Ecumenical Council, *Declaration on the Relation of the Church to Non-Christian Religions* (1966)

24 We believe that we may speak not only of the unknown God of the Greeks but also of the hidden Christ of Hinduism. Hidden and unknown, indeed! Yet present there, for he also is not far from any one of us.
Raymond Panikkar, *The Unknown Christ of Hinduism* (1964)

25 There is a common core of belief about ultimate reality — which I have termed a dual-aspect doctrine (or, with apologies to Buddhism, dual-aspect theism), present in each tradition.
Keith Ward, *Images of Eternity* (1987)

26 The *philosophia perennis* sees a unity which underlies the diversity of religious forms and practices.
Seyyed Hossein Nasr, 'The *Philosophia Perennis* and the Study of Religion' in *The World's Religious Traditions* (1984)

27 It seems to be quite true that the East is at the bottom of the spiritual change we are passing through today. Only this East is not a Tibetan monastery full of Mahatmas, but in a sense lies within us. It is from the depths

of our own psychic life that new spiritual forms will arise.
C.G. Jung, *Modern Man in Search of a Soul* (1933)

28 A particular religion can claim to be decisive for some people, and some people can claim that a particular religion is decisive for them, but no religion is justified in claiming that it is decisive for all.
Samuel J. Samartha, *Courage for Dialogue* (1981)

29 Not only does commitment to Jesus not exclude openness to others, but the greater the commitment to him, the greater will be one's openness to others.
Paul Knitter, *No Other Name* (1985)

30 The needed Copernican Revolution in theology involves . . . a shift from the dogma that Christianity is at the centre to the realisation that it is GOD who is at the centre and that all the religions of mankind, including our own, serve and revolve around him.
John Hick, *God and the Universe of Faiths* (1977)

31 Pluralism in the Christian theology of religions seeks to draw the faith of the world's religious past into a mutual recognition of one another's truths and values, in order for truth itself to come into proper focus.
Alan Race, *Christians and Religious Pluralism* (1983)

32 There can be no dialogue between 'religions', between Christianity and Hinduism, between one 'belief' and another. Dialogue can only take place between people.
Samuel J. Samartha, *Courage for Dialogue* (1981)

33 It would be impossible to find anywhere in the world a sincere Jew, Muslim or atheist who would not regard the assertion that he is an 'anonymous Christian' as presumptuous.
Hans Küng, *On Being a Christian* (1974)

II
THE SUPERNATURAL

20 GOD
See also 5. MONOTHEISM

1 The everlasting God, the LORD, the
Creator of the ends of the earth, fainteth
not, neither is weary. There is no searching
of his understanding.
Isaiah, 40, 28

2 O the depth of the riches both of the
wisdom and knowledge of God! How
unsearchable are his judgments, and his
ways past finding out!
Romans, 11, 33

3 In the Name of God, the Merciful, the
Compassionate.
Praise belongs to God, the Lord of the
worlds,
The Merciful, the Compassionate,
Master of the Day of Judgment.
Koran, 1, 1–3

4 I believe with perfect faith that the Creator,
blessed be his name, is not a body, and that
he is free from all the accidents of matter,
and that he has not any form whatsoever.
**Moses Maimonides, *Thirteen Principles*,
Article 3 (12th century)**

5 There is but one living and true God,
everlasting, without body, parts, or
passions; of infinite power, wisdom, and
goodness; the Maker and Preserver of all
things both visible and invisible.
**Book of Common Prayer, Articles of
Religion I**

6 Thou art the Primal God, the Ancient Spirit,
Thou art the Supreme Treasure-house of
this universe,
Thou art the knower, and the known, the
highest Home,
By thee the universe is pervaded, O thou of
infinite form.
Bhagavad Gita, 11, 38

7 The one God, hidden in all things,
All-pervading, the Inner Soul of all things.
Shvetashvatara Upanishad, 6, 11

8 There is one God, eternal truth is his name,
Creator of all things, and the all-pervading
spirit.
Fearless and without hatred, timeless and
formless.
Beyond birth and death, self-enlightened.
He is known by the grace of the Guru.
Guru Nanak, *Mul Mantra* (16th century)

9 The Wise Lord, as the Holy Spirit, shall give
us for Best Mind and deed and word true to
Righteousness,
Through Dominion and Devotion, Salvation
and Immortality.
Gathas, *Yasna*, 47

10 First of all believe that God is a being
incorruptible and blessed, just as in the
common idea of God which is engraved on
the mind, and do not assign to him anything
contrary to his incorruption or unsuited to
his blessedness.
**Epicurus, *Letter to Menoeceus*, 123 (4th
century BCE)**

11 The One must not be solely the solitary. If it
were, reality would remain buried and

shapeless since in the One there is no differentiation of forms. No beings would exist if the One remained shut up in itself.
Plotinus, *Enneads*, IV, 8 (3rd century)

12 There was something formlessly fashioned,
That existed before heaven and earth;
Without sound, without substance,
Dependent on nothing, unchanging,
All-pervading, unfailing.
One may think of it as the mother of all
        things under heaven.
Tao Te Ching, XXV

13 Man proposes, but God disposes.
Thomas Kempis, *Of the Imitation of Christ*, I, 19 (*c.* 1418)

14 God moves in a mysterious way
His wonders to perform;
He plants his footsteps in the sea,
And rides upon the storm.
William Cowper, *Olney Hymns*, 35 (1779)

15 The rich man in his castle,
The poor man at his gate,
God made them, high and lowly,
And order'd their estate.
Cecil Frances Alexander, *All Things Bright and Beautiful* (1848)

16 If God did not exist, it would be necessary to invent him.
Voltaire, *Epîtres*, 104 (1769)

17 Know then thyself, presume not God to
        scan,
The proper study of mankind is man.
Alexander Pope, *An Essay on Man* (1733)

18 An honest man's the noblest work of God.
Robert Burns, *The Cotter's Saturday Night* (1784)

19 God of our fathers, known of old,
Lord of our far-flung battle-line,
Beneath whose awful Hand we hold
Dominion over palm and pine —
Lord God of Hosts, be with us yet,
Lest we forget — lest we forget!
Rudyard Kipling, *Recessional* (1897)

20 God heard the embattled nations sing and
        shout
'Gott strafe England!' and 'God save the
        King!'
God this, God that, and God the other
        thing —
'Good God', said God, 'I've got my work
        cut out.'
J.C. Squire, *Epigrams* (1916)

21 The mills of God grind slowly, yet they grind exceeding small.
Friedrich von Logau, *Sinngedichte* (1653)

22 Those people should not be listened to who keep saying the Voice of the people is the Voice of God, since the riotousness of the crowd is always very close to madness.
Alcuin, *Letter to Charlemagne* (800)

23 In the faces of men and women I see God,
and in my own face in the glass,
I find letters from God dropt in the street,
and every one is signed by God's name.
Walt Whitman, *Leaves of Grass* (1855)

24 And all night long we have not stirred,
And yet God has not said a word!
Robert Browning, *Porphyria's Lover* (1842)

25 Thou mastering me,
God! giver of breath and bread;
World's strand, sway of the sea;
Lord of living and dead.
Gerard Manley Hopkins, *The Wreck of the Deutschland* (1876)

26 God be in my head,
And in my understanding.
Sarum Missal (1514)

27 He who knows about depth knows about God.
Paul Tillich, *The Shaking of the Foundations* (1962)

28 'Personal God' does not mean that God is 'a' person. It means that God is the ground of everything personal and that he carries within him the ontological power of personality. He is not a person, but he is not less than personal.
Paul Tillich, *Systematic Theology*, I (1951)

---

21 GODS
See also 6. POLYTHEISM

---

1 Thou shalt have no other gods before me.
Exodus, 20, 3

2 They be no gods, which are made with hands.
Acts, 19, 26

3 Allah will not forgive the association of anything with himself, though he forgives

anything short of that to whom he wills; he who associates anything with Allah has devised a mighty deed of guilt.
Koran, 4, 51

4 The gods are fond of the cryptic, and dislike the obvious.
Brihad-aranyaka Upanishad, 4, 2, 2

5 Worshippers of the gods go to the gods,
worshippers of the ancestors go to the
ancestors,
worshippers of the goblins go to the goblins,
worshippers of me also go to me.
Bhagavad Gita, 9, 25

6 How many are the Krishnas and Shivas,
How many are the Brahmas fashioning the
worlds,
Of many kinds and shapes and colours . . .
How many adepts, Buddhas and Yogis are
there,
How many goddesses and how many
images of goddesses,
How many gods and demons and how
many sages.
Hymns of Guru Nanak, *Dharam khand* (16th century)

7 Have the false gods ever been good masters?
Gathas, *Yasna*, 44, 20

8 The gods of most nations claim to have created the world. The Olympians make no such claim. The most they ever did was to conquer it . . . And when they have conquered their kingdoms, what do they do? Do they attend to the government? Do they promote agriculture? Do they practise trades and industries? Not a bit of it. Why should they do any honest work?
Gilbert Murray, *Five Stages of Greek Religion* (1925)

9 He says that Socrates is an evildoer who corrupts the youth, and who does not believe in the gods whom the city believes in.
Plato, *Apology*, 24b.

10 The gods ought to have made all men good, if they were truly concerned about the welfare of the human race, or at least they ought to have taken care of the good.
Cicero, *The Nature of the Gods*, 3, 79 (1st century BCE)

11 To those who ask you, Where have you seen the gods, or how do you who are so devout know for sure that the gods exist? I answer,

first of all, that even to the very eye, they are in some manner visible and apparent. Secondly, neither have I seen my own soul, and yet I respect and honour it. So then for the gods, by the daily experience that I have of their power and providence towards myself and others, I know certainly that they exist and therefore I worship them.
Marcus Aurelius, *Meditations*, 12, 21 (2nd century)

12 Whom the gods love dies young.
Menander, *Dis Exapaton*, 4 (4th century BCE)

13 To despise this sphere and the gods within it, or anything else that is lovely, is not the way to goodness.
Plotinus, *Enneads*, 2, 9, 16 (3rd century)

14 There was a rocky valley between Buxton and Bakewell . . . divine as the vale of Tempe; you might have seen the gods there morning and evening, — Apollo and the sweet Muses of the Light.
John Ruskin, *Praeterita*, III, iv (1889)

15 We, peopling the void air,
Make gods to whom to impute
The ills we ought to bear,
With God and Fate to rail at,
Suffering easily.
Matthew Arnold, *Empedocles on Etna*, 1, 2 (1852)

16 With an alien people clutching their gods.
I should be glad of another death.
T.S. Eliot, *Journey of the Magi* (1927)

17 Man is quite insane. He would not know how to create a maggot, and he creates gods by the dozen.
Michel de Montaigne, *Essais*, II, xii (1588)

18 'Twas only fear first in the world made gods.
Ben Jonson, *Sejanus*, II, ii (1603)

19 Before the gods that made the gods
Had seen their sunrise pass,
The White Horse of the White Horse Vale
Was cut out of the grass.
G.K. Chesterton, *Ballad of the White Horse*, i (1914)

20 I thank whatever gods may be
For my unconquerable soul.
W.E. Henley, *Echoes*, iv, 'Invictus' (1888)

22 GODDESSES

1 To burn incense unto the queen of heaven, and to pour out drink offerings unto her, as we have done, we, and our fathers, our kings, and our princes, in the cities of Judah, and in the streets of Jerusalem.
Jeremiah, 44, 17

2 That the temple of the great goddess Diana should be despised, and her magnificence should be destroyed, whom all Asia and the world worshippeth.
Acts, 19, 27

3 Have ye considered Al-Lat, and Al-Uzza, and the third, Manat, the other goddess? Have ye male issue and he female? In that case it is an unfair division. They are nothing but names which you and your fathers have used.
Koran, 53, 19–23

4 When on high the heaven had not been named, firm ground below had not been called by name, naught but primordial waters, their begetter, and Mother Tiamat, she who bore them all.
Enuma Elish, *When on high,* 1 (12–10th centuries BCE)

5 O mother earth, kindly set me down upon a well-founded place! With (father) heaven co-operating. O thou wise one, do thou place me into happiness and prosperity.
Atharva Veda, XII, 1

6 Of female powers I am Fame, Fortune, Speech, Memory, Wisdom, Steadfastness, Patience.
Bhagavad Gita, 10, 34

7 She has given us good shelter, strength and endurance, She, the consecrated of the Good Mind.
Gathas, *Yasna, 48, 6*

8 I pay homage to the Perfection of Wisdom. She is worthy of homage. She is unstained, and the entire world cannot stain her. She is a source of light, and from everyone in the triple world she removes darkness.
Ashta-sahasrika, VII, 170 (1st century)

9 Maya, the mythical goddess, sprang from the One, and her womb brought forth three acceptable disciples of the One: Brahma, Vishnu and Shiva.
Hymns of Guru Nanak, *eka mai* (16th century)

10 That which was the beginning of all things under heaven we may speak of as the 'mother' of all things.
He who apprehends the mother, thereby knows the sons.
Tao Te Ching, LII

11 When the Sun-goddess heard this she said: 'Though of late many prayers have been addressed to me, of none has the language been so beautiful as this'. So she opened a little the rock-door and peeped out. Thereupon the God . . . who was waiting beside the rock-door, forthwith pulled it open, and the radiance of the Sun-goddess filled the universe.
Nihongi, I, 45 (720)

12 I will sing of well-founded Earth, mother of all, eldest of all beings. She feeds all creatures that are in the world, all that go upon the goodly land, and all that are in the paths of the seas, and all that fly: all these are fed from her store. Through you, O Queen, men are blessed in their children and blessed in their harvests.
Homeric Hymns, XXX (8th–6th centuries BCE)

13 God rejoiceth that he is our Mother . . . Our Kind Mother, our Gracious Mother, for that he would all wholly become our Mother in all things, he took the Ground of his Works full low and full mildly in the Maiden's womb.
Julian of Norwich, *Revelations of Divine Love,* 52 and 60 (*c.* 1393)

14 The Gnostic interpretation of the Holy Ghost as the Mother contains a core of truth in that Mary was the instrument of God's birth and so became involved in the trinitarian drama as a human being. The Mother of God can, therefore, be regarded as a symbol of mankind's essential participation in the Trinity.
C.G. Jung, *Psychology and Religion* (1958)

15 Respectability has spread its leaden mantle over the whole country . . . and the man wins the race who can worship that great goddess with the most undivided devotion.
Leslie Stephen, *Sketches from Cambridge* (1865)

23 ANGELS

1 He shall give his angels charge over thee, to
keep thee in all thy ways.
Psalm, 91, 11

2 In heaven their angels do always behold the
face of my Father which is in heaven.
Matthew, 18, 10

3 If trouble befall a man, let him not cry to
Michael or Gabriel, but let him cry to Me
and I will answer him at once.
Mishnah, *Berachoth*, 13

4 When Adam was in the Garden of Eden, he
used to recline while the ministering angels
roasted flesh and filtered wine for him.
Mishnah, *Sanhedrin*, 59

5 The Night of Power is better than a
thousand months; in it the angels and the
spirit let themselves down, by the
permission of their Lord, with regard to
every affair.
Koran, 97, 3–4

6 When he confesses his sins, God saith to the
angels, 'Bring him back, for he never lost
hope of Me.'
Jalalu'l-Din Rumi, *Mathnawi*, V, 1815
(13th century)

7 O God thine angels are on their guard from
fear of thee, attentive, obeying thee, carrying
out thy command, and they cease not night
or day from thy praise.
Shi'a prayer, in Constance Padwick, *Muslim
Devotions* (1961)

8 The accuser angels below are busy all about
the world during the first three hours of the
night, but exactly at midnight the
accusations halt, for at this moment God
enters the Garden of Eden.
Zohar, *Genesis*, 'Midnight' (14th century)

9 They, above all, are pre-eminently worthy of
the name Angel because they first receive the
Divine Light, and through them are
transmitted to us the revelations which are
above us.
Dionysius the Areopagite, *The Celestial
Hierarchies*, IV (6th century)

10 An angel is a spiritual being, created by God
without a body, for the service of
Christendom and the Church.
Martin Luther, *Table Talk* (1569)

11 It is not known precisely where angels dwell
— whether in the air, the void, or the
planets. It has not been God's pleasure that
we should be informed of their abode.
Voltaire, *Philosophical Dictionary* (1764)

12 In this theatre of man's life it is reserved only
for God and angels to be lookers on.
Francis Bacon, *The Advancement of
Learning*, II, xx, 8 (1605)

13 Angels and ministers of grace defend us!
William Shakespeare, *Hamlet*, I, iv, 39
(c. 1603)

14 Matthew, Mark, Luke, and John,
The Bed be blest that I lie on,
Four angels to my bed,
Four angels round my head,
One to watch, and one to pray,
And two to bear my soul away.
Thomas Ady, *A Candle in the Dark* (1656)

15 At dusk three angels come down from the
sky to every house. One stands at the door,
another sits at the table, and a third watches
over the bed. They look after the house and
protect it. Neither wolves nor evil spirits can
enter the whole night long.
Carlo Levi, *Christ stopped at Eboli* (1947)

16 Then cherish pity, lest you drive an angel
from your door.
William Blake, *Songs of Innocence*, 'Holy
Thursday' (1789)

17 I heard a soft melodious voice, more pure
and harmonious than any I had heard with
my ears before; I believed it was the voice of
an angel who spake to the other angels.
John Woolman, *Journal* (1774)

24 SPIRITS

See also 26. SPIRIT-POSSESSION AND
EXORCISM, 172. GHOSTS AND APPARITIONS

1 Who maketh his angels spirits; his ministers
a flaming fire.
Psalm 104, 4

2 Believe not every spirit, but try the spirits
whether they are of God.
1 John, 4, 1

3 He created the jinn as a flame of fire.
Koran, 55, 14

4 Peace be to you, ye men of the mysterious

other world! Peace be to you ye sanctified
spirits! Ye lieutenant saints, ye overseeing
saints, ye saints of permutation. Ye pillars of
the earth.
Qadiriyya prayer, in Constance Padwick,
Muslim Devotions (1961)

5 Here is our food. All you spirits of our tribe,
invite each other. I do not say that you are
jealous, but you who have raised this sick
man, summon all the spirits.
Zulu prayer, in John S. Mbiti, *The Prayers
of African Religion* (1975)

6 *Glendower*: I can call spirits from the vasty
               deep.
Hotspur: Why, so can I, or so can any man;
But will they come when you do call for
          them?
William Shakespeare, *Henry IV, Part I*, III,
i, 53–5 (*c.* 1597)

7   For Spirits when they please
Can either Sex assume, or both; so soft
And uncompounded is their essence pure.
John Milton, *Paradise Lost*, I, 423–5 (1667)

8 Great spirits now on earth are sojourning;
He of the cloud, the cataract, the lake . . .
And other spirits there are standing apart
Upon the forehead of the age to come.
John Keats, *Sonnets*, 'Addressed to
Haydon', ii (1817)

9 I stood within the City disinterred;
And heard the autumnal leaves like light
               footfalls
Of spirits passing through the streets.
Percy Bysshe Shelley, *Ode to Naples* (1820)

10 The day of spirits; my soul's calm retreat
Which none disturb.
Henry Vaughan, *Silex Scintillans*, 'The
Night' (1655)

---

25 DEMONS AND DEVILS

1 They sacrificed unto devils, not to God; to
gods whom they knew not.
Deuteronomy, 32, 17

2 Your adversary the devil, as a roaring lion,
walketh about, seeking whom he may
devour.
1 Peter, 5, 8

3 The sounding of the ram's horn on the New
Year confounds Satan.
Mishnah, *Rosh Hashanah*, 16

4 When We said to the angels: 'Prostrate
yourselves to Adam'; they prostrated
themselves, with the exception of Iblis; he
refused in his pride and became one of the
unbelievers.
Koran, 2, 32

5 We acknowledge that Satan tempts man,
and suggests doubts to him, and deranges
him.
Al-Ash'ari, *Ibāna*, 54 (10th century)

6 Rābi'a said, 'My love for God leaves no
room for hating Satan.'
Attar, in Margaret Smith, *Rābi'a the Mystic*
(1928)

7 It is said in the Religion that when the
Destructive Spirit saw that he himself and
the demons were powerless on account of
the Blessed Man, he was thrown into a
stupor. For three thousand years he lay in a
stupor. And when he was thus languishing,
the demons with monstrous heads cried out
one by one (saying). 'Arise, O our father, for
we would join battle in the material world.'
Bundahishn, IV, in R.C. Zaehner, *The
Teachings of the Magi* (1956)

8   To whom th' Arch-Enemy,
And thence in Heav'n calld Satan, with bold
              words
Breaking the horrid silence thus began.
     If thou beest he; But O how fall'n! how
             chang'd
From him, who in the happy Realms of
              Light
Cloth'd with transcendent brightness didst
             outshine
Myriads though bright.
John Milton, *Paradise Lost*, 1, 81–7 (1667)

9 Here on earth they say of one who is not a
giver, who is not a believer, who is not a
sacrificer, 'Oh, devilish!' for such is the
doctrine of the devils.
Chandogya Upanishad, 8, 8, 5

10 There are two creations of beings in this
              world,
The divine and the demoniac.
Bhagavad Gita, 16, 6

11 God seeks comrades and claims love, the
Devil seeks slaves and claims obedience.
Rabindranath Tagore, *Fireflies* (1928)

12 The Devil is good in so far as he hath Being.
In this sense nothing is evil, or not good. But
sin is to will, desire, or love otherwise than
as God doth.
Theologia Germanica, 47 (1518)

13 I have always said, the first Whig was the
Devil.
Samuel Johnson, in Boswell, *Life of Johnson*
(1778)

14 He is — what we are; for sometimes
The Devil is a gentleman.
Percy Bysshe Shelley, *Peter Bell the Third*
(1819)

15 We may not pay Satan reverence, for that
would be indiscreet, but we can at least
respect his talents.
Mark Twain, in *Harper's Magazine* (1899)

16 An Apology for the Devil: It must be
remembered that we have only heard one
side of the case. God has written all the
books.
Samuel Butler, *Note-Books* (1912)

17 One is always wrong to open a conversation
with the devil, for, however he goes about it,
he always insists upon having the last word.
André Gide, *Journals* (1917)

18 This is a puzzling world, and Old Harry's
got a finger in it.
George Eliot, *The Mill on the Floss* (1860)

19 Readers are advised to remember that the
devil is a liar. Not everything that Screwtape
says should be assumed to be true even from
his own angle.
C.S. Lewis, *The Screwtape Letters* (1942)

20 I can't help thinking that if the devil doesn't
exist and, therefore man has created him, he
has created him in his own image and
likeness.
Just as he did God, you mean.
Fyodor Dostoyevsky, *The Brothers
Karamazov* (1880)

21 The devil is, undoubtedly, an awkward
figure: he is the 'odd man out' in the
Christian cosmos. That is why people would
like to minimize his importance by
euphemistic ridicule or by ignoring his
existence altogether; or, better still, to lay
the blame for him at man's door.
C.G. Jung, *Psychology and Religion* (1958)

22 The Devil was a great loss in the
preternatural world. He was always

something to fear and to hate; he supplied
the antagonist powers of the imagination,
and the arch of true religion hardly stands
firm without him.
William Hazlitt, *The Round Table* (1817)

23 The Dark Powers who are real terrors,
always on the verge of triumph, are
perpetually foiled by the steadfastness of
men.
Joseph Conrad, *Lord Jim* (1900)

---

26 SPIRIT-POSSESSION AND EXORCISM

---

1 Then said the woman, Whom shall I bring
up unto thee? And he said, Bring me up
Samuel. And when the woman saw Samuel,
she cried with a loud voice.
1 Samuel, 28, 11–12

2 A certain damsel possessed with a spirit of
divination met us, which brought her
masters much gain by soothsaying.
Acts, 16, 16

3 An ifrit, one of the jinn said: 'I shall bring it
thee.'
Koran, 27, 39

4 My wife woke in the water and suddenly,
changing her shape, became an Ifritah.
The Thousand and One Nights, 1, 3 (10th
century)

5 He had a wife possessed by a spirit. We
asked him: 'Who are you?'
Brihad-aranyaka Upanishad, 3, 7, 1

6 There is a widespread belief in possession by
evil spirits, which can be expelled by
exorcism . . . Only those possessed by an
evil spirit are affected by the fire, and, if
their skin is burnt, it is a sign of deliverance
from demoniacal possession.
L.S.S. O'Malley, *Popular Hinduism* (1935)

7 The removal of an illness is the occupation
of the 'devil-charmer' or exorcist, of the
magician who exorcises the planets, the
signs of the zodiac, and the moon-houses, of
the maker of amulets and talismans, and
finally, of the peoples' priest who plays the
part of mediator between the deities and
mankind.
P. Wirz, *Exorcism and the Art of Healing in
Ceylon* (1954)

8 The exorcist is both a caricature and an inversion of the orthodox Buddhist monk. He uses Buddhist sacred words for purposes diametrically opposed to those of the monk; the latter chants sacred words in order to teach morality and to transfer merit and blessings, whereas the exorcist uses sacred words to frighten spirits and drive them away.
S.J. Tambiah, *Buddhism and the Spirit Cults of North-East Thailand* (1970)

9 The malign spirit suddenly yielded after so many tenacious weeks and passed from Murasaki to the little girl who was serving as medium, and who now commenced to thresh and writhe and moan.
Murasaki Shikibu, *The Tale of Genji*, 35 (11th century)

10 The shamanic seance usually includes four stages: 1. evocation of the helping spirits; 2. discovery of the cause of the illness, usually an evil spirit that has stolen the patient's soul or entered his body; 3. expulsion of the evil spirit by threats, noise, etc.; and finally 4. the shaman's ascent to the sky.
Mircea Eliade, *Shamanism* (1951)

11 When the men of his village hold their Expulsion Rite, he puts on his Court dress and stands on the eastern steps.
Confucius, *Analects*, X, 10

12 Governmental discrimination against the shamans began in 31 B.C. when their seances were barred at court, and ended in their complete proscription from the Sung Dynasty onwards.
H. Welch, *The Parting of the Way* (1957)

13 May we see that . . . symptoms of malevolent spirit possession are an unconscious attempt by women to protest against neglect and oppression in a society largely dominated by men?
Carmen Blacker, *The Catalpa Bow* (1975)

14 Women's possession cults are also, I argue, thinly disguised protest movements directed against the dominant sex.
I.M. Lewis, *Ecstatic Religion* (1971)

15 Enjoying nothing so much as a good tussle with Belial or Beelzebub, he was forever fabricating and exorcizing demoniacs. Thanks to his efforts, Chinon was full of raving girls, bewitched cows, husbands unable, because of some sorcerer's malignant spells, to perform their conjugal duties.
Aldous Huxley, *The Devils of Loudun* (1952)

16 I command thee, unclean spirit, in the name of the father, of the son, and of the holy ghost, that thou come out, and depart from these infants.
First Prayer Book of Edward VI. Of the Administration of Public Baptism (1549)

17 Martin Bucer . . . also considers the exorcism to be objectionable, as implying that all unbaptized persons are demoniacs.
W.H. Frere, *A New History of the Book of Common Prayer* (1901)

18 There is an elaborate rite for the exorcism of evil spirits, the use of which is restricted to priests who have episcopal permission, contained in the 'Rituale Romanum'.
F.L. Cross, *The Oxford Dictionary of the Christian Church* (1957)

19 No exorciser harm thee!
Nor no witchcraft charm thee!
Ghost unlaid forbear thee!
Nothing ill come near thee!
William Shakespeare, *Cymbeline*, IV, ii, 277–80 (1609–10)

20 The black and merciless things that are behind the great possessions.
Henry James, *The Ivory Tower* (1917)

21 In our rich consumers' civilization we spin cocoons around ourselves and get possessed by our possessions.
Max Lerner, *The Unfinished Country*, i (1959)

22 The more popular kind of spiritualism is simply the old hankering after supernatural manifestations, which are always dear to semi-regenerate minds.
W.R. Inge, *Christian Mysticism* (1899)

III
THE NATURE OF GOD

27 BEING

1 To whom then will ye liken God? Or what likeness will ye compare unto him?
Isaiah, 40, 18

2 Every good gift and every perfect gift is from above, and cometh down from the Father of lights, with whom is no variableness, neither shadow of turning.
James, 1, 17

3 He who is everlasting, constant and in no way subject to change; immutable in his essence, and as he consists of nothing but his essence, he is mutable in no way whatsoever.
Moses Maimonides, *Guide for the Perplexed,* 23 (12th century)

4 He is God; there is no god but he, Knower
    of the hidden
and the revealed . . .
He is God; there is no god but he, the King,
    the Holy One,
the Perfect, the Faithful, the Protector, the
    Sublime,
the Over-ruling, the Majestic . . .
He is God; the Creator, the Maker, the
    Former;
to him belong the Most Beautiful Names.
Koran, 59, 22–4

5 We confess that God has two hands, without asking how, as he said: 'I have created with my two hands', and: 'On the contrary, both his hands are stretched wide.'
Al-Ash'ari, *Ibāna,* 9 (10th century)

6 He is, and there is with him no before or after, nor above nor below, nor far nor near, no union nor division, nor how nor where nor place. He is now as he was. He is the One without oneness and the Single without Singleness . . . whithersoever you turn, there is the Face of God.
Ibn al-Arabi, *Kitab al-Ajwiba,* 98, trans. Margaret Smith (1950)

7 I call upon thee, O God, by the Names inscribed around thy throne. I call upon thee by the Names written upon thy Seat. I call upon thee, O God, by the Name written upon the leaves of the olive tree.
Prayers of the Naqshabandi Order, trans. Kenneth Cragg, *Alive to God* (1970)

8 Of syllables I am the letter A,
Of compounded words the Dual,
I alone am immortal Time,
I am the Ordainer, with Faces in all
        directions.
Bhagavad Gita, 10, 33

9 He has no name, no dwelling-place, no
        caste;
He has no shape, or colour, or outer limits.
He is the Primal Being, Gracious and
        Benign,
Unborn, ever Perfect, Eternal.
Hymns of Guru Gobind Singh, *nam tham* (17th century)

10 God is a Being of perfect simplicity and truth, both in deed and word, and neither changes in himself nor imposes upon others.
Plato, *Republic,* II, 382

11 God is a living being, eternal, and infinitely good, since life and eternity without

interruption or pause is God's. Actually, this *is* God.
Aristotle, *Metaphysics*, VI, 9, 9

12 The divine One is a negation of negations, and a desire of desires. What does 'One' mean? Something to which nothing is to be added. The soul lays hold of the Godhead where it is pure, where there is nothing beside it, nothing else to consider.
Meister Eckhart, *Fragments*, trans. R.B. Blakney (1941)

13 God in eternity is without contradiction, suffering and grief, and nothing can hurt or vex him of all that is or befalleth. But with God, when he is made Man, it is otherwise.
Theologia Germanica, 40 (14th century)

14 The nature of God is a circle, of which the centre is everywhere and the circumference is nowhere.
Empedocles, attr., quoted in *Roman de la Rose* (13th century)

15 God is not a mixt and compounded Being, so that His Love is one thing and Himself another: but the most pure and simple of all Beings, all Act, and pure Love in the abstract.
Thomas Traherne, *Centuries of Meditations* (17th century)

16 It is essential to every theistic conception of God, and most of all to the Christian, that it designates and precisely characterizes Deity by the attributes Spirit, Reason, Purpose, Good Will, Supreme Power, Unity, Selfhood.
Rudolf Otto, *The Holy* (1917)

17 All God's names are hallowed, for in them He is not merely spoken about, but also spoken to.
Martin Buber, *I and Thou* (1937)

18 He who knows about depth knows about God.
Paul Tillich, *The Shaking of the Foundations* (1949)

19 Shall I say: Creator, Sustainer, Pardoner, Near One, Distant One, Incomprehensible One, God both of flowers and stars, God of the gentle wind and of terrible battles, Wisdom, Power, Loyalty and Truthfulness, Eternity and Infinity, you the All-Merciful, you the Just One, you Love itself?
Karl Rahner, *Prayers for Meditation* (1968)

28 TRANSCENDENCE

1 It is he that sitteth upon the circle of the earth, and the inhabitants thereof are as grasshoppers.
Isaiah, 40, 22

2 The blessed and only Potentate, the King of kings, and Lord of lords; who only hath immortality, dwelling in the light which no man can approach unto; whom no man hath seen, nor can see.
1 Timothy, 6, 16

3 God — there is no god but he, the Living, the Eternal . . . His throne extends over the heavens and the earth, to guard them does not weary him. He is the Exalted, the Mighty.
Koran, 2, 256

4 Why do you claim that the Creator is unlike creatures? If he were like them, his relation to temporal production would be the same as theirs. And if he were like them, he would have to be like them either in all respects or in some one respect . . . God Most High has said: 'There is nothing like unto him', and, 'No one is his equal.'
Al-Ash'ari, *Kitāb al-Luma*, 1, 7 (10th century)

5 No other higher thing whatsoever exists higher than Me, all this universe is strung on Me like heaps of pearls on a string.
Bhagavad Gita, 7, 7

6 The Lord differs from the soul which is embodied, acts and enjoys, and is the product of Nescience, in the same way as the real juggler who stands on the ground differs from the illusive juggler who climbs up to the sky by means of a rope.
Shankara, *Commentary on the Vedānta Sutras*, 1, 1, 17 (9th century)

7 Simply by being described in all Scripture as the 'Supreme Soul', the Supreme Person must be understood to be in a different category from all souls, whether bound or liberated.
Ramanuja, *Commentary on the Bhagavad Gita*, 15, 17 (11th century)

8 Manifest in all things, he is also the
                              Unmanifest Ground
of all things:

He is Formless. He is Transcendent.
Hymns of Guru Arjan, *sargun nirgun* (16th century)

9 We cannot grasp what God is, but only what he is not, and how other things are related to him.
Thomas Aquinas, *Summa contra Gentiles,* I, xxx (13th century)

10 Who am I, Lord, that I should presume to approach unto thee? Behold the Heaven of Heavens cannot contain thee, and thou sayest, 'Come ye all unto me.'
Thomas Kempis, *Of the Imitation of Christ,* IV, 1 (*c.* 1418)

11 Essence beyond essence, Nature increate, Framer of the world, I set thee, Lord, before my face. I lift up my soul to thee, I worship thee on my knees, and humble myself under thy mighty hand.
Lancelot Andrewes, *Private Devotions,* 1 (1648)

12 There is an infinitely qualitative difference between God and man. This means, or the expression for this is, that man is capable of nothing, it is God who gives everything, who gives man faith, and so on.
Søren Kierkegaard, *Papirer* (1849), P.A. Heiberg (ed.) (1924)

13 The nature of the numinous can only be suggested by means of the special way in which it is reflected in the mind in terms of feeling . . . We are dealing with something for which there is only one appropriate expression, *mysterium tremendum.*
Rudolf Otto, *The Holy* (1917)

14 Of course God is the 'wholly Other'; but He is also the wholly Same, the wholly Present. Of course He is the *Mysterium Tremendum* that appears and overthrows; but He is also the mystery of the self-evident, nearer to me than my *I.*
Martin Buber, *I and Thou* (1937)

---

29 IMMANENCE
See also 8. PANTHEISM

---

1 Whither shall I go from thy spirit?
Or whither shall I flee from thy presence?
If I ascend up into heaven, thou art there:
If I make my bed in hell, behold, thou art there.
Psalm, 139, 7–8

2 Where two or three are gathered together in my name, there am I in the midst of them.
Matthew, 18, 20

3 When ten people sit together and occupy themselves with the Torah, the Shechinah abides among them; as it is said, 'God stands in the congregation of the godly.'
Mishnah, *Pirke Aboth,* III, 7

4 Hast thou not seen that God knows what is in the heavens and what is in the earth? There is not a private conclave of three, but he is a fourth in it, nor of five but he is a sixth, nor of a lower number than that, nor of a higher, but he is with them wherever they may be.
Koran, 58, 8

5 If two persons sit together and scheme, King Varuna is there as a third, and knows it.
Atharva Veda, IV, 16, 2

6 Thou art woman. Thou art man.
Thou art the youth and the maiden too.
Thou as an old man totterest with a staff,
Being born, thou becomest facing in every direction.

Thou art the dark blue bird and the green parrot with red eyes.
Thou hast the lightning for thy child. Thou art seasons and seas.
Having no beginning, thou dost abide with immanence,
Wherefrom all beings are born.
Shvetashvatara Upanishad, 4, 3–4

7 Behind the Veil there's talk of ME and THEE;
Then falls the Veil — and no more THEE and ME.
Omar Khayyám, *Rubáiyát,* 32 (12th century)

8 All this universe is pervaded by Me, in the form of the unmanifested. All beings dwell in Me, but I do not subsist in them.
Bhagavad Gita, 9, 4

9 God is near you, with you, within you. A holy spirit sits within us, spectator of our evil and our good, our guardian.
Seneca, *Letters,* xli, 12 (1st century)

10 Man is merged with the Supreme, sunken

into it, one with it. Centre coincides with centre.
Plotinus, *Enneads*, 6, 9, 10 (3rd century)

11 If we say that all things are in God, we understand by this that, just as he is without distinction in his nature yet absolutely distinct from all things, so all things are in him in the greatest distinction and yet not distinct, because man is God in God.
Meister Eckhart, *Latin Sermon*, IV, 1 (13–14th centuries)

12 After this I saw God in a Point, that is to say, in mine understanding, — by which sight I saw that he is in all things.
Julian of Norwich, *Revelations of Divine Love*, 11 (*c.* 1393)

13 All things are in God, and depend upon him in such manner that without him they cannot possibly either exist or be conceived.
Baruch Spinoza, *Ethics*, I (1677)

14 There is an *omnipresent eternal Mind*, which knows and comprehends all things, and exhibits them to our view in such a manner, and according to such rules, as He Himself hath ordained, and by us they are termed the *laws of nature*.
George Berkeley, *Third Dialogue* (1713)

15 Teach me, my God and King,
In all things Thee to see.
George Herbert, *The Elixir* (1633)

16 O God within my breast,
Almighty! ever-present Deity!
Emily Brontë, *Last Lines* (1846)

17   And I have felt
A presence that disturbs me with the joy
Of elevated thoughts; a sense sublime
Of something far more deeply interfused,
Whose dwelling is the light of setting suns,
And the round ocean, and the living air,
And the blue sky, and in the mind of man,
A motion and a spirit, that impels
All thinking things, all objects of all
       thought,
And rolls through all things.
William Wordsworth, *Lines written above Tintern Abbey* (1798)

18 Speak to Him thou for He hears,
and Spirit with Spirit can meet —
Closer is He than breathing,
and nearer than hands and feet.
Alfred Tennyson, *The Higher Pantheism*, vi (1847)

19 Thou hast bound bones and veins in me,
      fastened me flesh,
And after it almost unmade, what with
      dread,
    Thy doing: and dost thou touch me
      afresh?
Over again I feel thy finger and find thee.
Gerard Manley Hopkins, *The Wreck of the Deutschland* (1876)

20 Even the enlightened person remains what he is, and is never more than his own limited ego before the One who dwells within him, whose form has no knowable boundaries, who encompasses him on all sides, fathomless as the abysms of the earth and vast as the sky.
C.G. Jung, *Psychology and Religion* (1958)

21 God as the ground of being infinitely transcends that of which he is the ground. He stands 'against' the world, in so far as the world stands against him, and he stands 'for' the world, thereby causing it to stand for him.
Paul Tillich, *Systematic Theology*, II (1957)

---

30 INCARNATION — AVATAR

---

1 The Word was made flesh, and dwelt among us, and we beheld his glory, the glory as of the only begotten of the Father, full of grace and truth.
John, 1, 14

2 Whenever there is a decline of Righteousness, and a rise of Unrighteousness, then I generate myself.
Bhagavad Gita, 7, 7

3 We take refuge in thee, thou art our only help. O Lord, we beseech thee to take birth as a man in order to destroy the enemy of man and gods.
Ramayana, 1, 15

4 The venerable ascetic Mahavira, the last of the Tirthakaras, took the form of an embryo in the womb of Devananda . . . He knew that he was to descend, he knew that he had descended, he knew not when he was descending.
Kalpa Sutra, 2 (3rd century BCE)

5 The Bodhisattva considered the matter of

the place in which he should be reborn. 'This king Shuddhodana', thought he, 'is worthy to be my father.' He then sought a mother who should be gracious, of good birth, pure of body, tender of passion, and short-lived.
Mahavastu, ii, 2 (1st century BCE)

6 The emphasis which Gurū Nānak lays upon God being *ajūni*, unborn, non-incarnated: Pervading all (as the heavens extend over all), infinite, absolute, not-incarnated.
W.H. McLeod, *Guru Nānak and the Sikh Religion* (1968)

7 For this mission God sent me into the world, And on the earth I was born as a mortal.
Hymns of Guru Gobind Singh, *mai apna* (17th century)

8 There is one physician, fleshly and spiritual, begotten and unbegotten, God in man, both of Mary and of God, first passible and then impassible.
Ignatius, *To the Ephesians*, vii, 2 (2nd century)

9 When a ray is projected from the sun it is a portion of the whole sun; but the sun will be in the ray because it is a ray of the sun; the substance is not separated but extended. So from spirit comes spirit, and God from God.
Tertullian, *Apology*, xxi (3rd century)

10 True God of true God, begotten not made, of one substance with the Father, through whom all things were made; who for us men and for our salvation came down from the heavens, and was made flesh of the Holy Spirit and the Virgin Mary, and became man.
Nicene Creed (4th century)

11 The Word, in a manner indescribable and inconceivable, united personally to himself flesh animated with a reasonable soul, and thus became man and was called the Son of man.
Cyril, *Epistle*, iv (5th century)

12 Why God became man.
Anselm, *Cur deus homo* (11th century)

13 Our God contracted to a span Incomprehensibly made man.
Charles Wesley, *A Collection of Hymns* (1779)

14 The eternal logos of God has a human heart, he risked the adventure of a human heart, until pierced by the sin of the world, it had

flowed out, until it had suffered to the end on the cross.
Karl Rahner, *Theological Investigations*, III (1967)

15 The incarnation, as I may say so, of a spiritual substance, is to me a kind of standing miracle.
T. Burnet, *The Earth* (1684)

16 Great men are the incarnations of the spirit of the age.
G.H. Lewes, *A Biographical History of Philosophy* (1847)

17 The avatar of Donne, as an intermediate power between Spenser and Milton, was so brief and partial.
D. Masson, *The Life of John Milton* (1859)

18 She ended with enjoying, and even abetting, this new avatar of the Church militant.
Leigh Hunt, *Autobiography*, ii (1850)

19 The kitchen-maid was an abstract personality, a permanent institution to which an invariable set of attributes assured a sort of fixity and continuity and identity throughout the long series of transitory human shapes in which that personality was incarnate; for we never found the same girl there two years running.
Marcel Proust, trans. C.K. Scott-Moncrieff, *Swann's Way* (1922)

31 TRIADS AND TRINITY

1 May the Sun protect us from the sky, the Wind from the air, the Fire from the earthly regions.
Rig Veda, X, 158

2 The threefold offspring of the Lord of Creatures — gods, men, and demons — dwelt with their father as students of sacred knowledge.
Brihad-aranyaka Upanishad, 5, 2

3 A holy trinity of Hinduism, the *Trimūrti* or triple form, was evolved, of Brahmā the creator, Viṣṇu the preserver, and Síva the destroyer . . . Early western students of Hinduism were impressed by the parallel between the Hindu trinity and that of Christianity. In fact the parallel is not very close, and the Hindu trinity, unlike the Holy

Trinity of Christianity, never really 'caught on'. All Hindu trinitarianism tended to favour one god of the three.
A.L. Basham, *The Wonder that was India* (1954)

4 Three acceptable disciples of the One: Brahma, Viṣṇu and Síva . . .
God makes them to work as He wills.
Hymns of Guru Nanak, *eka mai* (16th century)

5 The Body of Essence, the Body of Bliss, the Created Body — these are the bodies of the Buddhas. The first is the basis of the two others.
Mahayana-sutralankara, 9, 60 (4th century)

6 What help shall my soul expect from anyone . . . But in the Right, in thee Wise Lord, and the Best Mind.
Gathas, *Yasna*, 50, 1

7 Tao gave birth to One; One gave birth to Two; Two gave birth to Three; Three gave birth to the ten thousand things.
Tao Te Ching, XLII

8 There can be little doubt that the Taoists had intimate contact with Nestorian Christians at the capital during the T'ang dynasty. The really interesting question is where their trinity came from eight centuries previously.
J. Needham, *Science and Civilisation in China*, 2 (1956)

9 Baptizing them in the name of the Father, and of the Son, and of the Holy Ghost.
Matthew, 28, 19

10 Though the word 'Trinity', first used in its Greek form τριάς by Theophilus of Antioch (c. AD 180), is not found in Scripture, the conception is there both implicitly and explicitly.
F.L. Cross, *The Oxford Dictionary of the Christian Church* (1958)

11 The *Timaeus*, which was the first to propound a triadic formula for the God-image in philosophical terms, starts off with the ominous question: 'One, two, three — but . . . where is the fourth?'
C.G. Jung, *Psychology and Religion* (1958)

12 The Platonic formula for the triad contradicts the Christian Trinity in one essential point: the triad is built on opposition, whereas the Trinity contains no opposition of any kind, but is, on the contrary, a complete harmony in itself. The three Persons are characterized in such a manner that they cannot possibly be derived from Platonic premises, while the terms Father, Son and Holy Ghost do not proceed in any sense from the number three.
C.G. Jung, *Psychology and Religion* (1958)

13 With the one and with the other
There was equality,
So Three Persons, one Beloved,
Loved all, and they were three.
John of the Cross, *Romance, Upon the Gospel* (16th century)

14 Batter my heart, three person'd God; for,
    you
As yet but knock, breathe, shine, and seek to
    mend;
That I may rise, and stand, o'erthrow me,
    and bend
Your force, to break, blow, burn and make
    me new.
John Donne, *Holy Sonnets* (1633)

15 The *monotheistic faith* taken over from Israel and held in common with Islam must never be abandoned in any doctrine of the Trinity. There is no God but God.
Hans Küng, *On Being a Christian* (1974)

---

32 CREATOR
See also 43. IN THE BEGINNING, 44. CREATION

---

1 Where wast thou when I laid the
        foundations of the earth? . . .
When the morning stars sang together, and
        all the sons of
God shouted for joy?
Job, 38, 4 and 7

2 By him were all things created, that are in heaven, and that are in earth, visible and invisible, whether they be thrones, or dominions, or principalities, or powers: all things were created by him, and for him.
Colossians, 1, 16

3 In the same manner that the letter *beth* is closed on all sides and only open in front, similarly you are not permitted to inquire into what is before or what was behind, but only from the actual time of Creation.
Mishnah, *Chagigah*, 77

4 He is the eternal Lord, who reigned before
any creature had yet been fashioned; when
all was made according to his will, already
then his name was King. And after all has
ceased to be, still will he reign in solitary
majesty. He was, he is and he shall be in
glory.
Hebrew Prayer Book, *Adon Olam*, 1
(medieval)

5 He straightened himself up to the sky, which
was smoke, and said to it and to the earth:
'Come obediently, or unwillingly.' They
said: 'We come obediently,' And he finished
them as seven heavens in two days, and
inspired into each heaven its command.
Koran, 41, 10–11

6 We hold that there is no creator at all, save
God; and that the acts of creatures are
created and determined by God.
Al-Ash'ari, *Ibāna*, 18 (10th century)

7 That which is created must, as we affirm, of
necessity be created by a cause. But the
father and maker of all this universe is past
finding out, and even if we found him, to tell
of him to all men would be impossible.
Plato, *Timaeus*, 28

8 Some sages discourse of inherent Nature;
Others likewise, of Time. Deluded men!
It is the greatness of God in the world
by which this divine-wheel is caused to
                    revolve . . .
Ruled by him, his work revolves —
This which is regarded as earth, water, fire,
                    air and space!
He creates this work, and rests again.
Shvetashvatara Upanishad, 6, 1–3

9 From the Unmanifest all manifestations
come forth at the coming of day, and they
dissolve at the coming of night, in that same
one, known as the Unmanifest.
Bhagavad Gita, 8, 18

10 Thou art part and parcel of all things
                    equally, O Creator:
Thou must feel for all men and all nations.
Hymns of Guru Nanak, *Khurasan* (16th
century)

11 The Lord God of Israel, the Living and True
God, was from all Eternity, and from all
Eternity wanted like a God. He wanted the
communication of His divine essence, and
persons to enjoy it. He wanted Worlds, He
wanted Spectators, He wanted Joys, He

wanted Treasures. He wanted, yet He
wanted not, for He had them.
Thomas Traherne, *Centuries of Meditations*
(17th century)

12 When God at first made man,
Having a glass of blessings standing by;
Let us (said he) pour on him all we can:
Let the world's riches, which dispersed lie,
Contract into a span.
George Herbert, *The Pulley* (1633)

13 God is not finished. His highest divine
attribute is His creativeness and that which
is creative exists always in the beginning
stage. God is eternally in Genesis.
Isaac Bashevis Singer, *Love and Exile*
(1985)

---

33 PARENT
See also 22. GODDESSES

---

1 Thou art my Father, my God, and the rock
of my salvation.
Psalm, 89, 26

2 I thank thee, O Father, Lord of Heaven and
earth.
Matthew, 11, 25

3 Like father to a son, most kind, O Soma;
Thoughtful like friend to friend,
O thou of wide fame.
Rig Veda, VIII, 48, 4

4 He is the father of the active Good Mind
whose daughter is beneficent Devotion.
Gathas, *Yasna*, 45, 4

5 I am the father of this world,
The mother, the establisher, the grandsire.
Bhagavad Gita, 9, 17

6 Thou art my father, thou art my mother,
thou art my brother, thou art my kin,
In all places thou art my Saviour
Hymns of Guru Arjan, *tu mera pita* (16th
century)

7 By praying thus, with deep humility and
faith, thou wilt merge into the heart of . . .
the Divine Father–Mother, in a halo of
rainbow light, and attain Buddhahood.
The Tibetan Book of the Dead, 1, ii
(8th–9th centuries)

8 Caesar Augustus, Father of his own

Fatherland, divine Rome, Zeus Paternal, and Saviour of the whole human race, in whom Providence has not only fulfilled but even surpassed the prayers of all men.
Inscription at Halicarnassus, trans. F.C. Grant, *Ancient Roman Religion* (1957)

9 Our Father, it is thy universe, it is thy will, let us be at peace, let the souls of the people be cool; thou art our Father, remove all evil from our path.
E.E. Evans-Pritchard, *Nuer Religion* (1956)

10 He cannot have God for his father who has not the church for his mother.
Cyprian, *De Catholicae Ecclesiae Unitate*, vi (3rd century)

11 If you want to know, come unto Me and I will explain to you the origin of all things. I, God the Parent, reveal Myself and I will explain to you everything in detail; then the whole world will rejoice.
Henry van Straelen, *The Religion of Divine Wisdom*, 'Tenrikyo' (1954)

12 Jesus is our Very Mother in Nature by virtue of our first making; and he is our Very Mother in Grace, by taking our nature made. All the fair working, and all the sweet natural office of dearworthy Motherhood is impropriated to the Second Person.
Julian of Norwich, *Revelations of Divine Love*, 59 (*c.* 1393)

34 SPIRIT

See also 29. IMMANENCE

1 The spirit of the Lord shall rest upon him, the spirit of wisdom and understanding, the spirit of counsel and might, the spirit of knowledge and of the fear of the Lord.
Isaiah, 11, 2

2 God is spirit, and those who worship him must worship in spirit and truth.
John, 4, 24 (RSV)

3 The Holy Spirit wept and said, 'For these do I weep'.
Gemara, on 'Lamentations', 1, 16

4 They ask thee about the Spirit; say: 'The Spirit belongs to my Lord's affair.'
Koran, 17, 87

5 Thou art the Imperishable, the supreme Object of Knowledge,
Thou art the ultimate resting-place of this universe;
Thou art the immortal guardian of the Eternal Law,
Thou art the everlasting Spirit.
Bhagavad Gita, 11, 18

6 The universal and transcendent Cause of all things is neither without being nor without life, nor without reason and intelligence; nor is he a body, nor has he form or shape, quality, quantity or weight; nor has he any localized, visible or tangible existence . . . He suffers no change, corruption, division, privation or flux; none of these things can either be identified with or attributed to him.
Dionysius, *Mystical Theology*, IV (6th century)

7 The human will . . . receives also the Holy Spirit, through which there arises in his heart a delight in and a love of that supreme and unchangeable Good which is God.
Augustine of Hippo, *De spiritu et littera*, 5 (5th century)

8 The Holy Ghost has called me by the Gospel, and illuminated me with His gifts, and sanctified and preserved me in the true faith.
Martin Luther, *Short Catechism*, 2, 3 (1529)

9 The testimony of the Spirit is that alone by which the true knowledge of God hath been, is and can be only revealed.
The Chief Principles of the Christian Religion as Professed by the People Called the Quakers, II (1678)

10 I believe that the Holy Spirit should be able to break in at any time he chooses. When we lose this — we've lost everything.
F. Masserano, *A Study of Worship Forms in the Assemblies of God Denomination* (1966)

35 LIGHT

1 The LORD is my light and my salvation; whom shall I fear?
Psalm, 27, 1

2 This is the message which we have heard of

him, and declare unto you: that God is light, and in him is no darkness at all.
1 John, 1, 5

3 God is the light of the heavens and the earth, his light is like a niche in which is a lamp, the lamp in glass and the glass like a brilliant star, lit from a blessed tree, an olive neither of the East nor of the West whose oil would almost give light even though no fire touched it. Light upon light; God guides to his light whomsoever he wills.
Koran, 24, 35

4 If you keep your gaze fixed upon the Light, you will be delivered from dualism and the plurality of the finite body.
Jalalu'l-Din Rumi, *Mathnawi*, III, 1259 (13th century)

5 Everyone who perceives must have some relationship to the light, by which he is made able to perceive, and everything which is perceived has a relationship with God, who is Light, that is, all which perceives and all which is perceived.
Ibn al-Arabi, *Futuhut*, iii (13th century)

6 Thus is it revealed in the Good Religion. Ohrmazd was on high in omniscience and goodness: for infinite time he was ever in the light. The light is the space and place of Ohrmazd: some call it the Endless Light.
Bundahishn, I, 1 (9th century)

7 O everlasting Light, surpassing all created luminaries, flash forth thy lightning from above, piercing all the most inward parts of my heart.
Thomas Kempis, *Of the Imitation of Christ*, III, 34 (*c.* 1418)

8 There is in God — some say —
A deep, but dazzling darkness; as men here
Say it is late and dusky, because they
See not all clear.
O for that Night! where I in Him
Might live invisible and dim!
Henry Vaughan, *The Night* (1650)

2 They sing the song of Moses the servant of God, and the song of the Lamb, saying, Great and marvellous are thy works, Lord God Almighty, just and true are thy ways, thou King of saints.
Revelation, 15, 3

3 Everything is in the power of Heaven, except the fear of Heaven.
Mishnah, *Berachoth*, 33

4 To him belongs what is in the heavens and what is in the earth. He is the Lofty, the Mighty.
Koran, 42, 2

5 He is almighty by virtue of his power, his power being an eternal quality.
Fiqh Akbar, II, 2 (10th century)

6 O Thou of infinite might, thy prowess is unmeasured
Thou attainest all; therefore thou art All!
Bhagavad Gita, 11, 40

7 The world is charged with the grandeur of God.
It will flame out, like shining from shook foil;
It gathers to a greatness, like the ooze of oil Crushed.
Gerard Manley Hopkins, *God's Grandeur* (1876–89)

8 God contradicts Himself, which is the reason for so many contradictions in the Torah, in man, and in all nature. If God did not contradict Himself, He would be a congealed God, a once-and-for-all perfect being as Spinoza described Him.
Isaac Bashevis Singer, *Love and Exile* (1985)

9 A Protestant theologian has even had the temerity to assert 'God *can* only be good.' Yahweh could certainly have taught him a thing or two in this respect, if he himself is unable to see his intellectual trespass against God's freedom and omnipotence.
C.G. Jung, *Aion* (1959)

36 ALMIGHTY

1 Despise not thou the chastening of the Almighty: for he maketh sore, and bindeth up: he woundeth, and his hands make whole.
Job, 5, 17–18

37 OMNISCIENCE

1 O LORD, thou hast searched me, and known me. Thou knowest my downsitting,

and mine uprising, thou understandest my thought afar off.
Psalm, 139, 1–2

2 We speak the wisdom of God in a mystery, even the hidden wisdom, which God ordained before the world unto our glory.
1 Corinthians, 2, 7

3 No one in the heavens or the earth knows the unseen except God . . . Verily thy Lord knoweth what their breasts conceal and what they make public, and there is not a hidden thing in the heaven or the earth, but it is in a clear book.
Koran, 27, 66, 76–7

4 Why do you say that God is knowing? Well-made works can be wisely ordered only by one who is knowing . . . So when we behold in man an embodiment of wise organization, such as the life arranged in him by God, and his hearing and sight, and the ways in which food and drink are distributed in him, and his perfection and completeness, and when we behold the firmament with its sun, its moon, its stars, and their courses, we see in that proof that the maker of what we have mentioned could not have made it without knowing.
Al Ash'ari, *Kitāb al-Luma*, 1, 13 (10th century)

5 Thou art the Truth, and by the Truth is Truth affirmed. Thou art the Truth, and to Truth doth Truth return, and by Truth is Truth heard.
Abu Yazid, *Mi'raj*, 1, 132–6 (9th century)

6 Thou knowest thine own self by thy self alone, O Highest Spirit.
Bhagavad Gita, 10, 15

7 Not a shadow of imperfection, such as Unknowing, and so on, attaches to Brahman, the blameless, the absolutely blessed.
Ramanuja, *Commentary on Vedanta Sutras*, I, i, 13 (11th century)

8 Beat ever more on this Cloud of Unknowing that is betwixt thee and thy God with a sharp dart of longing love.
The Cloud of Unknowing, 12 (14th century)

9 The All-knowing Mother-Wisdom of the Most High God, is superessentially at once the substantiating Cause, the connecting Power, and the universal Consummation of all principles and things.
Dionysius, *Celestial Hierarchies*, 14 (6th century CE)

10 We did for one instant attain to touch it . . . in a flash of the mind attained to touch the eternal Wisdom which abides over all.
Augustine of Hippo, *Confessions* 9, 10, 23 (5th century)

11 Suppose we but once begin to raise our thoughts to God, and to ponder his nature, and how completely perfect are his righteousness, wisdom and power.
John Calvin, *The Institutes of the Christian Religion*, I, 1, 1 (1559)

12 It must be the Supreme Wisdom and Goodness of God our Creator and Lord, as it deigned to begin it, which will preserve, direct and carry forward in His holy service this least Society of Jesus.
Constitutions of the Society of Jesus, 1 (1560)

13 All is best, though we oft doubt,
What th'unsearchable dispose
Of highest wisdom brings about,
And ever best found in the close.
John Milton, *Samson Agonistes*, 1745–48 (1671)

14 Go, teach eternal wisdom how to rule —
Then drop into thyself, and be a fool!
Alexander Pope, *An Essay on Man*, II, i, 29 (1733)

15 With these celestial Wisdom calms the mind,
And makes the happiness she does not find.
Samuel Johnson, *The Vanity of Human Wishes*, 1, 351 (1749)

16 The wrath of the lion is the wisdom of God.
William Blake, *The Marriage of Heaven and Hell*, 8 (1793)

17 Wisdom requires no form; her beauty must vary, as varies the beauty of flame. She is no motionless goddess, for ever couched on her throne.
Maurice Maeterlinck, *Wisdom and Destiny* (1898)

38 GOODNESS AND GRACE

1 I had fainted, unless I had believed to see the

goodness of the LORD in the land of the living.
Psalm, 27, 13

2 Of his fulness have all we received, and grace for grace.
John, 1, 16

3 Recite, for thy Lord is the most generous,
Who taught by the pen,
Taught man what he did not know.
Koran, 96, 3–5

4 By showing grace to you, by my own power I have revealed to you my highest form.
Bhagavad Gita, 11, 47

5 Let me tell you why the Creator made this world of generation. He was good, and the good can never have any jealousy of anything.
Plato, *Timaeus*, 29d

6 Because it is the cause of good it cannot, then, be called the Good; yet in another sense it is the Good above all.
Plotinus, *Enneads*, VI, 9, 6 (3rd century)

7 As God is simple goodness, inner knowledge and light, he is at the same time also our will, love, righteousness and truth, the innermost of all virtues.
Theologia Germanica, 31 (14th century)

8 In confidence of thy goodness and great mercy, O Lord, I draw near, sick to the Healer, hungry and thirsty to the Fountain of life, needy to the King of Heaven.
Thomas Kempis, *Of the Imitation of Christ*, IV, 2 (*c.* 1418)

9 Yet God is good: I started sure of that, And why dispute it now?
Robert Browning, *Paracelsus*, II (1835)

10 The essential thing to know about God is that God is the Good. All the rest is secondary.
Simone Weil, *Pensées sans ordre* (1962)

11 Lord, I ascribe it to thy grace,
And not to chance, as others do,
That I was born of Christian race,
Isaac Watts, *Divine Songs for Children* (1715)

12 But for the grace of God there goes John Bradford.
John Bradford (1510–55), exclamation on seeing criminals taken to execution, in *Dictionary of National Biography*

39 COMPASSION AND MERCY
See also 137. FORGIVENESS, 167. JUDGEMENT

1 I desired mercy, and not sacrifice; and the knowledge of God more than burnt offerings.
Hosea, 6, 6

2 Go home to thy friends, and tell them how great things the Lord hath done for thee, and hath had compassion on thee.
Mark, 5, 19

3 May it be thy will that thy mercy may subdue Thy wrath; and may thy mercy prevail over thy attribute of justice, so that thou mayest deal with thy children in the quality of mercy and enter on their behalf within the line of strict justice.
Mishnah, *Berachoth*, 7

4 Some of the Bedouin believe in God and the Last Day . . . God will cause them to enter into his mercy; God is forgiving, compassionate.
Koran, 9, 100

5 It is said that written on the base of the Throne are the words: I have mercy on him that yearns for Me; I give to him that asks of Me.
Dala'ilu'l-khairat, in Constance Padwick, *Muslim Devotions* (1961)

6 As a father to his son, as a friend to his
        friend,
As a lover to his beloved, be pleased to show
        mercy, O God!
Bhagavad Gita, 11, 44

7 I am an ocean of boundless compassion, moral excellence, tenderness, generosity, and sovereignty, the refuge of the whole world without distinction of persons. I, the one ocean of tenderness to all who resort to me, take away the sorrows of my devotees.
Ramanuja, *Commentary on the Bhagavad Gita*, 6, 47 (11th century)

8 O thou who rejoicest in kindness having its source in compassion, thou great cloud of good qualities and of benevolent mind, thou quenchest the fire that vexes living beings, thou pourest out nectar, the rain of the Law.
Lotus of the True Law, 24, 22

9 I take refuge in the greatly compassionate

one, the Saviour of the world, omnipotent, omnipresent, omniscient.
Ashvaghosha, *The Awakening of Faith*, 1 (2nd century CE)

10 God plays and laughs in good deeds, whereas all other deeds, which do not make for the glory of God, are like ashes before him. Thus he says: 'Rejoice, O heavens! For the Lord hath comforted his people!'
Meister Eckhart, *Sermons*, 10 (13th–14th centuries)

11 Mercy is above this sceptered sway . . . It is an attribute to God himself.
William Shakespeare, *The Merchant of Venice*, IV, i, 187–9 (*c.* 1596–8)

12 The mercy of God extends not only to those that have made his will, in some degree, the rule of their actions . . . but even to those that have polluted themselves with studied and premeditated wickedness.
Samuel Johnson, *Sermons* (1788)

13 A God all mercy is a God unjust.
Edward Young, *The Complaint: Night Thoughts*, v, 176 (1745)

14 There is a tacit assumption that grace would be no longer grace if God became too free with it.
Karl Rahner, *Nature and Grace* (1963)

15 This, and only this, . . . can give us back a belief in God — in a compassionate, torn and sorrowing God who gave us free will out of love, and having forbidden Himself to interfere, must behold in agony what we do with our freedom.
Meyer Levin, *The Fanatic* (1964)

---

40 DIVINE LOVE

1 When Israel was a child, then I loved him, and called my son out of Egypt.
Hosea, 11, 1

2 Beloved, let us love one another: for love is of God; and every one that loveth is born of God, and knoweth God. He that loveth not knoweth not God; for God is love.
1 John, 4, 7–8

3 It is certain that his chastenings are

chastenings of love; as it is said, 'For whom the Lord loveth he correcteth.'
Mishnah, *Berachoth*, 5

4 A palace which is known as the Palace of Love sits amidst a vast rock, a most secret firmament. Here in this place the treasures of the King are kept, and all his kisses of love. Every soul loved by the Holy One, be blessed, enters into that palace.
Zohar, *The Destiny of the Soul* (14th century)

5 Ask forgiveness of your Lord, then repent towards him; verily my Lord is compassionate, loving.
Koran, 11, 92

6 Unqualified Divine Love for mankind is an idea completely alien to the Qur'ān. In fact 'to love' is too strong a phrase to convey the idea . . . which can be rendered equally well as 'to like or to approve.'
D. Rahbar, *God of Justice* (1960)

7 I have become the One I love, and he whom I love has become myself! We are two spirits, mingled in one body! Thus, to see me is to see him, and to see him is to see us.
Al-Hallāj, *Dīwān*, 57 (10th century)

8 Further, hear the highest secret of all, My supreme message. Because thou art greatly loved by Me, therefore I shall tell thee what is good for thee.
Bhagavad Gita, 18, 64

9 Whoever loves Me beyond measure, I will love him beyond measure. Unable to endure separation from him, I cause him to possess me. This is my true promise: you will come to me.
Ramanuja, *Commentary on the Bhagavad Gita*, 18, 65 (11th century)

10 The love that moves the sun and the other stars.
Dante Alighieri, *Paradiso*, XXXIII, 45 (1320)

11 Would you know our Lord's meaning in this thing? Know it well: Love was His meaning. Who showed it you? Love. What did he show you? Love. Why did he show it? For Love.
Julian of Norwich, *Revelations of Divine Love*, 86 (*c.* 1393)

12 A reciprocal love is actually formed between God and the soul, like the marriage union in

which the goods of both (the divine essence which each possesses freely by reason of the voluntary surrender between them) are possessed together by both.
John of the Cross, *The Living Flame of Love*, 3, 79 (16th century)

13 It follows that God, in so far as he loves himself, loves men; and, consequently, that the love of God towards men and the intellectual love of the mind towards God, is one and the same thing.
Baruch Spinoza, *Ethics*, 5, V, 36 (1677)

14 Love bade me welcome; yet my soul drew back,
Guilty of dust and sin.
But quick-ey'd Love, observing me grow slack
From my first entrance in
Drew nearer to me, sweetly questioning
If I lack'd any thing.
George Herbert, *The Temple*, 'Love' (1633)

15 His love unto Himself is His love unto them, and His love unto them is love unto Himself. They are individually one, which it is very amiable and beautiful to behold, because therein the simplicity of God doth evidently appear. The more He loveth them, the greater He is and the more glorious.
Thomas Traherne, *Centuries of Meditations*, IV, 65 (17th century)

16 He prayeth best, who loveth best
All things both great and small;
For the dear God who loveth us,
He made and loveth all.
Samuel Taylor Coleridge, *The Rime of the Ancient Mariner*, 647–50 (1798)

---

41 PROVIDENCE

---

1 Thou visitest the earth, and waterest it: thou greatly enrichest it with the river of God, which is full of water: thou preparest them corn, when thou hast so provided for it.
Psalm, 65, 9

2 God having provided some better thing for us, that they without us should not be made perfect.
Hebrews, 11, 40

3 During a third of the day he is occupied with sustaining the whole world, from the mightiest to the most insignificant of living beings.
Mishnah, *Abodah Zarah*, 3

4 God makes generous provision for whomsoever of his servants that he wills, or straightens things for them; truly God knows everything.
Koran, 29, 62

5 For protection of the good, and for destruction of evil-doers, to make a firm footing for Right, I come into being age after age.
Bhagavad Gita, 4, 8

6 He with his powerful knowledge beholds all creatures who are beset with many hundreds of troubles and afflicted by many sorrows, and thereby is a Saviour in the world.
Lotus of the True Law, 24, 17

7 'Providence', you say, 'does not concern itself with individual men,' No wonder! — since it does not care for cities. Not even for cities? No, nor for whole nations of peoples. If, therefore, it even despises whole nations, what wonder is there if it scorns the whole human race?
Cicero, *The Nature of the Gods*, III, 79–85 (1st century BCE)

8 Among all others, the rational creature is subject to divine providence in a more excellent way, in so far as he himself partakes of a share in providence, by being provident both for self and for others. Therefore he participates in eternal reason.
Thomas Aquinas, *Summa Theologica*, II, 1, 91 (13th century)

9 The doctrine of providence deals with the history of created being as such, in the sense that in every respect and in its whole span this proceeds under the fatherly care of God the Creator.
Karl Barth, *Church Dogmatics*, III, iii (1936)

10 That to the highth of this great argument
I may assert eternal Providence,
and justify the ways of God to men.
John Milton, *Paradise Lost*, L, 24–5 (1667)

11 The World was all before them, where to choose.
Their place of rest, and Providence their guide.

John Milton, *Paradise Lost*, XII, 646–7

12 Laugh where we must, be candid where we
       can,
    But vindicate the ways of God to man.
    Alexander Pope, *An Essay on Man*, i, 13
    (1733)

13 Behind a frowning providence
    He hides a smiling face.
    William Cowper, *Olney Hymns*, 35 (1779)

14 Dare trust in His providence; and be quiet;
    and go a-Angling.
    Izaak Walton, *The Compleat Angler*, 21
    (1653)

15 God tempers the wind, said Maria, to the
    shorn lamb.
    Laurence Sterne, *A Sentimental Journey*
    (1768)

16 We continually hear it recommended by
    sagacious people to complaining neighbours
    (usually less well placed in the world than
    themselves), that they should 'remain
    content in the station in which Providence
    has placed them.' There are perhaps some
    circumstances of life in which Providence
    has no intention that people *should* be
    content.
    John Ruskin, *Unto this Last*, IV (1860)

17 'Justice' was done, and the President of the
    Immortals (in Aeschylean phrase) had ended
    his sport with Tess.
    Thomas Hardy, *Tess of the D'Urbervilles*,
    59 (1891)

18 Man's religiosity makes him look in his
    distress to the power of God in the world:
    God is the *Deus ex machina*. The Bible
    directs man to God's powerlessness and
    suffering; only the suffering God can help.
    Dietrich Bonhoeffer, *Letters and Papers
    from Prison* (1967)

19 We are all falling. This hand's falling too —
    all have this falling-sickness none
                withstands.
    And yet there's one whose gently-holding
                hands
    this universal falling can't fall through.
    Rainer Maria Rilke, *Autumn*, trans. J.B.
    Leishman (1964)

20 They sounded like Truth, but he rejected
    them. Comfort can come too easily: he
    thought, those hands will never hold my
    fall: I slip between the fingers, I am greased

with falsehood, treachery: trust was a dead
language of which he had forgotten the
grammar.
Graham Greene, *The Heart of the Matter*,
(1948)

42 PREDESTINATION AND FATE
See also 109. FREEWILL

1 Before I formed thee in the belly I knew
   thee; and before thou camest forth out of
   the womb I sanctified thee, and I ordained
   thee a prophet unto the nations.
   Jeremiah, 1, 5

2 For whom he did foreknow, he also did
   predestinate . . . Moreover whom he did
   predestinate, them he also called: and whom
   he called, them he also justified: and whom
   he justified, them he also glorified.
   Romans, 8, 29–30

3 There will nothing befall us but what God
   hath written down for us. He is our patron
   and in God let believers put their trust.
   Koran, 9, 51

4 We know that what misses us could not
   have hit us, and that what hits us could not
   have missed us; and that creatures of
   themselves possess neither harm nor
   advantage, save what God wills.
   Al-Ash'ari, *Ibāna*, 21 (10th century)

5 There is much fatalism among those who
   are Muslims. But in the essential Islam of
   the Qur'ān fatalism is strenuously opposed,
   even though frequent expression is given to
   the truly religious sense of dependence on
   God for power to act and for protection
   from evil.
   W.M. Watt, *Free Will and Predestination in
   Early Islam* (1948)

6 The Moving Finger writes; and, having writ,
   Moves on: nor all thy Piety nor Wit
       Shall lure it back to cancel half a Line,
   Nor all thy Tears wash out a Word of it.
   Edward FitzGerald, *Rubáiyát of Omar
   Khayyám* (1859)

7 The Tradition that when Allah created
   Adam, He drew forth his posterity from his
   loins in two handfuls, one white as silver

and one black as coal, and said, 'These are in Paradise, and I care not; and these are in Hell and I care not.'
R.A. Nicholson, *The Idea of Personality in Ṣūfism* (1923)

8 The Lord ordains any one's acts, for whatever reason, and distributes the fruits of what men have previously done. When a man does anything, whether good or bad, know that it was ordained by the Placer.
Mahabharata, III, 33, 20

9 Everything has its own destiny, and it is for us to accept our destiny in its true form.
Mencius, VII, 2 (4th century BCE)

10 Thus saith the maiden Lachesis, the daughter of Necessity: 'Ye short-lived souls, a new generation of men shall here begin the cycle of its mortal existence. Your destiny shall not be allotted to you, but you shall choose it for yourselves . . . The responsibility lies with the chooser. Heaven is guiltless.'
Plato, *Republic*, X, 617

11 This is the predestination of saints, namely the foreknowledge and planning of God's kindnesses, by which they are most surely delivered, whoever are delivered. As for the rest, where are they left by God's righteous judgement save in the mass of perdition?
Augustine of Hippo, *De dono perseverantiae*, 35 (5th century)

12 By the decree of God, for the manifestation of His glory, some men and angels are predestinated unto everlasting life, and others foreordained to everlasting death.
The Westminster Confession of Faith, III (1643)

13 Predestination to Life is the everlasting purpose of God.
Book of Common Prayer, Articles of Religion XVII

14 I am aware that many have held and do hold the opinion that events are controlled by fate and by God so much that the prudence of men cannot modify them, and indeed that men have no influence whatever . . . Nevertheless, because free choice cannot be ruled out, I think it is probably true that fate controls half the things we do, and leaves the other half to be controlled by ourselves.
Niccolo Machiavelli, *The Prince*, 25 (1532)

15 All things have been predetermined by God; not, indeed, from the freedom of a will, or from an absolutely arbitrary decree, but from the absolute nature or infinite power of God.
Baruch Spinoza, *Ethics*, I (1677)

16 Great Destiny the Commissary of God.
John Donne, *Of the Progress of the Soul* (1601)

17 For those whom God to ruin has design'd, He fits for fate, and first destroys their mind.
John Dryden, *The Hind and the Panther*, iii, 1093 (1687)

18 I am the master of my fate: I am the captain of my soul.
W.E. Henley, *Echoes*, 'Invictus' (1888)

19 If an omnipotent and omniscient Creator ordains everything and foresees everything, we are brought face to face with a difficulty as insoluble as is that of free will and predestination.
Charles Darwin, *The Variation of Animals and Plants under Domestication* (1868)

20 God does not play dice.
Albert Einstein, in B. Hoffman, *Albert Einstein, Creator and Rebel*

21 For forty years he had fought against economic fatality. It was the central ill of humanity, the cancer which was eating into its entrails. It was there that one must operate; the rest of the healing process would follow.
Arthur Koestler, *Darkness at Noon* (1940)

22 The man who submits to his fate calls it the will of God: the man who puts up a hopeless and exhausting fight is more apt to see the devil in it.
C.G. Jung, *Psychology and Alchemy* (1953)

23 Belief in fate is mistaken from the beginning . . . the presence of the *Thou*, the becoming out of solid connexion is inaccessible to it. It does not know the reality of spirit; its scheme is not valid for spirit.
Martin Buber, *I and Thou* (1937)

IV
THE UNIVERSE

43 IN THE BEGINNING

1 In the beginning God created the heaven and the earth.
Genesis, 1, 1

2 In the beginning was the Word, and the Word was with God, and the Word was God. The same was in the beginning with God.
John, 1, 1–2

3 'In the beginning' — when the will of the King began to take effect, he engraved signs into the heavenly sphere. Within the most hidden recess a dark flame issued from the mystery of En Sof, the Infinite.
Zohar, *The Beginning*, 1 (14th century)

4 Which beginning of time according to our Chronologie, fell upon the entrance of the night preceding the twenty-third day of October in the year of the Julian Calendar, 710 [BCE 4004]
James Ussher, *The Annals of the World* (1658)

5 In the beginning nothing whatsoever was here. This was covered over with death, with hunger — for hunger is death . . . In the beginning this world was Soul, alone in the form of a Person. Looking around, he saw nothing else than himself. He said first: 'I am.'
Brihad-aranyaka Upanishad, 1, 1, 2; 1, 4, 1

6 In the beginning, my dear, this world was just Being, one only, without a second. To be sure, some people say: 'In the beginning this world was just Non-being, one only, without a second; from that Non-being Being was produced.' But verily, my dear, whence could this be? said he. How could Being be produced from Non-being? On the contrary, my dear, in the beginning this world was just Being, one only, without a second.
Chandogya Upanishad, 6, 2, 1–2

7 I am the beginning of creations, and the end, and the middle too.
Bhagavad Gita, 10, 32

8 In the beginning they established life and non-life, that at the last the worst existence should be for the wicked, but for the righteous one the Best Mind.
Gathas, *Yasna*, 30, 4

9 First of all, the Void came into being, next broad-bosomed Earth, the solid and eternal home of all, and Eros, the most beautiful of the immortal gods.
Hesiod, *Theogony*, 116 (8th century BCE)

10 Once upon a time there existed gods but no mortal creatures. When the appointed time came for these also to be born, the gods formed them within the earth out of a mixture of earth and fire.
Plato, *Protagoras*, 320

11 Io dwelt within the breathing-space of immensity.
The universe was in darkness, with water everywhere.
There was no glimmer of dawn, no clearness, no light.
Hare Hongi, *A Maori Cosmogony* (1907)

12 In the beginning there was no sun, no moon, no stars. All was dark, and everywhere there was only water. A raft came floating on the water. It came from the north, and in it were two persons — Turtle and Father-of-the-Secret-Society.
R.B. Dixon, *Maidu Myths* (1902)

44 CREATION
See also 32. CREATOR

1 He that created the heavens and stretched them out; he that spread forth the earth, and that which cometh out of it.
Isaiah, 42, 5

2 Thou hast created all things, and for thy pleasure they are and were created.
Revelation, 4, 11

3 God having determined to found a mighty state, first of all conceived its form in His mind, according to which form He made a world only perceptible to the intellect, and then completed one visible to the external senses, using the first one as a model.
Philo, *On the Creation of the World,* iv (1st century)

4 Ten things were created on the first day, viz. heaven and earth, Tohu and Bohu [waste and void], light and darkness, wind and water, the duration of day and the duration of night.
Mishnah, *Chagigah,* 12

5 Verily your Lord is God, who created the heavens and the earth in six days, then seated himself on the throne causing the night to cover the day, following day quickly, and the sun and the moon and the stars subjected to service by his command.
Koran, 7, 52

6 He, desiring to produce beings of many kinds from his own body, first with a thought created the waters, and placed his seed in them. That became a golden egg, in brilliancy equal to the sun; in that egg he himself was born as Brahma, the progenitor of the whole world.
Laws of Manu, i, 8–9

7 Neither death nor immortality was there then; there was no distinction of night or day. That One breathed without breath by inner power . . . by the might of its own fervour That One was born.
Rig Veda, 10, 129, 2–3

8 He who is without beginning and without end, in the midst of confusion, the Creator of all, of manifold form, the One embracer of the universe — By knowing God one is released from all fetters.
Shvetashvatara Upanishad, 5, 13

9 I take refuge in that same primal Spirit, whence issued forth of old the whole cosmic activity.
Bhagavad Gita, 15, 4

10 Ohrmazd, before the act of creation, was not Lord; after the act of creation he became Lord, eager for increase, wise, free from adversity, ever ordering aright, bounteous, all-perceiving.
Great Bundahishn, 1, 18 (9th century)

11 When God created the heavens, the earth and creatures, he did not *act.* He had nothing to do. He made no effort . . . When God made man, he put into his soul his equal, his active, everlasting masterpiece.
Meister Eckhart, *Sermons,* 27 (13th–14th centuries)

12 When the stars threw down their spears,
And water'd heaven with their tears,
Did he smile his work to see?
Did he who made the lamb make thee?
William Blake, *Tyger, Tyger* (1793)

13 All things began in order, so shall they end, and so shall they begin again; according to the ordainer of order and mystical mathematics of the city of heaven.
Thomas Browne, *The Garden of Cyrus,* 4 (1658)

14 God is the perfect poet,
Who in his person acts his own creations
Robert Browning, *Paracelsus,* II (1835)

15 Why is all around us here
As if some lesser god had made the world,
But had not force to shape it as he would?
Alfred Tennyson, *The Passing of Arthur* (1869)

16 Who made the world I cannot tell:
'Tis made, and here I am in hell.
My hand, though now my knuckles bleed,
I never soiled with such a deed.
A.E. Housman, *Collected Poems* (1939)

17 Creation — that is the great redemption from suffering, and life's growing light. But that the creator may be, suffering is needed and much change.
Friedrich Nietzsche, *Thus Spake Zarathustra* (1883)

18 The story of the creation and of original sin in Genesis is true. But other stories about the creation and original sin in other traditions are also true and also contain incomparably precious truths.
Simone Weil, *Letter to a Priest* (1953)

19 There is grandeur in this view of life, with its several powers, having been originally breathed by the Creator into a few forms or one; and that, while this planet has gone cycling on according to the fixed law of gravity, from so simple a beginning endless forms most beautiful and most wonderful have been and are being evolved.
Charles Darwin, *Of the Origin of Species* (1859)

---

45 NATURE

---

1 The earth is the Lord's, and the fulness thereof; the world, and they that dwell therein.
Psalm, 24, 1

2 The invisible things of him from the creation of the world are clearly seen, being understood by the things that are made, even his eternal power and Godhead.
Romans, 1, 20

3 He made for you the earth a carpet, and the heaven a dome; he sent down water from heaven, and thereby produced fruits as a provision for you.
Koran, 2, 20

4 In the cooing of the doves, in the hovering of birds, in the pasturing of cattle, in the excellence of the strong, in the might of the full-grown, in the sleeping of slumberers, in the brightening of morning, in the murmur of the winds.
Sufi prayer, in Constance Padwick, *Muslim Devotions* (1961)

5 You must know that both material Nature and the Spirit are without beginning, though changes and qualities spring from Nature.

Nature is declared the cause of anything that concerns action, means or result, while the Spirit is the cause of experience in pleasure and pain.
Bhagavad Gita, 13, 19–20

6 As a dancer ceases dancing when she has shown herself to the audience, so Nature ceases producing when she has revealed herself to the Spirit. Generous Nature, with its qualities, without benefit to herself, causes by many means benefit to the Spirit.
Samkhya-karika, 2, 60 (4th century)

7 The world is only a partial manifestation of the Godhead, it is not that Divinity. The Godhead is infinitely greater than any natural manifestation can be. By his very infinity, by his absolute freedom, he exists beyond all possibility of integral formulation in any scheme of worlds or extension of cosmic Nature, however wide, complex, endlessly varied this and every world may seem to us.
Aurobindo Ghose, *Essays on the Gita,* 2, 1, 9 (1920)

8 For the sake of the splendour, honour and glory of this life; for the sake of birth, death and final liberation; for the removal of pain, man acts sinfully towards the earth, or causes others to act so, or allows others to act so. This deprives him of happiness and perfect wisdom.
Acharanga Sutra, 1, 1 (3rd century BCE)

9 Heaven and Earth and all that lies between
    is like a bellows, in that it is
    empty, but gives a supply that
    never fails . . .
Heaven is eternal, the Earth everlasting.
How come they to be so? It is because they
    do not foster their own lives; that
    is why they live so long.
Tao Te Ching, V and VII

10 By the transformation of Yang and its union with Yin, the five agents arise: water, fire, wood, metal and earth. When these five forces are distributed in harmonious order, the four seasons run their course. The five agents constitute the system of Yin and Yang, and Yin and Yang constitute one Great Ultimate.
Chou Tun-yi, 1, 2 (11th century)

11 When I was a young man, I had a passionate desire for the wisdom that is called Physical Science. I thought it a splendid thing to

know the causes of everything: why a thing comes into being, and why it perishes, and why it exists . . . It seemed to me to be right that Mind should be the cause of all things, and I thought to myself, If this is so, then Mind will order and arrange each thing in the best possible way.
Plato, *Phaedo*, 96

12 What we call Nature is a Life-soul, born of a prior soul that lives a more powerful life than hers. She stands quietly gazing within herself, not looking either at what is above her or below, but steadfast in her own place, and in a kind of self-knowledge.
Plotinus, *Enneads*, 3, 8, 4 (3rd century)

13 I asked the earth and it answered me: 'I am not it', and all things whatsoever made the same confession. I asked the sea and the deeps and the creeping things and they answered me: 'We are not thy God; seek beyond us.'
Augustine of Hippo, *Confessions*, X, vi (5th century)

14 Whatever is well-fitting in you, O Universe, is fitting to me. Nothing can be early or late to me, which is seasonable to you. Whatever your seasons bring shall be happy fruit and increase to me. O Nature, all things come from you, all things exist in you. The poet says, Dear city of Cecrops; shall not I say, Dear city of God?
Marcus Aurelius, *Meditations*, 4, 19 (2nd century)

15 Here is the unity of blades of grass and bits of wood and stone, together with everything else . . . All that nature tries to do is to plunge into that unity, into the Father-nature, so that it may all be one, the one Son.
Meister Eckhart, *Sermons*, 11 (13th–14th centuries)

16 He showed me a little thing, the quantity of a hazel-nut, in the palm of my hand; and it was round as a ball. I looked thereupon with eye of my understanding, and thought: *What may this be?* And it was answered generally thus: *It is all that is made.*
Julian of Norwich, *Revelations of Divine Love*, V (c. 1393)

17 You never enjoy the world aright, till the Sea itself floweth in your veins, till you are clothed with the heavens, and crowned with the stars: and perceive yourself to be the sole

heir of the whole world, and more than so, because men are in it who are every one sole heirs as well as you.
Thomas Traherne, *Centuries of Meditations*, I, 29 (17th century)

18 By all these I prayed, by the rolling sun bursting through untrodden space, a new ocean of ether every day unveiled. By the fresh and wandering air encompassing the world; by the sea sounding on the shore — the green sea, white-flecked at the margin, and the deep ocean; by the strong earth under me.
Richard Jefferies, *The Story of my Heart* (1883)

19 God Almighty first planted a Garden. And indeed it is the purest of human pleasures. It is the greatest refreshment to the spirits of man; without which buildings and palaces are but gross handyworks.
Francis Bacon, *Essays*, 46 (1625)

20 He would adore my gifts instead of Me, And rest in Nature, not the God of Nature: So both should losers be.
George Herbert, *The Pulley* (1633)

21 Slave to no sect, who takes no private road, But looks through Nature, up to Nature's God.
Alexander Pope, *An Essay on Man*, iv (1733)

22 All things are artificial, for nature is the art of God.
Thomas Browne, *Religio Medici*, i (1643)

23 Nature is very consonant and conformable with herself.
Isaac Newton, *Opticks*, III, i (1730)

24 It is a happy world after all. The air, the earth, the water, teem with delighted existence. In a spring noon, or a summer evening, on whichever side I turn my eyes, myriads of happy beings crowd upon my view.
William Paley, *Natural Theology* (1802)

25 Theology at 120°F in the shade seems, after all, different from theology at 70°F . . . The theologian at 70°F in a good position presumes God to be happy and contented, well-fed and rested, without needs of any kind. The theologian at 120°F tries to imagine a God who is hungry and thirsty,

who suffers and is sad, who sheds perspiration and knows despair.
Klaus Klostermaier, *Hindu and Christian in Vrindaban* (1969)

26 The eternal silence of these infinite spaces frightens me.
Blaise Pascal, *Pensées* (1670)

27 Call the world if you please 'The Vale of Soul-Making.'
John Keats, letter to George and Georgiana Keats, 1819

28 All those bodies which compose the mighty frame of the world — have not any subsistence without a mind.
George Berkeley, *The Principles of Human Knowledge* (1710)

29 Bishop Berkeley destroyed this world in one volume octavo, and nothing remained, after his time, but mind; which experienced a similar fate from the hand of Mr Hume in 1739.
Sydney Smith, *Sketches of Moral Philosophy* (1850)

30 We stood talking for some time together of Bishop Berkeley's ingenious sophistry to prove the non-existence of matter . . . It is impossible to refute it . . . Johnson answered, striking his foot with mighty force against a large stone, till he rebounded from it, 'I refute it *thus.*'
James Boswell, *The Life of Samuel Johnson* (1791)

31 The chess-board is the world; the pieces are the phenomena of the universe; the rules of the game are what we call the laws of Nature.
T.H. Huxley, *Lay Sermons,* iii (1868)

32 The universe is not hostile, nor yet is it friendly. It is simply indifferent.
J.H. Holmes, *A Sensible Man's View of Religion* (1933)

33 That there is an America of secrets, and unknown Peru of Nature, whose discovery would richly advance them, is more than conjecture.
J. Glanvill, *The Vanity of Dogmatising* (1661)

34 The laws, the life, and the joy of beauty in the material world of God, are as eternal and sacred parts of His creation as, in the world of spirits, virtue; and in the world of angels, praise.
John Ruskin, *Modern Painters,* IX, xii (1888)

35 Are God and Nature then at strife
That Nature lends such evil dreams?
Alfred Tennyson, *In Memoriam,* LIV (1850)

36 The stuff of the universe, woven in a single piece according to one and the same system, but never repeating itself from one point to another, represents a single figure. Structurally it forms a Whole.
Pierre Teilhard de Chardin, *The Phenomenon of Man* (1959)

37 This secular world — formerly regarded as 'this' world, the wicked world *par excellence,* a neopagan world — today is not only taken into account in Christendom, but largely consciously approved and assisted in its development.
Hans Küng, *On Being a Christian,* i (1976)

46 THE FIRST HUMAN BEINGS

1 Adam said, This is now bone of my bones, and flesh of my flesh: she shall be called Woman, because she was taken out of Man.
Genesis, 2, 23

2 The first man Adam was made a living soul; the last Adam was made a quickening spirit.
1 Corinthians, 15, 45

3 Beloved is man, for he was created in the image of God; but it was by a special love that it was made known to him that he was created in the image of God.
Mishnah, *Aboth,* III, 18

4 If God is said to walk at eventide in the garden, and Adam to hide himself under the tree, I fancy that no one will question that these statements are figurative, declaring mysterious truths by the means of a seeming history, not one that took place in a bodily form.
Origen, *Peri Archon,* iv, 16 (3rd century)

5 Thou hast made us for thyself, and our heart is restless until it rest in thee.
Augustine of Hippo, *Confessions,* i (5th century)

6 Thy Lord said to the angels: 'See, I am going to create a human being from potter's clay, of mud ground down; So when I have formed him, and breathed my spirit into him, fall in obeisance to him.'
Koran, 15, 28–9

7 The female was fastened to the side of the male, and God cast the male into a deep slumber, and he lay on the side of the temple. God then cut the female from him and decked her as a bride and led her to him.
Zohar, *Creation of Man* (14th century)

8 He desired a second. He was, indeed, as large as a woman and a man closely embraced. He caused that self to fall into two pieces. Therefrom arose a husband and a wife. Therefore this is true: 'Oneself is like a half-fragment.'
Brihad-aranyaka Upanishad, i, 4, 3

9 There really was a man-woman in those days, a being which was half male and half female . . . Each of these beings was globular in shape, with rounded back and sides, four arms and four legs, and two faces, both the same, on a cylindrical neck . . . Zeus cut them all in half . . . Now when the work of bisection was complete it left each half with a desperate yearning for the other, and they ran together and flung their arms around each other's necks, and asked for nothing better than to be rolled into one.
Plato, *Symposium*, 189–91

10 Descending from heaven to this island, they erected a heavenly pillar and a spacious palace. At that time Izanagi asked his spouse Izanami saying: 'How is your body formed?' She replied saying: 'My body, formed though it be formed, has one place which is formed insufficiently.' Then Izanagi said: 'My body, formed though it be formed, has one place which is formed to excess. Therefore, I would like to take that place in my body which is formed to excess and insert it into that place in your body which is formed insufficiently, and thus give birth to the land . . . After they had finished saying this, they were united and bore a child.
Kojiki, i, 4–6 (712)

11 So passed they naked on, nor shunned the sight
of God or Angel, for they thought no ill:

So hand in hand they passed, the loveliest pair
That ever since in love's embraces met.
John Milton, *Paradise Lost*, IV, 319–22 (1667)

12 Here feel we but the penalty of Adam,
The seasons' difference.
William Shakespeare, *As You Like It*, II, i, 5–6 (*c.* 1599)

13 When Eve upon the first of Men
The apple press'd with specious cant,
Oh! what a thousand pities then
That Adam was not Adamant!
Thomas Hood, *A Reflection* (1827)

14 Adam and Eve had many advantages, but the principal one was that they escaped teething.
Mark Twain, *Pudd'nhead Wilson* (1894)

15 Oh, Adam was a gardener, and God who made him sees
That half a proper gardener's work is done upon his knees.
Rudyard Kipling, *The Glory of the Garden* (1886)

16 Of Adam's first wife, Lilith, it is told
(The witch he loved before the gift of Eve)
That, ere the snake's, her sweet tongue could deceive,
And her enchanted hair was the first gold.
Dante Gabriel Rossetti, *Lilith* (1870)

17 O wisest love! that flesh and blood
Which did in Adam fail,
Should strive afresh against their foe,
Should strive and should prevail.
John Henry Newman, *The Dream of Gerontius* (1865)

18 The romantic figure of the Noble Savage — gloriously glowing in rude but radiant physical health — was quickly banished into the realm of myth when Physical Medicine revealed that it was hardly possible to find in a primitive community any healthy person.
Margaret J. Field, *Search for Security* (1960)

47 PRIMEVAL FLOOD

1 God said unto Noah, The end of all flesh is come before me; for the earth is filled with

violence through them; and, behold, I will destroy them with the earth. Make thee an ark of gopher wood.
Genesis, 6, 13–14

2 As in the days that were before the flood they were eating and drinking, marrying and giving in marriage, until the day that Noah entered into the ark.
Matthew, 24, 38

3 It was suggested to Noah: 'No more of thy people will believe than have believed already, so be not distressed at what they have been doing. Make the Ark under our eyes.'
Koran, 11, 38–9

4 Tear down this house, build a ship!
Give up possessions, seek thou life.
Despise property and keep the soul alive!
Aboard the ship take thou the seed of all
        living things.
The Epic of Gilgamesh, Tablet XI
(1200–1000 BCE)

5 The fish said, 'in such and such a year that flood will come. Thou shalt then attend to me by preparing a ship; and when the flood has risen thou shalt enter into the ship, and I will save thee from it' . . . The flood then swept away all these creatures, and Manu alone remained here.
Shatapatha Brahmana, i, 8, 4–6

6 You must have an ark built, a sturdy one with a cable tied to it. You will embark on it with the seven seers. All the seeds of creatures I have enumerated before you should place in the ark and then wait for me.
Mahabharata, 3, 30

7 Zeus in disgust let loose a great flood on the earth, meaning to wipe out the whole race of man; but Deucalion, King of Phthia . . . built an ark, victualled it, and went aboard with his wife Pyrrha.
Robert Graves, The Greek Myths (1955)

8 *Athenian*: Then what view do you both take of the ancient legends? Have they any truth behind them?
Clinias: Which legends might you mean?
Athenian: Those which tell of repeated destructions of mankind by floods, pestilences, and from various other causes, which leave only a handful of survivors . . . The few who then escaped the general

destruction must all have been mountain shepherds, mere scanty embers of humanity.
Plato, Laws, 3, 677

9 A branch of one of your antediluvian families, fellows that the flood could not wash away.
William Congreve, Love for Love, V, ii (1695)

10 Theirs was the giant race before the flood.
John Dryden, Epistles, 'To Mr Congreve' (1693)

11 Après nous le déluge [after us the flood].
Madame de Pompadour, quoted in Madame de Hausset, Memoires (1766)

12 If I were called in
To construct a religion
I should make use of water.
Philip Larkin, The Whitsun Weddings (1964)

---

48 THE LAST DAYS
See also 167. JUDGEMENT

---

1 Then said I, O my Lord, what shall be the end of these things? And he said, Go thy way, Daniel: for the words are closed up and sealed till the time of the end.
Daniel, 12, 8–9

2 In those days shall be affliction, such as was not from the beginning of the creation which God created unto this time, neither shall be.
Mark, 13, 19

3 If you are worthy I will hasten it; if you are not worthy it will be in its time.
Mishnah, Sanhedrin, 98

4 When comes the great earthquake, and the earth brings forth its burdens, and man says: 'What is the matter with it?' That day it will tell its news, that thy Lord has prompted it.
Koran, 99, 1–5

5 For ninety days and nights did the spiritual gods do battle in the material world with the Destructive Spirit and the demons until they were routed and hurled into Hell.
Bundahishn, IV, 13 (9th century)

6 Lo, I am Time, that causes worlds to perish, grown mature, and come forth here to swallow up the worlds.
Bhagavad Gita, 11, 32

7 The cloud-capp'd towers, the gorgeous
　　　palaces,
The solemn temples, the great globe itself,
Yea, all which it inherit, shall dissolve
And, like this insubstantial pageant faded
Leave not a rack behind.
William Shakespeare, *The Tempest*, IV, i,
152–6 (1611)

8 In the light of today's perspectives we have
to say that what is involved in this
immediate expectation is not so much an
error as a time-conditioned, time-bound
world view.
Hans Küng, *On Being a Christian*, C, II, i
(1974)

9 In every moment slumbers the possibility of
being the eschatological moment: you must
awaken it.
Rudolf Bultmann, *Jesus and the Word*
(1934)

10 Many who are not yet 'in the Kingdom of
God' in its earthly manifestation, will enjoy
its ultimate fulfilment in a world beyond
this.
C.H. Dodd, *The Parables of the Kingdom*
(1936)

---

49 NEW WORLDS

1 It shall come to pass in the last days, that the
mountain of the LORD's house shall be
established in the top of the mountains, and
shall be exalted above the hills, and all
nations shall flow unto it.
Isaiah, 2, 1

2 I saw a new heaven and a new earth; for the
first heaven and the first earth were passed
away.
Revelation, 21, 1

3 This world is like a vestibule before the
World to Come; prepare yourself in the
vestibule that you may enter into the hall.
Mishnah, *Aboth*, 4

4 On the day when we shall roll up the heaven
like the rolling up of a scroll for the books,
as we made the creation at the first, we shall
restore it again.
Koran, 21, 104

5 When men shall roll up space, as it were a
piece of leather, then there will be an end of
evil.
Shvetashvatara Upanishad, 6, 20

6 This very same host of beings, coming into
existence over and over again, is dissolved at
the approach of night, willy-nilly, and
comes forth again at the approach of day.
Bhagavad Gita, 8, 19

7 The material world will become immortal
for ever and ever. This too is said, that this
earth will become flat, with neither hills nor
dales.
Bundahishn, in R.C. Zaehner, *The
Teachings of the Magi* (1956)

8 India will be quite flat everywhere . . . It will
have innumerable inhabitants, who will
commit no crimes or evil deeds, but will take
pleasure in doing good.
Maitreya-vyakarana, in E. Conze, *Buddhist
Scriptures* (1959)

9 All is heaven there; earth is heaven, and the
sea is heaven, and so are animals, plants and
men . . . Each walks there, as it were, on no
strange earth, but it is always in its own
place. Its starting-point accompanies it as it
hastens aloft, and it is not one thing and its
region another.
Plotinus, *Enneads*, 5, 8, 3 (3rd century)

10 In that City there shall be free will, the same
in all and indivisible in each, freed from all
evil and filled with all good . . . That is what
it shall be in the end that has no end. For
what else is our end, but to come to that
realm of which there is no end?
Augustine of Hippo, *The City of God*, 22,
30 (5th century)

11 The Utopian way of life provides not only
the happiest basis for a civilized community,
but also one which, in all human
probability, will last for ever.
Thomas More, *Utopia*, II (1516)

12 As we turn away from the flagstaff where
the new banner has just been run up; as we
depart, our ears yet ringing with the blare of
the heralds' trumpets that have proclaimed
the new order of things, what shall we turn
to then, what *must* we turn to then?
To what else, save to our work, our daily
labour?
William Morris, *Hopes and Fears for Art*
(1882)

13 I will not cease from Mental Fight,
Nor shall my Sword sleep in my hand
Till we have built Jerusalem
In England's green and pleasant Land.
William Blake, *Milton* (1804)

14 One God, one Law, one element,
And one far-off divine event,
To which the whole creation moves.
Alfred Tennyson, *In Memoriam,* cxxxi
(1850)

15 According to the first hypothesis which
expresses the hopes towards which we
ought in any case to turn our efforts as to an
ideal, evil on the earth at its final stage will
be reduced to a minimum . . . Some sort of
unanimity will reign over the entire mass of
the noosphere. The final convergence will
take place *in peace.*
Pierre Teilhard de Chardin, *The
Phenomenon of Man*
(1959)

V
HUMANITY
See also XVI MEN AND WOMEN

50 HUMAN NATURE

1 What is man, that thou art mindful of him?
and the son of man, that thou visitest him?
For thou hast made him a little lower than
      the angels,
and hast crowned him with glory and
      honour.
Psalm, 8, 4–5

2 What man knoweth the things of a man,
save the spirit of man which is in him?
1 Corinthians, 2, 11

3 Man was first created a single individual to
teach the lesson that whoever destroys one
life, Scripture ascribes it to him as though he
had destroyed a whole world; and whoever
saves one life, Scripture ascribes it to him as
though he had saved a whole world.
Mishnah, *Sanhedrin*, IV, 5

4 When thy Lord said to the angels: 'Lo, I am
going to place a viceroy [caliph] in the
earth'. They said: 'Wilt thou place in it one
who will work corruption and shed blood?
We sing hymns in thy praise and ascribe
holiness to thee.' He replied: 'I know what
ye know not.'
Koran, 2, 28

5 The aforesaid microcosmic being is named a
Man and a Viceroy. He is named a Man on
account of the universality of his organism
and because he comprises all realities.
Moreover, he stands to God as the pupil,
which is the instrument of vision, to the eye.

By means of him God beheld His creatures
and had mercy on them.
Ibn al-Arabi, *Fusus*, trans. R.A. Nicholson
(1907)

6 Of priests, warriors, artisans and serfs the
actions are distinguished by the qualities
that spring from their innate nature.
Bhagavad Gita, 18, 41

7 In dependence on the thirty-two parts of the
body and the five Elements of existence
there takes place this denomination
'Nagasena', this designation, this
conceptual term, a current appellation and a
mere name. In ultimate reality, however,
this person cannot be apprehended.
Buddhist, Milinda's Questions 28 (1st
century CE)

8 The nature of man is evil, his goodness is
acquired. His nature being what it is, man is
born, first, with a desire for gain. If this
desire is followed, strife will result and
courtesy will disappear. . . . Hence it is only
under the influence of teachers and laws and
the guidance of the rules of decorum and
righteousness that courtesy will be observed,
etiquette respected, and order restored.
Hsün Tzu, 23 (3rd century BCE)

9 Human nature is disposed to do good, just
as water flows downwards. There is no man
that does not show this tendency to
goodness.
Mencius, 6 (4th century BCE)

10 Many things there are, weird and
wonderful, none more so than man. He sails
beyond the seas, lashed white by winter

wind, piercing the waters roaring round . . .
In all things he finds him a way. Death is too
great for him, yet he devises healing of
sickness.
Sophocles, *Antigone*, 332ff. (441 BCE)

11 I am a man, I count nothing human foreign
to me.
Terence, *Heauton Timoroumenos*, 77 (2nd
century BCE)

12 Examine who you are. In the first place, a
man. That is, one who has nothing superior
to the faculty of choice, but all things subject
to this . . . Besides, you are a citizen of the
world, and a part of it; not a subservient but
a principal part. You are capable of
comprehending the divine order, and of
considering the connections of things.
Epictetus, *Discourses*, 2, 10 (1st century CE)

13 What is the chief end of man?
To glorify God and to enjoy him for ever.
The Shorter Catechism (1647)

14 What a piece of work is a man! How noble
in reason! how infinite in faculty! in form, in
moving, how express and admirable! in
action how like an angel! in apprehension
how like a god! the beauty of the world! the
paragon of animals!
William Shakespeare, *Hamlet*, II, ii, 324–8
(*c.* 1603)

15   Man, proud man,
Drest in a little brief authority,
Most ignorant of what he's most assur'd,
His glassy essence, like an angry ape,
Plays such fantastic tricks before high
heaven,
As make the angels weep.
William Shakespeare, *Measure for Measure*,
II, ii, 117–22 (*c.* 1604)

16 Know thyself.
Inscription in the temple of Delphi

17 From the gods comes the saying 'Know
thyself'.
Juvenal, *Satires*, xi, 27 (2nd century)

18 It is said, there came a voice from heaven,
saying, 'Man know thyself.' Thus that
proverb is still true, 'Going out were never
so good, but staying at home were much
better.'
Theologia Germanica, IX (14th century)

19 Within all of us there is another person, the
inner man, whom the Scripture calls the new

man, the heavenly man, the young person,
the friend, the Noble Man. And that is what
our Lord meant when he said that a
Nobleman went into a far country and got
himself a kingdom and then came back.
Meister Eckhart, *The Aristocrat* (13th–14th
centuries)

20 I have striven hard not to laugh at human
actions, not to weep at them, nor to hate
them, but to understand them.
Baruch Spinoza, *Tractatus Politicus*, iv
(1677)

21 To make judgements about great and high
things, a soul of the same stature is needed;
otherwise we ascribe to them that vice
which is our own.
Michel de Montaigne, *Essais*, I, xiv (1588)

22 Man is only a reed, the weakest thing in
nature; but he is a reed that thinks.
Blaise Pascal, *Pensées*, vi, 347 (1670)

23 I am — yet what I am, none cares or knows;
My friends forsake me like a memory lost:
I am the self-consumer of my woes —
They rise and vanish in oblivious host,
Like shadows in love's frenzied, stifled
              throes:–
And yet I am, and live — like vapours tost.
John Clare, *I am* (1844)

24 Man is the only animal that blushes. Or
needs to.
Mark Twain, *Following the Equator*, 27
(1897)

25 Man is, indeed, a being apart, since he is not
influenced by the great laws which
irresistibly modify all other organic beings
. . . Man has not only escaped natural
selection himself, but he is actually able to
take away some of that power from nature
which before his appearance she universally
exercised.
Alfred R. Wallace, *The Development of
Human Races under the Law of Natural
Selection* (1870)

---

51 THE HUMAN BODY

---

1 God created man in his own image, in the
image of God created he him; male and
female created he them.
Genesis, 1, 27

2 Know ye not that your body is the temple of
the Holy Ghost which is in you, which ye
have of God, and ye are not your own?
1 Corinthians, 6, 19

3 Recite in the name of thy Lord who created,
Created man from clots of blood.
Koran, 96, 1–2

4 The soul is utterly superior to the body, and
what gives each one of us his being is
nothing else but his soul, whereas the body
is no more than a shadow which keeps us
company.
Plato, *Laws*, XII, 959

5 Since the body, as possessed of life, is of a
compound character, the body itself would
not constitute the soul: for body is not
something attributed to a subject; it rather
acts as the underlying subject and the
material basis.
Aristotle, *On the Soul*, IV, 3

6 It would seem that our souls, charged with
the managing of bodies less perfect than
they, had to penetrate them if they were to
manage them truly.
Plotinus, *Enneads*, LV, 8 (3rd century)

7 In this ill-smelling, unsubstantial body,
which is a conglomerate of bone, skin,
muscle, marrow, flesh, semen, blood,
mucus, tears, rheum, faeces, urine, wind,
bile, and phlegm, what is the good of
enjoyment of desires?
Maitri Upanishad, 1, 3

8 This body, monks, is not yours, nor does it
belong to others. It should be regarded as
the product of former karma, effected
through what has been willed and felt.
Samyutta Nikaya, II, 64 (3rd century BCE)

9 The body is the temple, the mind is the
banner, fluttering in the wind of sensual
desires.
Sākhi, 29, in Charlotte Vaudeville, *Kabīr*
(1974)

10 Body am I entirely, and nothing else; and
soul is only a word for something about the
body.
Friedrich Nietzsche, *Thus Spake
Zarathustra* (1883)

11 I have said that the soul is not more than the
                          body,
And I have said that the body is not more
                  than the soul,

And nothing, not God, is greater to one than
                  one's self is.
Walt Whitman, *Leaves of Grass*, 'Song of
Myself' (1855)

12 Many years ago, I did not exist, but shortly
thereafter, because of my father and mother
who ate bread and meat, and garden
vegetables, I became a person. To this end,
my parents were not able to contribute
much but God made my body without any
help and created my soul like that which is
supreme.
Meister Eckhart, *Sermons* (13th–14th
centuries)

13 He that will have no *sensible* and *natural*
pleasure, shall have no *spiritual* pleasure.
Richard Baxter, *The Saints' Everlasting
Rest* (1650)

14 Know thou the soul as riding in a chariot,
The body as the chariot.
Know thou the intellect as the
                          chariot-driver,
And the mind as the reins.

The senses, they say, are the horses;
The objects of sense, what they range over,
The self combined with senses and mind
Wise men call 'the enjoyer.'

He who has not understanding,
Whose mind is not constantly held firm —
His senses are uncontrolled,
Like the vicious horses of a chariot-driver.
Katha Upanishad, 3, 3–5

15 The seven worlds which a man experiences:
At one year old he is like a king, placed in a
covered litter, and all embrace and kiss him.
At two or three he is like a pig which pokes
about the sewers. At ten he jumps about like
a kid. At twenty he is like a neighing horse;
he adorns his person and seeks a wife.
Having married, he is like an ass, bearing a
heavy burden. Then having become the
father of children, he grows bold like a dog
to procure sustenance for them. When
finally he has grown old, he is bent like a
monkey.
Midrash, on *Ecclesiastes*, 1, 2

16 And one man in his time plays many parts,
His acts being seven ages. At first the infant,
Mewling and puking in the nurse's
                          arms. . . .
                  Last scene of all,

That ends this strange eventful history,
Is second childishness, and mere oblivion,
Sans teeth, sans eyes, sans taste, sans
    everything.
William Shakespeare, *As You Like It*, II, vii,
143–4, 163–6 (*c.* 1599)

52 SOUL AND SPIRIT
  See also 105. REASON AND MIND

1 God breathed into his nostrils the breath of
life; and man became a living soul.
Genesis, 2, 7

2 What shall it profit a man, if he shall gain
the whole world, and lose his own soul? Or
what shall a man give in exchange for his
soul?
Mark, 8, 36–7

3 In the seventh heaven, are stored the spirits
and souls which have still to be created.
Mishnah, *Chagigah*, 12

4 The names and grades of the soul of man are
three: nefesh [vital soul], ruah [spirit],
neshamah [innermost soul, super-soul]. The
three are comprehended one within the
other, but each has its separate abode.
Zohar, G.G. Scholem (ed.) (1949)

5 How will it be when we gather them
together on a day about which there is no
doubt. And every soul shall be paid in full
what it has earned, without being wronged?
Koran, 3, 24

6 That soul is not this, it is not that. It is
unseizable, for it is not seized. It is
indestructible, for it is not destroyed. It is
unattached, for it does not attach itself. It is
unbound. It does not tremble. It is not
injured.
Brihad-aranyaka Upanishad, 3, 9, 26

7 This soul of mine within the heart is smaller
than a grain of rice, or a barley-corn, or a
mustard-seed, or a grain of millet, or the
kernel of a grain of millet. This soul of mine
within the heart is greater than the earth,
greater than the atmosphere, greater than
the sky, greater than these worlds.
Chandogya Upanishad, 3, 14, 3

8 As leaving aside his worn-out garments, a
man takes other new ones, so leaving aside
worn-out bodies the embodied soul goes to
other new ones.
Bhagavad Gita, 2,22

9 It is not born, nor does it ever die, nor
having come to be will it ever more
come not to be. Unborn, eternal,
everlasting, this ancient one [soul] is not
slain when the body is slain.
Bhagavad Gita, 2, 20

10 The soul cannot be understood as an
aggregate of many parts, for everywhere it is
apprehended as being other than the body,
being that which measures and of one form.
It is that which says in the body, 'I know
this.'
Ramanuja, *Commentary on the Bhagavad
Gita*, 2, 18 (11th century)

11 The Buddha never taught that the self 'is
not', but only that 'it cannot be apprehended.'
Edward Conze, *Buddhist Thought in India*
(1962)

12 You should know that the chief
characteristic of the soul is awareness, and
that its existence can be proved by all valid
means of proof. Souls may be classified as
transmigrant and liberated, or as embodied
in immobile and mobile beings.
Jinabhadra, *Ganadharavada*, 1, 32 (7th
century)

13 God did not make the soul after the body
. . . He made the soul in origin and
excellence prior to and older than the body,
to be the ruler and mistress, of whom the
body was to be the subject.
Plato, *Timaeus*, 34c

14 The soul must necessarily be a real
substance, as the form which determines a
natural body, possessed potentially of life.
Aristotle, *On the Soul*, IV, 3

15 Even as the eye could not behold the sun
unless it were itself sunlike, so neither could
the soul behold God if it were not Godlike.
Plotinus, *Enneads* i, 6, 9 (3rd century)

16 When God made man, he put into the soul
his equal, his active, everlasting masterpiece.
It was so great a work that it could not be
otherwise than the soul and the soul could
not be otherwise than the work of God.
God's nature, his being, and the Godhead
all depend on his work in the soul.
Meister Eckhart, *Sermons*, 27 (13th–14th
centuries)

17 Thinking is an attribute of the soul, and here

I discover what properly belongs to myself.
This alone is inseparable from me. I am, I
exist; this is certain.
René Descartes, *Discourse on Method*, 3, 2
(1637)

18 I do know that I, who am a spirit or thinking
substance, exist as certainly as I know my
ideas exist. Further, I know what I mean by
the terms *I* and *myself*; and I know this
immediately or intuitively, though I do not
perceive it as I perceive a triangle, a colour,
or a sound. The Mind, Spirit, or Soul is that
indivisible unextended thing which thinks,
acts, and perceives.
George Berkeley, *Three Dialogues*
(1713)

19 O soul, be changed into little water drops,
And fall into the ocean, ne'er be found:
My God, my God, look not so fierce on me.
Christopher Marlowe, *Doctor Faustus*, V,
ii, 179 (1588)

20 They that deny a God destroy man's
nobility; for certainly man is of kin to the
beasts by his body; and, if he be not of kin to
God by his spirit, he is a base and ignoble
creature.
Francis Bacon, *Essays*, 16 (1625)

21 For of the soul the body form doth take;
For soul is form, and doth the body make.
Edmund Spenser, *An Hymn in Honour of
Beauty*, 132 (1596)

22 Poor soul, the centre of my sinful earth —
William Shakespeare, *Sonnet* 146

23 My soul, sit thou a patient looker-on:
Judge not the play before the play is done.
Francis Quarles, *Emblems* (1635)

24   My soul
Smoothed itself out — a long-cramped scroll
Freshening and fluttering in the wind.
Robert Browning, *The Last Ride Together*,
iv (1842)

25 If you live and suffer long enough in a place,
you do not leave it altogether. Your spirit is
there.
Patrick White, *Voss* (1957)

26 The servant . . . being . . . an engine whose
motive power is a Soul, the force of this very
peculiar agent, as an unknown quantity,
enters into all the political economist's
equations, without his knowledge, and
falsifies every one of their results.
John Ruskin, *Unto This Last*, i (1860)

27 There is a soul above the soul of each,
A mightier soul, which yet to each belongs.
R.W. Dixon, *Humanity, Historical Odes*
(1864)

28 My own view is that nothing but dreams
and visions could have ever put into men's
minds such an idea as that of souls being
ethereal images of bodies.
E.B. Tylor, *Primitive Culture* (1871)

29 The theory has the quality of a just-so story
like 'how the leopard got his spots.' The
ideas of soul and spirit could have arisen in
the way Tylor supposed, but there is no
evidence that they did.
E.E. Evans-Pritchard, *Theories of Primitive
Religion* (1965)

30 Soul, when it is allowed an existence at all,
sits somewhat vaguely within the machine,
never defined. If anything goes wrong with
the machine, why, the soul is forgotten
instantly.
D.H. Lawrence, *Fantasia of the Unconscious*
(1923)

31 With Western man the value of the self sinks
to zero. Hence the universal depreciation of
the soul in the West. Whoever speaks of the
reality of the soul or psyche is accused of
'psychologism.'
C.G. Jung, *Psychology and Alchemy* (1953)

VI
THE SACRED

53 PLACES
See also 93. CHURCH

1 Put off thy shoes from off thy feet, for the place whereon thou standest is holy ground.
Exodus, 3, 5

2 Our fathers worshipped in this mountain; and ye say, that in Jerusalem is the place where men ought to worship.
John, 4, 20

3 Turn thy face in the direction of the Sacred Mosque, and wherever ye are, turn your faces in its direction.
Koran, 2, 139

4 They consecrated on the sacred grass this sacrifice, the Person, born in the beginning. With him the gods sacrificed.
Rig Veda, 10, 90, 7

5 The Beloved of the Gods, the king Piyadassi, when he had been consecrated twenty years, came in person and reverenced the place where Buddha Sákyamuni was born. He caused a stone enclosure to be made and a stone pillar to be erected.
Ashoka, *Rummindei Pillar Inscription* (3rd century BCE)

6 I adopt a word coined from the Latin *numen. Omen* has given us *ominous*, and there is no reason why from *numen* we should not similarly form a word *numinous*. I shall speak then of a unique 'numinous' category of value.
Rudolf Otto, *The Holy* (1917)

7 Whom dost thou worship in this lonely dark corner of a temple with doors all shut? Open thine eyes and see thy God is not before thee! He is there where the tiller is tilling the hard ground and where the pathmaker is breaking stone . . . Meet him and stand by him in toil and sweat of thy brow.
Rabindranath Tagore, *Gitanjali*, 11 (1913)

8 Thank God, there are still sacred places in India — sacred mountains and caves, sacred rivers and trees and plants and animals, sacred places where people go on pilgrimage. There are still temples where the old, sacred rites continue, and holy men to whom people go to find God. Always there is a sense of a transcendent Mystery, of an ultimate Reality behind the appearances.
Bede Griffiths, *Return to the Centre* (1976)

9 Kabir, they all go to the temple and there they bow their heads — But Hari dwells within the heart, so fasten yourself there!
Sākhi, 26, in Charlotte Vaudeville, *Kabir* (1974)

10 The province of Ise, of the divine wind, is the land whither repair the waves from the eternal world, the successive waves. It is a secluded and pleasant land. In this land I wish to dwell. In compliance, therefore, with the instruction of the Great Goddess, a shrine was erected to her in the province of Ise.
Nihongi, VI, 16 (720)

11 I am that Demeter who has share of honour and is the greatest help and cause of joy to the undying gods and mortal men. Now let all the people build me a great temple and

an altar below it . . . And I myself will teach my rites, that hereafter you may reverently perform them and so win the favour of my heart.
Homeric Hymns, 'to Demeter', II (700–500 BCE)

12 The existence of St Sophia is atmospheric; that of St Peter's, overpoweringly, imminently substantial. One is a church to God; the other a salon for his agents.
Robert Byron, *The Byzantine Achievement* (1929)

13 Addresses to the temple and serving God in the public communion of saints, is like rain from heaven.
Jeremy Taylor, *The Great Exemplar* (1649)

14 Churches are best for Prayer, that have least
      light:
To see God only, I go out of sight:
And to scape stormy days, I choose
An Everlasting night.
John Donne, *A Hymn to Christ* (1633)

54 SYMBOLS AND IMAGES

1 The LORD hath called by name Bezaleel . . . and he hath filled him with the spirit of God, in wisdom, in understanding, and in knowledge, and in all manner of workmanship; and to devise curious works, to work in gold, and in silver, and in brass.
Exodus, 35, 30–2

2 The brightness of his glory, and the express image of his person.
Hebrews, 1, 3

3 Let him pass by an image, turning his right hand towards it.
Laws of Manu, IV, 39

4 The divinity present in the symbols is regaled with incense and earthen lamps. Burning camphor is waved before it.
L.P. Vidyarthi, *The Sacred Complex in Hindu Gaya* (1961)

5 We define, with all care and exactitude, that the venerable and holy icons are set up in just the same way as the figure of the precious and life-giving cross . . . The more continually these are observed by means of such representations, so much the more will the beholders be aroused to recollect the originals.
Definition of the Second Council of Nicaea (787)

6 The confidence and faith of the heart alone make both God and an idol.
Martin Luther *Large Catechism*, I (1529)

7 I have spoken of the whole church as a great Book of Common Prayer; the mosaics were its illuminations, and the common people of the time were taught their Scripture history by means of them, more impressively perhaps, though far less fully, than ours are now by Scripture reading. They had no other Bible, and — Protestants do not often enough consider this — *could* have no other.
John Ruskin, *The Stones of Venice* (1853)

8 Protestants . . . are often unaware of the numinous power inherent in genuine symbols.
J.L. Adams, in *Tillich's Protestant Era* (1951)

9 There is no idolatry in the Mass. They believe God to be there, and they adore him.
Samuel Johnson, in Boswell, *Life of Samuel Johnson* (26 October 1769)

10 Even if they did happen to believe the divinity to be totally present in some stone or wood, it may be they were sometimes right. Do we not believe God is present in some bread and wine? Perhaps God was actually present in statues fashioned and consecrated according to certain rites.
Simone Weil, *Letter to a Priest* (1953)

11 [His] sense of religion . . . was shocked and disgusted at the tawdriness of the dressed-up saints in the cathedral — the worship, he called it, of wood and tinsel. But it seemed to me that he looked upon his own God as a sort of influential partner, who gets his share of profits in the endowment of churches. That's a sort of idolatry.
Joseph Conrad, *Nostromo* (1904)

55 RELICS

1 It came to pass, as they were burying a man, that, behold, they spied a band of men; and they cast the man into the sepulchre of

Elisha: and when the man was let down,
and touched the bones of Elisha, he revived,
and stood up on his feet.
2 Kings, 13, 21

2 From his body were brought unto the sick
handkerchiefs or aprons, and the diseases
departed from them.
Acts, 19, 12

3 The relic most eagerly sought after is hair
from the head or beard of Muhammed.
Imitating the examples handed down from
early times pious men have always been
fond of wearing such relics as amulets or
have asked for them to be put into their
graves.
Ignaz Goldziher, *Muslim Studies*, II (1971)

4 We are worthy to receive a portion of the
relics of the Exalted One. Over the remains
of the Exalted One will we put up a sacred
cairn, and in their honour will we celebrate a
feast . . . And he divided the remains of the
Exalted One into eight parts, with fair
division.
Maha Parinibbana Suttanta, 165–6
(3rd–1st centuries BCE)

5 Above the great relic-treasure did the
people, so far as they could, carry out the
enshrining of thousands of relics. Enclosing
all together the king completed the *thūpa*
[tumulus].
Mahavamsa, *Great Chronicle of Ceylon*,
xxxi (5th century)

6 What are the facts? The bone of a man long
since dead and decomposed is to be
admitted within the precincts of the Imperial
Palace. Confucius said, 'respect spiritual
beings but keep them at a distance' . . . Yet
now your Majesty is about to introduce
without reason a disgusting object,
personally taking part in the proceedings.
Han-Yü, (9th century), quoted in C. Eliot,
Hinduism and Buddhism, III (1921)

7 The Romish Doctrine concerning Purgatory,
Pardons, Worshipping and Adoration, as
well of Images as of Reliques, and also
invocation of Saints, is a fond thing vainly
invented, and grounded upon no warranty
of Scripture, but rather repugnant to the
Word of God.
Book of Common Prayer, Articles of
Religion XXII

8 Not every doctrine on these matters is a
'fond thing', but the *Romish* doctrine.

Accordingly the *Primitive* doctrine is not
condemned in it . . . What is opposed is the
received doctrine of the day.
Tracts for the Times, Tract XC (1841)

9 If any bishop from this time forward is
found consecrating a temple without holy
relics, he shall be deposed as a transgressor
of the ecclesiastical traditions.
Seventh General Council, Canon 7 (787)

10 Lord, who workest miracles by the relics of
thy saints, increase our faith in the
resurrection, and give us fellowship with
them in that undying glory of which their
reverend ashes are a pledge.
Roman Missal, November 5

---

56 HOLY DAYS
See also 4. HISTORICAL RELIGIONS

---

1 Remember the sabbath day, to keep it holy.
Six days shalt thou labour, and do all thy
work: but the seventh day is the sabbath of
the LORD thy God . . . For in six days the
LORD made heaven and earth, the sea, and
all that in them is, and rested the seventh
day: wherefore the LORD blessed the
sabbath day, and hallowed it.
Exodus, 20, 8–11

2 The sabbath was made for man, and not
man for the sabbath.
Mark, 2, 27

3 Two ministering angels accompany a man
on the Sabbath-eve from the Synagogue to
his house — one good and the other evil. On
entering the house and finding the
Sabbath-light burning, the table prepared
and the couch arranged, the good angel
exclaims, 'May it be his will that it might be
like this next Sabbath', and the wicked angel
is compelled to answer Amen.
Mishnah, *Shabbath*, 119

4 The six 'days' of the transcendent world
derive their blessings from the seventh day,
and out of that which it received from the
seventh day, each of the six supernal days
sends forth food to the world below.
Zohar, *Sabbath* (14th century)

5 We all hold our common meeting on the day
of the Sun, because it is the first day, on
which God changed the darkness and

matter in his making of the world, and Jesus Christ our Saviour on the same day rose from the dead.
Justin Martyr, *Apology*, i, 65–7 (2nd century)

6 When proclamation is made for the Prayer on the day of the assembly, endeavour to come to the remembrance of God and leave off bargaining.
Koran, 62, 8

7 The all-conquering Kaushitaki was wont to worship the rising sun — having performed the investiture with the sacred thread, having sipped water, thrice having sprinkled the water-vessel — saying: 'Thou art a snatcher! Snatch my sin!'
Kaushitaki Upanishad, 2, 7

8 Today is the Fast-day of the fifteenth day of the moon. If it appears the right time to the Assembly, let the Assembly perform the Fast-day service and recite the Patimokkha [binding] rules.
Vinaya, *Mahavagga*, II, 3

9 Seven whole days, not one in seven,
I will praise thee.
George Herbert, *The Temple*, 'Praise' (1633)

10 Anyone who performs any rite transcends profane time and space; similarly, anyone who 'imitates' a mythological model or even ritually assists at the retelling of a myth (taking part in it) is taken out of profane 'becoming' and returns to the Great Time.
Mircea Eliade, *Patterns in Comparative Religion* (1958)

---

57 FESTIVALS

See also 74. LITURGY AND RITUAL

---

1 Three times thou shalt keep a feast unto me in the year. Thou shalt keep the feast of unleavened bread . . . and the feast of harvest, the first fruits of thy labours . . . and the feast of ingathering.
Exodus, 23, 14–16

2 Christ our passover is sacrificed for us: therefore let us keep the feast.
1 Corinthians, 5, 7–8

3 We have appointed a pious rite, that they should make mention of the name of God over such beasts of the flocks as he hath provided them with.
Koran, 22, 35

4 It is a part of our religion to pray the Friday and festival prayers, and the other prayers and assemblies.
Al Ash'ari, *Ibāna*, 41 (10th century)

5 Some sacrifice with substance, others with austerity, others likewise sacrifice with Yoga, and religious men with strict vows sacrifice with study of knowledge and the sacred word.
Bhagavad Gita, 4, 28

6 Those who at the Lord's bidding feast, and take their fill of the Lord's holiness, attain peace and joy.
Thy minstrel spreads thy glory by singing thy word.
Guru Nanak, *haun dhadhi* (16th century)

7 The arrival of Baha'u'llah in the Najibiyyih Garden, subsequently designated by His followers the Garden of Ridvan, signalizes the commencement of what has come to be recognized as the holiest and most significant of all Baha'i festivals, the festival commemorating the Declaration of His Mission to His companions.
Shoghi Effendi, *God Passes By* (1945)

8 Christ's passion, death and resurrection are not simply *remembered* during the services of Holy Week; they really happen *then* before the eyes of the faithful. And a convinced Christian must feel that he is *contemporary* with these trans-historic events, for, by being re-enacted, the time of the theophany becomes actual.
Mircea Eliade, *Patterns in Comparative Religion* (1958)

9 Still to be neat, still to be drest,
As you were going to a feast.
Ben Jonson, *Epicoene* (1609)

10 Some say that ever 'gainst that season comes
Wherein our Saviour's birth is celebrated,
The bird of dawning singeth all night long;
And then, they say, no spirit can walk
　　　　abroad;
The nights are wholesome; then no planets
　　　　strike,
No fairy takes, nor witch hath power to
　　　　charm,
So hallow'd and so gracious is the time.
William Shakespeare, *Hamlet*, I, i, 158–64 (*c.* 1603)

58 ICONOCLASM

1 The workman melteth a graven image, and the goldsmith spreadeth it over with gold, and casteth silver chains. He that is so impoverished that he hath no oblation chooseth a tree that will not rot.
Isaiah, 40, 19–20

2 They became fools, and changed the glory of the uncorruptible God into an image made like to corruptible man, and to birds, and fourfooted beasts, and creeping things.
Romans, 1, 22–3

3 They told of thee in images, but not according to thine essence; they but likened thee in accordance with thy works. They figured thee in a multitude of visions; behold thou art One under all images.
Hebrew Prayer Book, 'Hymn of Glory'

4 O ye who have believed, wine, gambling, images, and divination are simply an abomination.
Koran, 5, 92

5 It is but an image of stone,
yet they adore it as the Creator!
Sākhi, 26, in Charlotte Vaudeville, *Kabīr* (1974)

6 He cannot be installed like an idol,
Nor can man shape His likeness.
Hymns of Guru Nanak, *thapia na* (16th century)

7 Pilgrimages, prayers, and offerings made to blind crosses or roods, and to deaf images of wood or stone, are pretty well akin to idolatry.
The Lollard Conclusions, 8 (1394)

8 The heathen in his blindness
Bows down to wood and stone.
Reginald Heber, *From Greenland's Icy Mountains* (1811)

9 The rule of wealth — the religion of gold. This is the obvious and natural idol of the Anglo-Saxon.
Walter Bagehot, *The English Constitution,* 4 (1867)

VII
SACRED PERSONS

59 CHARISMA

1 There are diversities of gifts [charismata], but the same Spirit . . . The manifestation of the Spirit is given to every man to profit withal.
1 Corinthians, 12, 4 and 7

2 He himself had the *charisma*, or spiritual gift of utterance
J.A. Robertson, *The Hidden Romance of the New Testament* (1920)

3 In *ex tempore* prayer he had a mysterious *charisma* of the Spirit.
N. Micklem, *Box and Puppets* (1957)

4 The term 'charisma' will be applied to a certain quality of an individual personality by virtue of which he is set apart from ordinary men and treated as endowed with super-natural, super-human, or at least specifically exceptional powers or qualities
A.M. Henderson and T. Parsons, trans. *Weber's Theory of Social and Economic Organization* (1947)

5 The skin of his face shone; and they were afraid to come nigh him . . . and till Moses had done speaking with them, he put a vail on his face.
Exodus, 34, 30–3

6 They were astonished at his doctrine: for he taught them as one that had authority, and not as the scribes.
Mark, 1, 22

7 The apostle, at the time when God willed to bestow His grace upon him and endow him with prophethood, would go forth for his affair and journey far afield until he reached the glens of Mecca and the beds of its valleys where no house was in sight; and not a stone or tree that he passed by but would say, 'Peace unto thee, O apostle of God.'
Ibn Ishaq, *Life of the Apostle of God* (9th century)

8 The Arabic word *baraka* means 'blessing.' In Morocco it is used to denote a mysterious wonder-working force which is looked upon as a blessing from God, a 'blessed virtue.' It may be conveniently translated into English by the word 'holiness.'
A person who possesses *baraka* in an exceptional degree is called by a term corresponding to our 'saint.'
E. Westermarck, *Ritual and Belief in Morocco* (1926)

9 The Yogi is higher than ascetics, he is also held to be higher than men of knowledge; the Yogi is higher than the men of ritual action; therefore be a spiritual athlete.
Bhagavad Gita, 6, 46

10 There comes the knowledge of the sounds of all living beings; by bringing residual potencies into consciousness comes the knowledge of previous lives, and the knowledge of other minds.
Patanjali, *Yoga Sutras*, 3, 17–19

11 Who, but the True Guru, could save a sinner like me?
Guru, thou art my father and my mother,
Thou art my friend, and hast wrought my salvation.
Hymns of Guru Ram Das, *Hamre man* (16th century)

12 The Exalted One, with clear and Heavenly
Ear, surpassing the hearing of men,
overheard the conversation among the
monks.
Mahapadana Suttanta, 1 (3rd–1st centuries
BCE)

13 Today I have seen Lao Tzu and can only
liken him to a dragon.
Quoted in Holmes Welch, *The Parting of the
Way* (1957)

14 His life was glorious, his death bewailed.
How can such a one ever be equalled.
Confucius, *Analects*, XIX, 25

15 She was discovered to possess miraculous
healing powers, particularly in the granting
of painless childbirth. Her fame spread
throughout the district and believers began
to flock round.
Carmen Blacker, *The Catalpa Bow* (1975)

16 They are believed to partake at times of the
nature of spirits; it is said that they can fly
through space unseen, and ascertain what is
happening at a distance.
A.P. Elkin, *The Australian Aborigines* (1945)

17 The prophet's powers are charismatic — an
individual inspiration . . . the representative
of the divine to man.
E.E. Evans-Pritchard, *Nuer Religion* (1956)

18 They seem to change the institutions of
Western democracy into a kind of tribal
form with a charismatic tribal leader.
The Listener (7 February 1963)

19 The Pentecostal experience is not a goal to
be reached, nor a place to stand, but a door
through which to go into a greater fullness
of life in the Spirit. It is an event which
becomes a way of life in which often
charismatic manifestations have a place.
W. Hollenweger, *The Pentecostals* (1972)

20 The Charismatic Renewal Movement is a
modern world-wide movement,
predominantly lay, now found among
members of all the major Christian
denominations, including the Roman
Catholic Church. Its distinctive feature is an
emphasis on practice of the charismatic gifts
described in the New Testament.
A.Q. Lister, in *A Dictionary of Christian
Spirituality* (1983)

21 Airy, in an airy manner in an airy parkland
walking,

Others take him by the hand, lead him, do
the talking.
But the Form, the airy One, frowns an airy
frown,
What they say he knows must be, but he
looks aloofly down.
Stevie Smith, *The Airy Christ* (1957)

---

60 PROPHETS
See also 61. SHAMANS, 78. MYSTICISM

---

1 Would God that all the LORD's people were
prophets, and that the LORD would put his
spirit upon them.
Numbers, 11, 29

2 He that prophesieth speaketh unto men to
edification, and exhortation, and comfort.
He that speaketh in an unknown tongue
edifieth himself; but he that prophesieth
edifieth the church.
1 Corinthians, 14, 3–4

3 Forty-eight prophets and seven prophetesses
spoke prophecies for Israel, and they neither
deducted from nor added to what was
written in the Torah, with the exception of
the law to read the book of Esther on the
Feast of Purim.
Mishnah, *Megillah*, 14

4 God raised up the prophets as bringers of
good tidings and warners, and with them he
sent down the Book with the truth to judge
among the people regarding that in which
they had differed.
Koran, 2, 209

5 The proof of the possibility of there being
prophecy and the proof that there has been
prophecy is that there is knowledge in the
world the attainment of which by reason is
inconceivable . . . Other properties of
prophetic revelation are apprehended only
by immediate experience from the practice
of the mystic way.
Al-Ghazali, *Deliverance from Error*,
139–40 (11th century)

6 Whenever I enter the prosperous townships
with these my followers, men and women
both, I am revered; they follow me in
countless numbers, asking where lies the
path to gain, some seeking prophecies, while
others, for many a day stabbed by grievous

pains, beg to hear the word that heals all manner of illness.
Empedocles, *Fragments*, 146 (5th century BCE)

7 We can only understand Nuer faith in their prophets, and also their fear of them, when we know that when they speak as prophets it is Spirit which speaks by their lips, theopneustic speech.
E.E. Evans-Pritchard, *Nuer Religion* (1956)

8 Do thou speak, O Lord God, the Inspirer and Enlightener of all the prophets; for thou alone without them canst perfectly instruct me, but they without thee will profit nothing.
Thomas Kempis, *Of the Imitation of Christ*, III, 3 (c 1418)

9 We hold that seeing prophesying is a part of spiritual worship: therefore in time of Prophesying it is unlawful to have a book as a help before the eye.
John Smyth, *The Differences of the Churches of the Separation* (1609)

10 Among all forms of mistake, prophecy is the most gratuitous.
George Eliot, *Middlemarch*, 10 (1871)

11 I will eat exceedingly, and prophesy.
Ben Jonson, *Bartholomew Fair*, I, vi (1614)

12   A man may prophesy,
With a near aim, of the main chance of things
As not yet come to life, which in their seeds
And weak beginnings lie intreasured.
William Shakespeare, *Henry IV, Part 2*, III, i, 82–5 (c. 1597)

13 Too many self-appointed 'elders' and 'spiritual teachers', exploiting what may be a genuine spiritual thirst and hunger, in fact lead their followers into dangerous spiritual dead ends.
Alexander Schmemann, *Of Water and the Spirit* (1976)

14 *The only satisfactory parallel to the prophetic experience is the phenomena of mysticism as described by writers like Teresa of Avila, John of the Cross and others. They affirm that the immediate experience of God is ineffable; like the prophets, they must employ imagery and symbolism to describe*

it, with explicit warnings that these are used.
J.L. McKenzie, *Dictionary of the Bible* (1965)

15 The prophetic element can (it does not have to) be connected with mystical experience.
Karl Rahner, *Encyclopedia of Theology* (1975)

16 I myself maintain that mysticism, as I have understood it, is the core and climax of all religious experience and that it expresses itself sometimes in a life of solitude and at other times in a prophetic life of powerful activity.
William Johnston, *The Inner Eye of Love* (1978)

61 SHAMANS
See also 12. MAGIC, 26. SPIRIT-POSSESSION

1 Shamanism in the strict sense is pre-eminently a religious phenomenon of Siberia and Central Asia. The word comes to us, through the Russian, from the Tungusic *šaman* . . . the shaman is a magician and medicine man: he is believed to cure, like all doctors, and to perform miracles of the fakir type, like all magicians, whether primitive or modern. But beyond this, he is a psychopomp, and he may also be priest, mystic, and poet.
Mircea Eliade, *Shamanism* (1964)

2 I taught them shamaning. Now I am going to teach you. The old shamans have died off, and there is no one to heal people. You are to become a shaman.
Leo Sternberg, *Divine Election in Primitive Religion* (1924)

3 The shaman sits down on the ground and, after drumming for a long time, invokes his tutelary spirits . . . Accompanied by his helping spirits, he had followed the road that leads to the Kingdom of Shadows.
Mircea Eliade, *Shamanism* (1964)

4 Both the medium and the ascetic are shamans because each in their particular manner of trance acts as a bridge between one world and another.
Carmen Blacker, *The Catalpa Bow* (1975)

5 The oldest shamanic figure of which we have any record [in Japan] is the Shinto *miko*. This powerful sacral woman — the term 'female shaman' conveys only feebly the probable majesty of her presence — served in shrines throughout the land.
Carmen Blacker, *The Catalpa Bow* (1975)

6 Many of the functions of the early shamans were later taken over by the Taoist priesthood.
W.A.C.H. Dobson, 'China' in G. Parrinder, *Man and his Gods* (1971)

7 The Buddhism of the Tibetan layman has absorbed many features of earlier, pre-Buddhistic religion. This was known as Bon, or Pön, and was a kind of shamanism, with worship of spirits and tutelary deities.
Trevor Ling, 'Buddhism' in *Man and his Gods* (1971)

8 Maori . . . priests were the mediums of their atua or local gods, and were in constant contact with them. As shamans they relayed messages from the gods who typically communicated by whistling.
L. Binet Brown, 'Early Australasia' in *Man and his Gods* (1971)

---

62 TEACHERS AND GURUS
See also 102. EDUCATION AND TEACHING

---

1 For a long season Israel hath been without the true God, and without a teaching priest, and without law.
2 Chronicles, 15, 3

2 God hath set some in the church, first apostles, secondarily prophets, thirdly teachers, after that miracles, then gifts of healing, helps, governments, diversities of tongues.
1 Corinthians, 12, 28

3 There were three hundred and ninety-four Courts of Justice in Jerusalem, and a corresponding number of Synagogues, Houses of Study, and elementary schools.
Mishnah, *Kethuboth*, 105

4 Do you intend to question your messenger as Moses was questioned aforetime?
Koran, 2, 102

5 I read the books of sound theologians and myself wrote some books on the subject. But it was a science, I found, which, though attaining its own aim, did not attain mine. Its aim was merely to preserve the creed of orthodoxy and to defend it against the deviations of heretics.
Al-Ghazali, *Deliverance from Error*, 80–1 (12th century)

6 To one who has the highest devotion for God, and for his Guru even as for God, to him these matters which have been declared become manifest if he is a great soul.
Shvetashvatara Upanishad, 6, 23

7 The Guru is the ladder, the dinghy, the raft by means of which one reaches God;
The Guru is the lake, the ocean, the boat, the sacred place of pilgrimage, the river.
Without the Guru there can be no bhakti, no love.
Hymns of Guru Nanak, *siri ragu* (16th century)

8 I offer myself in sacrifice to the Guru, a hundred times a day.
Sākhī, 1, 19, in Charlotte Vaudeville, *Kabīr* (1974)

9 The Master said, He who by reanimating the Old can gain knowledge of the New is fit to be a teacher.
Confucius, *Analects*, 2, 11

10 Banish wisdom, discard knowledge,
And the people will be benefited a
   hundredfold . . .
Give them Simplicity to look at,
the Uncarved Block to hold,
Give them selflessness and fewness of
   desires.
Tao Te Ching, XIX

11 Teaching a Christian how he ought to live does not call so much for words as for daily example.
Basil of Caesarea, *Oration*, II (4th century)

12 Let such teach others who themselves excel
And censure freely who have written well.
Alexander Pope, *An Essay on Criticism* (1711)

13 Those that do teach young babes
Do it with gentle means and easy tasks.
William Shakespeare, *Othello*, IV, ii, 112–13 (1602–4)

14 It is easier for a tutor to command than to teach.
John Locke, *Some Thoughts Concerning Education* (1693)

15 He who can, does. He who cannot, teaches.
George Bernard Shaw, *Man and Superman*
(1903)

16 He that teaches us anything which we knew
not before is undoubtedly to be reverenced
as a master.
Samuel Johnson, *The Idler* (1758)

17 The office of the scholar is to cheer, to raise,
and to guide men by showing them facts
amidst appearances.
R.W. Emerson, *The American Scholar*
(1837)

18 The humblest painter is a true scholar, and
the best of scholars — the scholar of nature.
William Hazlitt, *Table Talk* (1821)

19 But Cristes lore and his apostles twelve
He taught, but first he followed it himself.
Geoffrey Chaucer, *The Canterbury Tales,*
'Prologue', 527–8 (1387)

---

63 SAINTS

1 The saints of the most High shall take the
kingdom, and possess the kingdom for ever,
even for ever and ever.
Daniel, 7, 18

2 Just and true are thy ways, thou King of
saints.
Revelation, 15, 3

3 Verily upon the friends of God rests no fear,
neither do they grieve.
Koran, 10, 63

4 In every epoch after Mohammed a Saint
arises to act as his vicegerent . . . All
individual hearts are as the body in relation
to the universal Heart of the Saint.
Jalalu'l Din Rumi, *Mathnawi,* II, 815 (13th
century)

5 These are the real heroes of mystical
experience because God has revealed his
secrets to them, and they have taken up their
abode in his omnipotence, awaiting his
command, that God himself may fulfil a
deed performed.
Junayd, *Kitāb,* in R.C. Zaehner, *Hindu and
Muslim Mysticism* (1960)

6 Remain in the company of Saints,
though you get but chaff to eat.
Sākhi, 24, in Charlotte Vaudeville, *Kabir*
(1974)

7 God in his mercy, has made me encounter a
Saint.
My mind and body are joyous.
Hymns of Guru Arjan, *khojat* (16th
century)

8 The saint, with true vision, conceives
compassion for all the world, in east and
west and south and north, and so, knowing
the Sacred Lore, he will preach and proclaim
it.
Acharanga Sutra, 1, 6, 5 (3rd–1st centuries
BCE)

9 Great Seers and Perfected Ones in serried
ranks cry out,
'All Hail', and laud thee with abundant
hymns of praise.
Bhagavad Gita, 11, 21

10 In the communion of the saints
Is wisdom, safety and delight.
Richard Baxter, *Poetical Fragments,* 'He
wants not Friends' (1681)

11 Grace is indeed needed to turn a man into a
saint; and he who doubts it does not know
what a saint or a man is.
Blaise Pascal, *Pensées* (1670)

12 For Saints may do the same things by the
Spirit, in sincerity, which other men are
tempted to.
Samuel Butler, *Hudibras,* II, 2 (1663)

13 There are many (questionless) canonized on
earth, that shall never be Saints in Heaven.
Thomas Browne, *Religio Medici* (1643)

14 With thy quire of Saints for evermore,
I shall be made thy Music.
John Donne, *Hymn to God, my God, in my
sickness* (1635)

15 What do men seek from these saints except
what belongs to folly? Amongst all the
votive offerings you see covering the walls of
certain churches right up to the very roof,
have you ever seen one put up for an escape
from folly or for the slightest gain in
wisdom?
Desiderius Erasmus, *The Praise of Folly*
(1511)

16 Avenge, O Lord, thy slaughtered saints,
whose bones
Lie scattered on the Alpine mountains cold.
John Milton, *On the late Massacre in
Piedmont* (1645)

17 Many people genuinely do not wish to be

saints, and it is probable that some who achieve or aspire to sainthood have never felt much temptation to be human beings.
George Orwell, *Shooting an Elephant* (1950)

18 Can one be a saint without God? This is the only problem I know of today.
Albert Camus, *The Plague* (1947)

19 *Saint*, n. A dead sinner revised and edited.
Ambrose Bierce, *The Devil's Dictionary* (1911)

20 The only difference between the saint and the sinner is that every saint has a past, and every sinner has a future.
Oscar Wilde, *A Woman of No Importance* (1893)

21 The Orthodox have also, though by no means exclusively, made much of the sanctity of the simple and uneducated, the 'holy fools.' This is very much in the spirit of Matt. 11, 25, and is illustrated in Tolstoy's story of 'The Three Hermits', who could not learn the Lord's Prayer but could walk on the water.
Gordon S. Wakefield, 'Saints, Sanctity' in *A Dictionary of Christian Spirituality* (1983)

22 Far above us we see the saints moving on the snowy whiteness . . . and we follow after. *Any* man may climb.
W.E. Sangster, *The Pure in Heart* (1954)

---

64 MARTYRS

---

1 They that understand among thy people shall instruct many: yet they shall fall by the sword, and by flame, by captivity, and by spoil, many days.
Daniel, 11, 33

2 When the blood of thy martyr Stephen was shed, I also was standing by, and consenting unto his death.
Acts, 22, 20

3 The most admirable Polycarp . . . while at prayer fell into a trance three days before his arrest and saw his pillow set on fire. And he turned and said to his companions, 'I must needs be burned alive'.
The Martyrdom of Polycarp, V (155)

4 Their martyrdoms were divided into every form. For plaiting a crown of various colours and of all kinds of flowers, they presented it to the Father. It was proper therefore that the noble athletes, having endured a manifold strife, and conquered grandly, should receive the crown, great and incorruptible.
Eusebius, *Ecclesiastical History*, V, i (303)

5 The blood of the martyrs is the seed of the church. [Traditional rendering of: 'The more you mow us down, the more we grow, the seed is the blood of Christians'.]
Tertullian, *Apology* (197)

6 Be of good comfort, Master Ridley, and play the man. We shall this day light such a candle by God's grace in England, as (I trust) shall never be put out.
Hugh Latimer, in John Foxe, *Actes and Monuments* (1570)

7 He that will not live a saint can never die a martyr.
Thomas Fuller, *Gnomologia* (1732)

8 If a man is in doubt whether it would be better for him to expose himself to martyrdom or not, he should not do it. He must be convinced that he has a delegation from heaven.
Samuel Johnson, in Boswell, *Life of Samuel Johnson* (April 1773)

9 To die in agony upon a cross does not create a martyr; he must first will his own execution.
Henrik Ibsen, *Brand* 3 (1866)

10 The martyr endured tortures to affirm his belief in truth, but he never asserted his disbelief in torture.
G.K. Chesterton, *As I was Saying* (1936)

11 Martyrs, my friend, have to choose between being forgotten, mocked or used. As for being understood — never.
Albert Camus, *The Fall* (1956)

12 He shall be washed as white as snow,
By all the martyr'd virgins kist,
While the True Church remains below,
Wrapt in the old miasmal mist.
T.S. Eliot, *The Hippopotamus* (1920)

13 There are those who, for reasons of their own, would seek to deny that the Holocaust happened, or dispute the scale of Hitler's genocide. The evidence refutes them, and

the death camps now stand as tourist sights.
David J. Goldberg and John D. Rayner, *The Jewish People* (1987)

14 The simple eye of the camera shows us, at Belsen and Buchenwald, horrors that quite surpass Swift's powers — a vision of life turned back to its corrupted elements.
Lionel Trilling, *The Liberal Imagination* (1950)

65   PRIESTS AND CLERGY

1 Melchizedek king of Salem brought forth bread and wine: and he was the priest of the most high God.
Genesis, 14, 18

2 I wist not, brethren, that he was the high priest: for it written, Thou shalt not speak evil of the ruler of thy people.
Acts, 23, 5

3 A Brahmin reaches the highest goal by reciting prayers only; whether he perform other rites or neglect them, who befriends all creatures is declared to be a true Brahmin
Laws of Manu, 2, 87

4 Nobody must do anything that has to do with the church without the bishop's approval . . . When the bishop is present, there let the congregation gather.
Ignatius, *Ad Smyrn.,* vii (1st century)

5 Although in the visible Church the evil be ever mingled with the good, and sometimes the evil have chief authority in the Ministration of the Word and Sacraments, yet forasmuch as they do not the same in their own name, but in Christ's, and do minister by his commission and authority, we may use their Ministry, both in hearing the Word of God, and in receiving of the Sacraments.
Book of Common Prayer, Articles of Religion XXVI

6 The way appointed by Christ for the calling of any person, fitted and gifted by the Holy Ghost, unto the Office of Pastor, Teacher, or Elder in the Church, is that he be chosen there unto by the common suffrage of the Church itself.
The Savoy Declaration (1658)

7 New Presbyter is but old Priest writ large.
John Milton, *On the New Forcers of Conscience* (1646)

8 Male priests are allowed to marry — for there's nothing to stop a woman from becoming a priest, although women are not often chosen for the job, and only elderly widows are eligible.
Thomas More, *Utopia,* ii (1516)

9 Will no one revenge me of the injuries I have sustained from one turbulent priest?
Henry II, oral tradition in G. Lyttelton, *History of the Life of King Henry the Second* (1769)

10 I am one that had rather go with sir priest than sir knight.
William Shakespeare, *Twelfth Night,* III, iv, 258 (1601)

11 The youth, who daily farther from the east
Must travel, still is Nature's priest,
And by the vision splendid
Is on his way attended.
William Wordsworth, *Intimations of Immortality* (1807)

12 As I take my shoes from the shoemaker, and my coat from the tailor, so I take my religion from the priest.
Oliver Goldsmith, in Boswell, *Life of Samuel Johnson* (9 April 1773)

13 A man who is good enough to go to heaven, is good enough to be a clergyman.
Samuel Johnson, in Boswell, *Life of Samuel Johnson* (5 April 1772)

14 Clergy are men as well as other folks.
Henry Fielding, *Joseph Andrews* (1742)

15 There are three sexes — men, women, and clergymen.
Sydney Smith, in Lady Holland, *Memoir* (1855)

16 The clergyman is expected to be a kind of human Sunday.
Samuel Butler, *The Way of All Flesh* (1903)

17 The minister is coming down every generation nearer and nearer to the common level of the useful citizen — no oracle at all, but a man of more than average moral instincts, who, if he knows anything, knows how little he knows.
Oliver Wendell Holmes, *The Poet at the Breakfast Table* (1872)

18 The modalities of the sacred revealed by
Christianity are in fact more truly preserved
in the tradition represented by the priest
(however strongly coloured by history and
theology) than in the beliefs of the villagers
. . . This single man has kept more
completely, if not the original experience of
Christianity, at least its basic elements and
its mystical, theological and ritual values.
Mircea Eliade, *Patterns in Comparative
Religion* (1958)

66 PREACHERS

1 Because the preacher was wise, he still
taught the people knowledge; yea, he gave
good heed, and sought out, and set in order
many proverbs.
Ecclesiastes, 12, 9

2 How shall they hear without a preacher?
And how shall they preach, except they be
sent?
Romans 10, 14–15

3 O thou wrapped in thy mantle, rise and
warn, magnify thy Lord, purify thy
garments.
Koran, 74, 1–4

4 What is the use of preaching sermons, if one
does not put it into practice? It is like the
framework for a building, which crumbles
before our eyes.
Sākhī, 33, in Charlotte Vaudeville, *Kabīr*
(1974)

5 There are those who laudably desire the
office of preaching, whereas others no less
laudably are driven to it by compulsion.
Gregory the Great, *Pastoral Care*, I, 7 (6th
century)

6 He is a vain preacher of the word of God
without, who is not a hearer within.
Augustine of Hippo, *Sermons*, 129, (5th
century)

7 Preaching is not a natural but acquired
power, though a man may reach a high
standard, even then his power may forsake
him unless he cultivate it by constant
application and exercise.
John Chrysostom, *On the Priesthood*, V, 5
(4th century)

8 He that has but one word of God before him

and out of that cannot make a sermon, can
never be a preacher.
Martin Luther, *Table Talk*, 10 (1569)

9 The preaching of divines helps to preserve
well-inclined men in the course of virtue, but
seldom or never reclaims the vicious.
Jonathan Swift, *Thoughts on Various
Subjects* (1711)

10 A woman's preaching is like a dog's walking
on his hind legs. It is not done well, but you
are surprised to find it done at all.
Samuel Johnson, in Boswell, *Life of Samuel
Johnson* (13 July 1763)

11 Silent and amazed even when a little boy, I
remember I heard the preacher every Sunday
put God in his statements, as contending
against some being or influence.
Walt Whitman, *Leaves of Grass* (1855)

12 One of the earliest experiences I had with
Protestant preaching was its moralistic
character.
Paul Tillich, *The Protestant Era* (1948)

13 Sermons remain one of the last forms of
public discourse where it is culturally
forbidden to talk back.
Harvey Cox, *The Secular City*, 10 (1966)

14 I preached what I felt, what I smartingly did
feel.
John Bunyan, *Grace Abounding* (1666)

15 Let the preacher labour to be heard
intelligently, willingly, obediently. And let
him not doubt, that he will accomplish this
rather by the piety of his prayers, than the
eloquence of his speech.
Lancelot Andrewes, *Private Devotions*
(1648)

67 MONKS AND NUNS
See also 89. ASCETICISM

1 Jonadab the son of Rechab our father
commanded us, saying, Ye shall drink no
wine, neither ye, nor your sons for ever:
Neither shall ye build house, nor sow seed,
nor plant vineyard, nor have any: but all
your days ye shall dwell in tents.
Jeremiah, 35, 6–7

2 There be eunuchs, which have made

themselves eunuchs for the kingdom of
heaven's sake.
Matthew, 19, 12

3 Thou wilt find those of them who are
nearest in love to those who have believed to
be those who say: 'We are Nasara'; that is
because there are amongst them priests and
monks, and because they count not
themselves great.
Koran, 5, 85

4 No monkery in Islam.
Doubtful saying of Muhammad,
commented on by Jalalu'-Din Rumi,
Mathnawi, V, 574 (13th century)

5 He who will wear the yellow robe without
having cleansed himself from impurity, who
is devoid of truth and self-control, is not
deserving of the yellow robe.
Dhammapada, 9

6 As in the ocean's midmost depth no wave is
born, but all is still, so let the monk be still,
be motionless, and nowhere should he swell.
Sutta-nipata, 920 (3rd–1st centuries BCE)

7 If another insult him, a monk should not
          lose his temper,
For that is mere childishness . . .
Even if beaten he should not be angry, or
          even think
sinfully, but should know that patience is
          best, and
follow the Law.
Uttara-dhyayana Sutra, 2, 24 (3rd–1st
centuries BCE)

8 Idleness is the enemy of the soul. And
therefore, at fixed times, the brothers ought
to be occupied in manual labour; and again,
at fixed times, in sacred reading.
Rule of St Benedict, XIVIII (6th century)

9 This is the Rule and way of life of the
brothers minor; to observe the holy Gospel
of our Lord Jesus Christ, living in obedience,

without personal possessions, and in
chastity.
Rule of St Francis, I (1223)

10 A Monk there was, a fair for the mastery,
An out-rider, that loved venery,
A manly man, to be an abbot able.
Geoffrey Chaucer, *The Canterbury Tales,*
'Prologue', 169–71 (1387)

11 The devil was sick, the devil a monk would
          be;
The devil was well, and the devil a monk
          he'd be.
Francois Rabelais, *Gargantua and
Pantagruel*, iv, 24 (1534) trans. P.A.
Motteux (1693)

12 Cucullus non facit monachum [the cowl
does not make the monk]
William Shakespeare, *Twelfth Night*, I, v,
51 (1601)

13 The solitary monk who shook the world.
R. Montgomery, *Luther* (1842)

14 The holy time is quiet as a Nun
Breathless with adoration.
William Wordsworth, *Sonnets*, 'It is a
beauteous Evening' (1807)

15 Come, pensive Nun, devout and pure,
Sober, steadfast, and demure.
John Milton, *Il Penseroso* (1632)

16 The monastics could possess no private
property; they could save no money; they
could bequeath nothing. They lived,
received, and expended in common. The
monastery, too, was a proprietor that never
died and never wasted. The farmer had a
deathless landlord then; not a harsh
guardian, or a grinding mortgagee, or a
dilatory master in chancery . . . The monks
were, in short, in every district a point of
refuge for all who needed succour, counsel,
and protection.
Benjamin Disraeli, *Sybil* (1845)

VIII
SACRED WORDS

68 MYTHS AND LEGENDS

1 There were giants in the earth in those days.
Genesis, 6, 4

2 Neither give heed to fables and endless genealogies, which minister questions, rather than godly edifying which is in faith.
1 Timothy, 1, 4

3 Neither the violence of Antiochus, nor the arts of Herod, nor the example of the circumjacent nations, could ever persuade the Jews to associate with the institutions of Moses the elegant mythology of the Greeks.
Edward Gibbon, *The History of the Decline and Fall of the Roman Empire*, 15 (1776)

4 The story that by the caliph's order [general] 'Amr for six long months fed the numerous bath furnaces of the city with the volumes of the Alexandrian library is one of those tales which make good fiction but bad history. The great Ptolemaic Library was burnt as early as 48 B.C. by Julius Caesar. A later one, referred to as the Daughter Library, was destroyed about A.D. 389 as a result of an edict by the Emperor Theodosius. At the time of the Arab conquest, therefore, no library of importance existed in Alexandria and no contemporary writer ever brought the charge against 'Amr.
Philip K. Hitti, *History of the Arabs* (1937)

5 Once upon a time, Buddha relates, a certain king of Benares, desiring to divert himself, gathered together a number of beggars blind from birth and offered a prize to the one who should give him the best account of an elephant. The first beggar who examined the elephant chanced to lay hold of a leg, and reported that an elephant was a tree-trunk; the second, laying hold of the tail, declared that an elephant was like a rope; another, who seized an ear, insisted that an elephant was like a palm-leaf; and so on. The beggars fell to quarrelling with one another, and the king was greatly amused. Ordinary teachers who have grasped this or that aspect of truth quarrel with one another, while only a Buddha knows the whole.
Sarvepalli Radhakrishnan, *Eastern Religions and Western Thought* (1939)

6 Every myth, whatever its nature, recounts an event that took place *in illo tempore*, and constitutes as a result, a precedent and pattern for all the actions and 'situations' later to repeat that event. Every ritual, and every meaningful act that man performs, repeats a mythical archetype.
Mircea Eliade, *Patterns in Comparative Religion* (1958)

7 Myths are not believed in, they are conceived and understood.
George Santayana, *Little Essays* (1920)

8 I made my song a coat
Covered with embroideries
Out of old mythologies
From heel to throat.
W.B. Yeats, *Collected Poems*, 'A coat' (1933)

9 I expect you remember Bultmann's essay on the 'demythologizing' of the New Testament? My view of it today would be,

not that he went 'too far', as most people thought, but that he didn't go far enough. It's not only the 'mythological' concepts, such as miracle, ascension, and so on (which are not in principle separable from the concepts of God, faith, etc.) but 'religious' concepts generally, which are problematic.
Dietrich Bonhoeffer, *Letters and Papers from Prison* (1953)

10 The Gospels are expanded cult legends.
Rudolf Bultmann, *The History of the Synoptic Tradition* (1921)

11 With reference both to the 'first things' and to the 'last things', therefore, we cannot dispense with *demythologizing, not to eliminate but to interpret.*
Hans Küng, *On Being a Christian*, C, II, i (1978)

12 Our discourse necessarily brings us to Christ, because he is the still living myth of our culture. He is our culture hero, who, regardless of his historical existence, embodies the myth of the divine Primordial Man, the mystic Adam.
C.G. Jung, *Aion* (1959)

13 The myth of the god who dies and rises again, of the descent into the underworld, of the man who suffers for bringing fire from heaven, is revealed as history. It takes place at a definite point in space and time, 'under Pontius Pilate', and yet it has all the 'mystery' of the ancient myths.
Bede Griffiths, *Return to the Centre* (1976)

---

69 REVELATION

---

1 Surely the Lord GOD will do nothing but he revealeth his secret unto his servants the prophets.
Amos, 3, 7

2 I will come to visions and revelations of the Lord.
2 Corinthians, 12, 1

3 It belongs not to any human being that God should speak to him except by revelation or from behind a veil.
Koran, 42, 50

4 When God revealed the Torah, no bird chirped, no fowl beat its wings, no ox bellowed, the angels did not sing, the sea did not stir, no creature uttered a sound; the world was silent and still and the Divine Voice spoke.
Midrash, *Exodus Rabbah*, 29, 9

5 By Shruti [revelation] is meant the Veda, and by Smriti [tradition] the Institutes of the sacred law.
Laws of Manu, II, 10

6 To Arjuna in his despondency Krishna, faintly smiling, spoke these words.
Bhagavad Gita, 2, 10

7 Just as if a man were to set up that which has been thrown down, or were to reveal that which is hidden away, or were to point out the right road to him who has gone astray, or were to bring a lamp into the darkness so that those who have eyes could see external forms — just even so has the truth been made known to me, in many a figure, by the Blessed One.
Samanna-phala Sutta, 85 (3rd–1st centuries BCE)

8 If God is to speak his word to the soul, it must be still and at peace, and then he *will* speak his word and give himself to the soul and not a mere idea, apart from himself.
Meister Eckhart, *Sermons*, I (13–14th centuries)

9 The knowledge of man is as the waters, some descending from above, and some springing from beneath; the one informed by the light of nature, the other inspired by divine revelation.
Francis Bacon, *The Advancement of Learning*, II, v (1605)

10 Instead of complaining that God had hidden himself, you will give him thanks for having revealed so much of himself.
Blaise Pascal, *Pensées* (1670)

11 The pretending to extraordinary revelations and gifts of the Holy Ghost is a horrid thing, a very horrid thing.
Joseph Butler, to John Wesley (1739) in Wesley, *Works*, XIII

12 My own mind is the direct revelation which I have from God and far least liable to mistake in telling his will of any revelation.
R.W. Emerson, *Journals* (1831)

70 SCRIPTURES

See also 74. LITURGY AND RITUAL

1 I will shew thee that which is noted in the scripture of truth.
Daniel, 10, 21

2 From a child thou hast known the holy scriptures, which are able to make thee wise unto salvation.
2 Timothy, 3, 15

3 By the Book that makes clear. Lo, we have made it an Arabic Koran, maybe ye will understand. And lo, it is in the Mother of the Book in our presence, exalted, wise.
Koran, 43, 1–3

4 We hold that the Koran is the uncreated speech of God, and that he who holds the creation of the Koran is an unbeliever.
Al-Ash'ari, *Ibāna* 23 (10th century)

5 He who studies the Torah in order to learn and to do God's will acquires many merits; and not only that, but the whole world is indebted to him. He is cherished as a friend, a lover of God and of his fellow men.
Mishnah, *Pirke Aboth*, 6

6 The Torah releases one word, and comes forth from her sheath ever so little, and then retreats to concealment again. But this she does only for them who understand her and follow her precepts.
Zohar, *Lovers of the Torah* (14th century)

7 The deeper you dig into the Torah, the more treasures you uncover. Without the Torah the world would not exist. With the letters of the Torah, God has created Heaven and Earth.
Isaac Bashevis Singer, *Love and Exile* (1985)

8 Useful as a tank of water
when all round the water lies,
there's no more in all the Vedas
for a Brahmin who is wise.
Bhagavad Gita, 2, 46

9 The Vedas proclaim with one voice that He
is boundless,
The Semitic Books mention eighteen
hundred worlds;
But the Reality behind all is the One
Principle.
Hymns of Guru Nanak, *patala patal* (16th century)

10 There are Zen masters of a certain type who join in a chorus to deny that the sūtras contain the true teaching of the Buddha . . . Such statements represent the height of folly, they are the words of madmen.
Eto Sokuo, *Shuso to shite no Dogen Zenji* (1949)

11 The memoirs of the apostles or the writings of the prophets are read as long as time permits.
Justin Martyr, *Apology*, 67 (*c*. 155)

12 Holy Scripture containeth all things necessary to salvation.
Book of Common Prayer, Articles of Religion VI

13 The impregnable rock of Holy Scripture.
W.E. Gladstone, *The Impregnable Rock of Holy Scripture* (1890)

14 No man, who knows nothing else, knows even his Bible.
Matthew Arnold, *Culture and Anarchy*, iv (1869)

15 We must reject the assertion of neo-orthodox biblicism that the Bible is the 'only' source. The biblical message cannot be understood and could not have been received had there been no preparation for it in human religion and culture.
Paul Tillich, *Systematic Theology*, I (1951)

16 The Scripture in time of disputes is like an open town in time of war, which serves indifferently the occasions of both parties.
Alexander Pope, *Thoughts on Various Subjects* (1727)

17 Both read the Bible day & night,
But thou read'st black where I read white.
William Blake, *The Everlasting Gospel* (1818)

18 The English Bible, a book which, if everything else in our language should perish, would alone suffice to show the whole extent of its beauty and power.
T.B. Macaulay, *Essays and Biographies*, 'John Dryden' (1828)

19 Those who talk of the Bible as a 'monument of English prose' are merely admiring it as a monument over the grave of Christianity.
T.S. Eliot, *Religion and Literature* (1935)

20 It was subtle of God to learn Greek when he

wished to become an author — and not to learn it better.
Friedrich Nietzsche, *Beyond Good and Evil* (1886)

21 The works of Marx, as the source of revelation, have taken the place of the Bible and the Koran, although they are no freer from contradictions and obscurities than those earlier holy books.
Sigmund Freud, *New Introductory Lectures on Psycho-Analysis* (1933)

22 He opened the book beside the window. At that hour even the veiled panes seemed to grow translucent as crystal. So, while the true light remained to him, he continued to read, in such desperate and disorderly haste that he introduced here and there words and phrases, whole images of his own. His secret self was singing at last in great bursts:
'Praise ye Him, sun and moon: praise Him
          all ye stars of light,
Praise Him, ye heavens of heavens, and ye
          waters that be above the heavens:
And wires of aerials, and grey, slippery
          slates, praise, praise the Lord.'
Patrick White, *Riders in the Chariot* (1961)

71 BELIEF

See also 119. FAITH

1 He believed in the LORD; and he counted it to him for righteousness.
Genesis, 15, 6

2 Lord, I believe; help thou mine unbelief.
Mark, 9, 24

3 The believers are those whose hearts thrill with fear when God is mentioned, whose faith is increased by the recitation of his signs, and who rely on their Lord.
Koran, 8, 2

4 What is always, what is everywhere, what is by all people believed [Quod semper, quod ubique, quod ab omnibus creditum est].
Vincent of Lerins, *Commonitorium*, ii (c. 450)

5 My Lord, I do not believe. Help thou mine unbelief.
Samuel Butler, *Note Books*, G. Keynes and B. Hill (ed.) (1951)

6 I do not believe in Belief . . . Lord, I disbelieve — help thou my unbelief.
E.M. Forster, *Two Cheers for Democracy* (1951)

7 My dear child, you must believe in God in spite of what the clergy tell you.
Benjamin Jowett, in Margot Asquith, *Autobiography* (1922)

8 Nothing is so firmly believed, as what we least know.
Michel de Montaigne, *Essays* (1588)

9 It is natural for the mind to believe, and for the will to love; so that, for want of true objects, they must attach themselves to false.
Blaise Pascal, *Pensées* (1670)

10 We are so constituted that we believe the most incredible things, and, once they are engraved upon the memory, woe to him who would endeavour to erase them.
Johann Wolfgang von Goethe, *The Sorrows of Young Werther* (1774)

11 In view of the silliness of the majority of mankind, a widespread belief is more likely to be foolish than sensible.
Bertrand Russell, *Marriage and Morals* (1929)

12 Believe that life is worth living, and your belief will help create the fact.
William James, *The Will to Believe* (1896)

13 All things are possible to him that believes, more to him that hopes, even more to him that loves, and more still to him who practises and perseveres in these three virtues.
Brother Lawrence, *The Practice of the Presence of God* (1691)

14 Everything possible to be believed is an image of truth.
William Blake, *The Marriage of Heaven and Hell* (1790)

15 *We can believe what we choose.* We are answerable for what we choose to believe.
John Henry Newman, letter to Mrs Froude, 1848

16 I believe Christ's teaching; and this is what I believe. I believe that my welfare in the world will only be possible when all men fulfil Christ's teaching.
Leo Tolstoy, *What I Believe* (1884)

17 When I say 'I believe' I do not mean that I take over for myself what the Church says on these matters, affirming them as one might affirm empirical facts or geometrical theorems, but that, through love, I hold on to the perfect, unseizable, truth which these mysteries contain, and that I try to open my soul to it so that its light may penetrate into me.
Simone Weil, *Pensées sans ordre* (1963)

18 What do I believe? I am accused of not making it explicit. How to be explicit about a grandeur too overwhelming to express, a daily wrestling match with an opponent whose limbs never become material, a struggle from which the sweat and blood are scattered on the pages of anything the serious writer writes? A belief contained less in what is said than in the silences. In patterns on water. A gust of wind. A flower opening.
Patrick White, *Flaws in the Glass* (1981)

---

72 CREEDS

1 God was manifest in the flesh, justified in the Spirit, seen of angels, preached unto the Gentiles, believed on in the world, received up into glory.
1 Timothy, 3, 16

2 I believe in God almighty, and in Christ Jesus, his only son, our Lord . . .
Basis of the *Apostles' Creed*, from Marcellus of Ancyra (340)

3 We believe in One God the Father All-sovereign, maker of heaven and earth, and of all things visible and invisible . . .
Nicene Creed, found in Epiphanius (374)

4 The Catholick Faith is this: That we worship one God in Trinity, and Trinity in Unity; Neither confounding the Persons: nor dividing the substance . . .
Athanasian Creed, *Quicunque vult* (4th–5th centuries)

5 The heart of the confession of the unity of Allah and the true foundation of faith consist in this obligatory creed: I believe in Allah, his angels, his books, his Apostles, the resurrection after death, the decree of Allah the good and the evil thereof,

computation of sins, the balance, Paradise and Hell; and that all these are real . . .
Fiqh Akbar, II (10th century)

6 I believe with perfect faith that the Creator, blessed be his name, is the Author and Guide of everything that has been created, and that he alone has made, does make, and will make all things . . .
Creed or Principles of Moses Maimonides (12th century)

7 We make creeds arbitrarily, and explain them as arbitrarily. The Homoousion is rejected, and received, and explained away by successive synods. The partial or total resemblance of the Father and the Son is a subject for dispute for those unhappy times . . . The profane of every age have derided the furious contests which the difference of a single diphthong excited.
Edward Gibbon, *The Decline and Fall of the Roman Empire*, 21 (1776)

8 The Holy Scripture is the only sufficient, certain, and infallible rule of all saving knowledge, faith, and obedience . . .
Second Westminster Confession (1677)

9 We have a Calvinistic creed, a Popish liturgy, and an Arminian clergy.
William Pitt, speech in the House of Lords, 19 May 1772

10 Thou waitest for the spark from heaven!
and we,
Light half-believers in our casual creeds.
Matthew Arnold, *The Scholar-Gipsy* (1853)

11 Vain are the thousand creeds
That move men's hearts: unutterably vain.
Emily Brontë, *Last Lines* (1846)

12 Great God! I'd rather be
A Pagan suckled in a creed outworn.
William Wordsworth, 'The World is Too Much with Us' (1807)

13 Creeds are codified and dogmatized forms of original religious experience . . . This does not necessarily mean lifeless petrifaction. On the contrary, it may prove to be a valid form of religious experience for millions of people for thousands of years.
C.G. Jung, *Psychology and Religion* (1958)

14 If you have embraced a creed which appears to be free from the ordinary dirtiness of politics — a creed from which you yourself cannot expect to draw any material

advantage — surely that proves that you are in the right?
George Orwell, *Shooting an Elephant* (1950)

15 It is only in the lonely emergencies of life that our creed is tested: then routine maxims fail, and we fall back on our gods.
William James, *The Will to Believe* (1896)

16 For all the unity of the creed in the one Church, a pluralism of theologies has come to prevail within the one Church, which is far deeper, more far-reaching and more uncontrollable than formerly. This is something which in principle must by all means be considered a positive enrichment of the whole Church herself.
Karl Rahner, *Theological Investigations*, VII (1971)

IX
SACRED ACTIONS

73 WORSHIP

1 O come, let us worship and bow down: let us kneel before the LORD our maker.
Psalm, 95, 6

2 The hour cometh, and now is, when the true worshippers shall worship the Father in spirit and in truth: for the Father seeketh such to worship him.
John, 4, 23

3 Simon the Just . . . used to say, Upon three things the world is based: upon the Torah, upon divine worship, and upon acts of benevolence.
Mishnah, *Pirke Aboth*, 1, 2

4 A place of worship founded upon piety from the very first day is more appropriate for thee to stand in; in it are men who love to purify themselves, and God loveth those who purify themselves.
Koran, 9, 109

5 Public Worship is seventeen times better than private Worship.
Al-Ghazali, *The Beginning of Guidance*, 6 (12th century)

6 Those who attend permanently at the temple of his glory confess the imperfection of their worship and say: 'We have not worshipped thee according to the requirement of thy worship.'
Sa'di, *Gulistan*, trans. E. Rehatsek. (13th century)

7 When he begins to praise, then let the priest murmur the following:

From the unreal lead me to the real!
From darkness lead me to light!
From death lead me to immortality!
Brihad-aranyaka Upanishad, 1, 3, 28

8 I am both the recipient and the lord of all acts of worship.
Bhagavad Gita, 9, 24

9 A worshipper at any sacred centre at Gaya, as elsewhere in India, makes offerings of water, flowers, leaves, fruits and grains of rice.
L.P. Vidyarthi, *The Sacred Complex in Hindu Gaya* (1961)

10 By worshipping were it but with a single flower . . . by doing worship were it even with distracted thoughts, one shall in course of time see millions of Buddhas.
The Lotus of the True Law, 2, 93

11 Today they say: 'Tomorrow I shall adore', and the day after again: 'Tomorrow!'
Delaying thus from day to day
the chance will soon be lost.
Sākhī, 16, 24, in Charlotte Vaudeville, *Kabīr* (1974)

12 He worships God who knows him.
Seneca, *Letters to Lucilius* (1st century)

13 It is a thing plainly repugnant to the Word of God, and the custom of the Primitive Church, to have publick Prayer in the Church, or to minister the Sacraments in a tongue not understood of the people.
Book of Common Prayer, Articles of Religion XXIV

14 We hold that the worship of the New Testament properly so called is spiritual

proceeding originally from the heart.
John Smyth, *The Differences of the Churches of the Separation* (1609)

15 In service high, and anthems clear
As may, with sweetness, through mine ear,
Dissolve me into ecstasies,
And bring all Heaven before mine eyes.
John Milton, *Il Penseroso,* 163–6 (1632)

16 If you only make your addresses to God in
the morning and evening, and forget him all
the day, your hearts will grow indifferent in
worship.
Isaac Watts, *A Guide to Prayer* (1715)

17 This is the manner of their worship
[Quaker]. They are to wait upon the Lord,
to meet in the silence of flesh, and to watch
for the stirrings of his life, and the breakings
forth of his power among them.
Isaac Penington, *Inward Journey* (1681)

18 I remembered, He did say
Doubtless, that, to this world's end,
Where two or three should meet and pray,
He would be in their midst, their friend:
Certainly He was there with them.
Robert Browning, *Christmas-Eve and Easter-Day,* VIII (1850)

19 Worship is transcendent wonder.
Thomas Carlyle, *Heroes and Hero-Worship,* i (1841)

20 I like the silent church before the service
begins, better than any preaching.
R.W. Emerson, *Essays,* ii (1844)

21 Come all to church, good people', —
Oh, noisy bells, be dumb:
I hear you, I will come.
A.E. Housman, *A Shropshire Lad,* 'Bredon Hill' (1896)

22 Then someone said, 'Oh-oh! Time for the
worship service.' We all filed out over to the
vesper circle, the organ came in with its
tremolo, and we sang some songs about our
own souls. That was supposed to be
'worship'. But it wasn't!
Harvey Cox, *God's Revolution and Man's Responsibility* (1969)

23 The worship of God is not a rule of safety —
it is an adventure of the spirit, a flight after
the unattainable.
A.N. Whitehead, *Science and the Modern World* (1925)

24 Everyone has the right to freedom of
thought, conscience and religion; this right
includes freedom to change his religion or
belief, and freedom, either alone or in
community with others and in public or
private, to manifest his religion or belief in
teaching, practice, worship and observance.
Universal Declaration of Human Rights,
General Assembly of the United Nations,
Article 18 (1948)

---

74 LITURGY AND RITUAL
See also 75. SACRIFICE AND SACRAMENTS,
57. FESTIVALS

---

1 Concerning the feasts of the LORD, which
ye shall proclaim to be holy convocations.
Leviticus, 23, 2

2 As often as ye eat this bread, and drink this
cup, ye do shew the Lord's death till he
come.
1 Corinthians, 11, 26

3 When ye stand up for the Prayer, wash your
faces and your hands up to the elbows, and
wipe your heads and your feet up to the
ankles; and if you are polluted, purify
yourselves.
Koran, 5, 8

4 When the gods, with cosmic Man as
oblation, extended the sacrifice, Spring
became the butter for it, Summer the
firewood, Autumn the oblation. They
consecrated on the sacred grass this
sacrifice.
Rig Veda, 10, 90, 6–7

5 Such worship they say is of darkness, devoid
of faith, in which no injunction is observed
or food given out, no holy texts recited or
sacrificial fee paid.
Bhagavad Gita, 17, 13

6 The rites to which the Master gave the
greatest attention were those connected
with purification before sacrifice, with war
and with sickness.
Confucius, *Analects,* 7, 12

7 Rites rest on three bases: heaven and earth,
which are the source of all life; the
ancestors, who are the source of the human
race; sovereigns and teachers, who are the
source of government . . . It is through rites

that Heaven and earth are harmonious and sun and moon are bright.
Hsün Tzu, 19, 'On Rites' (3rd century BCE)

8 Of all rites the holiest rite
Is to cleanse one's soul in the company of the saints.
Hymns of Guru Arjan, *sarb dharm* (16th century)

9 The edges of the year have come round, we are about to celebrate the rites . . . do not permit any evil at all to come upon us and let the new year meet us peacefully.
R.S. Rattray, *Religion and Art in Ashanti* (1927)

10 Not in any *prescribed* form of prayer, or *studied* liturgie, but in such manner as the Spirit of grace and prayer teacheth all the people of God.
John Cotton, *The Way of the Churches of Christ in New England* (1645)

11 Not among the Greeks only, but throughout Orthodox Christendom the liturgy has remained at the very heart of the Church's life.
P. Hammond, *The Waters of Marah* (1956)

12 Baptism is not only a sign of profession, and mark of difference, whereby Christian men are discerned from others that be not christened, but it is also a sign of Regeneration or new Birth . . . The Baptism of young Children is in any wise to be retained in the Church.
Book of Common Prayer, Articles of Religion XXVII

13 As for Baptism, it is to be dispensed by a Minister of the Word unto a Believer professing his Repentance and his Faith.
John Cotton, *The True Constitution of a Particular Visible Church* (1642)

14 No noble rite nor formal ostentation.
William Shakespeare, *Hamlet*, IV, v, 215 (*c.* 1603)

15 *Ritualism*, n. A Dutch Garden of God where He may walk in rectilinear freedom, keeping off the grass.
Ambrose Bierce, *The Devil's Dictionary* (1911)

16 Every ritual has the character of happening *now*, at this very moment. The time of the event that the ritual commemorates or

re-enacts is made *present*, 're-presented' so to speak, however far back it may have been in ordinary reckoning.
Mircea Eliade, *Patterns in Comparative Religion* (1958)

17 We can build churches in native architecture, introduce African melodies into the liturgy, use styles of vestments borrowed from Mandarins or Bedouins, but real adaptation consists in the adaptation of our spirits to the spirits of these people.
Placide Tempels, *Bantu Philosophy* (1959)

18 It was long ago observed that 'rites of passage' play a considerable part in the life of religious man. Certainly, the outstanding passage rite is represented by the puberty initiation, passage from one age group to another (from childhood or adolescence to youth). But there is also a passage rite at birth, at marriage, at death, and it could be said that each of these cases always involves an initiation, for each of them implies a radical change in ontological and social status.
Mircea Eliade, *The Sacred and the Profane* (1959)

75 SACRIFICE AND SACRAMENT

1 Will the LORD be pleased with thousands of rams, or with ten thousands of rivers of oil? shall I give my firstborn for my transgression, the fruit of my body for the sign of my soul?
Micah, 6, 7

2 By him therefore let us offer the sacrifice of praise to God continually, that is, the fruit of our lips giving thanks to his name.
Hebrews, 13, 15

3 More beloved by me are the justice and righteousness which you perform than sacrifices.
Mishnah, *Berachoth*, 4

4 The sacrificial animals we have appointed to be amongst the manifestations of God for you, in which there is good for you; so make mention of the name of God over them.
Koran, 22, 37

5 If any devout soul offers me with devotion a

leaf or flower or fruit or water, I enjoy that
offering of devotion.
Bhagavad Gita, 9, 26

6 I offer myself in sacrifice to the Guru a
hundred times a day.
Sākhī, 1, 19, in Charlotte Vaudeville, *Kabīr*
(1974)

7 Spirits of the dead, receive this wine and
sheep, let no bad thing come upon us.
R.S. Rattray, *Religion and Art in Ashanti*
(1927)

8 *Question*: What meanest thou by this word
Sacrament?
Answer: I mean an outward and visible sign
of an inward and spiritual grace.
Book of Common Prayer, A Catechism

9 There are two Sacraments of Christ our
Lord in the Gospel, that is to say, Baptism,
and the Supper of the Lord. Those five
commonly called Sacraments, that is to say,
Confirmation, Penance, Orders, Matrimony
and extreme Unction, are not to be counted
Sacraments of the Gospel.
Book of Common Prayer, Articles of
Religion XXV

10 'Twas God the word that spake it,
He took the Bread and brake it;
And what the word did make it;
That I believe, and take it.
Elizabeth I, quoted in S. Clarke, *Marrow of
Ecclesiastical History* (1695)

11 They do make certain burnt offerings — of
incense and other aromatic substances, and
of innumerable candles. Of course they
realize that such things are no use to the
Divine Being, but they see no harm in them
as a form of tribute.
Thomas More, *Utopia*, ii (1516)

12 The body of Christ is not in this sacrament
according to the proper mode of spatial
dimension, but rather according to the mode
of substance . . . for the substance of
Christ's body takes the place of the
substance of bread.
Thomas Aquinas, *Summa Theologica*, iii,
lxxvi (13th century)

13 The Spiritual Presence cannot be received
without a sacramental element, however
hidden the latter might be.
Paul Tillich, *Systematic Theology*, III (1963)

76 MUSIC

1 Praise him with the sound of the trumpet:
praise him with the psaltery and harp.
Praise him with the timbrel and dance;
praise him with stringed instruments and
organs.
Praise him upon the loud cymbals:
praise him upon the high sounding cymbals.
Psalm, 150, 3–5

2 Speaking to yourselves in psalms and
hymns, singing and making melody in your
heart to the Lord.
Ephesians, 5, 19

3 It has been taught us that at the break of day
a chorus of a thousand and five hundred and
fifty myriads sing out hymns to God.
Zohar, *Hymns in Heaven* (14th century)

4 I was with the Prophet, and when he heard
the noise of a musical pipe, he put his fingers
into his ears.
Islamic Tradition, *Mishkat*, xxii, 9 (8th
century)

5 Do you think me ignorant of vocal music?
Listen to this: There are seven notes, three
scales, twenty-one modes, forty-nine
pitches, three measures, three pauses . . .
Nothing nobler than vocal song on earth or
in heaven is found, and the singing Devil
soothes the Lord when quivering strings
prolong the sound.
Pancha-tantra, *The Musical Ass* (3rd–7th
centuries)

6 A man who is not Good, what can he have
to do with music?
Confucius, *Analects*, III, 3

7 What else can I do, a lame old man, but sing
hymns to God? If I were a nightingale, I
would do the nightingale's part; if I were a
swan, I would do as a swan. But now I am a
rational creature, and I ought to praise God.
Epictetus, *Discourses*, I, xvi (2nd century)

8 How greatly did I weep in thy hymns and
canticles, deeply moved by the voices of thy
sweet-speaking church.
Augustine of Hippo, *Confessions*, ix, 6 (5th
century)

9 Music is one of the greatest gifts that God
has given us: it is divine and therefore Satan
is its enemy. For with its aid many dire

temptations are overcome; the devil does not stay where music is.
Martin Luther, *In Praise of Music* (1525)

10 Martin Luther . . . Like Wesley, Rowland Hill, General Booth, and a number of other religious leaders, he was the first to utter the famous dictum that the devil should not have all the best tunes.
Percy A. Scholes, *The Oxford Companion to Music* (1938)

11 That music itself is lawful, useful, and commendable, no man, no Christian dares deny, since the Scriptures, Fathers, and generally all Christians, all pagan authors extant, do with one consent aver it.
William Prynne, *Histriomastix* (1632)

12 We hold that seeing singing a psalm is a part of spiritual worship: therefore it is unlawful to have the book before the eye in time of singing a psalm.
John Smyth, *The Differences of the Churches of the Separation* (1609)

13 Glorious the song, when God's the theme.
Christopher Smart, *Song to David* (1763)

14 In Quires and Places where they sing, here followeth the Anthem.
Book of Common Prayer, Morning and Evening Prayer Rubrick

15 All the Heav'nly Quire stood mute,
And silence was in Heav'n.
John Milton, *Paradise Lost*, III, 217–18 (1667)

16 Let all the world in ev'ry corner sing
My God and King.
The Church with psalms must shout,
No door can keep them out.
George Herbert, *The Temple*, 'Antiphon' (1633)

17 Since I am coming to that holy room
Where, with thy Choir of Saints for
evermore,
I shall be made thy music.
John Donne, *Hymn to God my God, in my sickness* (1635)

18 So he passed over, and all the trumpets sounded for him on the other side.
John Bunyan, *Pilgrim's Progress* (1678)

19 Music, the greatest good that mortals know,
And all of heaven we have below.
Joseph Addison, *A Song for St Cecilia's Day* (1694)

20 I must despise the world which does not know that music is a higher revelation than all wisdom and philosophy.
Ludwig van Beethoven, quoted in Bettina von Arnim, *Letter to Goethe* (1810)

21 As some to church repair,
Not for the doctrine, but the music there.
Alexander Pope, *An Essay on Criticism* (1711)

22 1. In these hymns there is no doggerel; no botches; nothing put in to patch up the rhyme; no feeble expletives.
2. Here is nothing turgid or bombast, on the one hand, or low and creeping on the other.
3. Here are no *cant* expressions, no words without meaning . . . Here are, allow me to say, both the purity, the strength, and the elegance of the English language; and, at the same time, the utmost simplicity and plainness, suited to every capacity.
John Wesley, *A Collection of Hymns for the use of the People called Methodists*, 'Preface' (1779)

23 Music in England was ruined by *Hymns Ancient and Modern*.
Edward Elgar, quoted in Redwood, *An Elgar Companion* (1982)

24 In spite of myself, the insidious mastery of
song
Betrays me back, till the heart of me weeps
to belong
To the old Sunday evenings at home, with
winter outside
And hymns in the cosy parlour, the tinkling
piano our guide.
D.H. Lawrence, *Piano* (1928)

25 All music is praise of the Lord, which some people cannot or will not understand, the real jazz form of a spiritual soil, is truly the musical psalms of the twentieth-century man's torment in the tigerish growl of the trumpet.
The Indian Express (1963)

26 Then an astonishing thing happens. A stout woman dressed in black, with a forceful face, disengages herself from a bench and, bursting out into a hymn, moves towards the front, hip-swinging and dancing. The audience at once joins in, and soon we are all swaying in our seats, laughing and joking, faces happy in anticipation of the treat. The men beat the rhythm with feet and arms, and the whole congregation

resembles the audience at a variety concert.
Mia Brandel-Syrier, *Black Woman in Search of God* (1962)

27 Voss was jubilant as brass. Cymbals clapped drunkenly. Now he had forgotten words, but sang his jubilation in a cracked bass, that would not have disgraced temples because dedicated to God.
Patrick White, *Voss* (1957)

X
SPIRITUALITY

77 RELIGIOUS EXPERIENCE
See also 78. MYSTICISM

1 Before I formed thee in the belly I knew thee; and before thou camest forth out of the womb I sanctified thee, and I ordained thee a prophet to the nations.
Jeremiah, 1, 5

2 I know whom I have believed, and am persuaded that he is able to keep that which I have committed unto him.
2 Timothy, 1, 12

3 He stood straight on the high horizon,
then drew near and came down,
till he was two bow-lengths away or nearer,
and then he revealed to his servant what he
revealed.
Koran, 53, 6–10

4 By knowing God one is released from all fetters.
Shvetashvatara Upanishad, 1, 8

5 Filled with astonishment, his hair standing
on end,
Arjuna with folded hands bowed his head
before the God.
Bhagavad Gita, 11, 14

6 When a person has true spiritual experience, he may boldly drop external disciplines, even those to which he is bound by vows.
Meister Eckhart, *Sermons*, 3 (13th–14th centuries)

7 FIRE. God of Abraham, God of Isaac, God of Jacob, not of philosophers and scholars. Certainty. Certainty. Feeling. Joy. Peace.
Blaise Pascal, paper dated 23 November 1654, found in the lining of his coat after his death

8 Belief, ritual, and spiritual experience: these are the cornerstones of religion, and the greatest of them is the last.
I.M. Lewis, *Ecstatic Religion* (1971)

9 All authentic religion originates with mystical experience, be it the experience of Jesus, of the Buddha, or Mohammed, of the seers and prophets of the Upanishads.
William Johnston, *The Inner Eye of Love* (1978)

10 There is an experience of being in pure consciousness which gives lasting peace to the soul. It is an experience of the Ground or Depth of being in the Centre of the soul, an awareness of the mystery of being beyond sense and thought, which gives a sense of fulfilment, of finality, of absolute truth.
Bede Griffiths, *Return to the Centre* (1976)

11 A personal philosophical experience of moving out of a world of sense and arriving, dazed and disorientated for a while, into a universe of being.
Bernard Lonergan, *A Second Collection* (1974)

12 The language of religion is a set of formulas which register a basic spiritual experience.
Dag Hammarskjöld, *Markings* (1964)

13 The *Thou* meets me through grace — it is not found by seeking.
Martin Buber, *I and Thou* (1937)

14 Among all my patients in the second half of life — that is to say, over thirty-five — there

has not been one whose problem in the last resort was not that of finding a religious outlook on life.
C.G. Jung, *Modern Man in Search of a Soul* (1933)

15 I fled Him, down the nights and down the days;
I fled Him, down the arches of the years;
I fled Him, down the labyrinthine ways
Of my own mind; and in the mist of tears
I hid from Him, and under running laughter.
Francis Thompson, *The Hound of Heaven* (1893)

16 The sunset backed up against the sky, as they stood beneath the great swingeing trace-chains of its light. Perhaps she should have been made afraid by some awfulness of the situation, but she was not. She had been translated; she was herself a fearful beam of the ruddy, champing light.
Patrick White, *Riders in the Chariot* (1961)

17 I listened to the silence of the night and I felt as if I had all of a sudden penetrated the very heart of the universe. An immense happiness, such as I had never known, swept over me with a flow of fulfilment.
Carlo Levi, *Christ Stopped at Eboli* (1947)

---

78 MYSTICISM
See also 81. DEVOTION AND COMMUNION

---

1 I have loved thee with an everlasting love: therefore with lovingkindness have I drawn thee.
Jeremiah, 31, 3

2 The mystery which hath been hid from ages and from generations, but now is made manifest to his saints.
Colossians, 1, 26

3 We have created man, and we know what his soul whispers within him, for we are nearer to him than his jugular vein.
Koran, 50, 15

4 The complete mystic 'way' includes both intellectual belief and practical activity; the latter consists in getting rid of the obstacles in the self and in stripping off its base characteristics and vicious morals, so that the heart may attain to freedom from what is not God and to constant recollection of Him.
Al-Ghazali, *Deliverance from Error,* 122, 4 (12th century)

5 By love he comes to recognize my greatness, who I really am, and enters into me at once, by knowing me as I really am.
Bhagavad Gita, 18, 55

6 With the Tantras, an entirely new set of meditations comes to the fore, which no one has yet described in intelligible terms. Their rational content is negligible, and they are almost entirely concerned with concepts which pertain to the magical tradition of mankind . . . The original documents in which any study of Tantric thought must be based, are written in a code which no one has yet been able to break.
Edward Conze, *Buddhist Thought in India* (1962)

7 Happy is he among men upon earth who has seen these mysteries.
Hymn to Demeter, 480–2 (6th century BCE)

8 Among the signs by which those who are truly possessed by the gods may be known, the greatest is the fact that many are not burned, though fire is applied to them, since the deity breathing within them does not permit the fire to touch them.
Iamblichus, *On the Mysteries,* III, 4 (4th century)

9 It breaks forth, even from that which is seen and that which sees, and plunges the mystic into the Darkness of Unknowing, whence all perfection of understanding is excluded, and he is enwrapped in that which is altogether intangible and noumenal, being wholly absorbed in Him who is beyond all.
Dionysius, *Mystical Theology,* 1 (6th century)

10 The higher part of contemplation, as it may be had here, hangeth all wholly in this darkness and in this cloud of unknowing; with a loving stirring and a blind beholding unto the naked being of God Himself only.
The Cloud of Unknowing, 8 (14th century)

11 Mystical theology, that secret knowledge of God which spiritual persons call contemplation.
John of the Cross, *Spiritual Canticle,* 27, 5 (16th century)

12 Here I saw a great oneing betwixt Christ

and us, to mine understanding: for when He was in pain, we were in pain.
Julian of Norwich, *Revelations of Divine Love*, 18 (14th century)

13 No great works and wonder God has ever wrought or shall ever do in or through this created world, not even God himself in his goodness, will make me blessed if they remain outside of me.
Theologia Germanica, 9 (14th century)

14 Mysticism is the experience: mystical theology is reflection on this experience. The medievals did not make this distinction clearly.
William Johnston, *The Inner Eye of Love* (1978)

15 Zen literature speaks enthusiastically about such experience: we hear of people who reach deep enlightenment just by listening. It is all very wonderful. But is it mysticism? The answer is: No. For it is not knowledge that comes from love . . . The bodhisattva is in love with everyone he meets. This is unrestricted love. This is mysticism.
William Johnston, *The Inner Eye of Love* (1978)

16 It can be maintained that the strictly monotheistic religions do not naturally lend themselves to mysticism; and there is much to be said for this view. Christianity is the exception because it introduces into a monotheistic system an idea that is wholly foreign to it, namely, the Incarnation . . . Hindu mysticism differs from both the Christian and Muslim varieties in that it accepts the eternity of the soul as a fact of experience.
R.C. Zaehner, *Hindu and Muslim Mysticism* (1960)

17 In practice, mystics belonging to nearly all the religious traditions coincide to the extent that they can hardly be distinguished. They represent the truth of each of these traditions. The contemplation practised in India, Greece, China, etc., is just as supernatural as that of the Christian mystics.
Simone Weil, *Letter to a Priest* (1953)

18 The Jewish mystic almost invariably retains a sense of the distance between the Creator and His creature.
G.G. Scholem, *Major Trends in Jewish Mysticism* (1941)

19 Those who insist that mystical experience is not specifically different from the ordinary life of grace (as such) are certainly right.
Karl Rahner, *Encyclopedia of Theology* (1975)

20 Mysticism is the stressing to a very high degree, indeed the overstressing, of the non-rational or supra-rational elements in religion; and it is only intelligible when so understood.
Rudolf Otto, *The Holy*, IV (1917)

21 The Beatific Vision, *Sat Chit Ananda*, Being-Awareness-Bliss — for the first time I understood, not on a verbal level, not by inchoate hints or at a distance, but precisely and completely what those prodigious syllables referred to.
Aldous Huxley, *The Doors of Perception* (1954)

22 By a mystical experience Huxley seems to understand not only the experiences of all the recognized mystics, but experiences such as his own under the influence of mescalin; and, since he is honest, he would be forced to add, the experiences of madness.
R.C. Zaehner, *Mysticism, Sacred and Profane* (1957)

79 SALVATION AND CONVERSION

1 All the ends of the earth shall see the salvation of our God.
Isaiah, 52, 10

2 What must I do to be saved?
Acts, 16, 30

3 Whoever surrenders himself to God, being a well-doer, has his reward with his Lord, fears rests not upon him nor does he grieve.
Koran, 2, 106

4 Abandoning all duties, come to Me alone for refuge, I will save you from all evils, never fear.
Bhagavad Gita, 18, 66

5 With his powerful knowledge he beholds all creatures who are beset with many hundreds of troubles and afflicted by many sorrows, and thereby he is a Saviour in the world.
The Lotus of the True Law, 24, 17

6 I go to the Lord as a refuge, I go to the
Doctrine, and to the Order of monks.
Vinaya Pitaka, *Mahavagga*, 1, 22 (3rd–1st
centuries BCE)

7 Buddhism is above all a religion of
salvation. It claims to save man from the
illusions and snares and sufferings of human
existence.
William Johnston, *The Inner Eye of Love*
(1978)

8 I found stability and salvation
when the Satguru gave me firmness.
Sākhi, 1, 11, in Charlotte Vaudeville, *Kabir*
(1974)

9 He gives salvation or perdition
To those who are living or have been or
                    shall be:
The soul of the righteous rewarded with
                    Immortality.
Gathas, *Yasna*, 45, 7

10 Kom is a place that, excepting on the subject
of religion, and settling who are worthy of
salvation and who is to be damned, no one
opens his lips.
James Morier, *The Adventures of Hajji Baba
of Ispahan* (1824)

11 I seized, opened, and in silence read that
section, on which my eyes first fell: 'Not in
rioting and drunkenness, not in chambering
and wantonness, not in strife and envying;
but put ye on the Lord Jesus Christ, and
make not provision for the flesh, in
concupiscence.' No further would I read;
nor needed I; for instantly at the end of this
sentence, by a light as it were of serenity
infused into my heart, all the darkness of
doubt vanished away.
Augustine of Hippo, *Confessions*, VIII, 12
(5th century)

12 In the beginning of my conversion and
singular purpose, I thought that I would be
like the little bird that languishes for love of
his beloved, but is gladdened in his longing
when he that it loves comes and sings with
joy.
Richard Rolle, *The Fire of Love* (14th
century)

13   Consider this,
That in the course of justice none of us
Should see salvation.
William Shakespeare, *The Merchant of
Venice*, IV, i, 193–5 (*c.* 1596–8)

14 There is no expeditious road
To pack and label men for God,
And save them by the barrel-load.
Francis Thompson, *A Judgment in Heaven*
(1893)

15 The ordaining of salvation for man and of
man for salvation is the original and basic
will of God, the ground and purpose of His
will as Creator.
Karl Barth, *Church Dogmatics*, IV, i (1936)

16 The God-image in man was not destroyed
by the Fall but was only damaged and
corrupted ('deformed'), and can be restored
through God's grace.
C.G. Jung, *Aion* (1959)

17 Holy Scripture containeth all things
necessary to salvation.
Book of Common Prayer, Articles of
Religion VI

80 PIETY AND HOLINESS

1 Ye shall be holy: for I the LORD your God
am holy.
Leviticus, 19, 2

2 Be ye therefore perfect, even as your Father
which is in heaven is perfect.
Matthew, 5, 48

3 It is not piety that you should turn your
faces towards the East or the West. True
piety is this: to believe in God, and the Last
Day, the angels, the Book, and the prophets;
to give of one's substance, however
cherished, to relatives and orphans and the
poor, the traveller and beggars, and to
ransom captives; to perform the Prayer and
to pay the Alms.
Koran, 2, 172

4 *If* you are holy, only then are you Mine.
Mechilta Mishpatim, 20 (2nd century)

5 Being a knower, shaking off good and evil,
stainless, one attains supreme identity with
the Lord.
Mundaka Upanishad, 3, 1, 3

6 No one can be enlightened unless he be first
cleansed or purified or stripped. So also, no
one can be united with God unless he be
first enlightened. Thus there are three

stages: first, the purification; secondly, the enlightening; thirdly, the union.
Theologia Germanica, 14 (14th century)

7 Experience makes us see an enormous difference between piety and goodness.
Blaise Pascal, *Pensées* (1670)

8 Love of God is not always the same as love of good.
Hermann Hesse, *Narcissus and Goldmund* (1930)

9 For years I used almost as proverbs . . . 'Holiness rather than peace'.
John Henry Newman, *Apologia pro Vita sua* (1864)

10 It is rash to intrude upon the piety of others: both the depth and the grace of it elude the stranger.
George Santayana, *Dialogue in Limbo* (1925)

11 No one can make clear to another who has never had a certain feeling, in what the quality or worth of it consists. One must have musical ears to know the value of a symphony; one must have been in love oneself to understand a lover's state of mind.
William James, *The Varieties of Religious Experience* (1902)

12 So long as religion is only faith and outward form, and the religious function is not experienced in our own souls, nothing of any importance has happened.
C.G. Jung, *Psychology and Alchemy* (1953)

13 True piety is *acting what one knows*.
Matthew Arnold, *Notebooks* (1868)

---

81 DEVOTION AND COMMUNION
See also 78. MYSTICISM

---

1 I will betroth thee unto me in righteousness, and in judgment, and in lovingkindness, and in mercies.
Hosea, 2, 19

2 Abide in me, and I in you.
John, 15, 4

3 God will produce another people whom he loves and who love him.
Koran, 5, 59

4 That all 'I's' and 'thou's' might become one soul and at last be submerged in the Beloved.
Jalalu'i-Din Rumi, *Mathnawi*, 1, 1776 (13th century)

5 God dwells in the heart, according to the Tradition, 'Neither my earth nor my heaven contain me, but I am contained in the heart of my servant who believes.'
Ibn al-Arabi, *Tarjumanu al-Ashwaq*, VI, 1 (13th century)

6 Of Abu Yazīd it is recorded that he said: 'I sloughed off my self as a snake sloughs off its skin: then I looked into myself and lo! I was he.'
Quoted in R.C. Zaehner, *Hindu and Muslim Mysticism* (1960)

7 What is the love of God that is befitting? It is to love God with a great and exceeding love, so strong that one's soul shall be knit up with the love of God, and one should be continually enraptured by it.
Moses Maimonides, *Mishneh Torah*, x, 3 (12th century)

8 By undivided devotion, in such a form can I be known, and truly seen, and entered into.
Bhagavad Gita, 11, 54

9 Two birds, fast bound companions,
Clasp close the self-same tree.
Of these two, the one eats sweet fruit;
The other looks on without eating.

On the self-same tree a person, sunken,
Grieves for his impotence, deluded;
When he sees the other, the Lord, contented,
And his greatness, he becomes freed from
      sorrow.
Mundaka Upanishad, 3, 1, 1–2

10 Repeating 'Thou, Thou', I became Thou, in me, no 'I' remained.
Sākhī, 3, 6 in Charlotte Vaudeville, *Kabīr* (1974)

11 This is the path to Union:
Destroy sense of self, thou shalt find then
My Lord within thee.
Hymns of Guru Arjan, *mohan nind* (16th century)

12 Śaiva Siddhānta does not consider the non-dualist type of mysticism as having ultimate value in religious life . . . It proposes love of God as the key to the genuine religious experience.

M. Dhavamony, *Love of God according to Śaiva Siddhānta* (1971)

13 This is the life of the gods, and of divine and happy men, a liberation from all earthly concerns, a life unaccompanied with human pleasures, and a flight of the alone to the Alone.
Plotinus, *Enneads,* VI, ix (3rd century)

14 The core of the soul is sensitive to nothing but the divine Being, unmediated. Here God enters the soul with all he has and not in part, and nothing may touch that core except God himself.
Meister Eckhart, *Sermons,* 1 (13th–14th centuries)

15 I would fain be to the Eternal Goodness, what his own right hand is to a man.
Theologia Germanica, X (14th century)

16 There are two sorts of Devotion; the one essential and true; the other accidental and sensible. The essential is a promptitude of mind to do aright, to fulfil the commandments of God . . . Accidental and sensible Devotion exists when good desires are attended with a pleasant softness of heart.
Miguel de Molinos, *The Spiritual Guide,* I, v (1675)

17 Divine Union has its commencement, its progression, and its consummation. It is first an inclination and tendency towards God . . . on a nearer approach to God it adheres to him; and growing stronger and stronger in its adhesion, it finally becomes one; that is 'One Spirit with him.'
Madame Guyon, *A Short and Easy Method of Prayer,* xxi (1685)

18 To become Divine is the aim of life: then only can truth be said to be ours beyond the possibility of loss, because it is no longer outside of us, nor even in us, but we are it, and it is we.
H.F. Amiel, *Fragments d'un journal intime* (1884)

19 Look upon me till Thou are formed in me, that I may be a mirror of Thy brightness, a habitation of Thy love, and a temple of thy glory.
Thomas Traherne, *Centuries of Meditations,* i, 87 (17th century)

20 E'en so we met; and after long pursuit E'en so we join'd, we both became entire;

No need for either to renew a suit, For I was flax, and he was flames of fire. Our firm united souls did more than twine; So I my best beloved's am, so he is mine.
Francis Quarles, *Emblems,* v, 3 (1635)

21 Plunged in the Godhead's deepest sea, And lost in Thine immensity.
Charles Wesley, *A Collection of Hymns* (1779)

22 My brothers, the love of God is a hard love. It demands total self-surrender.
Albert Camus, *The Plague* (1947)

23 The ultimate spiritual union is probably as impossible to achieve as the perfect work of art or the unflawed human relationship.
Patrick White, *Flaws in the Glass* (1981)

---

82 MIRACLES

---

1 His miracles, and his acts, which he did in the midst of Egypt.
Deuteronomy, 11, 3

2 No man can do these miracles that thou doest, except God be with him.
John, 3, 2

3 They say: 'Why are not signs from his Lord sent down to him?' Say: 'Signs are with God only and I am only a clear warner.' Has it not sufficed them that we have sent down to thee the Book to be recited to them?
Koran, 29, 49–50

4 Moses our teacher was not believed in by the Israelites because of the miracles he wrought. One whose belief depends on miracles is of imperfect faith, since miracles can be wrought by magic and sleight-of-hand.
Moses Maimonides, *Mishneh Torah,* 'Foundations', viii, i (12th century)

5 The Master never talked of prodigies, feats of strength, disorders or spirits.
Confucius, *Analects,* VII, 20

6 Celsus . . . puts them on a level with the works of jugglers, on the ground that their professions are still more marvellous.
Origen, *Contra Celsum,* i, 68 (3rd century)

7 Since every friend to revelation is persuaded of the reality, and every reasonable man is convinced of the cessation, of miraculous

powers, it is evident that there must have been *some period* in which they were either suddenly or gradually withdrawn from the Christian church.
Edward Gibbon, *The History of the Decline and Fall of the Roman Empire*, 15 (1776)

8 A miracle is a violation of the laws of nature; and as a firm and unalterable experience has established these laws, the proof against a miracle, from the very nature of the fact, is as entire as any argument from experience can possibly be imagined.
David Hume, *Enquiry Concerning Human Understanding*, x (1748)

9 The laws of nature had sometimes been suspended by their Divine Author; and since what had happened once might happen again, a certain probability, at least no kind of improbability, was attached to the idea, taken in itself, of miraculous intervention in later times.
John Henry Newman, *Apologia pro Vita sua*, iii (1864)

10 The possibility cannot be excluded that some miracle stories offer *anticipated portrayals of the risen Christ*: epiphany stories, which frequently have an obvious point and — for the community — a symbolic meaning (rescue from the 'storm' of tribulation and so on).
Hans Küng, *On Being a Christian*, C, II, 2 (1974)

11 You can't, as Bultmann supposes, separate God and miracle, but you must be able to interpret and proclaim *both* in a 'non-religious' sense.
Dietrich Bonhoeffer, *Letters and Papers from Prison* (1953)

12 Miracles do not happen.
Matthew Arnold, *Literature and Dogma* (1883)

13 Seeing, hearing, feeling are miracles, and each part and tag of me is a miracle.
Walt Whitman, *Leaves of Grass*, 'Song of Myself' (1855)

14 Miracles appeal only to the understanding of those who cannot perceive the meaning. They are mere substitutes for the not understood reality of the spirit. The spirit and meaning of Christ are present and perceptible to us even without the aid of miracles.
C.G. Jung, *Answer to Job* (1952)

15 Scholars, and often the clergy in relation to the laity, are peculiarly reluctant to concede the innate human capacity to accept the marvellous, to delight in wonder and respond to the strongest claims made on the imagination.
Rachel Trickett, 'Imagination and Belief' in A.E. Harvey (ed.), *God Incarnate: Story and Belief* (1981)

83 VISIONS

1 In thoughts from the visions of the night, when deep sleep falleth on men, fear came upon me, and trembling, which made all my bones to shake. Then a spirit passed before my face; the hair of my flesh stood up.
Job, 4, 13–15

2 He was caught up into paradise, and heard unspeakable words, which it is not lawful for a man to utter.
2 Corinthians, 12, 4

3 He saw him, at a second descent . . . when the lotus tree was strangely enveloped. His eye swerved not, nor swept astray. Indeed, he saw one of the greatest signs of his Lord.
Koran, 53, 13–18

4 Buraq, the animal whose every stride carried it as far as its eye could reach, on which the prophets before him used to ride, was brought to the apostle and he was mounted on it. His companion [Gabriel] went with him to see the wonders between heaven and earth, until he came to Jerusalem's temple. There he found Abraham the friend of God, Moses, and Jesus assembled with a company of the prophets, and he prayed with them.
Ibn Ishaq, *The Life of the Apostle of God* (8th century)

5 With the first stage of the 'way' there begin the revelations and visions. The mystics in their waking state now behold angels and the spirits of the prophets; they hear these speaking to them and are instructed by them. Later, a higher stage is reached; instead of beholding forms and figures, they come to stages of the 'way' which it is hard to describe in language.
Al-Ghazali, *Deliverance from Error*, 133 (12th century)

6 In the Beatific Vision God manifests himself to the elect in a general epiphany, which, nevertheless, assumes various forms corresponding to the mental conceptions of God formed by the faithful on earth.
Ibn al-Arabi, *Futuhat*, III (13th century)

7 Because you cannot see me with your own natural eye, I will give you a celestial eye, behold my mystic power as Lord. Thus speaking, Hari, the Great Lord of Mystic Power, revealed his highest form as God.
Bhagavad Gita, 11, 8–9

8 Then did those who were assembled and sitting together in that congregation . . . all of them with their followers, gaze on the Lord in astonishment, in amazement, in ecstasy. And at that moment there issued a ray from within the circle of hair between the eyebrows of the Lord. It extended over eighteen hundred thousand Buddha-fields.
The Lotus of the True Law, 1

9 Can you wipe and cleanse your vision of the Mystery till it is all without blur?
Tao Te Ching, X

10 We pray that we may come into this Darkness which is beyond light, and, without seeing and without knowing, to see and to know that which is above vision and knowledge.
Dionysius, *Mystical Theology*, 2 (6th century)

11 This truly is the vision of God: never to be satisfied in the desire to see him. But one must always, by looking at what he can see, rekindle his desire to see more.
Gregory of Nyssa, *Life of Moses*, 239 (4th century)

12 Oh abundant grace, wherein I presumed to fix my gaze on the eternal light so long that I wearied my sight! Within its depths I saw gathered in, bound by love in one volume, the scattered leaves of all the universe.
Dante Alighieri, *Paradiso*, XXXIII, 82–7 (1320)

13 Visions or revelations of any manner of spirit, in bodily appearing or in imagining, sleeping or waking, or else any other feeling in the bodily senses . . . are not true contemplation; nor are they aught but simple and secondary.
Walter Hilton, *The Scale of Perfection*, X (14th century)

14 If the Soul after she has wearied herself by means of meditation, shall arrive at the stillness, tranquillity, and rest of contemplation, she ought then to put an end to all discursive thought, and repose in the loving contemplation and simple vision of God.
Miguel de Molinos, *The Spiritual Guide*, 1 (17th century)

15 Such a Beatific Vision is not for the present life, but is reserved for the final state of existence.
Bernard of Clairvaux, *The Song of Songs*, Sermon 29 (12th century)

16 The higher stages of the mystical life are very ordinary. There is no ecstasy, no rapture, no flash of light, no bells, no incense. I am now my true self.
William Johnston, *The Inner Eye of Love*, 13 (1978)

17 'What', it will be Question'd, 'When the Sun rises, do you not see a round disk of fire somewhat like a Guinea?' O no, no, I see an Innumerable company of the Heavenly host crying 'Holy, Holy, Holy is the Lord God Almighty.'
William Blake, *A Vision of the Last Judgment* (1810)

18 The Prophets Isaiah and Ezekiel dined with me, and I asked them how they dared so roundly to assert that God spoke to them; and whether they did not think at the time that they would be misunderstood, & so be the cause of imposition. Isaiah answer'd: 'I saw no God, nor heard any, in a finite organical perception; but my senses discover'd the infinite in every thing, and as I was then perswaded, & remain confirm'd, that the voice of honest indignation is the voice of God.
William Blake, *The Marriage of Heaven and Hell* (1793)

19 The Vision of Christ that thou dost see Is my Vision's Greatest Enemy: Thine has a great hook nose like thine, Mine has a snub nose like to mine.
William Blake, *The Everlasting Gospel* (1818)

20 That one Face, far from vanish, rather grows,
Or decomposes but to recompose,
Become my universe that feels and knows!
Robert Browning, *Epilogue* (1864)

21 Earth's crammed with heaven,
   And every common bush afire with God;
   But only he who sees, takes off his shoes,
   The rest sit round it and pluck blackberries.
   Elizabeth Barrett Browning, *Aurora Leigh*,
   vii (1857)

22 For I dipt into the future, far as human eye
                        could see,
   Saw the Vision of the world, and all the
                        wonder that would be.
   Alfred Tennyson, *Locksley Hall* (1842)

23 A damsel with a dulcimer
   In a vision once I saw.
   S.T. Coleridge, *Kubla Khan* (1798)

24 Anyone who has followed with attention the
   visions of Mary which have been increasing
   in number over the last few decades, and has
   taken their psychological significance into
   account, might have known what was
   brewing. The fact, especially, that it was
   largely children who had the visions might
   have given pause for thought, for in such
   cases the collective unconscious is always at
   work.
   C.G. Jung, *Psychology and Religion* (1958)

25 So, at last, the figure of her Lord and
   Saviour would stand before her in the
   chancel, looking down at her from beneath
   the yellow eyelids, along the strong, but
   gentle beak of a nose. She was content to
   leave then, since all converged finally upon
   the Risen Christ, and her own eyes had
   confirmed that the wounds were healed.
   Patrick White, *Riders in the Chariot* (1961)

---

84 DREAMS

---

1 The vision of that dream was this: He saw
  Onias, him that was high priest, a noble and
  good man, reverened in bearing, yet gentle
  in manner and well-spoken, and exercised
  from a child in all points of virtue, with
  outstretched hands invoking blessings on
  the whole body of the Jews.
  2 Maccabees, 15, 12

2 I have suffered many things this day in a
  dream because of him.
  Matthew, 27, 19

3 I have heard that the apostle used to say,
  'My eyes sleep while my heart is awake'.

Only God knows how revelation came and
he saw what he saw. But whether he was
asleep or awake, it was all true and actually
happened.
Ibn Ishaq, *The Life of the Apostle of God*
(8th century)

4 I saw the Prophet in a dream, and he said to
  me, 'O Rabi'a, dost thou love me?' I said, 'O
  Prophet of God who is there who does not
  love thee? But my love to God has so
  possessed me that no place remains for
  loving or hating any save him.'
  Margaret Smith, *Rabi'a the Mystic*, (1928)

5 When one goes to sleep, he takes along the
  material of this all-containing world, himself
  tears it apart, himself builds it up, and
  dreams by his own brightness, by his own
  light. Then this person becomes
  self-illuminated. There are no chariots there,
  no spans, no roads. But he projects from
  himself chariots, spans, roads . . . for he is a
  creator.
  Brihad-aranyaka Upanishad, 4, 3, 9–10

6 Once upon a time, I, Chuang Tzu, dreamt
  that I was a butterfly, fluttering hither and
  thither . . . Suddenly I awaked, and there I
  lay, myself again. Now I do not know
  whether I was then a man dreaming I was a
  butterfly, or whether I am now a butterfly
  dreaming I am a man.
  Chuang Tzu, 2 (4th century BCE)

7 The soul is present with us as much while
  we are asleep as while we are awake; and
  while waking resembles active observation,
  sleep resembles the implicit though not
  exercised possession of knowledge.
  Aristotle, *On the Soul*, IV, 3

8 The ancient belief that dreams reveal the
  future is not indeed entirely devoid of truth.
  By representing a wish as fulfilled the dream
  certainly leads us into the future.
  Sigmund Freud, *The Interpretation of
  Dreams* (1913)

9 Those who have likened our life to a dream
  were more right, by chance, than they
  realised. We are awake while sleeping, and
  waking sleep.
  Michel de Montaigne, *Essais*, III, xii (1588)

10   To die, to sleep;
   To sleep: perchance to dream: ay, there's
                        the rub;
   For in that sleep of death what dreams may
                        come

When we have shuffled off this mortal coil,
Must give us pause.
William Shakespeare, *Hamlet*, III, i, 64–8
(*c.* 1603)

11 Real are the dreams of Gods, and smoothly
        pass
Their pleasures in a long immortal dream.
John Keats, *Lamia*, i (1820)

12 He hath awakened from the dream of life.
Percy Bysshe Shelley, *Adonais*, XXXIX
(1821)

13 But I, being poor, have only my dreams;
I have spread my dreams under your feet;
Tread softly because you tread on my
        dreams.
W.B. Yeats, *He Wishes for the Cloths of
Heaven* (1899)

14 Judge of your natural character by what you
do in your dreams.
R.W. Emerson, *Journals* (1833)

15 I have a dream that one day this nation will
        rise up,
live out the true meaning of its creed.
Martin Luther King, speech at Washington,
27 August 1963

16 'If he left off dreaming about you, where do
you suppose you'd be?'
'Where I am now, of course,' said Alice.
'Not you!' Tweedledee retorted
contemptuously, 'You'd be nowhere. Why,
you're only a sort of thing in his dream!'
Lewis Carroll, *Through the Looking-Glass*
(1871)

XI
SPIRITUAL EXERCISES

85 PRAYER

1 This is the lover of the brethren, he who prayeth much for the people and the holy city, Jeremiah the prophet of God.
2 Maccabees, 15, 14

2 When thou prayest, enter into thy closet, and when thou hast shut the door, pray to thy Father which is in secret.
Matthew, 6, 6

3 The Holy One, blessed be he, longs for the prayer of the righteous.
Mishnah, *Jebamoth*, 64

4 Give glory with the praise of thy Lord before the rising of the sun, and before its setting, and in the intervals of the night, and at the ends of the day.
Koran, 20, 130

5 O Lord of Holy Utterance, may earth be gracious to us, gracious be our abode, kindly our couch. Let the breath of life be right here, in friendship with us.
Atharva Veda, 13, 17

6 Therefore, bowing and prostrating my body, O Lord to be revered, I beg grace from thee.
Bhagavad Gita, 11, 44

7 With hands outstretched in prayer, I will first ask of you, O Wise One with Righteousness, the acts of the Holy Spirit.
Gathas, *Yasna*, 28

8 Jalalu'l-Din was asked, 'Is there any way to God nearer than the ritual prayer?' 'No', he replied; 'but prayer does not consist in forms alone. Formal prayer has a beginning and an end, like all forms and bodies and everything that partakes of speech and sound; but the soul is unconditioned and infinite . . . Absorption in the Divine Unity is the soul of prayer.'
Fihi ma fihi, 15, in R.A. Nicholson, *Rūmī* (1950)

9 All men, Socrates, who have any degree of right feeling, at the beginning of every enterprise, whether small or great, always call upon God.
Plato, *Timaeus*, 27c.

10 Let us call upon God himself before we thus answer — not with uttered words, but reaching forth our souls in prayer to him; for thus alone can we pray, alone to him who is alone.
Plotinus, *Enneads*, V, 1, 6 (3rd century)

11 You ought to say fewer fixed prayers so that you may do more reading. Reading is good prayer. Reading teaches us how to pray, and what to pray for, and then prayer achieves it. In the course of reading, when the heart is pleased, there arises a spirit of devotion which is worth many prayers.
The Ancrene Riwle, 1 (13th century)

12 No thinking may well be got in beginners, without reading or hearing coming before: nor praying without thinking.
The Cloud of Unknowing, 35 (14th century)

13 Pray inwardly, though you think it savours not; for it is profitable, though you feel not, though you see nought, yea, though you think you cannot. For in dryness and in

barrenness, in sickness and in feebleness, then your prayer is well pleasing to me.
Julian of Norwich, *Revelations of Divine Love*, 41 (*c.* 1393)

14 When I pray for something, I do not pray; when I pray for nothing I really pray . . . To pray for anything except God might be called idolatry or injustice.
Meister Eckhart, *Fragments*, 34 (13th–14th centuries)

15 Lord, what particulars we pray for, we know not, we dare not, we humbly tender a blank into the hands of almighty God; write therein, Lord, what thou wilt, where thou wilt, by whom thou wilt.
Thomas Fuller, *Poems and Translations* (1868)

16 When I awake in the morning, which is always before it is light, I address myself to him, and converse with him, speak to him while I am lighting my candle and putting on my clothes.
Philip Doddridge, *On the Rise and Progress of Religion in the Soul* (1745)

17 Ere on my bed my limbs I lay.
It hath not been my use to pray
With moving lips or bended knees;
But silently, by slow degrees,
My spirit I to Love compose.
S.T. Coleridge, *The Pains of Sleep* (1816)

18 Churches are best for prayer, that have least light:
To see God only, I go out of sight:
And to scape stormy days, I choose
An Everlasting night.
John Donne, *A Hymn to Christ* (1633)

19 There are two sorts of prayer, the one tender, delightful, loving, and full of emotions; the other obscure, dry, desolate, tempted, and darksome. The first is of Beginners, the second of Proficients who are in the progress to Perfection. God gives the first to gain souls, the second to purify them.
Miguel de Molinos, *The Spiritual Guide* (1675)

20 If while making vocal prayer, you feel yourself drawn and invited to interior or mental prayer, do not refuse to go to it.
François de Sales, *Introduction to the Devout Life* (1608)

21 Accustom yourself gradually to let your mental prayer spread over all your daily external occupations. Speak, act, work quietly, as though you were praying, as indeed you ought to be.
François de la Mothe Fénelon, *Spiritual Letters* (1718)

22 God answers sharp and sudden on some prayers,
And thrusts the thing we have prayed for in our face,
A gauntlet with a gift in't.
Elizabeth Barrett Browning, *Aurora Leigh*, ii (1857)

23 I am just going to pray for you at St Paul's, but with no very lively hope of success.
Sydney Smith, quoted by Lady Holland, *Memoir*, 13 (1855)

24 Before we partake of the heavenly food there remains one last, essential and necessary, act: the *intercession . . .* The Church is not a society for escape — corporately or individually — from this world to taste of the mystical bliss of eternity . . . It is the very joy of the Kingdom that makes us *remember* the world and pray for it.
Alexander Schmemann, *The World as Sacrament* (1966)

25 More things are wrought by prayer
Than this world dreams of.
Alfred Tennyson, *Idylls of the King*, 'The Passing of Arthur' (1869)

26 Who rises from prayer a better man, his prayer is answered.
George Meredith, *The Ordeal of Richard Feverel* (1859)

27 This is my prayer to thee, my lord — strike, strike at the root of penury in my heart. Give me the strength lightly to bear my joys and sorrows.
Rabindranath Tagore, *Gitanjali* (1913)

28 Prayer is not an old woman's idle amusement. Properly understood and applied, it is the most potent instrument of action.
M.K. Gandhi, *Non-Violence in Peace and War* (1948)

86 PRAYER FOR THE DEAD

1 If he were not expecting that they that had

fallen would rise again, it were superfluous and idle to pray for the dead.
2 Maccabees, 12, 44

2 What shall they do which are baptized for the dead, if the dead rise not at all?
1 Corinthians, 15, 29

3 When the Negus died he prayed over him and begged that his sins might be forgiven.
Ibn Ishaq, *Life of the Apostle of God* (8th century)

4 We approve of almsgiving on behalf of the Muslim dead, and of prayer for them, and we believe that God benefits them thereby.
Al-Ash'ari, *Ibāna*, 48 (10th century)

5 Famed is this rite for the dead, called the sacrifice sacred to the ancestors, and performed on the day of the new moon.
Laws of Manu, III, 127

6 Someone asked for an explanation of the Ancestral Sacrifice. The Master said, I do not know. Anyone who knew the explanation could deal with all things under Heaven as easily as I lay this here; and he lay his finger upon the palm of his hand.
Confucius, *Analects*, III, 11

7 The practice of the Church in interceding for them [the Departed] at the Celebration of the Eucharist is so general and so ancient, that it cannot be thought to have come in upon imposture.
Herbert Thorndike, *Just Weights and Measures* (1662)

8 Lord God of mercies, grant to the souls of all thy servants a place of cool repose, the blessedness of quiet, the brightness of light: through our Lord.
Roman Missal, Second Collect for All Souls' Day

9 Lord of the living and dead; give to the living mercy and grace; to the dead, rest and light perpetual.
The Methodist Service Book (1975)

10 Fare well my dear child and pray for me, and I shall for you and all your friends that we may merrily meet in heaven.
Thomas More, last letter to his daughter Margaret Roper, 5 July 1535. He was executed next morning

11 I kept this day as the anniversary of my Tetty's death, with prayer and tears in the morning. In the evening, I prayed for her, conditionally if it were lawful . . . O Lord, so far as it may be lawful in me, I commend to thy fatherly goodness *the soul of my departed wife*; beseeching thee to *grant* her whatever is best in her *present state*, and *finally to receive her to eternal happiness.*
Samuel Johnson, in Boswell, *Life of Samuel Johnson* (28 March 1753)

12 It was so important to think quiet loving thoughts about people in idle moments, especially perhaps about the dead, who being substanceless so desperately need our thoughts.
Iris Murdoch, *The Sacred and Profane Love Machine* (1974)

87 MEDITATION
See also 88. YOGA AND ZEN

1 Be still, and know that I am God.
Psalm, 46, 10

2 Study to be quiet.
1 Thessalonians, 4, 11

3 The pious men of old used to wait an hour in silent meditation and then offer their prayer, in order to direct their heart to their Father in heaven.
Mishnah, *Berachoth*, v, 1

4 Do not shout thy prayer publicly, nor yet speak it low in secret, but seek between these a middle way.
Koran, 17, 110

5 We meditate on the lovely light of the sun, may it stimulate our thoughts.
Rig Veda, III, 62, 10 (the Gayatri mantra)

6 Taking as a bow the great weapon of the Upanishad,
One should put upon it an arrow sharpened by meditation.
Stretching it with a thought directed to the essence of That,
Penetrate that Imperishable as the mark.
Mundaka Upanishad, 2, 2, 3

7 Cultivating solitude, eating lightly, restraining speech, body and mind, constantly devoted to the discipline of meditation.
Bhagavad Gita, 18, 52

8 The sun shines by day, the moon lights up
the night, the warrior shines in his armour,
the Brahmin shines in his meditation.
Dhammapada, 387

9 Those who perform meditation for even one
    session
Destroy innumerable accumulated sins;
How should there be wrong paths for them?
Hakuin, *The Song of Meditation* (18th
century)

10 Those who know do not speak;
Those who speak do not know.
Block the passages, shut the doors.
Let all sharpness be blunted.
Tao Te Ching, LVI

11 In jesting we contemplate. One jests because
one wants to contemplate.
Plotinus, *Enneads*, III, 8 (3rd century)

12 Nowhere can man find a quieter or more
untroubled retreat than in his own soul.
Marcus Aurelius, *Meditations*, 4, 3 (2nd
century)

13 I will now close my eyes, I will stop my ears,
I will turn away my senses from their
objects, I will even efface from my
consciousness all the images of corporeal
things; or at least, because this can hardly be
accomplished, I will consider them as empty
and false; and thus, holding converse only
with myself, and closely examining my
nature, I will endeavour to obtain by degrees
a more intimate and familiar knowledge of
myself.
René Descartes, *Meditations on First
Philosophy*, III (1641)

14 Let all teachers hold their peace; let all
creatures be silent in thy sight; speak to me
thou alone.
Thomas Kempis, *Of the Imitation of Christ*,
I, 3 (1418)

15 The higher part of contemplation, as it may
be had here, hangs all wholly in this
darkness and in this cloud of unknowing.
The Cloud of Unknowing, VIII (14th
century)

16 After the action of the imagination, follows
the action of the understanding which we
call meditation, which is nothing else than
one or several considerations made in order
to move our affections to God and to divine
things, in which meditation is different from

study and other thoughts and
considerations.
François de Sales, *Introduction to the
Devout Life*, II, v (1608)

17 I believe that the best manner of meditating
is as follows: When, by an act of living faith,
you are placed in the Presence of God,
recollect some truth wherein there is
substance and food. Pause sweetly and
gently on it, not to employ the reason, but
merely to calm and fix the mind. For you
must observe, that your principal exercise
should always be the Presence of God.
Madame Guyon, *A Method of Prayer*, 2
(1685)

18 In true silence strength is renewed, and the
mind is weaned from all things, save as they
may be enjoyed in the Divine will; and a
lowliness in outward living, opposite to
worldly honour, becomes truly acceptable to
us.
John Woolman, *Journal* (1774)

19 Forbear to judge, for we are sinners all
Close up his eyes, and draw the curtain
        close;
And let us all to meditation.
William Shakespeare, *Henry VI, Part 2*, III,
iii, 31–3 (*c.* 1590–2)

20 Elected Silence, sing to me
And beat upon my whorlèd ear.
Gerard Manley Hopkins, *The Habit of
Perfection* (1875)

21 Come out of thy meditations and leave aside
thy flowers and incense! What harm is there
if thy clothes become tattered and stained?
Meet him and stand by him in toil and in
sweat of thy brow.
Rabindranath Tagore, *Gitanjali*, 11
(1913)

22 One can practise meditation simply by being
aware of one's body or of one's breathing or
of all the sensations that are going on inside
oneself, a practice which sounds very easy
but is extremely demanding.
William Johnston, *The Inner Eye of Love*
(1978)

23 Total surrender to the demands of the
human spirit: be attentive, be intelligent, be
reasonable, be responsible, be in love.
Bernard Lonergan, *Method in Theology*
(1972)

88 YOGA AND ZEN

1 This they consider as Yoga —
the firm holding back of the senses.
Mundaka Upanishad, 6, 11

2 The eights parts of Yoga are: self-control,
rules regulating life, bodily posture,
breath-control, withdrawal of the senses
from objects, fixed attention, meditation,
and concentration.
Yoga Sutras, 2, 29

3 This is the Noble Eightfold Path:
right views, right intention;
right speech, right action, right livelihood;
right effort, right mindfulness, right
          concentration
Samyutta Nikaya, v, 420 (3rd century BCE)

4 Let him establish a steady seat in a clean
place, neither too high nor too low, covered
with a cloth or a deer-skin or sacred grass.
Sitting there let him concentrate his mind on
a single point, restraining the activity of
thought and sense, and practise Yoga to
purify himself. Steady, holding his body,
head and neck motionless, gazing at the tip
of his nose and not looking round; with
tranquil soul, free from fear, firm in his vow
of chastity, with mind controlled, let him sit
yoked, with his thoughts on Me, absorbed
in Me.
Bhagavad Gita, 6, 11–14

5 The system of the *kung-an* (Japanese *koan*)
or 'Zen problem.' Literally, this term means
a 'public document' or 'case' in the sense of
a decision creating a legal precedent. Thus
the *koan* system involves 'passing' a series of
tests based on the *mondo* or anecdotes of
the old masters.
A.W. Watts, *The Way of Zen* (1957)

6 In almost all the *koan*, the striking
characteristic is the illogical or absurd act or
word. A monk once asked, 'What is
Buddha?' The master replied, 'Three pounds
of flax.' Or a Zen master remarked, 'When
both hands are clapped a sound is
produced; listen to the sound of one hand.'
Heinrich Dumoulin, *A History of Zen
Buddhism* (1963)

7 I deliberately undertook — to disengage a
number of practices from their matrix and
then to introduce them into Christian living

so as to form a Christianity both integrated
and whole . . . Everything in Yoga,
therefore, that promotes dialogue, the basic
Christian dialogue, may be boldly
considered as fit for adaptation.
J.-M. Déchanet, *Christian Yoga* (1960)

8 This it the goal of a Christian yoga. Body
and soul are to be transfigured by the divine
life and to participate in the divine
consciousness.
Bede Griffiths, *Return to the Centre* (1976)

9 The Sermon on the Mount has (and very
justly I believe) been compared to Zen in
that it describes the undifferentiated
consciousness of one who lives in the
here-and-now with joy and without care.
William Johnston, *The Inner Eye of Love*
(1978)

89 ASCETICISM AND WORLD-DENIAL
See also 67. MONKS AND NUNS

1 Hide thyself by the brook Cherith, that is
before Jordan. And it shall be, that thou
shalt drink of the brook; and I have
commanded the ravens to feed thee.
1 Kings, 17, 3–4

2 Love not the world, neither the things that
are in the world.
1 John 2, 15

3 Every year during that month the Apostle
would pray in seclusion and give food to the
poor that came to him. And when he
completed the month and returned from his
seclusion, first of all before entering his
house he would go to the Ka'ba and walk
round it seven times or as often as it pleased
God.
Ibn Ishaq, *Life of the Apostle of God*, trans.
A. Guillaume (1955)

4 Having passed the third part of life in the
forest, he may live as an ascetic during the
fourth part of his existence, after
abandoning attachment to worldly objects.
Laws of Manu, VI, 33

5 He who controls his limbs through which he
acts, but sits pondering sensual objects in his
mind, is rightly called a hypocrite.
Bhagavad Gita, 3, 6

6 If a monk feels sick, and is unable duly to
mortify the flesh, he should regularly

diminish his food. Mindful of his body, immovable as a beam, the monk should strive to waste his body away . . . Overcoming manifold hardships and troubles, with trust in his religion he performs this terrible penance. Thus in due time he puts an end to his existence.
Acharanga Sutra, 1, 7, 6

7 How difficult it is for the man who dwells at home to live the higher life in all its fullness, purity, and perfection. Free as the air is the life of him who has renounced all worldly things.
Digha Nikaya, 1, 62

8 What is the use of matted hair, O fool, what of the raiment of goat-skins? Thine inward nature is full of wickedness; the outside thou makest clean.
Dhammapada, 394

9 The path was still alarmingly red and smoking by the time my turn came, but so effective apparently were the *yamabushi's* [ascetic's] spells that the embers underfoot felt no more than pleasantly warm to the soles . . . My feet are rather sensitive and my mind at the time was in turmoil, yet a mild warmth was all that I felt.
Carmen Blacker, *The Catalpa Bow* (1975)

10 O man, practise asceticism in the following manner: Think no more of thy house in the city, than if it were a forest abode; and remain always a hermit in thine heart! Instead of matted hair, cultivate continence; wash thyself daily in unity of will with God.
Hymns of Guru Gobind Singh, *re man* (17th century)

11 If you want to make Pythocles happy, add not to his possessions but take away from his desires.
Epicurus, *Fragment,* 28 (3rd century BCE)

12 This fellow [Epicurus] is bringing in a new philosophy; he preaches hunger and his disciples follow him. They get but a single roll, a dried fig to relish it, and water to wash it down.
Clement of Alexandria (150–215), *Stromateis,* ii, 493

13 If you wish to follow Him you must take the cross upon you. The cross is the same as the Christ life and that is a bitter cross for a natural man.
Theologia Germanica, 51 (14th century)

14 What is the sense of struggling to be virtuous, denying yourself the pleasant things of life, and deliberately making yourself uncomfortable, if there is nothing you hope to gain by it? And what *can* you hope to gain by it, if you receive no compensation after death for a thoroughly unpleasant, that is, a thoroughly miserable life?
Thomas More, *Utopia,* 2 (1516)

15 Dear Mother, dear Mother, the Church is cold,
But the Ale-house is healthy & pleasant & warm . . .
But if at the Church they would give us some Ale,
And a pleasant fire our souls to regale,
We'd sing and we'd pray all the live-long day,
Nor ever wish once from the Church to stray.
William Blake, *The Little Vagabond* (1794)

16 Oh would I could subdue the flesh
Which sadly troubles me!
And then perhaps could view the flesh
As though I never knew the flesh
And merry misery.
John Betjeman, *Senex* (1940)

17 My austerities, fastings, and prayers are, I know, of no value if I rely upon them for reforming me. But they have an inestimable value if they represent, as I hope they do, the yearnings of a soul striving to lay his weary head in the lap of his maker.
M.K. Gandhi, in *Harijan,* 18 April 1936

90 FASTING

1 It is such a fast that I have chosen? a day for a man to afflict his soul? is it to bow down his head as a bulrush, and to spread sackcloth and ashes under him? wilt thou call this a fast, and an acceptable day to the LORD? Is not this the fast that I have chosen? to loose the bands of wickedness, to undo the heavy burdens, and to let the oppressed go free, and that ye break every yoke? Is it not to deal thy bread to the hungry, and that thou bring the poor that are cast out to thy house?
Isaiah, 58, 5–7

2 Thou, when thou fastest, anoint thine head, and wash thy face; that thou appear not

unto men to fast, but unto thy Father which
is in secret.
Matthew, 6, 17–18

3 The Elder of the congregation addressed the
worshippers with words of admonition:
'Brethren, it is not said of the men of
Nineveh, "And God saw their sackcloth and
their fasting", but, "God saw their works,
that they turned from their evil way."'
Mishnah, *Taanith*, II, 1

4 Fasting is prescribed for you as it was for
those before you, maybe you will show
piety. . . . The month of Ramadan, in which
the Koran was sent down as guidance for
the people . . . so whoever of you is at home
during the month let him fast in it; but if
anyone is sick or on a journey let him fast a
number of other days. God wishes to make
it easy for you.
Koran, 2, 179–81

5 Our wise men prohibited self-mortification
by fasting. Concerning this and similar
excesses Solomon exhorts us: 'be not
righteous over much.'
Moses Maimonides, *Mishneh Torah*, 1
(12th century)

6 Fasting is the penance for omitting the daily
rites prescribed by the Veda.
Laws of Manu, XI, 204

7 He who eats too much has no yogic
discipline, nor he who does not eat at all;
neither he who sleeps too much, nor he who
is ever wakeful; but he that is moderate in
food and recreation.
Bhagavad Gita, 6, 16–17

8 The Fast-day is of great fruit, of great
blessing, of great splendour, and of great
influence . . . For this night and day, I will
eat only at one mealtime, abstaining from
eating at night, and avoiding untimely food.
With this I imitate the monks.
Anguttara Nikaya, iv, 248 (3rd–1st
centuries BCE)

9 As regards fasting, it constitutes, together
with the obligatory prayers, the two pillars
that sustain the revealed Law of God. They
act as stimulants to the soul, strengthen,
revive, and purify it, and thus ensure its
steady development.
Principles of Baha'i Administration (1976)

10 It is no mastery to wake and fast till thine
head ache, nor to run to Rome and to

Jerusalem upon thy bare feet, nor to start
about and preach as if thou wouldst turn all
men by thy preaching . . . But it is a great
mastery for a man to love his
fellow-Christian in charity, and wisely to
hate the sin of him and love the man.
Walter Hilton, *The Scale of Perfection*, 1, 65
(1494)

11   One who never feels
The wanton stings and motions of the sense,
But doth rebate and blunt his natural edge
With profits of the mind, study and fast.
William Shakespeare, *Measure for Measure*,
I, iv, 58–61 (*c.* 1604)

12 Forget thyself to Marble, till
With a sad Leaden downward cast
Thou fix them on the earth as fast.
And join with thee calm Peace, and Quiet,
Spare Fast, that oft with gods doth diet.
John Milton, *Il Penseroso*, 42–6 (1632)

13 The murmuring poor, who will not fast in
peace.
George Crabbe, *The Newspaper* (1785)

91 PILGRIMAGE

1 This man went up out of his city yearly to
worship and to sacrifice unto the LORD of
hosts.
1 Samuel, 1, 3

2 His parents went to Jerusalem every year at
the feast of the passover.
Luke, 2, 41

3 Proclaim the Pilgrimage among the people;
let them come to thee on foot or on any lean
mount, that they may be present at things of
benefit to them, and make mention of the
name of God on certain specified days . . .
Then let them make an end of their
uncleanness and fulfil their vows, and
perform the circuit of the ancient House.
Koran, 22, 28–30

4 The first time I made the pilgrimage I saw
the House, and the second time I made it I
saw the Lord of the House, but not the
House, but the third time I made it I saw
neither the House nor the Lord of the
House.
Abu Yazid, in al-Sarraj. *Kitab al-Luma* (9th
century)

5 Two fellows went on a pilgrimage,
the fickle Mind and the hypocrite Soul:
they could not get rid of a single sin,
and they took on two hundredweights
                                more!
Sākhī, 26, in Charlotte Vaudeville, *Kabīr*
(1974)

6 Pilgrimages, penances, compassion and
                                almsgiving
Bring a little merit, the size of sesame seed,
But he who hears and believes and loves the
                                Name
Shall bathe and be made clean
In a place of pilgrimage within him.
Hymns of Guru Nanak, *tirath tap* (16th
century)

7 Do not imagine that the journey is short;
one must have the heart of a lion to follow
this unusual road, for it is very long and the
sea is deep. One plods along in a state of
amazement, sometimes smiling sometimes
weeping. As for me, I shall be happy to
discover even a trace of Him. That would
indeed be something, but to live without
Him would be a reproach. A man must not
keep his soul from the beloved but must be
in a fitting state to lead his soul to the court
of the King.
'Attar, *The Conference of the Birds*, i (13th
century)

8 Days and months are travellers of eternity.
So are the years that pass by . . . I myself
have been tempted for a long time by the
cloud-moving wind – filled with a strong
desire to wander.
Basho, *The Narrow Road to the Deep
North*, i (17th century)

9 On this mountaintop, at the holiest spot of
this sprawling complex of temples, in the
shadow of these towering cedars, one stands
before the tomb of the saint whose life and
legacy inspire the pilgrimage. Here one asks
his blessing, his guidance and protection, *his
company*, on the pilgrimage to come.
Oliver Statler, *Japanese Pilgrimage* (1983)

10 There can still be found a few men and
women who spend the greater part of their
time in peripatetic wandering . . .
Sometimes these follow the prescribed

course of recognised pilgrimages routes, the
Eighty-eight Places of Shikoku or the
Thirty-three Places of the Western
Provinces.
Carmen Blacker, *The Catalpa Bow* (1975)

11 Pilgrimage is a basic exercise in Hindu
religion. Each place has its own attractions:
here a man may get rid of his sins, there he
finds 'deliverance.' But only in Vrindaban is
it possible to achieve gopi-bhakti, the
highest form of love for Krishna.
Klaus Klostermaier, *Hindu and Christian in
Vrindaban* (1969)

12 If thou covet to come to this blessed sight of
very peace and be a true pilgrim to
Jerusalem-ward, though it be so that I were
never there, nevertheless as far forth as I can
I shall set thee on the way thitherward.
Walter Hilton, *The Scale of Perfection*, 2, 21
(1494)

13 Give me my scallop-shell of quiet,
My staff of faith to walk upon,
My scrip of joy, immortal diet,
My bottle of salvation,
My gown of glory, hope's true gage
And thus I'll take my pilgrimage.
Walter Raleigh, *The Passionate Man's
Pilgrimage* (1603)

14 Than longen folk to goon on pilgrimages.
Geoffrey Chaucer, *The Canterbury Tales*,
·'Prologue', 12 (*c.* 1387)

15 There's no discouragement
Shall make him once relent
His first avow'd intent
To be a pilgrim.
John Bunyan, *The Pilgrim's Progress* (1678)

16 Of what avail is it to go across the sea to
Christ if all the time I lose the Christ that is
within me here?
Leo Tolstoy, *Master and Man*, 'Two Old
Men' (1895)

17 All of us are pilgrims on this earth, I have
even heard people say that the earth itself is
a pilgrim in the heavens.
Maxim Gorky, *The Lower Depths* (1903)

18 Ere the days of his pilgrimage vanish,
How pleasant to know Mr Lear!
Edward Lear, *Nonsense Songs* (1871)

XII
RELIGIOUS COMMUNITY

92 PEOPLE

1 Thou art an holy people unto the LORD thy God, and the LORD hath chosen thee to be a peculiar people unto himself, above all the nations that are upon the earth.
Deuteronomy, 14, 2

2 Ye are a chosen generation, a royal priesthood, an holy nation, a peculiar people . . . Which in time past were not a people, but are now the people of God.
1 Peter, 2, 9–10

3 Three precious gifts did the Holy One, blessed be he, bestow upon Israel, and all of them he gave only through the medium of suffering: they are the Torah, the land of Israel, and the World to Come.
Mishnah, *Berachoth*, 5

4 There is a community of the People of the Book which is steadfast reciting the signs of God . . . Ye have become the best community ever produced for the people, urging what is reputable and restraining from what is disreputable, and believing in God.
Koran, 3, 109, 106

5 All the Faithful are equal as to knowledge, subjective certainty, trust, love, inner quiet, fear, hope and faith.
Fiqh Akbar, II, 19 (10th century)

6 In order to protect this universe he, the most resplendent one, assigned separate occupations to those who sprang from his mouth, arms, thighs, and feet . . . As the

Brahmin sprang from his mouth, as he was the first-born, and as he possesses the Veda, he is by right the lord of this whole creation.
Laws of Manu, 1, 87–93

7 He who takes refuge in the Buddha, the Law, and the Order, he perceives, in his clear wisdom, the Four Noble Truths . . . Blessed is the birth of the awakened; blessed is the teaching of the true Law; blessed is concord in the Order.
Dhammapada, 190, 194

8 Great Yamato [Japan] is a divine country. It is only our land whose foundations were first laid by the divine ancestor. It alone has been transmitted by the Sun Goddess to a long line of her descendants. There is nothing of this kind in foreign countries. Therefore it is called the divine land.
Kitabatake Chicafusa, *Jinkoshotoku* (14th century)

9 This royal throne of kings, this scepter'd isle,
This earth of majesty, this seat of Mars,
This other Eden, demi-paradise,
This fortress built by Nature for herself
Against infection and the hand of war . . .
This blessed plot, this earth, this realm, this England.
William Shakespeare, *Richard II*, II, i, 40–4; 50 (1595)

10 I am the Martyr of the People.
Charles I, in J. Rushworth, *Historical Collections*, vi (1708)

11 If by the people you understand the multitude, the *hoi polloi*, 'tis no matter what they think; they are sometimes in the right,

and sometimes in the wrong: their judgement is a mere lottery.
John Dryden, *Essay of Dramatic Poesy* (1688)

12 I am not one of those who think that the people are never in the wrong. They have been so, frequently and outrageously, both in other countries and in this. But I do say, that in all disputes between them and their rulers, the presumption is at least upon a par in favour of the people.
Edmund Burke, *Thoughts on the Cause of the Present Discontents* (1770)

13 When wilt thou save the people?
        Oh, God of Mercy! when?
The people, Lord, the people!
        Not thrones and crowns, but men!
Ebenezer Elliott, *The People's Anthem* (1846)

14 I am a part of all that I have met.
Alfred Tennyson, *Ulysses* (1842)

15 While the people retain their virtue and vigilance, no administration, by any extreme of wickedness or folly, can very seriously injure the government in the short space of four years.
Abraham Lincoln, *First Inaugural Address* (1861)

16 Smile at us, pay us, pass us; but do not quite
        forget.
For we are the people of England, that never
        have spoken yet.
G.K. Chesterton, *The Secret People* (1915)

17 Mankind has become so much one family that we cannot insure our own prosperity except by insuring that of everyone else.
Bertrand Russell, 'The Science to Save Us from Science' (1950)

18 It is always possible to bind together a considerable number of people in love, so long as there are other people left over to receive the manifestations of their aggressiveness.
Sigmund Freud, *Civilization and its Discontents* (1930)

19 Everyone has duties to the community in which alone the free and full development of his personality is possible.
Universal Declaration of Human Rights, Article 29, General Assembly of the United Nations (1948)

93 CHURCH

1 Thou art Peter, and upon this rock I will build my church; and the gates of hell shall not prevail against it.
Matthew, 16, 18

2 What the soul is in a body, this the Christians are in the world. The soul is spread through all the members of the body, and Christians through the divers cities of the world. The soul has its abode in the body, and yet it is not of the body.
Epistle to Diognetus, 5–7 (2nd century)

3 We ought in the first place to set in order the conditions of the reverence paid to the Divinity, by giving to the Christians and all others full authority to follow whatever worship any man has chosen.
Constantine and Licinius, *Edict of Milan* (313)

4 It is our desire that all the various nations which are subject to our Clemency and Moderation, should continue in the profession of that religion which was delivered to the Romans by the divine Apostle Peter.
Theodosius I, *Cunctos Populos* (380)

5 Choose, therefore, from each Church those things that are pious, religious, and seemly, and when you have, as it were, incorporated them, let the minds of the English be accustomed thereto.
Gregory I, *Epistles*, xi, 64, to Augustine of Canterbury (601)

6 The visible Church of Christ is a congregation of faithful men, in the which the pure Word of God is preached, and the Sacraments be duly ministered.
Book of Common Prayer, Articles of Religion XIX

7 Grounded upon the doctrine of the prophets and apostles, having the same antiquity that the Kirk of the Apostles has as concerning doctrine, prayers, administration of sacraments and all things requisite to a particular Kirk.
Scottish Confession (1560)

8 That the English Church shall be free.
Magna Carta, 1 (1215)

9 God is decreeing to begin some new and

great period in His Church, even to the reforming of Reformation itself. What does He then but reveal Himself to His servants, and as His manner is, first to His Englishmen.
John Milton, *Areopagitica* (1644)

10 I am afraid he has not been in the inside of a church for many years; but he never passes a church without pulling off his hat. This shews that he has good principles.
Samuel Johnson, of Dr John Campbell, in Boswell, *Life of Samuel Johnson* (1763)

11 Politics and the pulpit are terms that have little agreement. No sound ought to be heard in the church but the healing voice of Christian charity.
Edmund Burke, *Reflections on the Revolution in France* (1790)

12 Kneeling ne'er spoil'd silk stockings; quit
            thy state;
All are equal within the Church's gate.
George Herbert, *The Temple,* 'The Church Porch' (1633)

13 Wherever God erects a house of prayer,
The Devil always builds a chapel there;
And 'twill be found, upon examination,
The latter has the largest congregation.
Daniel Defoe, *The True-Born Englishman,* i (1701)

14 The hippotamus's day
Is passed in sleep; at night he hunts;
God moves in a mysterious way —
The Church can sleep and feed at once.
T.S. Eliot, *The Hippopotamus,* (1920)

15 Broad of Church and broad of mind,
Broad before and broad behind.
John Betjeman, *The Wykehamist* (1932)

16 I like a church; I like a cowl;
I love a prophet of the soul . . .
Yet not for all his faith can see
Would I that cowlèd churchman be.
R.W. Emerson, *The Problem* (1867)

17 It is the lower classes which do the really creative work, forming communities on a genuinely religious basis. They alone unite imagination and simplicity of feeling with a non-reflective habit of mind, a primitive energy, and an urgent sense of need.
Ernst Troeltsch, *The Social Teaching of the Christian Churches* (1912)

18 I am firmly convinced that a vast number of

people belong to the fold of the Catholic Church and nowhere else, because they are most suitably housed there . . . I believe, too, that there must be protestants against the Catholic Church, and also protestants against Protestantism.
C.G. Jung, *Modern Man in Search of a Soul* (1933)

19 Her Christianity belonged in a social context: good works, regular church attendance, and a visiting card framed in brass on the end of the pew.
Patrick White, *Flaws in the Glass* (1981)

20 The *name* itself shows how much the Church would be committed, is committed, to the cause of its Lord . . . Its source was the Byzantine popular form *Kyrike* and thus means 'belonging to the Lord' or, in a wider sense, 'house of the Lord.'
Hans Küng, *On Being a Christian* (1974)

21 The Church is people, fallible and sinful people, and if it is no better than any other human institution it is certainly no worse. It is nonsense to pretend that we could have our religion without it; and though it has fallen into grave error from time to time, I doubt if it has done as much harm as nationalism, materialism, colonialism, capitalism, communism, fascism, militarism and apathy.
Gerald Priestland, *Priestland's Progress* (1981)

94 ORTHODOXY AND ESTABLISHMENT
See also 17. DOGMATISM

1 Ye shall be unto me a kingdom of priests, and a holy nation . . . If thou shalt indeed obey his voice, and do all that I speak; then I will be an enemy unto thine enemies, and an adversary unto thine adversaries.
Exodus, 19, 6; 23, 22

2 I will give unto thee the keys of the kingdom of heaven: and whatsoever thou shalt bind on earth shall be bound in heaven: and whatsoever thou shalt loose on earth shall be loosed in heaven
Matthew, 16, 19.

3 The Holy One, blessed be he, inverted Mount Sinai over them like a huge vessel and declared, 'If you accept the Torah, well and good; if not, here shall be your sepulchre.'
Mishnah, *Shabbath*, 88

4 Those to whom we have given the Book and who recite it as it should be recited — they believe in it; those who disbelieve in it — they are the losers.
Koran, 2, 115

5 When a man is uncertain concerning any of the subtleties of theology, it is his duty to cling for the time being to the orthodox faith.
Fiqh Akbar, II, 28 (10th century)

6 Those men who constantly follow this my doctrine, full of faith and not murmuring, they are freed from the effect of actions. But those who murmur against it and do not follow my doctrine, these fools, deluded in all knowledge, you must know they are lost.
Bhagavad Gita, 3, 32

7 This is the path; there is none other that leads to the purifying of insight. Follow this, and it will be to escape from death.
Dhammapada, 274

8 What Tao plants cannot be plucked,
What Tao clasps, cannot slip . . .
Apply it to yourself and by its power you
         will be freed
from dross . . .
Apply it to the kingdom, and the kingdom
         shall thereby be
made to flourish.
Tao Te Ching, LIV

9 There is no salvation outside the church.
Augustine of Hippo, *De Baptismo*, IV, xvii (5th century). See also Cyprian, *De Catholicae Ecclesiae Unitate*, 6, see 17, 8

10 We authorize the followers of this law to assume the title of Catholic Christians; but as for the others, since, in our judgement, they are foolish madmen, we decree that they shall be branded with the ignominious name of heretics, and shall not presume to give to their conventicles the name of churches.
Theodosius I, *Cunctos Populos* (380)

11 The king our sovereign lord, his heirs and successors, kings of this realm, shall be taken, accepted, and reputed the only supreme head in earth of the Church of England, called *Anglicana Ecclesia*
Henry VIII, *The Supremacy Act* (1534)

12 I recognize the Holy Catholic and Apostolic Roman Church as the mother and mistress of all churches.
Bull of Pius IV, *Injunctum nobis* (1564) (Council of Trent Profession of Faith)

13 Always to be ready to obey with mind and heart, setting aside all judgement of one's own, the true spouse of Jesus Christ, our holy mother, our infallible and orthodox mistress, the Catholic Church, whose authority is exercised over us by the hierarchy.
Ignatius Loyola, *Spiritual Exercises*, II (1534) (of Jesuits)

14 The Roman pontiff, when he speaks *ex cathedra* (that is, when — fulfilling the office of Pastor and Teacher of all Christians — on his supreme Apostolical authority, he defines a doctrine concerning faith and morals to be held by the Universal Church), through the divine assistance promised him in blessed Peter, is endowed with that infallibility, with which the Divine Redeemer has willed that His Church — in defining doctrine concerning faith or morals, should be equipped.
Vatican Council I, on Papal Infallibility (1870)

15 Orthodoxy is my doxy; heterodoxy is another man's doxy.
William Warburton, in J. Priestley, *Memoirs* (1807)

16 Every church is orthodox to itself; to others, erroneous or heretical.
John Locke, *A Letter concerning Toleration* (1689–92)

17 The great estate of the church, which, whatever its articles of faith, belonged and still belongs to the people, was seized at various times, under various pretences, by an assembly that continually changed the religion of their country and their own by a parliamentary majority, but which never refunded the booty.
Benjamin Disraeli, *Sybil* (1845)

18 If we compare the old and the new teaching, we cannot fail to notice an epoch-making reversal of the attitude to those outside the 'holy Roman Church'. What has happened

here? Not much, some Catholic theologians soothingly claim, only a new 'interpretation' of the infallible, ancient dogma.
Hans Küng, *On Being a Christian* (1974)

19 The real ecumenical crisis today is not between Catholics and Protestants, but between traditional and experimental forms of church life.
Harvey Cox, *The Secular City* (1966)

20 The church must be reminded that it is not the master or the servant of the state, but rather the conscience of the state.
Martin Luther King, *Strength to Love* (1963)

21 Two orders of mankind are the enemies of church and state: the king without clemency, and the holy man without learning.
Sa'di, *Gulistan* (1258)

95 SCHISM, SECTS AND REFORM

1 Ahijah caught the new garment that was on him, and rent it in twelve pieces: And he said to Jeroboam, Take these ten pieces: for thus saith the LORD, the God of Israel, Behold, I will rend the kingdom out of the hand of Solomon, and will give ten tribes to thee.
1 Kings, 11, 30–1

2 That ye all speak the same thing, and that there be no divisions among you; but that ye be perfectly joined together in the same mind, and in the same judgement.
1 Corinthians, 1, 10

3 Had God so willed, he would have made you one community. But he has not done so, in order that he might try you in regard to what has come to you. So strive to be foremost in what is good. It is to God that you return, all of you, and he will announce to you that in which you have been differing.
Koran, 5, 53

4 These two-and-seventy sects will remain till the Resurrection: the heretic's talk and argument will not fail.
Jalalu'l-Din Rumi, *Mathnawi,* V, 3221 (13th century)

5 The Grape that can with Logic absolute
The Two-and-Seventy jarring Sects confute.
Edward Fitzgerald, *Rubáiyát of Omar Khayyám,* 43 (1859)

6 Difference of opinion in the community is a token of divine mercy.
Fiqh Akbar, 1, 7 (8th century)

7 Let him not honour heretics, even by a greeting, or men who follow forbidden occupations.
Laws of Manu, IV, 30

8 They say the world is without truth, without religious basis, without a God; not originating in regular causation but motivated by desire alone . . . These wicked ones proceed to the lowest place.
Bhagavad Gita, 16, 8–20

9 This entire theory rests on a fictitious foundation of altogether hollow and vicious arguments, incapable of being stated in definite logical alternatives, and devised by men who are destitute of those particular qualities which cause individuals to be chosen by the Supreme Being.
Ramanuja, *Commentary on the Vedānta Sūtras,* I, 1, i (11th century)

10 No one is to cause dissension in the Order. The Order of monks and nuns has been united, and this unity should last for as long as my sons and great grandsons, and the moon and the sun. Whoever creates a schism in the Order, whether monk or nun, is to be dressed in white garments, and to be put in a place not inhabited by monks or nuns.
Ashoka, *Schism Edict* (conflated) (3rd century BCE)

11 My congregation has been cleared from the chaff, freed from the trash; it is firmly established in the strength of faith. It is good that those proud ones are gone away.
Lotus of the True Law, II, 36

12 Long has the wicked prophet delayed me,
He who has broken away from
        Righteousness.
He has not taken care that Holy Devotion
        be his,
Nor has he taken counsel with the Good
        Mind, O Wise One.
Gathas, *Yasna,* 49

13 Let them be entirely excluded even from the

thresholds of churches, since we permit no
heretics to hold their unlawful assemblies in
the towns.
Theodosius I, *Nullus haereticus* (381)

14 With regard to heretics, two considerations
are to be kept in mind: 1. on their side, 2. on
the side of the Church. 1. There is the sin,
whereby they deserve not only to be
separated from the Church by
excommunication, but also to be shut off
from the world by death . . . 2. But on the
side of the Church there is mercy, with a
view to the conversion of them that are in
error.
Thomas Aquinas, *Summa Theologica*, ii,
Q.xi, Article III (13th century)

15 I beseech you, in the bowels of Christ, think
it possible you may be mistaken.
Oliver Cromwell, to the General Assembly
of the Church of Scotland (1650)

16 They that approve a private opinion, call it
opinion; but they that mislike it, heresy: and
yet heresy signifies no more than private
opinion.
Thomas Hobbes, *Leviathan*, 11 (1651)

17 As the Church of *Jerusalem, Alexandria,*
and *Antioch,* have erred; so also the Church
of *Rome* hath erred, not only in their living
and manner of Ceremonies, but also in
matters of Faith.
Book of Common Prayer, Articles of
Religion XIX

18 Because about the manner and order of this
government, whether it ought to be
Presbyterial, or Prelatical, such endless
questions, or rather uproar is arisen in this
land, as may be justly termed, what the fever
is to the physicians, the eternal reproach of
the divines.
John Milton, *The Reason of Church
Government Urged against Prelaty* (1641)

19 Bid me to live, and I will live
Thy Protestant to be.
Robert Herrick, *To Anthea, Who May
Command Him Anything* (1648)

20 He who begins by loving Christianity better
than Truth will proceed by loving his own
sect or church better than Christianity, and
end by loving himself better than all.
S.T. Coleridge, *Aids to Reflection* (1825)

21 All protestantism, even the most cold and
passive, is a sort of dissent. But the religion
most prevalent in our northern colonies is a
refinement on the principle of resistance; it
is the dissidence of dissent, and the
protestantism of the Protestant religion.
Edmund Burke, *Speech on Conciliation with
America* (1775)

22 Almost every sect of Christianity is a
perversion of its essence, to accommodate it
to the prejudices of the world.
William Hazlitt, *The Round Table*
(1817)

23 She [the Church of Rome] thoroughly
understands what no other church has ever
understood, how to deal with enthusiasts.
T.B. Macaulay, *Von Ranke* (1840)

24 How can what an Englishman believes be
heresy? It is a contradiction in terms.
George Bernard Shaw, *St Joan,* iv (1923)

25 There is nothing in the whole world so
unbecoming in a woman as a
Nonconformist conscience.
Oscar Wilde, *Lady Windermere's Fan*, III
(1891)

26 It is not permissible to designate as
'unchurched' those who have become
alienated from organized denominations
and traditional creeds. In living among these
groups for half a generation I learned how
much of the latent Church there is within
them.
Paul Tillich, *On the Boundary* (1967)

27 Lapsed Orthodox Jews no longer feel bound
to accept many of the theological beliefs
inherent in the Torah, nor the principles of
the Jewish faith as enshrined in
Maimonides' formulation of the thirteen
cardinal beliefs of Judaism. Doctrines such
as the resurrection of the dead, final
judgement, and reward and punishment in
the Hereafter have been largely ignored or
discarded.
D. Cohn-Sherbok, 'Ranking Religions', in
Religious Studies (1986)

28 'A few on both sides are coming to realise
that while we are divided in faith, we are
divided within the same faith.' – 'this
division within the self-same faith' is
'between people who believe otherwise but
in no Other.'
Hans Küng, *Justification* (1981)

96 PERSECUTION

1 Whoso falleth not down and worshippeth
shall the same hour be cast into the midst of
a burning fiery furnace.
Daniel, 3, 6

2 If they have persecuted me, they will also
persecute you; if they have kept my saying,
they will keep yours also. But all these
things will they do unto you for my name's
sake, because they know not him that sent
me.
John, 15, 20–1

3 When there are righteous in a generation,
the righteous are punished for the sins of
that generation.
Mishnah, *Shabbath*, 33

4 Fight them, until there is no persecution,
and the religion is God's; then if they
refrain, let there be no enmity, except
against wrong-doers.
Koran, 2, 189

5 If outsiders should speak against me, or
against the Doctrine, or against the Order,
you should not on that account bear malice,
or suffer heart-burning, or feel ill will. If you
are angry or hurt on that account, that will
stand in the way of your own self-conquest.
Digha Nikaya, 3 (3rd century BCE)

6 Nero put in his own place as culprits and
punished with every refinement of cruelty
the men whom the common people hated
for their secret crimes. They called them
Christians . . . Hence commiseration arose
. . . on the ground that they were not
destroyed for the good of the state, but to
satisfy the cruelty of an individual.
Tacitus, *Annales*, xv, 44 (115)

7 We are told that when blessed Peter saw his
wife led away to death he was glad that her
call had come and that she was returning
home, and spoke to her in the most
encouraging and comforting tones,
addressing her by name: 'My dear,
remember the Lord.' Such was the marriage
of the blessed, and their consummate feeling
towards their dearest.
Clement of Alexandria, *Miscellanies*, vii
(2nd century)

8 They are not to be sought out; but if they
are accused and convicted, they must be
punished.
Emperor Trajan, in Pliny, *Epistles*, x, 96
(111)

9 Notwithstanding any provisions concerning
the Christians in our former instructions, all
who choose that religion are to be permitted
to continue therein without any let or
hindrance, and are not to be in any way
troubled or molested.
Constantine and Licinius, *Edict of Milan*
(313)

10 If he be found still stubborn, the Church
gives up hope of his conversion and takes
thought for the safety of others by
separating him from the Church by sentence
of excommunication; and, further, leaves
him to the secular court to be
exterminated from the world by death.
Thomas Aquinas, *Summa Theologica*, ii,
Q.xi, Article III (13th century)

11 Them, before the people, in a high place
cause to be burnt, that such punishment
may strike fear to the minds of others.
Henry IV, *De Haeritico Comburendo* (1401)

12 The Kirishitan [Christian] band have come
to Japan, not only sending their merchant
vessels to exchange commodities, but also
longing to disseminate an evil law, to
overthrow right doctrine . . . These must be
instantly swept out, so that not an inch of
soil remains to them in Japan on which to
plant their feet, and if they refuse to obey
this command they shall suffer the penalty.
Iyeyasu, *Proclamation against Christians*
(1614)

13 We decree that Jews and Saracens of both
sexes, in every Christian province and at all
times, shall be clearly and visibly
differentiated from other peoples by the
character of their dress . . . We forbid Jews
to be given preferment in public office.
Fourth Lateran Council (1215)

14 While we were talking came by several poor
creatures carried, by constables, for being at
a conventicle . . . I would to God they
would either conform, or be more wise, and
not be catched!
Samuel Pepys, *Diary* (7 August 1664)

15 It were better to be of no Church, than to be
bitter for any.
William Penn, *Some Fruits of Solitude* (1693)

16 I never saw, heard, nor read, that the clergy
    were beloved in any nation where
    Christianity was the religion of the country.
    Nothing can render them popular, but some
    degree of persecution.
    Jonathan Swift, *Thoughts on Religion*
    (1768)

17 Religious persecution may shield itself under
    the guise of a mistaken and over-zealous
    piety.
    Edmund Burke, Speech, (17 February 1788)

18 When suave politeness, tempering bigot
              zeal,
    Corrected *I believe* to *One does feel.*
    Ronald Knox, *Absolute and Abitofhell*
    (1913)

19 Progress towards the welfare of mankind is
    made not by the persecutors but by the
    persecuted . . . Only goodness, meeting evil
    and not infected by it, conquers evil.
    Leo Tolstoy, *What I Believe* (1884)

20 The bare fact is that truth cannot be tolerant
    and cannot admit compromise or
    limitations, that scientific research looks on
    the whole field of human activity as its own,
    and must adopt an uncompromisingly
    critical attitude towards any other power
    that seeks to usurp any part of its province.
    Sigmund Freud, *New Introductory Lectures
    on Psycho-Analysis* (1933)

97 TOLERATION
See also 109. FREEWILL, 126. CONSCIENCE

1 Thou hast had pity on the gourd, for the
   which thou hast not laboured, neither
   madest it grow; which came up in a night,
   and perished in a night: And should not I
   spare Nineveh, that great city?
   Jonah, 4, 10–11

2 Refrain from these men, and let them alone:
   for if this counsel or this work be of men, it
   will come to nought: But if it be of God, ye
   cannot overthrow it.
   Acts, 5, 38–9

3 There is no compulsion in religion.
   Koran, 2, 257

4 One should honour another man's sect, for

by doing so one increases the influence of
one's own sect and benefits that of the other
man.
Ashoka, *Major Rock Edict,* XII (3rd century
BCE)

5 When you perceive that we have made this
   grant to the said Christians, your Devotion
   understands that to others also freedom for
   their own worship and observance is
   likewise left open and freely granted, as
   befits the quiet of our times.
   Constantine and Licinius, *Edict of Milan*
   (313)

6 Let no one be at variance, or do wrong to
   another; neither you that are in error to
   those who worship the gods, as is right and
   proper, in the manner handed down from
   earliest antiquity.
   Julian (the Apostate), *Epistles,* LII (362)

7 The Arians soon perceived the danger of
   their situation, and prudently assumed those
   modest virtues which, in the fury of civil and
   religious dissensions, are seldom practised,
   or even praised, except by the weaker party.
   They recommended the exercise of
   Christian charity and moderation.
   Edward Gibbon, *The History of the Decline
   and Fall of the Roman Empire,* 2 (1781)

8 That the men in our realm have and hold all
   the aforesaid liberties, rights, and grants,
   well and in peace, freely and quietly, fully
   and wholly.
   Magna Carta, 63 (1215)

9 We permit those of the so-called Reformed
   Religion to live and abide in all the towns
   and districts of this our Realm . . . free from
   inquisition, molestation or compulsion to
   do anything in the way of Religion, against
   their conscience.
   Henry IV of France, *Edict of Nantes,* VI
   (1598)

10 It hath been the wisdom of the Church of
    England, ever since the first compiling of her
    publick Liturgy, to keep the mean between
    the two extremes, of too much stiffness in
    refusing, and of too much easiness in
    admitting any variation from it.
    Book of Common Prayer, the Preface,
    Revision of 1662

11 In necessary things, unity; in doubtful
    things, liberty; in all things, charity.
    Richard Baxter, (1615–91) Motto

12 Nobody ought to be compelled in matters of religion either by law or force.
John Locke, *Letters Concerning Toleration* (1689–92)

13 The duty of the civil authorities is to regard all peaceable inhabitants of the realm as being good subjects.
P. Bayle, *Dictionnaire historique et critique*, ii (1702)

14 It is dishonourable to pass a hard censure on the religions of all other countries: it concerns them to look to the reasonableness of their own faith; and it is sufficient for us to be establish'd in the truth of our own.
T. Sprat, *The History of the Royal Society* (1667)

15 We shall be wary therefore what persecutions we raise against the living labours of public men, how we spill the seasoned life of man preserved and stored up in books.
John Milton, *Areopagitica* (1644)

16 The only purpose for which power can be rightfully exercised over any member of a civilized community, against his will, is to prevent harm to others. His own good, either physical or moral, is not a sufficient warrant.
John Stuart Mill, *On Liberty* (1859)

17 The English Jews are, as far as we can see, precisely what our Government has made of them. They are precisely what any sect, what any class of men, treated as they have been treated, would have been . . . Let them enjoy personal security; let their property be under the protection of the law.
T.B. Macaulay, *Civil Disabilities of the Jews* (1831)

18 Neither the ghetto nor special taxation were ever foisted on the Jews and the door of social acceptability was soon opened to those wealthy enough, or adaptable enough, to take advantage of that peculiarly English diffidence about religion which helps make it such a tolerant country.
David J. Goldberg and John D. Rayner, *The Jewish People* (1987)

19 Letting a hundred flowers blossom, and a hundred schools of thought contend, is the policy for promoting the progress of the arts and the sciences.
Mao Zedong, *Quotations*, Little Red Book (1966)

20 Everyone has the right to freedom of thought, conscience and religion; this right includes freedom to change his religion or belief, and freedom, alone or in community with others and in public or private, to manifest his religion or belief in teaching, practice, worship and observance.
Universal Declaration of Human Rights, Article 18, General Assembly of the United Nations (1948)

---

98 PROSELYTIZATION AND MISSIONS

1 Arise, go to Nineveh, that great city, and cry against it.
Jonah, 1, 2

2 Go ye into all the world, and preach the gospel to every creature.
Mark, 16, 15

3 If they repent, and establish the Prayer and pay the Alms, they are your brothers in religion.
Koran, 9, 11

4 The governments of the world should know that Islam cannot be defeated. Islam will be victorious in all the countries of the world, and Islam and the teachings of the Koran will prevail all over the world.
Ayatollah Khomeini, speech in 1979, quoted in V.S. Naipaul, *Among the Believers* (1981)

5 Thus spake God unto me:
I have cherished thee as my son
And ordained thee to spread the Faith.
Go and extend true religion throughout the world
And divert the people from the evil paths.
Hymns of Guru Gobind Singh, *mai apna* (17th century)

6 May the reverend Lord teach the Doctrine, may the Happy One teach the Doctrine. There are beings of little impurity that are falling away through not hearing the Doctrine.
Majjhima Nikaya, i, 167 (3rd century BCE)

7 My own being and my pleasures, all my righteousness in the past, present, and future, I surrender indifferently, that all creatures may win to their end.
Shanti-deva, *Chary-avatara* (7th century)

8 Mark is said to have been the first man to set out for Egypt and preach there the gospel which he had himself written down, and the first to establish churches in Alexandria itself.
Eusebius, *History of the Church*, 14, 16 (4th century)

9 About the one hundred and fiftieth year after the coming of the English to Britain, Pope Gregory was inspired by God to send his servant Augustine with several other God-fearing monks to preach the word of God to the English nation.
Bede, *A History of the English Church and People*, 23 (8th century)

10 An Enquiry into the obligations of Christians to use means for the Conversion of the Heathens.
William Carey, title of book (1792)

11 We have now before us a pleasing spectacle, Christians of different denominations although differing in points of church government, united in forming a society for propagating the gospel among the heathen. This is a new thing in the Christian church.
D. Bogue, *Sermons Preached in London at the Formation of the Missionary Society* (1795)

12 The sole object shall be to encourage a wider circulation of the Holy Scriptures without note or comment.
W. Canton, *History of the British and Foreign Bible Society*, I, 11 (1910)

13 A concern arose to spend some time with the Indians, that I might feel and understand their life and the spirit they live in, if haply I might receive some instruction from them, or they might be in any degree helped forward by my following the leadings of truth among them.
John Woolman, *Journal*, (1774)

14 I adapt myself to their ideas just as Saint Paul adapted himself to the ideas of the Athenians, regarding the unknown God . . . This facilitates conversions, for, once they have recognized me as their guru, they come willingly and even gladly to my instructions.
Roberto de Nobili (1577–1656), letters quoted in V. Cronin, *A Pearl to India* (1959)

15 One of Ricci's greatest difficulties was to disentangle the authentic teaching of Confucius from the heteroclite system known as Confucianism. From a study of the *Analects* he became convinced that Confucius had taught a reverence for Heaven, upon which all earthly things depend, and that this religion was untainted by idolatry.
V. Cronin, *The Wise Man from the West* (1955)

16 Every one was free to practise what religion he liked, and to try and convert other people to his own faith, provided he did quietly and politely, by rational argument.
Thomas More, *Utopia*, ii (1516)

17 Mrs Jellyby . . . was a pretty, very diminutive, plump woman, of from forty to fifty, with handsome eyes, though they had a curious habit of seeming to look a long way off. As if . . . they could see nothing nearer than Africa! . . . Miss Jellyby . . . 'I wish Africa was dead!' she said, on a sudden.
I was going to remonstrate.
'I do!' she said. 'Don't talk to me . . . I hate and detest it. It's a beast!'
Charles Dickens, *Bleak House* (1853)

18 I must break out on the subject of Hubbards . . . These garments are usually made at working parties in Europe; and what idea the pious ladies in England, Germany, Scotland and France can have of the African figure I cannot think, but evidently part of their opinion is that it is very like a tub.
Mary Kingsley, *Travels in West Africa* (1897)

19 Sex plays a significant part in Bantu life and thought, and should, therefore, also do so in Bantu religion. 'Christianity is only skin deep', the missionaries sigh, but — in all honesty — has it ever tried to reach the more vital parts?
Mia Brandel-Syrier, *Black Woman in Search of God* (1962)

20 Nothing great was ever achieved without enthusiasm.
R.E. Emerson, *Essays, First Series* (1841)

21 Belief in a Divine mission is one of the many forms of certainty that have afflicted the human race.
Bertrand Russell, *Unpopular Essays* (1952)

22 At least two thirds of our miseries spring from human stupidity, human malice, and those great motivators and justifiers of malice and stupidity, idealism, dogmatism

and proselytizing zeal on behalf of religious or political idols.
Aldous Huxley, *Tomorrow and Tomorrow and Tomorrow* (1956)

23 The missionaries — even the martyrs among them — are too closely accompanied by guns and battleships for them to be true witnesses of the Lamb. I have never heard that the Church has ever officially condemned punitive expeditions undertaken to avenge the missionaries. Personally, I should never give even as much as a sixpence towards any missionary enterprise.
Simon Weil, *Letter to a Priest* (1953)

24 While approving of any attempt to save the souls of other men, he did appreciate the comfort of his own.
Patrick White, *Voss* (1957)

25 People who abuse missionaries have not seen their medical work. The whole health of Khorasan depends on them.
Robert Byron, *The Road to Oxiana* (1937)

26 Some of the old ethics will disappear with the old gods, but new gods will create new ethical values, and new ethical values in turn will create new conceptions of deity.
C.K. Meek, *Law and Authority in a Nigerian Tribe* (1937)

27 The missions of the higher religions are not competitive; they are complementary. We can believe in our own religion without having to feel that it is the sole repository of truth.
Arnold Toynbee, *An Historian's Approach to Religion* (1956)

28 From ancient times down to the present day there is found in various peoples a certain recognition of that hidden power which is present in history and human affairs . . . The Catholic Church rejects nothing which is true and holy in these religions . . . She therefore urges her sons, using prudence and charity, to join members of other religions in discussions and collaboration.
Second Vatican Council, *Declaration of the Relation of the Church to Non-Christian Religions* (1966)

29 Man is never saved through any religious system. Only God can save man through the influence of his saving grace . . . These religions are a providential means of salvation for their adherents.
J. Neuner, *Christian Revelation and World Religions* (1967)

99 UNITY AND ECUMENISM
See also 19. RELATIONS BETWEEN RELIGIONS

1 Behold, how good and how pleasant it is for brethren to dwell together in unity!
Psalm, 133, 1

2 That they all may be one; as thou, Father, art in me, and I in thee, that they also may be one in us: that the world may believe that thou hast sent me.
John, 17, 21

3 Lo, this community of yours is one community, and I am yours Lord, so show piety towards me.
Koran, 23, 54

4 There is indeed, but one Vehicle; there is no second, nor a third anywhere in the world . . . The Chief of the world appears in the world to reveal the Buddha-knowledge. He has but one aim, indeed, no second.
Lotus of the True Law, 2, 53–4

5 A common danger unites even the bitterest enemies.
Aristotle, *Politics,* 5, 5

6 Plurality which is not reduced to unity is confusion. Unity which does not depend on plurality is tyranny.
Blaise Pascal, *Pensées,* 870 (1670)

7 We must all hang together, or assuredly we shall all hang separately.
Benjamin Franklin, on the Declaration of Independence (1776)

8 With firmness in the right as God gives us to see the right, let us strive on to finish the work we are in, to bind up the nation's wounds.
Abraham Lincoln, *Second Inaugural Address* (1865)

9 Here are Episcopalians, Methodists, Presbyterians, and Independents, all united in one society, all joining to form its laws, to

regulate its institutions, and manage its various concerns.
D. Bogue, *Sermons Preached in London at the Formation of the Missionary Society* (1795)

10 No expression of opinion should be sought from the Conference on any matter involving any ecclesiastical or doctrinal question on which those taking part in the Conference differed among themselves.
The History and Records of the World Missionary Conference, Edinburgh (1910)

11 We do not ask that any one Communion should consent to be absorbed in another. We do ask that all should unite in a new and great endeavour to recover and to manifest to the world the unity of the Body of Christ for which he prayed.
Lambeth Conference, letter 'To All Christian People', (1920)

12 The World Council of Churches has come into existence because we have already recognised a responsibility to one another's churches . . . We cannot rest content with our present divisions.
World Council of Churches, report of the first Assembly, Amsterdam (1948)

13 It is not enough for the whole *oikoumene*, both Rome and the World Council of Churches, to address fine speeches to the 'outer world', to society at large, and 'inside' between the Churches, merely to set up everlasting mixed commissions, arrange polite mutual visits, indulge in endless academic dialogue without practical consequences. There must be genuine, increasing integration of the different Churches.
Hans Küng, *On Being a Christian* (1974)

14 If the great religions continue to waste their energies in a fratricidal war instead of looking upon themselves as friendly partners in the supreme task of nourishing the spiritual life of mankind, the swift advance of secular humanism and moral materialism is assured.
S. Radhakrishnan, *Eastern Religions and Western Thought* (1940)

---

100 DECLINE OF RELIGION
See also 16. AGNOSTICISM, 15. ATHEISM

---

1 O priests, that despise my name. And ye say,

Wherein have we despised thy name? Ye offer polluted bread upon mine altar; and ye say, Wherein have we polluted thee? In that ye say, The table of the LORD is contemptible.
Malachi 1, 6–7

2 Many false prophets shall rise, and shall deceive many. And because iniquity shall abound, the love of many shall wax cold.
Matthew, 24, 11–12

3 Meeting-places for study will be turned into brothels, the learning of the scribes will decay, and sin-fearing men will be contemned.
Mishnah, *Sanhedrin,* 97

4 Verily those who have disbelieved of the People of the Book, and the Polytheists, are in the fire of Gehenna.
Koran, 98, 5

5 Among other things, there is a drying up of great oceans, the falling away of mountain peaks, the deviation of the fixed pole-star, the cutting of the cords of the winds, the submergence of the earth, the retreat of the celestials from their stations.
In this sort of cycle of existence, what is the good of enjoyment of desires, when after a man has fed on them there is seen repeatedly his return here to earth? Please deliver me. In this cycle of existence I am like a frog in a waterless well.
Maitri Upanishad, 1, 4

6 There will be five disappearances. What five? The disappearance of attainment, the disappearance of proper conduct, the disappearance of learning, the disappearance of the outward form, the disappearance of the relics.
Anagata-vamsa, 1, 87 (1st–3rd centuries)

7 The next stage of the journey towards liberty will be refusal to submit to the magistrates, and on this will follow emancipation from the authority and correction of parents and elders; then, as the goal of the race is approached, comes the effort to escape obedience to the law, and when that goal is all but reached, contempt for oaths, for the plighted word, and all religion.
Plato, *Laws,* III, 701

8 The sea of Faith
Was once, too, at the full, and round earth's shore

Lay like the folds of a bright girdle furl'd.
But now I only hear
Its melancholy, long, withdrawing roar,
Retreating, to the breath
Of the night-wind, down the vast edges
          drear
And naked shingles of the world.
Matthew Arnold, *Dover Beach* (1867)

9 Every day, every week, every month, every
quarter, the most widely read journals seem
just now to vie with each other in telling us
that the time for religion is past, that faith is
a hallucination or an infantile disease, that
the gods have at last been found out and
exploded.
Max Müller, *Lectures on the Origin and
Growth of Religion* (1878)

10 The opinion is everywhere gaining ground
that religion is a mere survival from a
primitive and mythopoeic age, and its
extinction only a matter of time.
A.E. Crawley, *The Tree of Life* (1905)

11 More recently the standard secular attitude
has been that its religions do not matter —
that progress consists in leaving behind 'the
shackles of the past', and substituting valves
for values.
W.C. Smith, 'The Christian and the
Religions of Asia' in *Changing Asia* (1959)

12 A false spirit of arrogance, hysteria,
woolly-mindedness, criminal amorality, and
doctrinaire fanaticism, a purveyor of shoddy
spiritual goods, spurious art, philosophical
stutterings, and Utopian humbug, fit only to
be fed wholesale to the mass man of today.
That is what the post-Christian spirit looks
like.
C.G. Jung, *Aion* (1959)

---

101 RENEWAL OF RELIGION
See also 49. NEW WORLDS

---

1 The ransomed of the LORD shall return,
and come to Zion with songs and
everlasting joy upon their heads: they shall
obtain joy and gladness, and sorrow and
sighing shall flee away.
Isaiah, 35, 10

2 Behold the tabernacle of God is with men,

and he will dwell with them, and they shall
be his people.
Revelation, 21, 3

3 Then will the days of the Messiah occur;
and the Holy One, blessed be He, will not
renew the world until after seven thousand
years.
Mishnah, *Sanhedrin,* 97

4 When the help of God comes, and victory,
and you see men entering God's religion in
crowds, then proclaim the praise of your
Lord.
Koran, 110, 1–3

5 The rising of the sun from the place where it
sets, the descent of Jesus from Heaven, as
well as the other eschatological signs
according to the description thereof in
authentic Tradition, are a reality that will
take place.
Fiqh Akbar, II, 29 (10th century)

6 My delusion is destroyed, and by thy grace
I understand, and stand secure,
And doubts dispersed I shall obey thy
          word.
Bhagavad Gita, 18, 73

7 After wandering and wandering, O Lord,
I have come at last to take refuge in Thee.
Nanak's humble prayer is –
'Let me be busy in thy service.'
Hymns of Guru Arjan, *Ashtapadi,* 21, 1
(16th century)

8 Maitreya, the best of men, will preach the
true Dharma, which is compassionate
towards all living beings. And when he has
disciplined in his true Dharma hundreds and
hundreds of millions of living beings, then
that leader will at last enter Nirvana.
Maitreya-vyakarana, 102 (1st–5th
centuries)

9 True peace shall be there, where no man
shall suffer trouble from himself or from any
other. God himself, who has given virtue,
shall be the reward there.
Augustine of Hippo, *The City of God,* 22
(5th century)

10 Mr Ready-to-Halt called for his fellow
pilgrims and told them, saying, 'I am sent
for, and God shall surely visit you also.'
John Bunyan, *The Pilgrim's Progress* (1678)

11 True religion is slow in growth, and, when
once planted, is difficult of dislodgement;
but its intellectual counterfeit has no root in

itself: it springs up suddenly, it suddenly withers.
John Henry Newman, *The Idea of a University* (1858)

12 Men have torn up the roads which led to Heaven, and which all the world followed; now we have to make our own ladders.
Joseph Joubert, *Pensées*, 17, 5 (1842)

13 The cosmic religious experience is the strongest and the noblest driving force behind scientific research.
Albert Einstein, quoted in obituary (19 April 1955)

14 Religion will not regain its old power until it can face change in the same spirit as does science.
A.N. Whitehead, *Science and the Modern World* (1925)

15 The means by which we live have outdistanced the ends for which we live. Our scientific power has outrun our spiritual power. We have guided missiles and misguided men.
Martin Luther King, *Strength to Love* (1963)

16 Religion will never disappear into the sea of its own errors, as Marx and Freud supposed. It will always pick itself up and dust itself down, precisely because of what goes on in the love of God and of one's neighbour as oneself.
John Bowker, in Gerald Priestland, *Priestland's Progress* (1981)

17 The Church as community of faith . . . in these days must not be concerned primarily with the observance of ritual, disciplinary and moral regulations, but with men being able to live and receive from one another what they need in order to live.
Hans Küng, *On Being a Christian* (1974)

18 Even the most sceptical cling to the aesthetics, the history of Orthodoxy, until in a crisis, whether some personal quarrel or national disaster, the blood and tears of faith come pouring out.
Patrick White, *Flaws in the Glass* (1981)

19 It seems to be ordained that a secularised Christianity should always be followed by the counter-thrust of a vigorously eschatological, a narrow and restricted by that of an open and free.
Karl Barth, *Church Dogmatics*, III, iii (1936)

20 These have all been actual renewals. They have not been accomplished without new errors and apostasy, but from the standpoint of the basis of the Church they still have to be recognised as necessary renewals, in which the Church as a whole has come to life again.
Karl Barth, *Church Dogmatics*, III, iii (1936)

102 EDUCATION AND TEACHING
See also 62. TEACHERS AND GURUS

1 Therefore shall ye lay up these my words in your heart . . . and ye shall teach them your children, speaking of them when thou sittest in thine house.
Deuteronomy, 11, 18–19

2 Let him that is taught in the word communicate unto him that teacheth in all good things.
Galatians, 6, 6

3 Joshua ben Gamala came and instituted that teachers should be appointed in every province and in every city, and children about the age of six or seven placed in their charge.
Mishnah, *Baba Bathra*, 21

4 A good word is like a good tree whose root is firmly fixed, and whose top is in the sky; which produces its edible fruit every season.
Koran, 14, 30

5 Sure and certain knowledge is that knowledge in which the object is disclosed in such a fashion that no doubt remains along with it.
Al-Ghazali, *Deliverance from Error*, i (12th century)

6 He then, having become a pupil at the age of twelve, having studied all the Vedas, returned at the age of twenty-four, conceited, thinking himself learned, proud. Then his father said to him: 'Shvetaketu, my dear, since now you are conceited, think yourself learned, and are proud, did you also ask for that teaching whereby what has not been heard of becomes heard of, what has not been thought of becomes thought of, what has not been understood becomes understood?'
Chandogya Upanishad, 6, 1, 2–3

7 If I were to teach the Doctrine, and others did not understand it, it would be a weariness to me, a vexation . . . Then Brahma, knowing the deliberation of my mind . . . said, 'May the reverend Lord teach the Doctrine.'
Majjhima Nikaya, i, 240–1 (3rd century BCE)

8 The Master said, He who learns but does not think is lost. He who thinks but does not learn is in great danger . . . Shall I teach you what knowledge is? When you know a thing, to recognize that you know it; and when you do not know a thing, to recognise that you do not know it. That is knowledge.
Confucius, Analects, II, 15–17

9 Banish learning, and there will be no more grieving.
What after all is the difference between 'yea' and 'aye'?
Can it be compared to the difference between good and bad?
Tao Te Ching, XX

10 Education is not in reality what some people proclaim it to be in their professions. What they aver is that they can put true knowledge into a soul that does not possess it, as if they were inserting vision into blind eyes . . . But our present argument indicates that the true analogy for this indwelling power in the soul and the instrument whereby each of us apprehends is that of an eye that could not be converted to the light from the darkness except by turning the whole body.
Plato, *Republic*, VII, 518

11 Much learning does not teach understanding.
Heraclitus, *Fragments* (6th century BCE)

12 Only the educated are free.
Epictetus, *Discourses*, 2, 1 (2nd century)

13 Learning is its own exceeding great reward.
William Hazlitt, *The Plain Speaker* (1826)

14 The things taught in colleges and schools are not an education, but the means of education.
R.W. Emerson, *Journals* (1831)

15 Education is the leading human souls to what is best, and making what is best out of them; and these two objects are always attainable together, and by the same means; the training which makes men happiest in themselves also makes them most serviceable to others.
John Ruskin, *The Stones of Venice*, 3 (1853)

16 There's a new tribunal now
Higher than God's – the educated man's!
Robert Browning, *The Ring and the Book* (1869)

17 In the first place God made idiots. This was for practice. Then he made school boards.
Mark Twain *Following the Equator* (1897)

18 The dons are too busy educating the young men to be able to teach them anything.
Samuel Butler, *Note-Books* (1912)

19 The first duty of a lecturer – to hand you after an hour's discourse a nugget of pure truth to wrap up between the pages of your notebooks and keep on the mantelpiece for ever.
Virginia Woolf, *A Room of One's Own* (1929)

20 An education which does not cultivate the will is an education that depraves the mind.
Anatole France, *The Crime of Sylvestre Bonnard* (1881)

21 Voluntary renunciation of time-conditioned and obsolete privileges (for instance, in the matter of Catholic schools) should be considered in certain, especially Catholic countries (not to speak of Northern Ireland).
Hans Küng, *On Being a Christian* (1974)

---

103 CARE OF THE SICK
See also 108. SUFFERING

---

1 The LORD heard the voice of Elijah; and the soul of the child came into him again, and he revived.
1 Kings, 17, 22

2 Jesus went forth, and saw a great multitude, and was moved with compassion toward them, and he healed their sick.
Matthew, 14, 14

3 Everywhere the two medical services of the Beloved of the Gods, the king Piyadassi, have been provided. These consist of the medical care of man and the care of animals. Medicinal herbs whether useful to man or to

beast, have been brought and planted wherever they did not grow.
Ashoka, *Major Rock Edict*, II (3rd century BCE)

4 This hospital, the first in Islam, was created by Hārūn al-Rashīd at the beginning of the ninth century, following the Persian model . . . Not long afterwards other hospitals to the number of thirty-four grew up throughout the Moslem world.
P.K. Hitti, *History of the Arabs* (1937)

5 Before all things, and above all things, care must be taken of the sick; so that the brethren shall minister to them as they would to Christ himself; for he said: 'I was sick and ye visited me.'
Rule of St Benedict, 36 (6th century)

6 There was never yet philosopher
That could endure the toothache patiently.
William Shakespeare, *Much Ado About Nothing*, v, i, 35–6 (*c.* 1598–9)

7 Diseases crucify the soul of man, attentuate our bodies, dry them, wither them, shrivel them up like old apples, make them so many anatomies.
Robert Burton, *The Anatomy of Melancholy*, i (1621)

8 For the world, I count it not an inn, but an hospital, and a place, not to live, but to die in.
Thomas Browne, *Religio Medici*, ii (1643)

9 How sickness enlarges the dimensions of a man's self to himself! he is his own exclusive object. Supreme selfishness is inculcated upon him as his own duty.
Charles Lamb, *Last Essays of Elia*, 'The Convalescent' (1833)

10 A bodily disease, which we look upon as whole and entire within itself, may, after all, be but a symptom of some ailment in the spiritual part.
Nathaniel Hawthorne, *The Scarlet Letter*, 10 (1850)

11 We forget ourselves and our destinies in health, and the chief use of temporary sickness is to remind us of these concerns.
R.W. Emerson, *Journals* (1821)

12 Both sin and sickness are error, and Truth is their remedy.
Mary Baker Eddy, *Science and Health* (1875)

13 Disease makes men more physical, it leaves them nothing but body.
Thomas Mann, *The Magic Mountain*, 4, 10 (1924)

14 Let us a little permit Nature to take her own way; She better understands her own ways than we.
Michel de Montaigne, *Essays*, 'Of Experience' (1588)

XIII
RELIGIOUS PHILOSOPHY

---

104 PHILOSOPHY

---

1 Where shall wisdom be found? and where is the place of understanding?
Job, 28, 12

2 Beware lest any man spoil you through philosophy and vain deceit, after the tradition of men.
Colossians, 2, 8

3 To what is a scholar like? A flask containing aromatic ointment. When it is unstopped the fragrance is diffused; when it is stopped up the fragrance is not diffused.
Mishnah, *Abodah Zarah*, 35

4 To teach them the Book and the Wisdom, and to purify them by almsgiving; verily Thou art the Sublime, the Wise.
Koran, 2, 123

5 Every student of mathematics admires its precision and the clarity of its demonstrations. This leads him to believe in the philosophers, and to think that all their sciences resemble this one in clarity and demonstrative cogency. Further, he has already heard the accounts on everyone's lips of their unbelief, their denial of God's attributes, and their contempt for revealed truth.
Al-Ghazali, *Deliverance from Error*, 90 (12th century)

6 All those traditions and all those despicable systems of philosophy, which are not based on the Veda, produce no reward after death;

for they are declared to be founded on Darkness.
Laws of Manu, XII, 95

7 Do not question too much, lest your head fall off. In truth, you are questioning too much about a divinity about which further questions cannot be asked. Gargi, do not over-question. Thereupon [the female philosopher] Gargi held her peace.
Brihad-aranyaka Upanishad, 3, 6

8 This I ask thee, O Lord, answer me truly:
That I may make my wisdom from thy
            instruction, O Wise One,
And from the words which I have received
            from the Good Mind.
Gathas, *Yasna*, 44

9 The Master said, Give me a few more years, so that I may have spent a whole fifty in study, and I believe that after all I should be fairly free from error.
Confucius, *Analects*, VII, 16

10 He who has been earnest in the love of knowledge and of true wisdom, and has exercised his intellect more than any other part from him, must have thoughts immortal and divine, if he attain truth, and in so far as human nature is capable of sharing in immortality, he must be altogether immortal.
Plato, *Timaeus*, 90

11 It is because of wonder that men, anciently as now, philosophized. They wondered initially at the obvious problems of every day, and then little by little they progressed

to the point of expressing difficulties of a more demanding sort.
Aristotle, *Metaphysics*, i, 3

12 Philosophy before the coming of the Lord was necessary to the Greeks for righteousness, but now it is profitable for piety, seeing that it is a sort of training for those who by means of demonstration have the enjoyment of faith . . . This was a schoolmaster to the Greek world, as the Law was to the Hebrews.
Clement of Alexandria, *Stromateis*, 1, 5 (2nd century)

13 When you understand physics, you have entered the hall; and when, after completing the study of natural philosophy, you master metaphysics, you have entered the innermost court and are with the king in the same palace.
Moses Maimonides, *The Guide for the Perplexed*, 51, 385 (12th century)

14 Although the truth of the Christian faith surpasses the capacity of human nature, yet those things which reason has inherently in possession cannot be contrary to the Christian truth.
Thomas Aquinas, *Summa contra Gentiles*, i, vii (13th century)

15 The philosophers, cloaked and bearded to command respect, insist that they alone have wisdom and all other mortals are but fleeting shadows. Theirs is certainly a pleasant form of madness, which sets them building countless universes.
Desiderius Erasmus, *In Praise of Folly*, 52 (1511)

16 There is nothing so strange and so unbelievable that it has not been said by one philosopher or another.
René Descartes, *Discourse on Method*, 2 (1639)

17 To make light of philosophy is to be a true philosopher.
Blaise Pascal, *Pensées*, 4 (1670)

18 A little philosophy inclineth man's mind to Atheism, but depth in philosophy bringeth men's minds about to religion.
Francis Bacon, *Essays*, 'Atheism' (1625)

19 To believe only possibilities, is not faith, but mere Philosophy.
Thomas Browne, *Religio Medici* (1643)

20 No man was ever yet a great poet, without being at the same time a profound philosopher.
S.T. Coleridge, *Biographia Literaria* (1817)

21 To a philosopher no circumstance, however trifling, is too minute.
Oliver Goldsmith, *The Citizen of the World*, 30 (1762)

22 The various opinions of philosophers have scattered through the world as many plagues of the mind as Pandora's box did those of the body; only with this difference, that they have not left hope at the bottom.
Jonathan Swift, *A Critical Essay upon the Faculties of the Mind* (1707)

23 There was never a tutor that did professly teach Felicity, though that be the mistress of all other sciences.
Thomas Traherne, *Centuries of Meditations* (17th century)

24 I have tried too in my time to be a philosopher; but, I don't know how, cheerfulness was always breaking in.
Oliver Edwards, in Boswell, *Life of Samuel Johnson* (17 April 1778)

25 Pretend what we may, the whole man within us is at work when we form our philosophical opinions.
William James, *The Will to Believe* (1896)

26 Philosophy begins in wonder. And, at the end, when philosophic thought has done its best, the wonder remains.
A.N. Whitehead, *Modes of Thought* (1938)

27 There are more things in heaven and earth, Horatio,
Than are dreamt of in your philosophy.
William Shakespeare, *Hamlet*, 1, v, 166–7

---

105 REASON AND MIND
See also 52. SOUL AND SPIRIT

---

1 O ye simple, understand wisdom; and, ye fools, be ye of an understanding heart.
Proverbs, 8, 5

2 What man knoweth the things of a man, save the spirit of man which is in him?
1 Corinthians, 2, 11

3 A certain group of men have made ignorance their capital. Finding reasoning and inquiry into religious beliefs too

burdensome, they incline towards the easy way of servile sectarianism. They calumniate him who scrutinizes the basic dogmas of religion and accuse him of deviation.
Al-Ash'ari, *A Vindication of the Science of Kalām* (10th century)

4 He who has not understanding,
Whose mind is not constantly held firm –
His senses are uncontrolled.
Like the vicious horses of a chariot-driver.
Katha Upanishad, 3, 5

5 As the lion, king of beasts, is reckoned chief among animals, for his strength, speed and bravery, so is the faculty of wisdom reckoned chief among mental states helpful to enlightenment.
Samyutta Nikaya, V, 227 (3rd century BCE)

6 Enlightenment is the movement of man out of his minority state, which was brought about by his own fault. The minority state means the incapacity to make use of one's understanding without the guidance of another . . . Have the courage to make use of your own understanding is thus the motto of Enlightenment.
Immanuel Kant, *What is Enlightenment?* (1784)

7 The understanding, like the eye, whilst it makes us see and perceive all things, takes no notice of itself; and it requires art and pains to set it at a distance and make it its own subject.
John Locke, *An Essay Concerning Human Understanding,* 1, 1 (1690)

8 The mind is its own place, and in it self
Can make a Heaven of Hell, a Hell of Heaven.
John Milton, *Paradise Lost,* i, 254 (1667)

9 The mind is a dangerous weapon, even to the possessor, if he knows not discreetly how to use it.
Michel de Montaigne, *Essays* (1588)

10 Man has been endowed with reason, with the power to create, so that he can add to what he's been given. But up to now he hasn't been a creator, only a destroyer. Forests keep disappearing, rivers dry up, wild life's become extinct, the climate's ruined and the land grows poorer and uglier every day.
Anton Chekhov, *Uncle Vanya* (1900)

11 Mind is a light which the Gods mock us with,
To lead those false who trust it.
Matthew Arnold, *Empedocles on Etna,* 1, 2 (1852)

12 What is the price of Experience? do men buy it for a song?
Or wisdom for a dance in the street? No, it is bought with the price
Of all that a man hath, his house, his wife, his children.
Wisdom is sold in the desolate market where none come to buy,
And in the wither'd field where the farmer plows for bread in vain.
William Blake, *Vala or The Four Zoas,* 2 (1797)

13 We should take care not to make the intellect our god; it has, of course, powerful muscles, but no personality.
Albert Einstein, *Out of My Later Years* (1950)

14 True ideas are those that we can assimilate, validate, corroborate and verify. False ideas are those that we can not.
William James, *Pragmatism* (1907)

15 Has it not yet been observed that all religious statements contain logical contradictions and assertions that are impossible in principle, that this is in fact the very essence of religious assertion?
C.G. Jung, *Psychology and Alchemy* (1953)

16 I am the son of a midwife . . . My art of midwifery is in general like theirs, the only difference is that my patients are men, not women, and my concern is not with the body but with the soul that is in travail of birth.
Socrates, in Plato, *Theaetetus,* 149–50

106 QUESTIONS AND SPECULATION

1 Hath God forgotten to be gracious? hath he in anger shut up his tender mercies?
Psalm, 77, 9

2 What shall I do that I may inherit eternal life?
Mark, 10, 17

3 Who provides for you from the heaven and the earth, or who has power over the hearing and the sight?
Koran, 10, 32

4 What is the cause? Is it Brahma? Whence are we born? Whereby do we live? And on what are we established? Over-ruled by whom, in pains and
  pleasures,
Do we live our various conditions, O ye
  theologians?
Is it time, or inherent nature, or necessity, or
  chance,
Or the elements, or a female womb, or a
  male person,
that are to be considered as the cause?
It is not a combination of these,
because of the existence of the soul.
Shvetashvatara Upanishad, 1, 1–2

5 This I ask thee, O Lord, answer me truly:
Who set the Earth in its place below, and the
  sky of the
clouds, that it shall not fall?
Who the waters and the plants?
Who yoked the two steeds to wind and
  clouds?
Who, O Wise One, is the creator of the
  Good Mind?
Gathas, *Yasna*, 44

6 Whether the world is eternal I have not explained, or whether the world is not eternal . . . Whether a Buddha is both non-existent and not non-existent after death, I have not explained. And why have I not explained this? Because this is not useful, is not concerned with the principle of a religious life, does not conduce to aversion, absence of passion, cessation, tranquillity, supernatural faculty, perfect knowledge, or Nirvana, and therefore I have not explained it.
Majjhima Nikaya, 1, 426 (3rd century BCE)

7 I was constantly veering to and fro, puzzling primarily over this sort of question. Is it when heat and cold produce fermentation, as some have said, that living creatures are bred? Is it with the blood that we think, or with the air or the fire that is in us? Or is it none of these, but the brain that supplies our senses of hearing and sight and smell, and from these memory and opinion arise? . . . However, I once heard someone reading from a book, as he said, by Anaxagoras, and asserting that it is mind that produces order

and is the cause of everything. This explanation pleased me.
Plato, *Phaedo*, 96–7

8 Myself when young did eagerly frequent
Doctor and Saint, and heard great
    Argument
About it and about; but evermore
Came out by the same Door where in I
    went.
Edward Fitzgerald, *Rubáiyát of Omar
    Khayyám*, 27 (1859)

9 In arguing too, the person own'd his skill,
For e'en though vanquish'd, he could argue
    still;
While words of learned length, and
    thund'ring sound
Amazed the grazing rustics rang'd around,
And still they gaz'd, and still the wonder
    grew,
That one small head could carry all he
    knew.
Oliver Goldsmith, *The Deserted Village*
(1770)

10 Weary and toiled with rowing up and down on the seas of questions.
Jeremy Taylor, *The great Exemplar* (1649)

11   Those obstinate questionings
Of sense and outward things,
Fallings from us, vanishings:
Blank misgivings of a creature
Moving about in worlds not realised.
William Wordsworth, *Ode: Intimations of
Immortality* (1807)

12 He is the one man who will always be the most surprised, the most affected, the most apprehensive and the most joyful in the face of events. He will not be like an ant which has foreseen everything in advance, but like a child in a forest, or on Christmas Eve: one who is always rightly astonished by events, by the encounters and experiences which overtake him.
Karl Barth, *Church Dogmatics*, IV, i (1936)

13 Does this good exist? What does it matter? The things of this world exist, but they are not the good. Whether the good exists or not, there is no other good than the good.
Simone Weil, *First and Last Notebooks*
(1956)

14 Galileo, who held a scientific truth of great importance, abjured it with the greatest ease as soon as it endangered his life. In a certain

sense, he did right. That truth was not worth the stake. Whether the earth or the sun revolves around the other is a matter of profound indifference. To tell the truth, it is a futile question. On the other hand, I see many people die because they judge that life is not worth living.
Albert Camus, *The Myth of Sisyphus* (1942)

107 SCIENCE

1 Well favoured and skilful in all wisdom, and cunning in knowledge, and understanding science.
Daniel, 1, 4

2 Oppositions of science, falsely so called.
1 Timothy, 6, 20

3 Just as it is not a condition of religion to reject medical science, so likewise the rejection of natural science is not one of its conditions . . . Nature is in subjection to God most high, not acting of itself but serving as an instrument in the hands of its Creator.
Al-Ghazali, *Deliverance from Error*, 95 (11th–12th centuries)

4 Just as by one piece of clay everything made of clay may be known – the modification is merely a verbal distinction, a name; the reality is just 'clay' – so is that teaching.
Chandogya Upanishad, 6, 1, 4

5 All phenomena have their causes. If one does not know these causes, although one may happen to be right about the facts, it is as if one knew nothing, and in the end one will be bewildered . . . For everything there must be a reason. Therefore the sage does not inquire about endurance or decay, nor about goodness or badness, but about the reasons for them.
Master Lü, *Spring and Autumn Annals* (3rd century BCE)

6 It is not the life according to knowledge which makes men act rightly and be happy, not even if it be knowledge of all the sciences, but one science only, that of good and evil.
Plato, *Charmides*, 174

7 Geometry (which is the only science that it

hath pleased God hitherto to bestow on mankind).
Thomas Hobbes, *Leviathan*, i, 4 (1651)

8 An undevout astronomer is mad.
Edward Young, *Night Thoughts*, 9 (1746)

9 O ye Religious, discountenance every one among you who shall pretend to despise Art & Science!
William Blake, *Jerusalem*, Plate 77 (1804)

10   To thee
Science appears but, what in truth she is,
Not as our glory and our absolute boast,
But as a succedaneum, and a prop to our
            infirmity.
William Wordsworth, *The Prelude*, ii (1850)

11 The religion that is afraid of science dishonours God and commits suicide.
R.W. Emerson, *Journals* (1831)

12 If they [scientists] are worthy of the name, they are indeed about God's Path and about his bed and spying out all his ways.
Samuel Butler, *Note-Books* (1912)

13 Philosophy is not opposed to science, it behaves itself as if it were a science, and to a certain extent makes use of the same methods; but it parts company with science, in that it clings to the illusion that it can produce a complete and coherent picture of the universe.
Sigmund Freud, *New Introductory Lectures on Psycho-Analysis* (1933)

14 Between theology and science there is a No Man's Land, exposed to attack from both sides; this No Man's Land is philosophy. Almost all the questions of most interest to speculative minds are such as science cannot answer . . . Why, then, you may ask, waste time on such insoluble problems? To this one may answer as a historian, or as an individual facing the terror of cosmic loneliness.
Bertrand Russell, *History of Western Philosophy* (1946)

15 Religion will not regain its old power until it can face change in the same spirit as does science. Its principles may be eternal, but the expression of those principles requires continual development.
A.N. Whitehead, *Science and the Modern World*, 12 (1925)

16 Science without religion is lame, religion

without science is blind.
Albert Einstein, *Out of My Later Years*
(1950)

108 SUFFERING

1 Verily I have cleansed my heart in vain, and
washed my hands in innocency. For all the
day long have I been plagued, and chastened
every morning.
Psalm, 73, 13–14

2 This is thankworthy, if a man for conscience
toward God endure grief, suffering
wrongfully.
1 Peter, 2, 19

3 Whoever rejoices in the sufferings that come
upon him in this life brings salvation to the
world.
Mishnah, *Taanith*, 8

4 When a misfortune has fallen upon you, and
you had inflicted twice as much, will you
say: 'How is this?' Say rather: 'You are
yourselves to blame; God has power over all
things.'
Koran, 3, 159

5 God said: 'Yea; a favourite and chosen slave
of Mine fell sick. I am he. Consider well: His
infirmity is My infirmity; his sickness is My
sickness.'
Jalalu'l-Din Rumi, *Mathnawi*, II, 2156
(13th century)

6 To what land shall I flee? Where bend my
                          steps?
I am thrust out from family and tribe;
I have no favour from the village to which I
                    would belong,
Nor from the wicked rulers of the country:
How then, O Lord, shall I obtain thy
                    favour?
Gathas, *Yasna*, 46

7 As one breaks wood with wood, stone with
stone, iron with iron, the inert with the
insentient, so the blessed God, the
self-existent great-grandfather, hurts
creatures with creatures, hiding behind a
disguise . . . When I see noble, moral, and
modest people harassed in their way of life,
and the ignoble happy, I stagger with
wonder. I condemn the God who allows
such outrages!
Mahabharata, 3, 31

8 If any sickness should come and he suffers
pain, he should cheerfully steady his mind
and bear the ills that attack him . . . If
someone strikes a monk who is restrained
and subdued, he should think, 'It might be
worse, I have not lost my life.'
Uttara-dhyayana Sutra, 2, 27–32 (3rd
century BCE)

9 The Four Noble Truths: Suffering, the origin
of suffering, the cessation of suffering, and
the Noble Eightfold Path which leads to the
cessation of suffering.
Dhammapada, 190–1

10 Prosperity doth best discover vice, but
adversity doth best discover virtue.
Francis Bacon, *Essays*, 'Of Adversity'
(1625)

11 All is for the best in the best of possible
worlds.
Voltaire, *Candide*, 30 (1759)

12 I was not met as in intercourse with my
fellow-men by the cold platitudes that fall so
lightly from the lips of those whose hearts
have never known one real pang, nor whose
lives one crushing blow. I was not told that
all things were ordered for the best, nor
assured that the overwhelming disparities of
life were but apparent, but I was met from
the eyes and brow of Him who was indeed
acquainted with grief, by a look of solemn
recognition.
Dora Greenwell, *Colloquia Crucis* (1871)

13 Something even more sickening, the silence
of God. In face of this terrible sacrifice . . .
Like the sea, God was silent. The silence of
God was something I could not fathom.
Shusaku Endo, *Silence* (1976)

14 How can great wisdom care so little about
the torments of innocent creatures? This
question, which began to agonize me when I
was six or seven years old, still haunts me
today. I still cannot accept the ruthlessness
of nature, God, the Absolute . . . How can a
merciful God allow all this to happen and
keep silent?
Isaac B. Singer, *Love and Exile* (1985)

15 Thou art indeed just, Lord, if I contend
With thee; but, sir, so what I plead is just.
Why do sinners' ways prosper? and why
                    must
Disappointment all I endeavour end?
Gerard Manley Hopkins, *Thou art Indeed
Just, Lord* (1889)

16 About suffering they were never wrong,
The Old Masters: how well they understood
Its human position; how it takes place
While someone else is eating or opening a
        window
Or just walking dully along.
W.H. Auden, *Musée des Beaux Arts* (1930)

17 In the judgement of Christianity and the
Mahāyāna, even the extremity of Suffering
is not too high a price to pay for following
Love's lead; for, in their judgement,
Selfishness, not Suffering, is the greatest of
all evils, and Love, not release from
Suffering, is the greatest of all goods.
Arnold Toynbee, *An Historian's Approach
to Religion* (1956)

18 Religion in a time of plague could not be the
religion of every day. While God might
accept and even desire that the soul should
take its ease and rejoice in happier times, in
periods of extreme calamity He laid extreme
demands on it.
Albert Camus, *The Plague* (1947)

19 God is weak and powerless in the world,
and that is precisely the way, the only way,
in which he is with us and helps us . . . Only
the suffering God can help.
Dietrich Bonhoeffer, *Letters and Papers
from Prison* (1967)

109 FREEWILL
See also 42. PREDESTINATION AND FATE,
161. SLAVERY

1 I have chosen the way of truth: thy
judgments have I laid before me.
Psalm, 119, 30

2 If the Son therefore shall make you free, ye
shall be free indeed.
John, 8, 36

3 When the Pharisees say that all things
happen by fate, they do not take away from
men the freedom of acting as they think fit;
since their notion is that it has pleased God
to mix up the decrees of fate and man's will,
so that man can act virtuously or viciously.
Josephus, *Antiquities*, 18, 1, 3 (1st century)

4 Do not say with regard to anything: 'I am

going to do that tomorrow', except with the
reservation that God so will.
Koran, 18, 23

5 We hold that no one can do a thing before
he does it, and that no one is independent of
God, or able to evade God's knowledge.
Al-Ash'ari, *Ibana*, 17 (10th century)

6 Held fast by your own natural action, what
through delusion you seek not to do, you
shall do even against your will.
Bhagavad Gita, 18, 60

7 Every human being has been given free-will.
If he wishes to incline himself towards the
good way and to be righteous, he is free to
do so; and if he wishes to incline himself
towards the evil way and to be wicked he is
free to do that . . . Every individual is
capable of being righteous like Moses or
wicked like Jeroboam, wise or foolish,
merciful or cruel, mean or generous.
Moses Maimonides, *Mishneh Torah*, 5.1–3
(12th century)

8 Your destiny shall not be allotted to you, but
you shall choose it for yourselves. Let him
who draws the first lot be the first to choose
a life, which shall be his irrevocably. Virtue
owns no master: he who honours her shall
have more of her, and he who slights her,
less.
Plato, *Republic*, X, 617

9 He is free who lives as he likes; who is not
subject to compulsion, restraint or violence;
whose pursuits are unhindered, his desires
successful, his aversions never met.
Epictetus, *Discourses*, 4, 1 (2nd century)

10 A Christian is no-one's servant, subject to
none; and he is every-one's servant, subject
to all.
Martin Luther, *The Liberty of a Christian
Man*, 1 (1520)

11 No free man shall be taken or imprisoned or
dispossessed, or outlawed or exiled, or in
any way destroyed.
Magna Carta (1215)

12 Dr Johnson shunned tonight any discussion
of the perplexed question of fate and free
will, which I attempted to agitate: 'Sir, (said
he,) we *know* our will is free, and *there's* an
end of't.'
James Boswell, *Life of Johnson*, 10 October
1769

13 If some great Power would agree to make me always think what is true and do what is right, on condition of being turned into a sort of clock and wound up every morning before I got out of bed, I should instantly close with the offer.
T.H. Huxley, *On Descartes' Discourse on Method* (1870)

14 'I don't want comfort. I want God. I want poetry. I want real danger, I want freedom, I want goodness, I want sin.'
'In fact', said Mustapha Mond, 'you're claiming the right to be unhappy.'
'All right, then', said the Savage defiantly, 'I'm claiming the right to be unhappy.'
Aldous Huxley, *Brave New World* (1932)

15 The Party denied the free will of the individual – and at the same time it exacted his willing self-sacrifice. It denied his capacity to choose between two alternatives – and at the same time it demanded that he should constantly choose the right one. It denied his power to distinguish good and evil – and at the same time it spoke pathetically of guilt and treachery.
Arthur Koestler, *Darkness at Noon* (1940)

16 You know the alternative: either we are not free and God the all-powerful is responsible for evil. Or we are free and responsible but God is not all-powerful. All the scholastic subtleties have neither added anything to nor subtracted anything from the acuteness of this paradox.
Albert Camus, *The Myth of Sisyphus* (1942)

17 For free will to exist, evil had to exist, in order that man's choice might be his own. God could not thereafter permit Himself to interfere in man's actions, for then there would be an end to free will and an end to the ascending revelation of life . . . For man to become truly free, God had to put man's will beyond even divine intervention.
Meyer Levin, *The Fanatic* (1964)

18 We who lived in concentration camps can remember the men who walked through the huts comforting others, giving away their last piece of bread. They may have been few in number, but they offer sufficient proof that everything can be taken from a man but one thing: the last of the human freedoms – to choose one's attitude in any given circumstances, to choose one's own way.
Viktor Frankl, *Man's Search for Meaning.* (1959)

110 DOUBT
See also 16. AGNOSTICISM AND HUMANISM

1 I gave my heart to know wisdom, and to know madness and folly: I perceived that this also is vexation of spirit. For in much wisdom is much grief: and he that increaseth knowledge increaseth sorrow.
Ecclesiastes, 1, 17–18

2 Him that is weak in the faith receive ye, but not to doubtful disputations.
Romans, 14, 1

3 Do ye really disbelieve in him who created the earth in two days, and to him do yet set up peers?
Koran, 41, 8

4 There is this doubt in regard to a man deceased: 'He exists', say some. 'He exists not', say others.
Katha Upanishad, 1, 20

5 An uninstructed ordinary person is not wisely reflecting if he thinks: 'In the past was I, was I not, what was I, what was I like, having been what what was I?'
Majjhima-nikaya, 1, 8 (3rd century BCE)

6 Doubt has devoured the whole world but none has ever eaten Doubt.
Sākhī, 1, 7, in Charlotte Vaudeville, *Kabir* (1974)

7 I alone seem to have lost everything,
Mine is indeed the mind of a very idiot,
So dull am I.
The world is full of people that shine;
I alone am dark.
Tao Te Ching, XX

8 A castle, called Doubting Castle, the owner whereof was Giant Despair.
John Bunyan, *The Pilgrim's Progress*, i (1678)

9 If a man will begin with certainties, he shall end in doubts; but if he will begin with doubts, he shall end in certainties.
Francis Bacon, *The Advancement of Learning*, I, i, 3 (1605)

10 Ten thousand difficulties do not make one doubt.
John Henry Newman, *Apologia pro Vita sua* (1864)

11 There lives more faith in honest doubt,

Believe me, than in half the creeds.
Alfred Tennyson, *In Memoriam*, (1850)

12 All we have gained then by our unbelief
Is a life of doubt diversified by faith,
For one of faith diversified by doubt:
We called the chess-board white – we call it
black.
Robert Browning, *Bishop Blougram's Apology* (1855)

13 I am the doubter and the doubt,
And I the hymn the Brahmin sings.
R.W. Emerson, *Brahma* (1857)

14 Faith which does not doubt is dead faith.
Miguel de Unamuno, *La Agonia del Christianismo*

15 I emerged from my encounters with the
Church and Bible reassured by the
uncertainties I had met, and by the honesty
with which churchmen had confessed them.
Gerald Priestland, *Priestland's Progress* (1981)

---

111 PROOFS OF GOD
See also 5. MONOTHEISM, 44. CREATION

---

1 He hath made everything beautiful in his
time: also he hath set the world in their
heart, so that no man can find out the work
that God maketh from the beginning to the
end.
Ecclesiastes, 3, 11

2 For the invisible things of him from the
creation of the world are clearly seen, being
understood by the things that are made,
even his eternal power and Godhead.
Romans, 1, 20

3 Among his signs are the night and the day,
the sun and the moon; do obeisance neither
to the sun nor to the moon, but do
obeisance to God, who created them.
Koran, 41, 37

4 What is the proof that creation has a maker
who made it and a governor who wisely
ordered it?
The proof of that is that the completely
mature man was originally semen, then a
clot, then a small lump, then flesh and bone
and blood.
Al-Ash'ari, *Kitāb al-Luma* (10th century)

5 The one who rules over every single source,

In whom this whole world comes together
and dissolves,
The Lord, the blessing-giver, God
adorable —
By revering him one goes for ever to this
peace.
Shvetashvatara Upanishad, 4, 11

6 We know from Scripture that there is a
Supreme Being whose nature is absolute
bliss and goodness; who is fundamentally
antagonistic to all evil; who is the cause of
the origination, sustentation, and
dissolution of the world.
Ramanuja, *Commentary on the Vedanta Sutras*, IV, 4, 22 (11th century)

7 That which is created must, as we affirm, of
necessity be created by a cause. But the
father and maker of all this universe is past
finding out.
Plato, *Timaeus*, 28

8 That the Final Cause is among things
unmoved is shown by logical distinction,
since it exists for the sake of something
which desires it; and of these two, one is
unmoved while the other which desires it is
not. The Final Cause then causes movement
as beloved, and something moved by it
moves all other things.
Aristotle, *Metaphysics*, L, 10

9 If that than which no greater can be
conceived were only in the understanding,
there would be something still greater than
it, which assuredly is impossible.
Something, therefore, without doubt, exists
than which no greater can be conceived, and
it is both in the understanding and in reality.
Anselm, *Proslogium*, ii (11th century)

10 That God exists can be proved in five Ways:—
The first and most evident Way is the
argument from Motion. . . . The second
Way is from consideration of efficient
Causes . . . The third Way is taken from
consideration of the possible and the
necessary . . . The fourth Way is the
consideration of the grades of stages which
are found in all things . . . The fifth Way is
the consideration of the government of
things.
Thomas Aquinas, *Summa Theologica*, I, ii,
3 (13th century)

11 Twenty-four scholars got together and tried
to say what God is and were unable to do it
. . . God is something that must transcend

being. Anything which has being, date and location does not belong to God, for he is above them all and although he is in all creatures, yet he is more than all of them.
Meister Eckhart, *Sermons* (13th–14th centuries)

12 I conceive God as actually infinite, so that nothing can be added to his perfection. And, in fine, I readily perceive that the objective being of an idea cannot be produced by a being that is merely potentially existent, which, properly speaking, is nothing, but only by a being existing formally and actually.
René Descartes, *Meditations on First Philosophy,* III (1641)

13 I have unfolded the nature of God and his properties, namely, that he is that which exists of necessity; that he is one, that he exists and acts from the sole necessity of his own nature; that he is the free cause of all things.
Baruch Spinoza, *Ethics,* I (1677)

14 From my own being, and from the dependency I find in myself and my ideas, I do, by an act of reason, necessarily infer the existence of a God, and of all created things in the mind of God.
George Berkeley, *Third Dialogue* (1713)

15 From the beautiful connexion and rigid observance of established rules, we drew the chief argument for theism; and from the same principles are enabled to answer the principal objections against it.
David Hume, *Dialogues concerning Natural Religion,* 6 (1779)

16 The extreme difficulty or rather impossibility of conceiving this immense and wonderful universe, including man with his capacity of looking far backwards and far into futurity, as the result of blind chance or necessity. When thus reflecting I feel compelled to look to a First Cause having an intelligent mind in some degree analogous to that of man.
Charles Darwin, *Autobiography* (1887)

17 Two things fill the mind with ever new and increasing wonder and awe, the more often and the more seriously reflection concentrates upon them: the starry heaven above me and the moral law within me.
Immanuel Kant, *Critique of Practical Reason* (1788)

18 I do not myself believe that Philosophy can either prove or disprove the truth of religious dogmas, but ever since Plato most philosophers have considered it part of their business to produce 'proofs' of immortality and the existence of God.
Bertrand Russell, *History of Western Philosophy* (1946)

19 Either God exists or he does not. But to which side shall we lean? Reason can decide nothing, there is an infinite chaos which separates us. A game is being played, at the extremity of this infinite distance, where heads or tails will fall. What will you bet?
. . . If you win, you win everything. If you lose, you lose nothing. Bet then that he exists, without hesitating.
Blaise Pascal, *Pensées,* 3, 233 (1670)

20 If we put obedience to God above everything else, unreservedly, with the following thought: 'Suppose God is real', then our gain is total . . . If one follows this rule of life, then no revelation at the moment of death can cause any regrets; because if chance or the devil govern all worlds we would still have no regrets for having lived this way. This is greatly preferable to Pascal's wager.
Simone Weil, *Pensées sans Ordre* (1962)

XIV
VIRTUE AND THE GOOD

112 LISTS OF VIRTUES

1 The spirit of the LORD shall rest upon him,
the spirit of wisdom and understanding, the
spirit of counsel and might, the spirit of
knowledge and of the fear of the LORD.
Isaiah, 11, 2

2 The fruit of the Spirit is love, joy, peace,
longsuffering, gentleness, goodness, faith,
meekness, temperance.
Galatians, 5, 22

3 There are seven marks of a wise man. The
wise man does not speak before him who is
greater than he in wisdom; and does not
break in upon the speech of his fellow; he is
not hasty to answer; he questions according
to the subject matter; and answers to the
point; he speaks upon the first thing first,
and the last last; regarding that which he
has not understood he says, I do not
understand it, and he acknowledges the
truth.
Mishnah, *Pirke Aboth*, 5

4 Islam is built upon five things: on confessing
that there is no god but God, performing
prayers, giving the legal alms, going on
pilgrimage to the House, and fasting during
the month of Ramadan.
Al-Malati, *Kitab al-Tanbih* (10th century)

5 On the destruction of impurity by the
practice of the parts of Yoga, there comes
enlightenment leading up to discriminative
knowledge . . . The self-controls are:

non-violence, truth, honesty, chastity and
abstinence.
Yoga Sutras, 2, 28–30

6 The Five Precepts:
I undertake to observe the rule
to abstain from taking life;
to abstain from taking what is not given;
to abstain from sensual misconduct;
to abstain from false speech;
to abstain from intoxicants as tending to
cloud the mind.
Edward Conze, *Buddhist Scriptures* (1959)

7 The Four Great Vows [of a Bodhisattva]:
However innumerable beings are, I vow to
save them;
However inexhaustible the passions are, I
vow to extinguish them;
However immeasurable the Teachings are, I
vow to master them;
However incomparable the Buddha-truth is,
I vow to attain it.
D.T. Suzuki, *Manual of Zen Buddhism*
(1950)

8 Master K'ung said, He who could put the
Five into practice everywhere under Heaven
would be Good.
Tzu-Chang begged to hear what these were.
The Master said, Courtesy, breadth, good
faith, diligence, and clemency.
Confucius, Analects, XVII, 6

9 Here are my three treasures. Guard and
keep them!
The first is pity; the second, frugality; the
third, refusal to be 'foremost of all things
under heaven.'
Tao Te Ching, LXVII

10 A man should be of good cheer about his soul . . . if he has earnestly pursued the pleasure of learning, and adorned his soul with the adornment of temperance, and justice, and courage, and freedom, and truth.
Plato, *Phaedo*, 114

11 Virtue is a state apt to exercise deliberate choice, being in the relative mean, determined by reason, and as a man of practical wisdom would determine . . . In respect of fears and confidence or boldness, the Mean state is Courage.
Aristotle, *Ethics*, 2, 1106

12 I cannot praise a fugitive and cloistered virtue, unexercised and unbreathed, that never sallies out and sees her adversary, but slinks out of the race, where that immortal garland is to be run for, not without dust and heat.
John Milton, *Areopagitica* (1644)

13 Lord, turn my necessities into virtues; the works of nature into the works of grace, by making them orderly, temperate, subordinate, and profitable to ends beyond their own proper efficacy.
Jeremy Taylor, *The Rule and Exercise of Holy Living* (1650)

14 Medieval churchmen . . . held that faith, hope and love are the fundamental Christian virtues and that the cardinal virtues (prudence, justice, temperance, fortitude) are needed to express faith, hope and love in all the varying circumstances of life in the world.
R.E.C. Browne, in *A Dictionary of Christian Ethics* (1967)

113 THE RIGHT

See also 118. GOODNESS AND MERCY

1 Depart from evil, and do good; seek peace, and pursue it.
Psalm, 34, 14

2 Why callest thou me good? There is none good but one, that is, God.
Mark, 10, 18

3 He perfects his goodness upon you . . .

Verily God commands justice and kindness.
Koran, 16, 83–92

4 The highest good is like that of water. The goodness of water is that it benefits the ten thousand creatures; yet itself does not scramble, but is content with the places that all men disdain. It is this that makes water so near to the Way.
Tao Te Ching, VIII

5 The Master said, It is Goodness that gives to a neighbourhood its beauty. One who is free to choose, yet does not prefer to dwell among the Good – how can he be accorded the name of wise?
Confucius, *Analects*, IV, 1

6 Human nature is disposed to goodness, just as water flows downwards. There is no water but flows down, and no men but show this tendency to good.
Mencius, VI (4th century BCE)

7 The greatest thing to learn is the idea of good, by reference to which just things and all the rest become useful and beneficial.
Plato, *Republic*, VI, 505

8 The cause of all existing things cannot be any one of them. Because it is the cause of good it cannot, then, be called the Good; yet in another sense it is the Good above all.
Plotinus, *Enneads*, VI, 9 (3rd century)

9 In ethics they discuss the same problems as we do. Having distinguished between three types of 'good', psychological, physiological, and environmental, they proceed to ask whether the term is strictly applicable to all of them or only to the first.
Thomas More, *Utopia*, II (1516)

10 The whole course of our life must be subject to moral maxims; but this is impossible, unless with the moral law, which is a mere idea, reason connects an efficient cause which ordains to all conduct which conforms to the moral law an issue either in this or another life, which is in exact conformity with our highest aims.
Immanuel Kant, *Critique of Pure Reason*, 2, 2, 2, (1781)

11 There is nothing either good or bad but thinking makes it so.
William Shakespeare, *Hamlet*, II, ii, 249 (*c*.1603)

12 It is good to be tired and wearied by the vain

search after the true good, that we may stretch out our arms to the Redeemer.
Blaise Pascal, *Pensées* (1670)

13 Our will is always for our own good, but we do not always see what that is.
Jean-Jacques Rousseau, *The Social Contract*, 2, 3 (1762)

14 Evil be thou my Good.
John Milton, *Paradise Lost*, iv (1667)

15 Good, but not religious good.
Thomas Hardy, *Under the Greenwood Tree* (1872)

16 The Christian ideal has not been tried and found wanting. It has been found difficult; and left untried.
G.K. Chesterton, *What's Wrong with the World*, i, 5 (1910)

---

114 DUTY

---

1 He hath shewed thee, O man, what is good; and what doth the LORD require of thee, but to do justly, and to love mercy, and to walk humbly with thy God?
Micah, 6, 8

2 When ye shall have done all those things which are commanded you, say, We are unprofitable servants: we have done that which it was our duty to do.
Luke, 17, 10

3 Serve God, and do not associate anything with him; show parents kindness; also to relatives, and the poor, and the person under your protection be he relative or not, to the companion by your side, to the follower of the way, and to what your right hands possess.
Koran, 4, 40

4 Better do one's own duty, though imperfect, than do another's duty well; it is better to die in one's own duty, the duty of other men is perilous.
Bhagavad Gita, 3, 35

5 He whose evil conduct is covered by good conduct lights up this world like the moon when freed from a cloud.
Dhammapada, 173

6 This is the duty of a true man –
to shelter all, as a tree from the fierce sun,

and to labour that many may enjoy what he earns,
like the fruit of a fertile tree.
Tamil Quatrains, 202 (6th century)

7 The Master said, a young man's duty is to behave well to his parents at home and to his elders abroad, to be cautious in giving promises and punctual in keeping them, to have kindly feelings towards everyone, but to seek the intimacy of the Good. If, when all that is done, he has any energy to spare, then let him study the polite arts.
Confucius, *Analects*, 1, 6

8 Athenians, I hold you in the highest regard and love; but I will obey God rather than you: and as long as I have breath and strength I will not cease from philosophy, and from exhorting you, and declaring the truth to every one of you whom I meet.
Plato, *Apology* [of Socrates], XVII

9 The views of Aristotle on ethics represent, in the main, the prevailing opinions of educated and experienced men of his day . . . The book appeals to the respectable middle-aged, and has been used by them, especially since the seventeenth century, to repress the ardours and enthusiasms of the young.
Bertrand Russell, *History of Western Philosophy* (1946)

10 The whole subject of duties, in its greatest latitude, is comprehended under two parts: the first is taken up in explaining what is good, and what our greatest good. The second is in certain directions and precepts, according to which on all occasions it is our duty to govern our lives and actions.
Cicero, *Offices*, 1, 3 (1st century BCE)

11 Our duty is to be useful, not according to our desires but according to our powers.
H.F. Amiel, *Fragments d'un journal intime* (1883)

12 It is a part of special prudence never to do anything because one has an inclination to do it; but because it is one's duty, or is reasonable.
Matthew Arnold, *Notebooks* (1868)

13 Do all the good you can, by all the means you can.
John Wesley, *Rule of Conduct* (1774)

14 Stern Daughter of the Voice of God!
O Duty! if that name thou love

Who art a Light to guide, a Rod
To check the erring, and reprove.
William Wordsworth, *Ode to Duty* (1807)

15 Of Law there can be no less acknowledged,
than that her seat is the bosom of God, her
voice the harmony of the world.
Richard Hooker, *Of the Laws of
Ecclesiastical Polity* (1594)

16 Let us have faith that right makes might;
and in that faith let us to the end, dare to do
our duty as we understand it.
Abraham Lincoln, speech, 27 February
1860

17 The moral laws lead through the conception
of the *summum bonum* as the object and
final end of pure practical reason to religion,
that is, to the recognition of all duties as
divine commands.
Immanuel Kant, *Critique of Practical
Reason*, II, 2, 5 (1788)

18 'Do the duty which lies nearest thee', which
thou knowest to be a duty! Thy second
duty will already have become clearer.
Thomas Carlyle, *Sartor Resartus*, 9 (1833)

19 In practice it is seldom very hard to do one's
duty when one knows what it is, but it is
sometimes exceedingly difficult to find this
out.
Samuel Butler, *Note-Books* (1912)

20 As for Doing-good, that is one of the
professions which are full. Moreover, I have
tried it fairly, and, and, strange as it may seem,
am satisfied that it does not agree with my
constitution.
H.D. Thoreau, *Walden* (1854)

21 If all experiences are indifferent, that of duty
is as legitimate as any other.
Albert Camus, *The Myth of Sisyphus* (1942)

22 There is no duty we so much underrate as
the duty of being happy.
R.L. Stevenson, *Virginibus Puerisque* (1881)

---

115 TRUTH AND WISDOM
See also 105. REASON AND MIND

---

1 Great is truth, and strong above all things.
1 Esdras, 4, 41

2 Great is truth, and shall prevail.
T. Brooks, *The Crown and Glory of
Christianity* (1662)

3 Ye shall know the truth, and the truth shall
make you free.
John, 8, 32

4 By three things is the world preserved: by
truth, by judgement, and by peace . . . The
three are really one; if judgement is
executed, truth is vindicated and peace
results.
Mishnah, *Aboth*, 1, 18, and *Taanith*, 68

5 This is the truth:
The works which the sages saw in the sacred
                    sayings
Are manifoldly spread forth in the Vedas.
Follow them constantly, ye lovers of truth!
This is your path to the world of good
                    deeds.
Mundaka Upanishad, 1, 2, 1

6 The true lover of knowledge must, from
childhood up, be most of all a striver after
truth in every form.
Plato, *Republic*, 6, 485

7 All human beings by nature have an urge to
know.
Aristotle, *Metaphysics*, 1, 1

8 Fortunate are those who have come to know
the causes of things.
Virgil, *Georgics*, 2, 490 (1st century BCE)

9 Life is that Wisdom by which all things are
made, both the things that have been and
the things that are yet to be . . . We did for
one instant attain to touch it . . . in a flash
of the mind attained to touch the eternal
Wisdom which abides over all.
Augustine of Hippo, *Confessions*, 9, 10,
23–5 (5th century)

10 From the feeling of our own ignorance,
vanity, poverty, infirmity, and – what is
more – depravity and corruption, we
recognize that the true light of wisdom,
sound virtue, full abundance of every good,
and purity of righteousness rest in the Lord
alone.
John Calvin, *Institutes of the Christian
Religion*, 1, 1(1536)

11 A recognised factor in the making of this age
is the gradual secularisation of the idea of
'wisdom', and consequently of the ideal of
the good life, in some ways a necessary

secularisation, a necessary recognition of the relative autonomy of merely human values.
J. Durkan, in D. McRoberts (ed.), *Essays on the Scottish Reformation* (1962)

12 What is truth? Truth is something so noble that if God could turn aside from it, I could keep to the truth and let God go.
Meister Eckhart, *Fragments* (13th–14th centuries)

13 What is truth? said jesting Pilate, and would not stay for an answer.
Francis Bacon, *Essays*, 'Of Truth' (1625)

14 Let her and Falsehood grapple; who ever knew Truth put to the worse, in a free and open encounter?
John Milton, *Areopagitica* (1644)

15 And diff'ring judgements serve but to declare
That truth lies somewhere. If we knew but where.
William Cowper, *Hope* (1782)

16 When I tell any Truth it is not for the sake of convincing those who do not know it, but for the sake of defending those who do.
William Blake, Public Address (1810)

17 Truth from his lips prevail'd with double sway,
And fools, who came to scoff, remain'd to pray.
Oliver Goldsmith, *The Deserted Village* (1770)

18 The truth is rarely pure, and never simple.
Oscar Wilde, *The Importance of Being Ernest* I, (1895)

19 Man with his burning soul
Has but an hour of breath
To build a ship of truth
In which his soul may sail —
Sail on the sea of death,
For death takes toll
Of beauty, courage, youth,
Of all but truth.
John Masefield, *Truth* (1914)

20 And is it True? It is not True.
And if it were it wouldn't do,
For people such as me and you.
Hilaire Belloc, *Cautionary Tales*, 'Upon being asked by a Reader whether the verses contained in this book were true' (1907)

21 And is it true? And is it true.
This most tremendous tale of all.
John Betjeman, *Christmas* (1954)

---

116 BEAUTY AND ART
See also 76. MUSIC

---

1 In the cutting of stones, to set them, and in carving of wood, to make any manner of cunning work . . . of the embroiderer, in blue, and in purple, in scarlet, and in fine linen.
Exodus, 35, 33–5

2 Whatsoever things are true, whatsoever things are just, whatsoever things are pure, whatsoever things are lovely, whatsoever things are of good report; if there be any virtue, and if there be any praise, think on these things.
Philippians, 4, 8

3 To him belong the Most Beautiful Names; to him whatever is in the heavens and the earth gives glory.
Koran, 59, 24

4 Wearing marvellous garlands and garments,
With marvellous perfumes and ointments,
Made up of all wonders, this God,
The Infinite, faced in all directions.
Bhagavad Gita, 11, 11

5 Thou watchest all creation,
Where sounds of musical melodies,
Of instruments playing, minstrels singing,
Are joined in divine harmony.
Hymns of Guru Nanak, *sodar tera* (16th century)

6 It is because everyone under Heaven recognizes Beauty as Beauty, that the idea of ugliness exists . . . For truly Being and Not-being grow out of one another.
Tao Te Ching, II

7 Since God Almighty has sealed me with the stamp of beauty, I desire that men should behold it and recognise His grace towards me, and I will not veil it.
Tradition of Ayesha, wife of Muhammad, quoted in Margaret Smith, *Rābi'a the Mystic* (1928)

8 Purity and beauty always go hand in hand.
E.V. Gatenby, *The Cloud-men of Yamato*
(1929)

9 Begin with the assumption that there exists
an absolute beauty, and an absolute good
. . . It appears to me that if anything besides
absolute beauty is beautiful, it is so simply
because it partakes of absolute beauty.
Plato, *Phaedo*, XLIX

10 Light (God's eldest daughter) is a principal
beauty in building.
Thomas Fuller, *The Holy State and the
Profane State*, 'Of Building' (1642)   .

11 He that will have no *sensible* and *natural*
pleasure, shall have no *spiritual pleasure*.
Richard Baxter, *The Saint's Everlasting Rest*
(1650)

12 God made the country, and man made the
town.
William Cowper, *The Task*, i (1785)

13 Beauty in things exists in the mind which
contemplates them.
David Hume, *Essays*, 'Of Tragedy' (1742)

14 Beauty is Nature's coin, must not be hoarded,
But must be current, and the good thereof
Consist in mutual and partaken bliss.
John Milton, *Comus* (1634)   .

15 'Beauty is truth, truth beauty', — that is all
Ye know on earth, and all ye need to know.
John Keats, *Ode on a Grecian Urn* (1820)

16 Spirit of BEAUTY, that dost consecrate
With thine own hues all thou dost shine
                 upon
Of human thought or form — where art
            thou gone?
Percy Bysshe Shelley, *Hymn to Intellectual
            Beauty* (1817)

17 God make thee good as thou art beautiful.
Alfred Tennyson, *The Idylls of the King*,
'The Holy Grail' (1869)

18 The innocent and the beautiful
Have no enemy but time.
W.B. Yeats, *In Memory of Eva Gore-Booth
and Con Markiewicz* (1933)

19 I love all beauteous things,
I seek and adore them;
God hath no better praise,
And man in his hasty days
Is honoured for them.
Robert Bridges, *I Love All Beauteous Things*
(1876)

20 I have never known a man who seemed
altogether right and calm in faith, who
seriously cared about art; and when casually
moved by it, it is quite impossible to say
beforehand by what class of art this
impression will on such men be made. Very
often it is by a theatrical commonplace,
more frequently still by false sentiment.
John Ruskin, *The Stones of Venice* (1853)

21 It is amazing how complete is the delusion
that beauty is goodness.
Leo Tolstoy, *The Kreutzer Sonata* (1889)

22 Things are pretty, graceful, rich, elegant,
handsome, but, until they speak to the
imagination, not yet beautiful.
R.W. Emerson, *The Conduct of Life*,
'Beauty' (1860)

23 Beauty is one of the rare things that do not
lead to doubt of God.
Jean Anouilh, *Becket*, i (1959)

---

117 JUSTICE
See also 118. GOODNESS AND MERCY

---

1 Let judgment run down as waters, and
righteousness as a mighty stream.
Amos, 5, 24

2 Judge not, and ye shall not be judged:
condemn not, and ye shall not be
condemned: forgive, and ye shall be
forgiven.
Luke, 6, 37

3 Those who have believed and wrought the
works of righteousness, they receive a
reward that is rightfully theirs. What then
after that will declare you false in regard to
the Judgement? Is not God the best of
judges?
Koran, 95, 6–8

4 Justice, being violated, destroys; justice,
being preserved, preserves: therefore justice
must not be violated, lest violated justice
destroy us.
Laws of Manu, VIII, 15

5 The Master said, If the ruler himself is
upright, all will go well though he does not
give orders. But if he himself is not upright,

even though he gives orders, they will not be obeyed.
Confucius, *Analects*, XIII, 6

6   Zeus, fearing the total destruction of our race, sent Hermes to impart to men the qualities of respect for others and a sense of justice, so as to bring order into our cities and create a bond of friendship and union.
Plato, *Protagoras*, 322

7   All virtue is summed up in dealing justly.
Aristotle, *Nicomachean Ethics*, 5, 1

8   Grant unto her whole Council, and to all that are put in authority under her, that they may truly and indifferently minister justice, to the punishment of wickedness and vice, and to the maintenance of thy true religion, and virtue.
Book of Common Prayer, Prayer for the Church Militant in The Communion

9   Earthly power doth then show likest God's When mercy seasons justice.
William Shakespeare, *The Merchant of Venice*, IV, i, 191–2 (*c.* 1596–8)

10   I shall temper so Justice with Mercy, as may illustrate most Them fully satisfied, and thee appease.
John Milton, *Paradise Lost*, X, 77–9 (1667)

11   Fiat justitia et ruant coeli. Let justice be done though the heavens fall.
William Watson, *A Decacordon* (1602). First citation in an English work of a famous maxim

12   Justice will not condemn even the Devil himself wrongfully.
Thomas Fuller, *Gnomologia* (1732)

13   We see neither justice nor injustice which does not change its nature with change in climate. Three degrees of latitude reverse all jurisprudence: a meridian decides the truth.
Blaise Pascal, *Pensées*, 294 (1670)

14   It is not, what a lawyer tells me I *may* do; but what humanity, reason, and justice tell me I ought to do.
Edmund Burke, *Speech on Conciliation with America* (1775)

15   Justice is truth in action.
Benjamin Disraeli, speech, 11 February 1851

16   No human actions ever were intended by

the Maker of men to be guided by balances of expediency, but by balances of justice.
John Ruskin, *Unto this Last* (1860)

---

118 GOODNESS AND MERCY
See also 117. JUSTICE

---

1   Most men will proclaim every one his own goodness, but a faithful man who can find?
Proverbs, 20, 6

2   The fruit of the Spirit is love, joy, peace, longsuffering, gentleness, goodness, faith, meekness, temperance.
Galatians, 5, 22–3

3   Seven qualities avail before the Throne of Glory: faith, righteousness, justice, lovingkindness, mercy, truth, and peace.
Aboth d'Rabbi Nathan, 37 (2nd century)

4   Verily God commands justice and kindness, and giving to kindred; and he forbids indecency, and disreputable conduct, and greed.
Koran, 16, 92

5   The gift that is said to be of Goodness, is one that is given because it is a sacred duty, to one from whom no favour is expected in return, at the right place and time.
Bhagavad Gita, 17, 20

6   If among thoughts they value those that are profound,
If in friendship they value gentleness,
In words, truth; in government, good order;
In deeds, effectiveness; in actions, timeliness —
In each case it is because they prefer what does not lead to strife.
Tao Te Ching, VIII

7   Of divine goods, the first and chiefest is wisdom; and next after it, sobriety of spirit; a third, resultant from the blending of both these with valour, is righteousness; and valour itself is fourth.
Plato, *Laws*, i, 631

8   There is a difference between justice and consideration in one's relations to one's fellow men. It is the function of justice not to do wrong to one's fellow men; of considerateness, not to wound their feelings.
Cicero, *De Officiis*, 1, 28 (1st century BCE)

9 Seek not good from without: seek it within yourselves, or you will never find it.
Epictetus, *Discourses*, 3, 24 (2nd century)

10 Live not as though there were a thousand years ahead of you. Fate is at your elbow, make yourself good while life and power are still yours.
Marcus Aurelius, *Meditations*, 4, 17 (2nd century)

11 If to do were as easy as to know what were good to do, chapels had been churches, and poor men's cottages princes' palaces. It is a good divine that follows his own instructions.
William Shakespeare, *The Merchant of Venice*, 1, ii, 11–13 (*c.* 1596–8)

12 There is no man so good, who, were he to submit all his thoughts and actions to the laws, would not deserve hanging ten times in his life.
Michel de Montaigne, *Essays*, 'Of Vanity' (1588)

13 We see neither justice nor injustice which does not change its nature with change in climate. Three degrees of latitude reverse all jurisprudence: a meridian decides the truth.
Blaise Pascal, *Pensées*, 294 (1670)

14 The inclination to goodness is imprinted deeply in the nature of man: insomuch, that if it issue not towards men, it will take unto other living creatures.
Francis Bacon, *Essays*, 'Goodness' (1625)

15 Justice is always violent to the party offending, for every man is innocent in his own eyes.
Daniel Defoe, *The Shortest Way with the Dissenters* (1702)

16 Teach me to feel another's woe,
To hide the fault I see;
That mercy I to others show,
That mercy show to me.
Alexander Pope, *The Universal Prayer*, 10 (1738)

17 As I know more of mankind I expect less of them, and am ready now to call a man a good man upon easier terms than I was formerly.
Samuel Johnson, in Boswell, *Life of Samuel Johnson* (September 1783)

18 By perfection, I mean the humble, patient,

gentle love of God and our neighbour, ruling our tempers, words and actions.
John Wesley, *A Plain Account of Christian Perfection* (1765)

19 What makes it so difficult to do justice to others is, that we are hardly sensible of merit, unless it falls in with our own views and line or pursuit; and where this is the case, it interferes with our own pretensions.
William Hazlitt, *Characteristics* (1823)

20 Every actual state is corrupt. Good men must not obey the laws too well.
R.W. Emerson, *Essays, Second Series*, 'Politics' (1844)

21 Jail does not teach anyone to do good, nor Siberia, but a man — yes! A man can teach another man to do good — believe me!
Maxim Gorky, *The Lower Depths* (1903)

22 I am afraid that good people do a great deal of harm in this world. Certainly the greatest harm they do is that they make badness of such extraordinary importance.
Oscar Wilde, *Lady Windermere's Fan*, I (1892)

23 Somehow, our sense of justice never turns in its sleep till long after the sense of injustice in others has been thoroughly aroused.
Max Beerbohm, *And Even Now*, 'Servants' (1920)

24 We hand folks over to God's mercy, and show none ourselves
George Eliot, *Adam Bede*, 42 (1859)

25 Only God can tell the saintly from the suburban,
Counterfeit values always resemble the true.
W.H. Auden, *New Year Letter* (1941)

---

119 FAITH
See also 71. BELIEF

---

1 The just shall live by his faith
Habakkuk, 2, 4

2 Faith is the substance of things hoped for, the evidence of things not seen . . . Through faith we understand that the worlds were framed by the word of God, so that things which are seen were not made of things which do appear.
Hebrews, 11, 1–3

3 Those who have faith are prosperous; who ·
are humble in their prayers, who turn away
from idle talk, and who are active in
almsgiving.
Koran, 23, 1–4

4 There is no faith without Islam and Islam
without faith cannot be found. The two are
as back and belly.
Fiqh Akbar, II, 18 (10th century)

5 The faith of every man accords with his
essential nature; man here is made up of
faith; as a man's faith is, so is he.
Bhagavad Gita, 17, 3

6 By faith you shall be free, and go beyond the
realm of death.
Sutta Nipata, 1146 (3rd century BCE)

7 I do not seek to understand in order that I
may believe, but I believe in order that I may
understand.
Anselm, *Proslogium* (11th century)

8 Methinks there be not impossibilities
enough in Religion for an active faith.
Thomas Browne, *Religio Medici*, i (1643)

9 Faith is not a notion, but a real strong
essential hunger, an attracting or magnetic
desire of Christ, which as it proceeds from a
seed of the divine nature in us, so it attracts
and unites with its like.
William Law, *Grounds and Reasons of
Christian Regeneration* (1750)

10 There is a faith which is of a man's self, and
a faith which is the gift of God; or a power
of believing which is found in the nature of
fallen man, and a power of believing which
is given from above.
Isaac Penington, *The Inward Journey* (1761)

11 That willing suspension of disbelief for the
moment, which constitutes poetic faith.
S.T. Coleridge, *Biographia Literaria*, 14
(1817)

12 Faith consists in believing when it is beyond
the power of reason to believe. It is not
enough that a thing be possible for it to be
believed.
Voltaire, *Questions sur l'Encyclopédie*
(1764)

13 I felt I did trust in Christ, Christ alone for
salvation: and an assurance was given me
that he had taken away *my* sins, even *mine*,
and saved me from the law of sin and death.
John Wesley, *Journal* (24 May 1738)

14 Man is capable of nothing, it is God who
gives everything, who gives man faith.
Søren Kierkegaard, *Journal* (1849)

15 Faith is a state of the mind and the soul . . .
The language of religion is a set of formulas
which register a basic spiritual experience.
Dag Hammarskjöld, *Markings* (1964)

16 We live in an age which asks for faith, pure
faith, naked faith, mystical faith.
William Johnston, *The Inner Eye of Love*
(1978)

---

120 HOPE

1 Hope in God: for I shall yet praise him, who
is the health of my countenance, and my
God.
Psalm, 43, 5

2 The faith of Abraham . . . who against hope
believed in hope.
Romans, 4, 18

3 Why, at the dawn of the new era, at the very
beginning of the fratricidal twentieth
century, was I given the name Nadezhda
[Hope]?
Nadezdha Mandelstam, *Hope against Hope*
(1970)

4 Even now I am full of hope, but the end lies
in God.
Pindar, *Odes* (5th century BCE)

5 Ten thousand men possess ten thousand
hopes —
A few bear fruit in happiness; the others go
awry.
Euripides, *The Bacchae* (5th century BCE)

6 'Abandon all hope, ye that enter.' These
words in a dark colour I saw written above a
gate.
Dante Alighieri, *Inferno*, III, 9–11 (1320)

7 Oh, what a valiant faculty is hope, that in a
mortal subject, and in a moment, makes
nothing of usurping infinity, immensity,
eternity, and of supplying its master's
indigence, at its pleasure, with all things he
can imagine or desire!
Michel de Montaigne, *Essays*, 'Of Names'
(1588)

8 True hope is swift and flies with swallow's

wings; Kings it makes gods, and meaner creatures kings.
William Shakespeare, *Richard III,* V, ii, 23–4 (1591)

9 Never give out while there is hope; but hope not beyond reason, for that shows more desire than judgment.
William Penn, *Some Fruits of Solitude* (1693)

10 Hope springs eternal in the human breast: Man never Is, but always To be blest.
Alexander Pope, *An Essay on Man,* i (1734)

11 Hope is necessary in every condition. The miseries of poverty, sickness, of captivity, would, without this comfort, be insupportable.
Samuel Johnson, *The Rambler,* 67 (1752)

12 Hope is the best possession. None are completely wretched but those who are without hope, and few are reduced so low.
William Hazlitt, *Characteristics,* 33 (1823)

13 Hopeless hope hopes on and meets no end, Wastes without springs and homes without a friend.
John Clare, *The Exile* (1841)

14 Experience bows a sweet contented face, Still setting to her seal that God is true . . .
While Hope, who never yet hath eyed the goal,
With arms flung forth, and backward floating hair,
Touches, embraces, hugs the invisible.
Christina Rossetti, *Verses* (1893)

15 I should go with him in the gloom, Hoping it might be so.
Thomas Hardy, *The Oxen* (1915)

16   Cry *I can no more.* I can:
Can something, hope, wish day come, not choose not to be.
Gerard Manley Hopkins, *Carrion Comfort* (1889)

17 Because I do not hope to turn again
Because I do not hope
Because I do not hope to turn.
T.S. Eliot, *Ash Wednesday,* 1 (1930)

18 Friends and loves we have none, nor wealth, nor blessed abode,
But the hope of the City of God at the other end of the road.
John Masefield, *The Seekers* (1910)

121 CHARITY
See also 163. ALMSGIVING

1 I was eyes to the blind, and feet was I to the lame. I was a father to the poor: and the cause which I knew not I searched out.
Job, 29, 15–16

2 Above all things have fervent charity among yourselves: for charity shall cover the multitude of sins.
1 Peter, 4, 8

3 Whoever runs after charity to practise it, the Holy One, blessed be He, provides him with the means wherewith to do it.
Mishnah, *Baba Bathra,* 9

4 We must observe the commandment to give charity with greater care than any other positive precept. For charity is the sign of the righteous man.
Moses Maimonides, *Code,* 'Gifts to the Poor' (12th century)

5 A kind word with forgiveness is better than charity followed by injury; God is rich and gracious. O you who believe, do not make your charity worthless by obligation and insult.
Koran, 2, 265–6

6 He should feed children, married daughters, old relatives, pregnant women, sick people, and also guests and servants, and only afterwards should the householder and his wife eat the food that remains.
Yajnavalkya Lawbook (4th century)

7 Only those rich men are truly wealthy Who relieve the need of their neighbours.
Tamil Quatrains, 170 (6th century)

8 When travelling priests arrive, the old resident priests go out to welcome them and carry for them their clothes and alms-bowls, giving them water for washing and oil for anointing their feet, as well as the liquid food allowed out of hours.
Travels of Fa-hsien (4th century)

9 Help people in distress as you would help a fish in a dried-up rut . . . Respect the aged and have pity on the poor. Collect food and clothing and relieve those who are cold and hungry along the road.
Yin-chih Wen, or The Silent Way of Recompense (11th century)

10　When men fight, after the first blow, charity is broken. And whoever dies without charity goes the straight road to hell.
Lollard Conclusions, 10 (1394)

11　In faith and hope the world will disagree, But all mankind's concern is charity.
Alexander Pope, *An Essay on Man*, 3, 303 (1734)

12　I believe there is no sentiment he has such faith in as that 'charity begins at home.'
R.B. Sheridan, *The School for Scandal*, 5, 2 (1777)

13　With malice toward none, with charity for all.
Abraham Lincoln, *Second Inaugural Address* (1865)

14　Charity and Mercy. Not unholy names, I hope?
Charles Dickens, *Martin Chuzzlewit*, 9 (1844)

15　Charity, dear Miss Prism, charity! None of us are perfect. I myself am peculiarly susceptible to draughts.
Oscar Wilde, *The Importance of Being Earnest*, II (1895)

16　Charity and personal force are the only investments worth anything.
Walt Whitman, *Leaves of Grass*, 'Song of Prudence' (1855)

---

122 LOVE

1　Thou shalt love thy neighbour as thyself: I am the LORD.
Leviticus, 19, 18

2　He that loveth not his brother whom he hath seen, how can he love God whom he hath not seen?
1 John, 4, 20

3　If you love him, I am faithful to repay you a good reward; but if you do not love him, I am the Judge to exact a penalty.
Aboth d'Rabbi Nathan, 16 (2nd century)

4　I ask you for no reward in return, except love towards the kinsfolk.
Koran, 42, 22

5　Such a Yogi's mind, from the excess of love he bears me, is lost in me because I am different in essence from all else. Out of the

excess of his love for me, he cannot continue to exist without me.
Ramanuja, *Commentary on the Bhagavad Gita*, 6, 47 (11th century)

6　Mencius said: To feed a person without loving him is to treat him like a pig. To love without respecting him is to treat him like a domestic pet.
Mencius, VII (4th century BCE)

7　Love conquers all things: Let us too give in to Love.
Virgil, *Eclogues*, x, 69 (1st century BCE)

8　Love is all we have, the only way that each can help the other.
Euripides, *Orestes* (408 BCE)

9　Love and do what you will.
Augustine of Hippo, *Tractatus in Ep. Joannis*, vii (5th century)

10　　　　Love alone
Is the true seed of every merit in you,
And of all acts for which you must atone.
Dante Alighieri, *Purgatorio*, 17 (1320)

11　In the beginning of my conversion and singular purpose, I thought that I would be like the little bird that languishes for love of his beloved but is gladdened in his longing when he that it loves comes and sings with joy.
Richard Rolle, *The Fire of Love* (14th century)

12　Nothing is sweeter than Love, nothing stronger, nothing higher, nothing wider, nothing more pleasant, nothing fuller nor better in Heaven and earth.
Thomas Kempis, *Of the Imitation of Christ*, 3, 5 (1418)

13　Love is a circle that doth restless move
In the same sweet eternity of love
Robert Herrick, *Hesperides* (1648)

14　Love, all alike, no season knows, nor clime, Nor hours, days, months, which are the rags of time.
John Donne, *Songs and Sonnets* (1633)

15　We have just enough religion to make us hate, but not enough to make us love one another.
Jonathan Swift, *Thoughts on Various Subjects* (1706)

16　We never, then, love a person, but only qualities.
Blaise Pascal, *Pensées*, 323 (1670)

17 To love nothing is not to live; to love but
feebly is to languish rather than live.
François Fénelon, *A un homme du monde*
(1699)

18 Love seeketh not itself to please,
Nor for itself hath any care,
But for another gives its ease,
And builds a Heaven in Hell's despair.
William Blake, *Songs of Experience*
(1794)

19 Love had he found in huts where poor men
lie;
His daily teachers had been woods and rills.
William Wordsworth, *Song at the Feast of
Brougham Castle* (1807)

20 God gives us love. Something to love
He lends us; but, when love is grown
To ripeness, that on which it throve
Falls off, and love is left alone.
Alfred Tennyson, *To J.S.* (1833)

21 A pity beyond all telling
Is hid in the heart of love.
W.B. Yeats, *The Pity of Love* (1893)

22 Where there is no love there is no sense
either.
Fyodor Dostoevsky, *Notes from
Underground* (1864)

23 Each man kills the thing he loves,
By each let this be heard,

Some do it with a bitter look,
Some with a flattering word.
Oscar Wilde, *The Ballad of Reading Gaol*, i,
7 (1898)

24 Love consists in this, that two solitudes
protect and border and salute each other.
Rainer Maria Rilke, *Letters to a Young Poet*
(1904)

25 Love is an endless mystery, for it has
nothing else to explain it.
Rabindranath Tagore, *Fireflies* (1928)

26 Even as love crowns you so shall he crucify
you. Even as he is for your growth so is he
for your pruning.
Kahlil Gibran, *The Prophet* (1923)

27 Love is union with somebody, or
something, outside oneself, under the
condition of retaining the separateness and
integrity of one's own self.
Erich Fromm, *The Sane Society* (1955)

28 And you, who speak in me when I speak
well,
withdraw not your grace, leave me not dry
and cold.
I have praised you in the pain of love, I
would praise you still
in the slowing of the blood, the time when I
grow old.
Judith Wright, *The Other Half*, 'Prayer'
(1966)

XV
MORALITY

123 THE WAY

1 Blessed are the undefiled in the way, who
walk in the law of the Lord.
Psalm, 119, 1

2 If he found any of this way, whether they
were men or women, he might bring them
bound unto Jerusalem.
Acts, 9, 2

3 Guide us in the straight path, the path of
those upon whom thou hast bestowed good.
Koran, 1, 5–6

4 This wisdom has been revealed to you in
theory;
listen now to how it should be practised.
Bhagavad Gita, 2, 39

5 What is this Middle Way, the knowledge of
which the Buddha has gained, which leads
to insight, which leads to wisdom, which
conduces to calm, to knowledge, to insight,
to Nirvana? It is the Noble Eightfold Path.
Mahavagga, 1, 6 (3rd–1st centuries BCE)

6 In the pursuit of the Way the first essential is
sitting still . . . Simply to spend time in
sitting still, without any thought of gain,
even without a feeling of gaining
enlightenment — that is our Founder's Way.
Shobo Genzo Zuimonki (13th century)

7 The Master said, Set your heart upon the
Way, support yourself by its power, lean
upon Goodness, seeks distraction in the
arts.
Confucius, *Analects,* VII, 6

8 When the Great Way was practised, the
world was shared by all alike. The worthy
and the able were promoted to office, and
men practised good faith and lived in
affection . . . Now the great way has
become hid and the world is the possession
of private families.
Book of Rites, 9 (1st century BCE)

9 The Way is like an empty vessel, that yet
may be drawn from without ever
needing to be filled.
It is bottomless; the very progenitor of all
things in the world.
Tao Te Ching, IV

10 Where is what the ancients call the system of
the Way to be found? It is everywhere.
Where does the spiritual come from? Where
does the intelligent come from? . . . They all
have their origin in the One.
Chuang Tzu, 33 (4th century BCE)

11 There is a narrow path which will bring us
safely to our journey's end, with reason as
our guide.
Plato, *Phaedo,* XI

12 Enlightened men keep the middle path,
which is also the best.
Theologia Germanica, 39 (14th century)

13 What is this little way which you would
teach souls? It is the way of spiritual
childhood, the way of trust and absolute
surrender.
Thérèse of Lisieux, *Novissima Verba* (1898)

14 I have often admired the mystical way of
Pythagoras, and the secret magic of
numbers.
Thomas Browne, *Religio Medici,* i (1643)

15 That is the Path of Wickedness,
Though some call it the Road to Heaven.
Ballad of Thomas the Rhymer, xii (13th
century)

16 Then I saw that there was a way to Hell,
even from the gates of heaven.
John Bunyan, *The Pilgrim's Progress* (1678)

17 Through a wise and salutary neglect, a
generous nature has been suffered to take
her own way to perfection.
Edmund Burke, *Speech on Conciliation with
America* (1775)

124 THE GOLDEN RULE

1 All things whatsoever ye would that men
should do to you, do ye even so to them.
Matthew, 7, 12

2 What thou thyself hatest, do to no man.
Tobit, 4, 15

3 Hillel said: What is hateful to you, do not do
to your fellow man; that is the essence of the
Torah, the rest is commentary: go and learn.
Mishnah, *Shabbat*, 31a

4 Repel the evil with what is better, and lo, he
between whom and thee there is enmity will
be as if he were a warm friend.
Koran, 41, 34

5 Against an angry man let him not in return
show anger, let him bless when he is cursed.
Laws of Manu, VI, 48

6 Tzu-kung asked saying, Is there any single
saying that one can act upon all day and
every day?
The Master said, Perhaps the saying about
consideration: Never do to others what you
would not like them to do to you.
Confucius, *Analects*, XV, 23

7 We ought not to repay wrong with wrong or
do harm to any man, no matter what we
may have suffered from him.
Plato, *Crito*, X

8 He that returns a good for evil obtains the
victory.
Thomas Fuller, *Gnomologia* (1732)

9 Not all of those to whom we do good love

us, neither do all those to whom we do evil
hate us.
Joseph Roux, *Meditations of a Parish Priest*
(1886)

10 The Golden Rule is that there are no golden
rules.
George Bernard Shaw, *Man and Superman*,
iv (1903)

125 COMMANDMENTS
See also 114. DUTY, AND 153. THE STATE AND
RULERS

1 Fear God, and keep his commandments: for
this is the whole duty of man.
Ecclesiastes, 12, 13

2 If there be any other commandment, it is
briefly comprehended in this saying,
namely, Thou shalt love thy neighbour as
thyself.
Romans, 13, 9

3 Greater is he who performs the
commandments from love than he who
performs them from fear.
Mishnah, *Sotah*, 31

4 When Moses came . . . We wrote for him in
the Tablets of everything as admonition,
and a distinct setting forth of everything.
Koran, 7, 139–42

5 When a man knows these things and
practises them, that man shall be called
great in the kingdom of heaven, according
to the witness of Jesus (peace be upon him).
Al-Ghazali, *The Beginning of Guidance*, i,
16 (12th century)

6 The same thing does the divine voice here,
the thunder, repeat: *Da! Da! Da!* That is,
restrain yourselves, give, be compassionate.
Brihad-aranyaka Upanishad, 5, 2

7 Then spoke the thunder
DA
Datta: what have we given?
T.S. Eliot, *The Waste Land* (1922)

8 The one ceremony which has great value is
that of *Dhamma*. This ceremony includes,
regard for slaves and servants, respect for
teachers, restrained behaviour towards
living beings, and donations.
Ashoka, *Major Rock Edict*, IX (3rd century
BCE)

9 The Master said, Govern the people by regulations, keep order among them by chastisements, and they will flee from you, and lose all self-respect. Govern them by moral force, keep order among them by ritual, and they will keep their self-respect and come to you of their own accord.
Confucius, *Analects*, II, 3

10 The path of duty lies close at hand, yet we seek for it afar. Our business lies in what is simple, yet we seek for it in what is difficult. If every man would love his parents and treat his elders as they should be treated, the Empire would be at peace.
Mencius, IV (4th century BCE)

11 One who is poor in spirit and of a humble mind does not despise or make light of law, order, precepts and holy customs, nor yet of those who observe and cleave wholly to them.
Theologia Germanica, 26 (14th century)

12 They have very few laws, because, with their social system, very few laws are required.
Thomas More, *Utopia*, ii (1516)

13 Love, and do what you will.
Augustine of Hippo, *Epist. Joannis Tractatus*, vii (5th century)

14 The laws of God, the laws of man,
He may keep that will and can.
A.E. Housman, *Last Poems*, 'Lancer' (1922)

15 There is a very real evil consequent on ascribing a supernatural origin to the received maxims of morality. That origin consecrates the whole of them and protects them from being discussed or criticized.
John Stuart Mill, *Three Essays on Religion* (1874)

16 A state of temperance, sobriety and justice without devotion is a cold, lifeless, insipid condition of virtue, and is rather to be styled philosophy than religion.
Joseph Addison, *The Spectator*, 201 (1711)

---

126 CONSCIENCE

---

1 There was silence, and I heard a voice saying, Shall mortal man be more just than God?
Job, 4, 16–17

2 The work of the law written in their hearts, their conscience also bearing witness.
Romans, 2, 15

3 O God, thou hast endowed conscience with no material force to compel man's reluctant obedience. So give them inwardly a spiritual compulsion in which they will follow it out of choice and delight.
M. Kamel Hussein, *City of Wrong* (1959)

4 This selfsame breathing spirit, even the intelligent self, has entered this bodily self up to the hair and fingernail tips. Just as a razor might be hidden in a razor-case, or fire in a fire-receptacle.
Kaushitaki Upanishad, 4, 20

5 The Master said, Heaven begat the power that is in me.
Confucius, *Analects*, VII, 22

6 I have a certain divine sign from God . . . I have had it from childhood: it is a kind of voice, which whenever I hear it, always turns me back from something which I was going to do.
Plato, *Apology* [of Socrates], XIX

7 There is an agent in my soul which is perfectly sensitive to God. I am as sure of this as I am that I am alive.
Meister Eckhart, *Sermons*, 6 (13th–14th centuries)

8 My conscience is taken captive by God's word, I cannot and will not recant anything, for to act against our conscience is neither safe for us, nor open to us.
On this I take my stand. I can do no other. God help me. Amen.
Martin Luther, final answer at the Diet of Worms, 1521

9 God alone is Lord of the conscience; and hath left it free from the doctrines and commandments of men . . . So that to believe such doctrines or to obey such commands out of conscience, is to betray true liberty of conscience.
The Westminster Confession of Faith, XX (1643)

10 Since God hath assumed to himself the power and dominion of the conscience, who alone can rightly instruct and govern it,

therefore it is not lawful for any whatsoever, by virtue of any authority or principality they bear in the government of this world, to force the consciences of others.
The Chief Principles of the Christian Religion, as Professed by the People called the Quakers, XIV (1678)

11 Give me the liberty to know, to utter, and to argue freely according to conscience, above all liberties.
John Milton, *Areopagitica* (1644)

12 Look to your health; and if you have it, praise God, and value it next to a good conscience.
Izaak Walton, *The Compleat Angler*, 21 (1653)

13 Thus conscience doth make cowards of us all;
And thus the native hue of resolution Is sicklied o'er with the pale cast of thought.
William Shakespeare, *Hamlet*, III, i, 83–5 (*c.* 1603)

14 The establishment of this one thing [toleration] would take away all ground of complaints and tumults on account of conscience.
John Locke, *A Letter Concerning Toleration* (1692)

15 Conscience is a coward, and those whose faults it has not strength enough to prevent it seldom has justice enough to accuse.
Oliver Goldsmith, *The Vicar of Wakefield*, 13 (1766)

16 In many walks of life, a conscience is a more expensive encumbrance than a wife or a carriage.
Thomas de Quincey, *Confessions of an English Opium-Eater* (1822)

17 The Nonconformist Conscience makes cowards of us all.
Max Beerbohm, *King George the Fourth* (1894)

18 We see whither it has brought us . . . making strictness of the moral conscience so far the principal thing, and putting off for hereafter and for another world the care of being complete at all points.
Matthew Arnold, *Culture and Anarchy* (1869)

19 Conscience is the inner perception of objections to definite wish impulses that exist in us; but the emphasis is put upon the fact that this rejection does not have to depend on anything else, that it is sure of itself. This becomes even plainer in the case of a guilty conscience, where we become aware of the inner condemnation of such acts which realized some of our definite wish impulses.
Sigmund Freud, *Totem and Taboo* (1913)

20 There is another man within me, that's angry with me, rebukes, commands, and dastards me.
Thomas Browne, *Religio Medici*, i (1643)

21 The more faithfully you listen to the voice within you, the better you will hear what is sounding outside.
Dag Hammarskjöld, *Markings* (1961)

127 INDIVIDUAL BEHAVIOUR
See also 152. SOCIAL BEHAVIOUR

1 Keep thy tongue from evil, and thy lips from speaking guile. Depart from evil, and do good; seek peace, and pursue it.
Psalm, 34, 13–14

2 Whatsoever things are true, whatsoever things are honest, whatsoever things are just, whatsoever things are pure, whatsoever things are lovely, whatsoever things are of good report; if there be any virtue, and if there be any praise, think on these things.
Philippians, 4, 8

3 Fortunate are the believers, those who in their prayer are humble, those who turn away from vain talk, those who are active for almsgiving, those who restrain themselves.
Koran, 23, 1–5

4 He who controls the senses with the mind, and undertakes the Yoga of action with the action-senses, but is unattached to the fruits of action, he is the best.
Bhagavad-Gita, 3, 7

5 The eschewing of all evil, the perfecting of good deeds, the purifying of one's mind, this is the teaching of the Buddhas.
Dhammapada, 183

6 Tzu-kung asked about the true gentleman. The Master said, He does not preach what

he practises till he has practised what he preaches.
Confucius, *Analects*, II, 13

7 The Sage puts himself in the background; but is always to the fore. Remains outside; but is always there.
Is it not just because he does not strive for any personal end that all his personal ends are fulfilled?
Tao Te Ching, VII

8 They also serve who only stand and wait.
John Milton, *On His Blindness* (1673)

9 I am never to act otherwise than so *that I could also will that my maxim should become a universal law.*
Immanuel Kant, *Groundwork to a Metaphysics of Morals* (1785)

10 He who would do good to another man must do it in Minute Particulars: General Good is the plea of the scoundrel, hypocrite & flatterer, For Art & Science cannot exist but in minutely organized Particulars, And not in generalizing Demonstrations of the Rational Power. The Infinite alone resides in Definite and Determinate Identity.
William Blake, *Jerusalem*, Plate 55 (1804)

128 KARMA

1 When the voice of a dead man goes into fire . . . what then becomes of this person? . . . The two went away and deliberated. What they said was *karma* (action). What they praised was *karma*. Verily, one becomes good by good action, bad by bad action.
Brihad-aranyaka Upanishad, 3, 2, 13

2 On Karma alone be your interest, never on its fruits; let not the results of Karma be your motive, nor be your attachment to inaction.
Bhagavad Gita, 2, 47

3 It is because of the deeds one does, whether pure or impure, by means of this psycho-physical organism, that one is once again linked with another psycho-physical organism, and is not freed from one's evil deeds.
Milinda's Questions, 5, 420 (1st century)

4 Notwithstanding their pleasures and

relations, all men must suffer in due time the fruit of their works; as a coconut detaching itself from its stalk falls down, so life will end when its time is spent.
Sutra Kritanga, 1, 2, 1 (3rd century BCE)

5 Kabir, this body is like a forest and your own *karma* is like an axe: it is you who will destroy yourself, Kabir knows it very well!
Sākhi, 15, 60, in Charlotte Vaudeville, *Kabir* (1974)

129 EVIL AND SIN

1 I acknowledge my transgressions: and my sin is ever before me. Against thee, thee only, have I sinned, and done this evil in thy sight.
Psalm, 51, 3–4

2 It is no more I that do it, but sin that dwelleth in me.
Romans, 7, 17

3 To God belongs what is in the heavens and what is in the earth, that he may recompense those who do evil for what they have done, and may recompense those who do well, with the best reward.
Koran, 53, 32

4 Arjuna said: What impels this man to commit sin, even against his will, as if constrained by force?
The Blessed Lord said: It is desire, it is anger, arising from the element of passion; all-consuming, very sinful, know this to be your enemy on earth.
Bhagavad Gita, 3, 36–7

5 Man, cease from sins! For the life of man will come to an end. Men who are drowned in lust, as it were, and addicted to pleasure will acquire Karma which results in delusion.
Sutra-kritanga, 1, 2, 1 (3rd century BCE)

6 A man does not sin by commission only, but often by omission.
Marcus Aurelius, *Meditations*, 9, 5 (2nd century)

7 We have left undone those things which we ought to have done; And we have done

those things which we ought not to have done; And there is no health in us.
Book of Common Prayer, General Confession

8 A man's free choice avails only to lead him to sin, if the way of truth is hidden from him. And when it is plain to him what he should do and to what he should aspire, even then, unless he feels love and delight therein, he does not perform his duty, nor undertake it, nor attain to the good life.
Augustine of Hippo, *Of Spirit and Letter*, 5, (5th century)

9 We are not born in our full development, but with a capacity for good and evil; we are begotten as well without virtue as without vice, and before the activity of our own personal will there is nothing in man but what God has stored in him.
Pelagius, in Augustine, *Of Original Sin*, 14 (5th century)

10 Original sin is seen to be a hereditary depravity and corruption of our nature, diffused into all parts of the soul.
John Calvin, *Institutes of the Christian Religion*, ii, 31 (1559)

11 Be a sinner and sin strongly, but more strongly have faith and rejoice in Christ.
Martin Luther, *Epistolae*, i, 345 (1556)

12 Our religion is made so as to wipe out vices; it covers them up, nourishes them, incites them.
Michel de Montaigne, *Essais*, ii, xii (1580)

13 I saw not *sin*: for I believe it has no manner of substance nor no part of being, nor could it be known but by the pain it is cause of.
Julian of Norwich, *Revelations of Divine Love*, 13 (*c.* 1393)

14 Wilt thou forgive that sin where I begun,
  Which is my sin, though it were done
            before?
  Wilt thou forgive those sins through which I
            run,
  And do them still: though still I do deplore?
  When thou hast done, thou hast not done,
  For, I have more.
John Donne, *A Hymn to God the Father* (1633)

15 I never wonder to see men wicked, but I often wonder to see them not ashamed.
Jonathan Swift, *Thoughts on Various Subjects* (1706)

16 We must soften into a credulity below the milkiness of infancy to think all men virtuous. We must be tainted with a malignity truly diabolical, to believe all the world to be equally wicked and corrupt.
Edmund Burke, *Thoughts on the Cause of the Present Discontents* (1770)

17 Pleasure's a sin, and sometimes Sin's a pleasure.
Lord Byron, *Don Juan*, i, 133 (1824)

18 There is no sin except stupidity.
Oscar Wilde, *The Critic as Artist* (1891)

19 Really to sin, you have to be serious about it.
Henrik Ibsen, *Peer Gynt*, 5 (1867)

20 But evil is wrought by want of thought,
  As well as want of heart!
Thomas Hood, *The Lady's Dream* (1844)

21 Who has not a hundred times found himself committing a vile or stupid action, for no other reason than because he knows he should *not*? Have we not a perpetual inclination, in the teeth of our best judgement, to violate that which is *Law*, merely because we understand it to be such.
E.A. Poe, *The Black Cat* (1843)

22 Or, Lord, if too obdurate I,
  Choose thou, before that spirit die,
  A piercing pain, a killing sin,
  And to my dead heart run them in!
R.L. Stevenson, *The Celestial Surgeon* (1887)

23 It's harder to confess the sin that no one
            believes in
  Than the crime that everyone can
            appreciate.
  For the crime is in relation to the law
  And the sin is in relation to the sinner.
T.S. Eliot, *The Elder Statesman*, 3 (1958)

---

130 FALSEHOOD
See also 131. OATHS

---

1 They have taught their tongue to speak lies, and weary themselves to commit iniquity.
Jeremiah, 9, 5

2 The devil . . . when he speaketh a lie, he speaketh of his own: for he is a liar, and the father of it.
John, 8, 44

3 The penalty of the liar is that he is not
believed even when he speaks the truth.
Mishnah, *Sanhedrin*, 89

4 Look how they devise falsehood against
God; it is sufficient as a manifest deed of
guilt.
Koran, 4, 53

5 The rulers of the state are the only ones who
should have the privilege of lying for the
benefit of the state; no others may have
anything to do with it.
Plato, *Republic*, III, 389

6 To tell a falsehood is like the cut of a sabre,
for though the wound may heal, the scar of
it will remain.
Sa'di, *Gulistan*, 8, 98 (1258)

7 The devil can cite Scripture for his purpose.
An evil soul, producing holy witness,
Is like a villain with a smiling cheek,
A goodly apple, rotten at the heart.
William Shakespeare, *The Merchant of
Venice*, I, iii, 93–6 (*c.* 1596–8)

8 It is not the lie that passeth through the
mind, but the lie that sinketh in, and settleth
in it, that doth the hurt.
Francis Bacon, *Essays*, 'Of Truth' (1625)

9 And, after all, what is a lie? 'Tis but
The truth in masquerade, and I defy
Historians — heroes — lawyers — priests,
              to put
A fact without some leaven of a lie.
Lord Byron, *Don Juan*, 11, 37 (1824)

10 A falsehood is, in one sense, a dead thing;
but too often it moves about, galvanized by
self-will, and pushes the living out of their
seats.
S.T. Coleridge, *Aids to Reflection* (1825)

11 As hypocrisy is said to be the highest
compliment to virtue, the art of lying is the
strongest acknowledgment of the force of
truth.
William Hazlitt, *Table Talk* (1822)

12 The best liar is he who makes the smallest
amount of lying go the longest way.
Samuel Butler, *The Way of All Flesh* (1903)

13 Every violation of truth is not only a sort of
suicide in the liar, but is a stab at the health
of human society.
R.W. Emerson, *Essays* (1841)

14 The falsehood lies deep in the necessities of

existence, in secret fears and half-formed
ambitions, in the secret confidence
combined with a secret mistrust of
ourselves, in the love of hope and the dread
of uncertain days.
Joseph Conrad, *Under Western Eyes* (1911)

---

131 OATHS
See also 130. FALSEHOOD

---

1 Ye shall not swear by my name falsely,
neither shalt thou profane the name of thy
God: I am the LORD.
Leviticus, 19, 12

2 Swear not at all; neither by heaven; for it is
God's throne: nor by the earth; for it is his
footstool.
Matthew, 5, 34–5

3 God will not take you to task for vain words
in your oaths, but he will take you to task
for what your hearts have earned; God is
forgiving, gracious.
Koran, 2, 225

4 Let no wise man swear an oath falsely, even
in a trifling matter; for he who swears an
oath falsely is lost in this world and after
death.
Laws of Manu, VIII, 111

5 They were mere amateurs in legislative
work, or they could hardly have fancied an
oath a guarantee of moderation.
Plato, *Laws*, III, 692

6 We judge that Christian Religion doth not
prohibit, but that a man may swear when
the Magistrate requireth, in a cause of faith
and charity, so it be done according to the
Prophet's teaching, in justice, judgement
and truth.
Book of Common Prayer, Articles of
Religion XXXIX

7 I understand that Christ's injunction
concerning oaths is not at all so
insignificant, easy, and unimportant as it
had seemed to me when, among the oaths
prohibited by Christ, I had not included
oaths demanded by the State. And I asked
myself: Is it not said here that the oath is
also forbidden for which the Church
commentators are so anxious to make an
exception. Is not the oath here forbidden,

that very oath without which the separation of men into nations is impossible, and without which a military class is impossible?
Leo Tolstoy, *What I Believe* (1884)

8 Oaths are but words, and words but wind, Too feeble implements to bind.
Samuel Butler, *Hudibras*, 2, 2 (1663)

9 An oath, an oath, I have an oath in heaven: Shall I lay perjury upon my soul?
William Shakespeare, *The Merchant of Venice*, IV, i, 223–4 (*c.* 1596–8)

---

132 PRIDE, ENVY AND THEFT

1 Pride goeth before destruction, and a haughty spirit before a fall.
Proverbs, 16, 18

2 From within, out of the heart of men, proceed evil thoughts, adulteries, fornications, murders, thefts, covetousness, wickedness, deceit, lasciviousness, an evil eye, blasphemy, pride, foolishness.
Mark, 7, 21–2

3 Whoever exalts himself by means of words of the Torah, to what is he like? To a carcass flung into the road from which passers-by protect their nose and keep away.
Aboth d'Rabbi Nathan, xi (2nd century)

4 Do not walk boisterously upon the earth; verily thou wilt not make a hole in the earth, nor yet reach the mountains in stature.
Koran, 17, 39

5 Self-conceited, haughty, full of pride and arrogance of wealth, they do acts of religious worship in name alone.
Bhagavad Gita, 16, 17

6 All around I see Nothing pretending to be Something,
Emptiness pretending to be Fulness.
Confucius, *Analects*, VII, 25

7 Victorious warfare often enough leads men to pride, and through pride they take the taint of other vices innumerable.
Plato, *Laws*, 641

8 Pride, arrogance, boastfulness. This is the chronic disease. It is man's consideration of himself with the eye of self-glorification and self-importance and his consideration of others with the eye of contempt. The result as regards the tongue is that he says, 'I . . . I . . .'; as accursed Satan said: 'I am better than Adam; Thou hast created me of fire, but him Thou hast created of clay.'
Al-Ghazali, *The Beginning of Guidance*, 36 (12th century)

9 Sheer pride thinks to know and understand more than all men besides, therefore she chooses to prate more than all other men, and would fain have her opinions and speeches to be alone regarded and listened to, and counts all that others think and say to be wrong, and holds it in derision as a folly.
Theologia Germanica, 25 (1350)

10 None are more taken in by flattery than the proud, who wish to be the first and are not.
Baruch Spinoza, *Ethics*, 4 (1677)

11 He that is proud eats up himself: pride is his own glass, his own trumpet, his own chronicle; and whatever praises itself but in the deed, devours the deed in the praise.
William Shakespeare, *Troilus and Cressida*, II, iii, 150–3 (1602)

12 Discourses on humility are a source of pride to the vain, and of humility to the humble; few speak of humility humbly.
Blaise Pascal, *Pensées*, 377 (1670)

13 It is a fine thing to rise above pride, but you must have pride in order to do so.
Georges Bernanos, *The Diary of a Country Priest* (1936)

14 He that is down needs fear no fall,
He that is low no pride.
He that is humble ever shall
Have God to be his guide.
John Bunyan, *The Pilgrim's Progress* (1678)

15 Pride is seldom delicate; it will please itself with very mean advantages.
Samuel Johnson, *Rasselas* (1759)

16 A proud man is satisfied with his own good opinion, and does not seek to make converts to it.
William Hazlitt, *Characteristics* (1823)

17 Such boastings as the Gentiles use,
Or lesser breeds without the Law.
Rudyard Kipling, *Recessional* (1897)

18 Thou shalt not steal; an empty feat,
When it's so lucrative to cheat.
A.H. Clough, *The Latest Decalogue* (1862)

19 The faults of the burglar are the qualities of
the financier.
George Bernard Shaw, *Major Barbara*
(1905)

20 All stealing is comparative. If you come to
absolutes, pray who does not steal?
R.W. Emerson, *Essays, Second Series* (1844)

---

133 DRUNKENNESS AND GAMBLING

---

1 Wine is a mocker, strong drink is raging;
and whosoever is deceived thereby is not
wise.
Proverbs, 20, 1

2 Use a little wine for thy stomach's sake and
thine often infirmities.
1 Timothy, 5, 23

3 The tree from which Adam ate was the vine,
for there is nothing which brings
lamentation upon man so much as wine.
Mishnah, *Sanhedrin,* 70

4 They will ask thee about wine and
gambling; say: 'In both of them there is
great guilt, and also uses for the people, but
their guilt is greater than their usefulness.'
Koran, 2, 216

5 A Brahmin, stupefied by drunkenness, might
fall on something impure, or improperly
pronounce Vedic texts, or commit some
other act which ought not to be committed.
Laws of Manu, XI, 97

6 Drink, which even pious laymen had not
given up,
He, perfect of soul, will forbid
everywhere . . .
Gambling, which even great princes could
not abandon,
He will utterly put an end to, like the name
of his worst enemy.
Hemachandra, *Mahavira-charita,* 12, 59
(12th century)

7 These are the people who show politeness to
Islam. Often you see one of them reading
the Koran, attending the Friday assembly

and public Worship and praising the sacred
Law. Neverthless he does not refrain from
drinking wine and from various wicked and
immoral practices.
Al-Ghazali, *Deliverance from Error,* 149
(12th century)

8 Possibly a person may say: 'since envy,
cupidity and ambition are evil qualities and
lead to a man's ruin, I shall avoid them to
the uttermost and seek their contraries.' A
person following this principle will not eat
meat, nor drink wine, nor marry nor dwell
in a decent house, nor wear comely apparel
. . . This too is the wrong way, not to be
followed. Whoever persists in such a course
is termed a sinner.
Moses Maimonides, *Mishneh Torah,*
'Deoth', iii (12th century)

9 Drink moderately, for drunkenness neither
keeps a secret, nor observes a promise.
Miguel de Cervantes, *Don Quixote,* 2, 4
(1615)

10 Too much and too little wine. Give him
none, he cannot find truth; give him too
much, the same.
Blaise Pascal, *Pensées,* 71 (1670)

11 Drink not the third glass, which thou canst
not tame,
When once it is within thee.
George Herbert, *The Temple,* 'The Church
Porch', 5 (1633)

12 Malt does more than Milton can,
To justify God's way to man.
A.E. Housman, *A Shropshire Lad* (1896)

13 And Noah he often said to his wife when he
sat down to dine,
'I don't care where the water goes if it
doesn't get into the wine.'
G.K. Chesterton, *Wine and Water*
(1915)

14 Drunkenness is never anything but a
substitute for happiness. It amounts to
buying a dream of a thing when you have
not enough money to buy the dreamed-of
thing materially.
André Gide, *Journals* (1896)

15 Gambling is the great leveller. All men are
equal — at cards.
Nikolai Gogol, *Gamblers* (1842)

16 Adventure upon all the tickets in the lottery,
and you lose for certain; and the greater the

numbers of your tickets the nearer you approach to this certainty.
Adam Smith, *The Wealth of Nations*, 1, 10 (1776)

---

134 KILLING
See also 135. SUICIDE, 155. WAR

---

1 Thou shalt not kill.
Exodus, 20, 13

2 Ye have heard that it was said by them of old time, Thou shalt not kill: and whosoever shall kill shall be in danger of the judgement: But I say unto you, That whosoever is angry with his brother without a cause shall be in danger of the judgement.
Matthew, 5, 21–2

3 If one comes to kill you, be first and kill him.
Mishnah, *Sanhedrin*, 72

4 Do not kill the person whom God has made inviolable except with justification.
Koran, 17, 35

5 It was a great wickedness that we had resolved to commit, in that greedy for the joys of kingship we undertook to slay our kinsfolk. So if the enemy should come with weapons in their hands and slay me in battle, it would be a safer course for me to have no weapons and be unresisting.
Bhagavad Gita, 1, 45–6

6 All men tremble at punishment, all men fear death.
Likening others to oneself, one should neither slay nor cause to slay.
Dhammapada, 129

7 All breathing, existing, living, sentient creatures should not be slain, nor treated with violence, nor abused, nor tormented, nor driven away.
Acharanga Sutra, 1, 4, 1 (3rd century BCE)

8 All of a sudden he asked me: How can the Empire be brought to peace? I replied: By being united.
Who can give it unity? — I said: A man with no lust for killing men.
But who could place it in the charge of such a man? — Everybody in the Empire will help to do so.
Mencius, I (4th century BCE)

9 Who kills a man kills a reasonable creature, God's image; but he who destroys a good book, kills reason itself, kills the image of God, as it were in the eye.
John Milton, *Areopagitica* (1644)

10 Thou shalt not kill; but need'st not strive Officiously to keep alive.
A.H. Clough, *The Latest Decalogue* (1862)

11 Our life has so diverged from the teaching of Christ that that very divergence has become the chief hindrance to our understanding his teaching. We have so disregarded and forgotten all he said about our way of life — his injunction not merely not to kill, but not even to hate any man; not to defend ourselves but to turn the other cheek and to love our enemies.
Leo Tolstoy, *What I Believe* (1884)

12 Literally speaking, Ahimsa means 'non-killing.' But to me it has a world of meaning, and takes me into realms much higher, infinitely higher. It really means that you may not offend anybody; you may not harbour an uncharitable thought, even in connection with one who may consider himself to be your enemy.
M.K. Gandhi, in C.F. Andrews, *Mahatma Gandhi's Ideas* (1929)

---

135 SUICIDE
See also 134. KILLING

---

1 Saul took a sword, and fell upon it.
1 Samuel, 31, 4

2 He cast down the pieces of silver in the temple, and departed, and went and hanged himself.
Matthew, 27, 5

3 A person may not do injury to himself; some authorities declare that he may. But in view of the text, 'Surely your blood, the blood of your lives, will I require', which was interpreted to mean self-destruction, it is different.
Mishnah, *Baba Kamma*, 91

4 Do not kill yourselves. Surely God is compassionate to you, but whosoever does that in transgression and wrongfully, we shall one day roast in fire.
Koran, 4, 33–4

5 Libations of water shall not be offered to those who have committed suicide.
Laws of Manu, V, 89

6 To run away from trouble is a form of cowardice and, while it is true that the suicide braves death, he does it not for some noble object but to escape some ill.
Aristotle, *Nicomachean Ethics*, 3, 7

7 Amid the sufferings of life on earth, suicide is God's best gift to man.
Pliny the Elder, *Natural History*, 2 (1st century)

8 O! that this too too solid flesh would melt,
Thaw and resolve itself into a dew;
Or that the Everlasting had not fix'd
His canon 'gainst self-slaughter!
William Shakespeare, *Hamlet*, I, ii, 129–32 (*c.* 1603)

9 The thought of suicide is a great source of comfort: with it a calm passage is to be made across many a night.
Friedrich Nietzsche, *Beyond Good and Evil*, IV (1886)

10 There is but one truly serious philosophical problem and that is sucide. Judging whether life is or is not worth living amounts to answering the fundamental question of philosophy.
Albert Camus, *The Myth of Sisyphus* (1942)

11 The question is whether it is the way out, or the way in.
R.W. Emerson, *Journals* (1839)

---

136 REPENTANCE AND CONFESSION

1 I have heard of thee by the hearing of the ear: but now mine eye seeth thee. Wherefore I abhor myself, and repent in dust and ashes.
Job, 42, 5–6

2 Bring forth therefore fruits worthy of repentance.
Luke, 3, 8

3 Who says, 'I will sin and repent, and again sin and repent', will be denied the power of repenting.
Mishnah, *Joma*, 8, 9

4 Turn penitently to God as a body, O believers, maybe you will prosper.
Koran, 24, 31

5 What has been my chief transgression, that thou wouldst slay the friend who sings thy praises? Tell me, unconquerable Lord, and quickly I will approach thee sinless with my homage. Loose us from the sins committed by our fathers, and from those wherein we ourselves have offended.
Rig Veda, VII, 86

6 If I treated thee disrespectfully . . . for that I beg forgiveness of thee.
Bhagavad Gita, 11, 42

7 Every one, throughout the year, should regard himself as if he were half innocent and half guilty; and should regard the whole of mankind as half innocent and half guilty. If then he commits one more sin, he presses down the scale of guilt against himself and the whole world and causes its destruction.
Moses Maimonides, *Mishneh Torah*, 'Repentance' (12th century)

8 Whiteness most white. Ah, to be clean again
In mine own sight and God's most holy
                    sight!
To reach thro' any flood or fire of pain
Whiteness most white.
Christina Rossetti, *Verses* (1893)

9 Remorse sleeps during prosperity but awakes to bitter consciousness during adversity.
Jean-Jacques Rousseau, *Confessions* (1770)

10 You cannot lay remorse upon the innocent nor lift it from the heart of the guilty,
Unbidden shall it call in the night, that men may wake and gaze upon themselves.
Kahlil Gibran, *The Prophet* (1923)

11 If you have behaved badly, repent, make what amends you can and address yourself to the task of behaving better next time. On no account brood over your wrongdoing. Rolling in the muck is not the best way of getting clean.
Aldous Huxley, *Brave New World* (1932)

12 It is better to trust in God in humiliated repentance than to revel in the sense of sinlessness.
P.T. Forsyth, *Christian Perfection* (1899)

13 One had to practise the role of a penitent to be able to end up as a judge . . . I stand before all humanity recapitulating my shame without losing sight of the effect I am producing.
Albert Camus, *The Fall* (1956)

14 He said, 'I don't know how to repent.' That
was true: he had lost the faculty. He
couldn't say to himself that he wished his sin
had never existed, because the sin seemed to
him now so unimportant — and he loved
the fruit of it.
Graham Greene, *The Power and the Glory*
(1940)

---

137 FORGIVENESS
See also 39. COMPASSION AND MERCY

---

1 Hear thou in heaven thy dwelling place: and
when thou hearest forgive.
1 Kings, 8, 30

2 If ye forgive not men their trespasses, neither
will your Father forgive your trespasses.
Matthew, 6, 15

3 Whoever is compassionate towards his
fellow-creatures (and forgives wrongs done
to him), compassion is shown to him from
Heaven; and whoever is not compassionate
towards his fellow-creatures, compassion is
not shown to him from Heaven.
Mishnah, *Shabbath*, 151

4 The recompense of an evil deed is an evil
like it, so if anyone pardons and makes
peace, it rests with God to reward him.
Koran, 42, 38

5 Revenge is not always better, but neither is
forgiveness; learn to know them both, son,
so that there be no problem. Son, a man
who is always forgiving finds many things
wrong; his servants despise him, and so do
outsiders. No creatures ever bow to him,
and that is why the learned criticize being
always forgiving.
Mahabharata, 3, 29

6 'He abused me, he struck me, he overcame
me, he robbed me' — in those who harbour
such thoughts hatred will never cease. 'He
abused me, he struck me, he overcame me,
he robbed me' — in those who do not
harbour such thoughts hatred will cease.
Dhammapada, 3–4

7 The Beloved of the Gods believes that one
who does wrong should be forgiven as far as
it is possible to forgive him. And the Beloved
of the Gods conciliates the forest tribes of
his empire, but he warns them that he has

power even in his remorse, and he asks them
to repent, lest they be killed.
Ashoka, *Major Rock Edict*, XIII (3rd
century BCE)

8 God may pardon you, but I never can.
Elizabeth I, to the Countess of Nottingham,
in David Hume, *History of England under
the House of Tudor* (1759)

9 To err is human, to forgive divine.
Alexander Pope, *An Essay on Criticism*, 2,
325 (1711)

10 Forgiveness to the injured does belong, For
they ne'er pardon who have done the
wrong.
John Dryden, *The Conquest of Granada*, 2,
1, 2 (1671)

11 It is easier to forgive an enemy than to
forgive a friend.
William Blake, *Jerusalem* (1804)

12 You ought certainly to forgive them as a
christian, but never to admit them in your
sight, or allow their names to be mentioned
in your hearing.
Jane Austen, *Pride and Prejudice*, 57 (1813)

13 Wilt thou forgive that sin by which I won
Others to sin? and, made my sin their door?
Wilt thou forgive that sin which I did shun
A year, or two: but wallowed in, a score?
When thou hast done, thou hast not done,
For, I have more.
John Donne, *A Hymn to God the Father*
(1633)

14 Forgiveness is the answer to the child's
dream of a miracle by which what is broken
is made whole again, what is soiled is again
made clean.
Dag Hammarskjöld, *Markings* (1964)

---

138 RECONCILIATION AND
ATONEMENT

---

1 Make an atonement for thyself, and for the
people: and offer the offering of the people,
and make an atonement for them.
Leviticus, 9, 7

2 If thou bring thy gift to the altar, and there
rememberest that thy brother hath ought
against thee; leave there thy gift before the
altar, and go thy way; first be reconciled to

thy brother, and then come and offer thy gift.
Matthew, 5, 23–4

3 For transgressions between a man and his fellow man, the Day of Atonement does not atone unless he has first reconciled his fellow man.
Mishnah, *Yoma*, 8, 9

4 Wounds are an occasion for retaliation; so if anyone remit it as a gift, it is an expiation for him.
Koran, 5, 49

5 Ay' madam; he desires to make atonement
Between the Duke of Gloucester and your
    brothers.
William Shakespeare,*Richard III*, 1, iii, 36–7 (1591)

6 We must not come to make an attonement

with God . . . before we have made attonement with our Brother.
Samuel Clarke, *The marrow of ecclesiastical historie* (1650)

7 Strange to see how a good dinner and feasting reconciles everybody.
Samuel Pepys, *Diary,* 9 November 1685

8 That temple of silence and reconciliation where the enmities of twenty generations lie buried, in the Great Abbey.
T.B. Macaulay, *Warren Hastings* (1841)

9   There is a dark
Inscrutable workmanship that reconciles
Discordant elements, makes them cling
        together
In one society.
William Wordsworth, *The Prelude*, i (1850)

XVI
MEN AND WOMEN

139 PARENTS AND CHILDREN

1 Honour thy father and thy mother: that thy
days may be long upon the land which the
LORD thy God giveth thee.
Exodus, 20, 12

2 Children, obey your parents in the Lord: for
this is right . . . And, ye fathers, provoke not
your children to wrath: but bring them up in
the nurture and admonition of the Lord.
Ephesians, 6, 1–4

3 With parents exercise kindness, whether one
or both of them attain old age with thee; say
not to them 'Fie!' neither chide them, but
speak to them respectfully. And lower to
them the wing of humility out of
compassion and say: 'My Lord, have mercy
upon them as they brought me up when I
was young' . . . And slay not your children
for fear of poverty; We will provide for you
and them.
Koran, 17, 24–5, 33

4 When a family is destroyed, the eternal laws
of the family perish.
Bhagavad Gita, 1, 40

5 Good behaviour towards slaves and
servants, obedience to mother and father,
generosity towards friends, acquaintances,
and relatives, and towards ascetics and
priests, and abstention from killing living
beings. Father, son, brother, master, friend,
acquaintance, relative, and neighbour
should say, 'this is good, this we should do.'
Ashoka, *Major Rock Edict*, XI (3rd century
BCE)

6 The Master said, In serving his father and
mother a man may gently remonstrate with
them. But if he sees that he has failed to
change their opinion, he should resume an
attitude of deference and not thwart them.
He may feel discouraged, but not resentful.
Confucius, *Analects*, IV, 18

7 Which is the greatest service? The service of
parents is the greatest. Which is the greatest
of charges? The charge of oneself is the
greatest. I have heard of keeping oneself,
and thus being able to serve one's parents.
But I have not heard of failing to keep
oneself, and yet being able to serve one's
parents.
Mencius, IV, 19 (4th century BCE)

8 As fast as the children are born, they will be
received by the officers appointed for the
purpose, whether men or women, or both
. . . bringing the mothers to the nursery
when their breasts are full, but taking every
precaution that no mother shall know her
own child.
Plato, *Republic*, 5, 460

9 The oldest of all societies, and the only
natural one, is the family. Yet children are
tied to their father by nature only as long as
they need him for survival. When this needs
ends, the natural bond is dissolved. When
the children are freed from the obedience
they owed to their father, and he is freed
from responsibility towards them, both
parties regain their independence.
Jean-Jacques Rousseau, *The Social
Contract*, 2 (1762)

10 This is the reason why mothers are more
devoted to their children than fathers: it is

that they suffer more in giving them birth and are more certain that they are their own.
Aristotle, *Nicomachean Ethics*, 9, 7

11 Men are generally more careful of the breed of their horses and dogs than of their children.
William Penn, *Some Fruits of Solitude* (1693)

12 Parentage is a very important profession: but no test of fitness for it is ever imposed in the interests of the children.
George Bernard Shaw, *Everybody's Political What's What* (1944)

13 The joys of parents are secret, and so are their griefs and fears: they cannot utter the one, nor will they not utter the other.
Francis Bacon, *Essays* (1625)

14 You may give them your love but not your thoughts. For they have their own thoughts. You may house their bodies but not their souls. For their souls dwell in the house of tomorrow, which you cannot visit, even in your dreams.
Kahlil Gibran, *The Prophet* (1923)

15 A child's nature is too serious a thing to admit of its being regarded as a mere appendage to another being.
Charles Lamb, *Essays of Elia* (1823)

16 In the little world in which children have their existence, whosoever brings them up, there is nothing so finely perceived and so finely felt, as injustice.
Charles Dickens, *Great Expectations* (1861)

17 Children are completely egoistic; they feel their needs intensely and strive ruthlessly to satisfy them.
Sigmund Freud, *The Interpretation of Dreams* (1899)

---

140 WIDOWS AND ORPHANS

---

1 I delivered the poor that cried, and the fatherless, and him that had none to help him. The blessing of him that was ready to perish came upon me: and I caused the widow's heart to sing for joy.
Job, 29, 12–13

2 If any widow have children or nephews, let them learn first to shew piety at home, and to requite their parents.
1 Timothy, 5, 4

3 'Blessed is he that doeth righteousness at all times'; this refers to one who well nourishes his children while they are young. Another Rabbi declared that it refers to one who brings up orphans in his house and gets them married.
Mishnah, *Kethuboth*, 50

4 Did he not find an orphan and give thee
    shelter?
Did he not find thee erring, and guide thee?
Did he not find thee poor, and enrich thee?
So as for the orphan, be not overbearing;
And as for the beggar, scold not;
And as for the goodness of thy Lord,
    discourse of it.
Koran, 93, 6–11

5 Care must be taken of barren women, of those who have no sons, of those whose family is extinct, of wives and widows faithful to their lords.
Laws of Manu, VIII, 28

6 Do justice as long as thou abidest on earth. Calm the weeper and oppress not the widow. Do not oust a man from the property of his father.
Instruction for King Meri-ka-re (*c.* 2000 BCE)

7 Some undone widow sits upon my arm,
And takes away the use of 't; and my sword,
Glued to my scabbard with wrong'd
    orphans' tears
Will not be drawn.
Philip Massinger, *A New Way to Pay Old Debts* (1632)

8 Oh! teach the orphan-boy to read,
Or teach the orphan-girl to sew.
Alfred Tennyson, *Lady Clara Vere de Vere* (1842)

9 As God gives us to see the right, let us strive on to finish the work we are in: to bind up the nation's wounds; to care for him who shall have borne the battle, and for his widow and his orphan.
Abraham Lincoln, *Second Inaugural Address* (1865)

---

141 MAN
See also 50. HUMAN NATURE

---

1 The LORD God formed man of the dust of the ground, and breathed into his nostrils

the breath of life; and man became a living soul . . . but for Adam there was not found an help meet for him.
Genesis, 2, 7, 20

2 The husband is head of the wife, even as Christ is the head of the church.
Ephesians, 5, 23

3 Blessed art thou, O lord our God, King of the universe, who hast not made me a woman.
Hebrew Authorized Daily Prayer Book

4 We created man of an extract of clay, then we made him a drop in a sure receptacle, then we created the drop a clot, then we created the clot a morsel, then we created the morsel bones, and we clothed the bones with flesh, then we produced him, another creature.

5 It behoves a man to be 'male and female' always, so that his faith may remain stable, and in order that the Presence may never leave him.
Zohar, *Male and Female* (14th century)

6 He only is a perfect man who consists of three persons united: his wife, himself, and his offspring.
Laws of Manu, IX, 45

7 Verily, not for love of the husband is a husband dear, but for love of the Soul a husband is dear.
Brihad-aranyaka Upanishad, 2, 4, 5

8 The sense of mercy is found in all men; the sense of shame is found in all men; the sense of respect is found in all men; the sense of right and wrong is found in all men.
Mencius, VI (4th century BCE)

9 Man, when perfected, is the best of animals, but, when separated from law and justice, he is the worst of all.
Aristotle, *Politics*, 1, 2

10 Each man carries the vestiges of his birth — the slime and eggshells of his primeval past — with him to the end of his days. Some never become human, remaining frog, lizard, ant. Some are human above the waist, fish below.
Hermann Hesse, *Demian* (1919)

11 Man as we know him is a poor creature, but he is half-way between an ape and a god, and he is travelling in the right direction.
W.R. Inge, *Outspoken Essays*, Second Series (1922)

12 Man is an exception, whatever else he is. If he is not the image of God, then he is a disease of the dust.
G.K. Chesterton, *All Things Considered* (1908)

13 Man is amazing, but he is not a masterpiece . . . Perhaps the artist was a little mad. Eh? What do you think? Sometimes it seems to me that man is come where he is not wanted, where there is no place for him; for if not, why should he want all the place?
Joseph Conrad, *Lord Jim* (1900)

14 Men are but children of a larger growth.
John Dryden, *All for Love* (1678)

142 WOMAN
See also 50. HUMAN NATURE

1 Who can find a virtuous woman? for her price is far above rubies. The heart of her husband doth safely trust in her, so that he shall have no need of spoil.
Proverbs, 31, 10–11

2 Blessed art thou among women, and blessed is the fruit of thy womb.
Luke, 1, 42

3 Scripture places men and women on an equality with regard to all the laws of the Torah.
Mishnah, *Baba Kamma*, 15

4 The self-surrendering men and the self-surrendering women, the believing men and the believing women, the obedient men and the obedient women, the truthful men and the truthful women . . . God has prepared forgiveness for them and a mighty reward.
Koran, 33, 35

5 Though destitute of virtue, or seeking pleasure, or devoid of good qualities, yet a husband must be constantly worshipped as a god by a faithful wife.
Laws of Manu, V, 154

6 In the mornings all I have time to do is to stand at the bottom of his bed and say: 'Utha-Utha!' (up you get!), and after that I am far too busy cooking for him to have any time to waste in worshipping him!
Brahmin lady, quoted by S. Stevenson, *The Rites of the Twice-born* (1920)

7 How are we to conduct ourselves, lord, with
   regard to womankind?
As not seeing them, Ananda.
But if we should see them, what are we to
   do?
No talking, Ananda.
But if they should talk to us, lord, what are
   we to do?
Keep wide awake, Ananda.
Digha Nikaya, ii, 141 (3rd century BCE)

8 A monk should not trust women, knowing
   that they are full of deceit.
Sutra Kritanga, 1, 4, 1 (3rd century BCE)

9 A beautiful woman is like a snake:
   those who touch it get bitten!
But it dares not come near
those enamoured of the feet of Rām.
Sākhī, 30, in Charlotte
Vaudeville, *Kabir*, (1974)

10 The Valley Spirit never dies
   It is named the Mysterious Female.
And the Doorway of the Mysterious Female
Is the base from which Heaven and Earth
   sprang.
Tao Te Ching, VI

11 We shall have to select duly qualified
   women also, to share in the life and official
labours of the duly qualified men; since we
find that they are competent to the work,
and of kindred nature with the men.
Plato, *Republic*, 5, 456

12 I know that a woman is a dish for the gods,
   if the devil dress her not.
William Shakespeare, *Anthony and
Cleopatra*, v, ii, 71 (*c.* 1606–7)

13 Woman was God's second blunder.
Friedrich Nietzsche, *The Antichrist* (1888)

14 The nakedness of woman is the work of
   God.
William Blake, *The Marriage of Heaven and
Hell* (1793)

15 God made the rose out of what was left of
   woman at the creation. The great difference
is, we feel the rose's thorns when we gather
it, and the other's when we have had it some
time.
W.S. Landor, *Imaginary Conversations*
(1829)

16 There is in every true woman's heart a spark
   of heavenly fire, which lies dormant in the
broad daylight of prosperity, but which

kindles up and beams and blazes in the dark
hour of adversity.
Washington Irving, *The Sketch Book of
Geoffrey Crayon, Gent* (1820)

17 No coward soul is mine,
   No trembler in the world's storm-troubled
      sphere:
I see Heaven's glories shine,
And faith shines equal, arming me from
   fear.
Emily Brontë, *Last Lines* (1846)

18 A sexual theology . . . is the awareness of a
   variety of needs: — The need to recognize
that in the very midst of our current sexual
chaos and floundering there exists an
immense amount of longing for more
meaningful and more human sexual
relationships. — The need to wrestle with
the vastly important insights of recent
feminist theology concerning the sexist
limitations of much in Christian life and
thought.
J.B. Nelson, *Embodiment* (1978)

143 MARRIAGE

1 Therefore shall a man leave his father and
   his mother, and shall cleave unto his wife:
and they shall be one flesh.
Genesis, 2, 24

2 He that is married careth for the things that
   are of the world, how he may please his
wife.
1 Corinthians, 7, 33

3 Never have I called my wife by that word,
   but always 'my Home.'
Mishnah, *Shabbath*, 118

4 Among his signs is that he has created for
   you of your own species spouses that you
may dwell with them, and has set love and
mercy between you.
Koran, 30, 20

5 A twice-born man shall marry a wife of
   equal caste who is endowed with auspicious
bodily marks.
Laws of Manu, III, 4

6 If Heaven and Earth were not mated, the
   myriad things would not have been born. It
is by means of the great rite of marriage that

mankind subsists throughout the myriad generations.
Book of Rites, 50 (1st century BCE)

7 It would be an immense advantage for the wives and children to be common to all, if it were possible. But I expect there would be most controversy about the practicability of the scheme . . . Manifestly then our next care will be to make the marriage-union as sacred a thing as we possibly can: and this sanctity will attach to the marriages which are most for the public good.
Plato, *Republic*, 5, 457 8

8 Bourgeois marriage is in reality a system of wives in common and thus, at the most, what the Communists might possibly be reproached with, is that they desire to introduce, in substitution for a hypocritically concealed, an openly legalized community of women.
Karl Marx, *Communist Manifesto*, 2 (1848)

9 A Table of Kindred and Affinity wherein whosoever are related are forbidden in Scripture and our Laws to marry together. A man may not marry his Grandmother . . .
Book of Common Prayer (1662)

10 Church teachers were practically unanimous in teaching that the ministers of the sacrament are the contracting parties themselves, the nuptial blessing being an accessory.
G.H. Joyce, *Christian Marriage* (1948)

11 Holy men and women have used many mutual caresses in their marriage, truly loving but chaste caresses, tender but sincere.
François de Sales, *Introduction to the Devout Life* (1609)

12 How can a bishop marry? How can he flirt? The most he can say is, 'I will see you in the vestry after service.'
Sydney Smith, in Lady Holland, *Memoir* (1855)

13 Single life makes men in one instance to be like angels, but marriage in very many things makes the chaste pair to be like Christ.
Jeremy Taylor, *Holy Living* (1650)

14 One was never married, and that's his hell, another is, and that's his plague.
Robert Burton, *The Anatomy of Melancholy* (1621)

15 There is no more lovely, friendly and charming relationship, communion or company than a good marriage.
Martin Luther, *Table Talk* (1569)

16 Never marry but for love, but see that thou lovest what is lovely.
William Penn, *Some Fruits of Solitude* (1693)

17 A good marriage is that in which each appoints the other guardian of his solitude.
Rainer Maria Rilke, *Letters* (1910)

18 The joys of marriage are the heaven on
    earth,
Life's paradise, great princess, the soul's
    quiet.
John Ford, *The Broken Heart* (1633)

19 For the rest let him attend to his work, be glad in it, love his wife, be glad in her, bring up his children with joyfulness, love his fellow men, rejoice in life.
Søren Kierkegaard, *Training in Christianity* (1850)

20 He had loved Harriet. But he had married her in a muddled compromising impure deliberately blinded state, thinking this to be the best possible. He had committed the sin against the Holy Ghost.
Iris Murdoch, *The Sacred and Profane Love Machine* (1974)

144 POLYGAMY

1 Solomon clave unto these in love. And he had seven hundred wives, princesses, and three hundred concubines: and his wives turned away his heart.
1 Kings, 11, 2–3

2 A bishop then must be blameless, the husband of one wife.
1 Timothy, 3, 2

3 A man may marry as many wives as he pleases.
Mishnah, *Jebamoth*, 65

4 If you fear that you may not act with equity in regard to the orphans, marry such of the women as seem good to you, two or three or four. But if you fear that you may not be fair, then only one.
Koran, 4, 3

5 For the first marriage of twice-born men wives of equal caste are recommended; but for those who through desire proceed to marry again the following females, chosen according to the direct order of the castes, are most approved.
Laws of Manu, III, 12

6 There was a Brahmin who had four daughters. These four were wooed by four persons. The Brahmin could not decide to whom to give them, so he thought he would tell the matter to the Supreme Buddha . . . and he gave him all his daughters.
Jataka Tales, 200 (5th century)

7 According to the Rites man has the right to marry more than one wife, but woman shall not follow two masters. For it is said: 'A husband is Heaven, and Heaven cannot be shirked.' Therefore a wife cannot leave her husband.
Lady Pan Chao, *Women's Precepts*, V (2nd century)

8 It is, for instance, common to say that one sex is more 'monogamic' than the other sex, especially that men are 'polygamic' while women are 'monogamic.' Strictly speaking, such statements are meaningless. At the outset, it is obvious that since the sexes are born nearly equal in number (with, at the start, a preponderance of males), the natural order in a civilized society cannot work out as two wives for every male, and in the societies which recognize polygamy it is only practised by a small wealthy class.
Havelock Ellis, *The Psychology of Sex* (1936)

145 DIVORCE

1 Let him write her a bill of divorcement, and give it in her hand, and send her out of his house.
Deuteronomy, 24, 1

2 Whosoever shall put away his wife, saving for the cause of fornication, causeth her to commit adultery.
Matthew, 5, 32

3 He that desires to be divorced from his wife for any cause whatever (and many such causes happen among men), let him in writing give assurance that he will never cohabit with her any more.
Josephus, *Antiquities*, iv, viii, 23 (1st century)

4 When you divorce women, divorce them at their prescribed period; count the prescribed period and show piety towards God your Lord; do not expel them from their houses . . . and call as witnesses two persons of probity from amongst you.
Koran, 65, 1–2

5 The Prophet, peace and blessings of God be on him, said, 'The thing which is lawful but most disliked by God is divorce.'
A'bu Dawud, *Traditions*, 13, 3 (9th century)

6 Divorce both Faith and Reason from my Bed,
And take the Daughter of the Vine to spouse.
Omar Khayyám, *Rubáiyát*, 40 (11th century)

7 Neither by sale nor by repudiation is a wife released from her husband.
Laws of Manu, IX, 45

8 A loveless marriage is nothing but the empty husk of an outside matrimony, as undelightful and unpleasing to God as any other kind of hypocrisy.
John Milton, *The Doctrine and Discipline of Divorce* (1643)

9 Our marriage is dead, when the pleasure is fled:
'Twas pleasure first made it an oath.
John Dryden, *Songs* (1673)

10 What God hath joined together no man shall put asunder: God will take care of that.
George Bernard Shaw, *Getting Married* (1908)

11 Divorce is probably of nearly the same date as marriage. I believe, however, that marriage is some weeks more ancient.
Voltaire, *Philosophical Dictionary* (1764)

12 Seal then this bill of my Divorce to All
On whom those fainter beams of love did fall;
Marry those loves, which in youth scattered be
on Fame, Wit, Hopes (false mistresses) to thee.
John Donne, *A Hymn to Christ* (1633)

146 SEX
See also 46. THE FIRST HUMAN BEINGS

1 Let him kiss me with the kisses of his mouth: for thy love is better than wine.
The Song of Solomon, 1, 2

2 The wife hath not power of her own body, but the husband: and likewise also the husband hath not power of his own body, but the wife. Defraud ye not one the other.
1 Corinthians, 7, 4–5

3 Your women are to you as furrows; so come to your furrows as you wish, and forward for your souls; and fear God, and know that you shall meet him.
Koran, 2, 223

4 He comes to her and says:
I am this man; thou art that woman.
That woman, thou; this man am I . . .
I am the heaven; thou, the earth.
Come, let us two clasp together.
Brihad-aranyaka Upanishad, 6, 4, 20

5 In the beginning, the Lord of Beings created men and women, and in the form of commandments in a hundred thousand chapters, he laid down rules for regulating their existence with regard to Right, Gain, and Love . . . Sexual intercourse being a thing dependent on man and woman requires the application of proper means by them, and these means are to be learnt from the Kama Sutra. The non-application of proper means, which we see in the brute creation, is caused by their being unrestrained.
Kama Sutra, 1, 1; 2, 1–4 (5th century)

6 The Master said, I have never yet seen anyone whose desire to build up his moral power was as strong as sexual desire.
Confucius, *Analects*, IX, 17

7 The Tao of husband and wife represents the harmonious blending of Yin and Yang, it establishes man's communion with the spirits, it reaffirms the vast significance of Heaven and Earth, and the great order of human relationships.
Lady Pan Chao, *Women's Precepts* (2nd century)

8 As long as I have life,
I shall never forget
My beloved, with whom I slept.
Kojiki, i, 45 (712)

9 Augustine's theory of the transmission of original sin by way of the sexual urge which is the typical form of 'concupiscence', the lusting of flesh against spirit, has had a most disastrous influence upon much of traditional Christian ethics.
J. Burnaby, 'Augustine' in *A Dictionary of Christian Ethics* (1967)

10 The marriage act that is done out of sensuous pleasure is a lesser sin than fornication.
Thomas Aquinas, *Summa Theologica*, II, 9, 154 (13th century)

11 The Apostle doth confess, that concupiscence and lust hath of itself the nature of sin.
Book of Common Prayer, Articles of Religion IX

12   Nor turned I ween
Adam from his fair Spouse, nor *Eve* the Rites
Mysterious of connubial Love refus'd:
Whatever Hypocrites austerely talk
Of purity and place and innocence,
Defaming as impure what God declares
Pure, and commands to some, leaves free to all.
John Milton, *Paradise Lost*, IV, 742–7

13 Since sex-teaching was done in the initiation schools when the Africans were still heathens, and since all that and the sex-behaviour that went with it now belongs to the bad old ways we have left behind us, they now associate all sex-talks with heathenism, and they think that since they are now Christians it has become something not to talk about, and certainly not with religion and in church.
Mia Brandel-Syrier, *Black Woman in Search of God* (1962)

14 Chastity is the most unpopular of the Christian virtues. There is no getting away from it: the Christian rule is, 'Either marriage, with complete faithfulness to your partner, or else total abstinence.'
C.S. Lewis, *Mere Christianity* (1952)

15 To drive home the close parallel between the sexual act and the mystical union with God may seem blasphemous today. Yet the blasphemy is not in the comparison, but in the degrading of the one act of which man is capable that makes him like God both in the intensity of his union with his partner and in the fact that by this union he is a co-creator with God.
R.C. Zaehner, *Mysticism Sacred and Profane* (1957)

16 The sexual embrace can only be compared with music and with prayer.
Havelock Ellis, *On Life and Sex* (1937)

17 Coitus is a recurrent act of thanksgiving.

Enjoyable intercourse, far from leading to
reduced frequency, seeks repetition.
J. Dominian, *The Tablet,* 'Love's Enemy'
(1983)

18 With the new understanding of the dignity
of woman, and her place in society, there
has been an appreciation of the value of love
in marriage and of the meaning of intimate
married life in the light of that love.
Papal Encyclical, *Humanae Vitae,* 29 July
1968

19 Parents need to remember that having
children is a venture in faith, requiring a
measure of courage and confidence in God's
goodness. Too cautious a reckoning of the
costs may be as great an error as failure to
lift the God-given power of procreation to
the level of ethical decision.
**United States National Council of
Churches,** statement on Responsible
Parenthood (1961)

20 One of the greatest mistakes of Christian
thinking through the centuries has been that
sharp separation so many theologians and
spiritual guides have made between 'love
carnal' and 'love seraphick.' There are really
no sharp lines of distinction between
'sacred' and 'profane' love.
Joseph Needham, address at Caius Chapel,
Cambridge (1976)

---

147 CONTRACEPTION

1 He spilled it on the ground, lest that he
should give seed to his brother. And the
thing which he did displeased the LORD:
wherefore he slew him also.
Genesis, 38, 9–10

2 The time is short: it remaineth, that both
they that have wives be as though they had
none.
1 Corinthians, 7, 29

3 It does not matter if you do not do it, for
every soul that is to be born up to the day of
resurrection will be born.
Mishkat, 13, 6 (14th century)

4 Tantra represents a thoroughgoing practical
system for manipulating and focusing
human libido, enhancing it, and then
withdrawing it completely from the passing

and valueless phenomena of the world and
directing it instead to a transcendent object.
Philip Rawson, *The Art of Tantra* (1973)

5 Yang is modelled after fire, Yin after water.
Just as water can quench fire, so Yin can
diminish Yang. If the contact lasts too long,
the Yin essence will grow stronger than his
own Yang essence, whereby the latter will
be harmed.
Fang-nei-pu-i, *Healthy Sex Life* (7th
century)

6 Jewish law and tradition look upon it as
wrong. The blessing of God is not to be
wasted for any reason.
M. Lamm, *The Jewish Way in Love and
Marriage* (1980)

7 The commitment to responsible parenthood
requires that husband and wife, keeping a
right order of priorities, recognize their own
duties towards God, themselves, their
families and human society. From this it
follows that they are not free to act as they
choose in the service of transmitting life . . .
Excluded is any action, which either before,
at the moment of, or after sexual
intercourse, is specifically intended to
prevent procreation.
Papal Encylical, *Humanae Vitae* (1968)

8 Is it beautiful, for instance, is it productive
        of good
That the Roman Catholic hierarchy should
        be endlessly discussing at this
        moment
Their shifting theology of birth control, the
        Vatican
Claiming the inspiration of the Holy Spirit?
        No, it is not good.
Stevie Smith, *How do you see?* (1972)

9 Holding that the purpose of the marital act
is to serve the 'one-flesh' union, the
Protestant consensus rejects any bondage to
the biological function. Husbands and wives
are free to use the gifts of science to promote
or to defer conception.
R.M. Fagley, 'Procreation' in *A Dictionary
of Christian Ethics* (1967)

---

148 INFIDELITY AND ADULTERY

1 The adulterer and the adulteress shall surely
be put to death.
Leviticus, 20, 10

2 He that is without sin among you, let him
first cast a stone at her.
John, 8, 7

3 Whoso engages in much gossip with women
brings evil upon himself, neglects the study
of the Torah, and will in the end inherit
Gehinnom.
Mishnah, *Pirke Aboth*, 1, 5

4 The fornicatress and the fornicator —
scourge each of them with a hundred
stripes; let no pity affect you in regard to
them.
Koran, 24, 2

5 Men who commit adultery with the wives of
others, the king shall cause to be marked by
punishments which cause terror, and
afterwards banish.
Laws of Manu, VIII, 352

6 Liaison with another's wife
is just like eating garlic:
You may eat it in a corner,
But in the end, it will be found out!
Sākhi, 30, 1, in Charlotte Vaudeville, *Kabir*
(1974)

7 It is natural for a woman to be wild with her
husband when he goes in for secret love.
Euripides, *Medea* (5th century BCE)

8 Thou shalt not die: die for adultery! No:
The wren goes to't, and the small gilded fly
Does lecher in my sight.
William Shakespeare, *King Lear*, IV, vi,
111–13 (1604–5)

9 Do not adultery commit;
Advantage rarely comes of it.
A.H. Clough, *The Latest Decalogue* (1862)

10 Adultery is an evil only inasmuch as it is a
theft; but we do not steal that which is given
to us.
Voltaire, *Philosophical Dictionary* (1764)

11 What men call gallantry, and gods adultery,
Is much more common where the climate's
sultry.
Lord Byron, *Don Juan*, i (1819)

---

149 PROSTITUTION

---

1 Their mother hath played the harlot: she
that conceived them hath done shamefully:
for she said, I will go after my lovers.
Hosea, 2, 5

2 Know ye not that he which is joined to an
harlot is one body? for two, saith he, shall
be one flesh.
1 Corinthians, 6, 16

3 Avoid fornication, verily it has become an
indecency, and is bad as a way.
Koran, 17, 34

4 When a courtesan takes up with a man from
love, the action is natural; but when she
resorts to him for the purpose of getting
money, her action is artificial or forced.
Even in the latter case, however, she should
conduct herself as if her love were indeed
natural, because men repose their
confidence on those women who apparently
love them.
Kama Sutra, VI, 1 (5th century)

5 Take away the sewer and you will fill the
palace with pollution . . . Take away
prostitutes from the world and you will fill it
with sodomy.
Thomas Aquinas, *De regimine principium*,
1, 14 (13th century)

6 Men make necessities of their own, and then
find ways to satisfy them.
Jeremy Taylor, *Holy Living* (1650)

7 Prisons are built with stones of law, brothels
with bricks of religion.
William Blake, *The Marriage of Heaven and
Hell* (1790)

8 It is self-evident that the abolition of the
present system of production must bring
with it the abolition of the community of
women springing from that system, i.e., of
prostitution both public and private.
Karl Marx, *The Communist Manifesto*, 2
(1848)

9 Men will pay large sums to whores, for
telling them they are not bores.
W.H. Auden, *New Year Letter* (1940)

10 What if I am a prostitute, what business has
society to abuse me? . . . If I am a hideous
cancer in society, are not the causes of the
disease to be sought in the rottenness of the
carcass?
Letter in *The Times* (24 February 1858)

150 CELIBACY
See also 67. MONKS AND NUNS, 89.
ASCETICISM AND WORLD-DENIAL

1 Thou shalt not take thee a wife, neither shalt thou have sons or daughters in this place.
Jeremiah, 16, 2

2 The unmarried and widows, It is good for them if they abide even as I.
1 Corinthians, 7, 8

3 Monasticism, they invented it, We did not prescribe it for them, except it arose out of desire for the satisfaction of God.
Koran, 57, 27

4 Brahmins who know such a soul overcome desire for sons, desire for wealth, desire for worlds, and live the life of mendicants.
Brihad-aranyaka Upanishad, 3, 5

5 He whose passions are destroyed, who is indifferent to food, who has perceived the nature of release and unconditioned freedom, his path is difficult to understand like that of birds through the sky.
Dhammapada, 93

6 I strictly charge all the brethren not to hold conversation with women so as to arouse suspicion, nor to take counsel with them.
Rule of St Francis, 11 (1223)

7 Bishops, Priests, and Deacons, are not commanded by God's Law, either to vow the estate of single life, or to abstain from marriage: therefore it is lawful for them, as for all other Christian men, to marry at their own discretion, as they shall judge the same to serve better to godliness.
Book of Common Prayer, Articles of Religion XXXII

8 A virgin priest the altar best attends,
A state the Lord commands not, but
    commends.
Thomas Ken, *Hymns* (1695)

9 Marriage has many pains, but celibacy has no pleasures.
Samuel Johnson, *Rasselas* (1759)

10 Chastity is not chastity in an old man, but a disability to be unchaste.
John Donne, *Sermons* (1619)

11 The essence of chastity is not the suppression of lust, but the total orientation of one's life towards a goal.
Dietrich Bonhoeffer, *Letters and Papers from Prison* (1953)

12 Anarchists don't marry. It's well known. They can't. It would be apostasy.
Joseph Conrad, *The Secret Agent* (1907)

151 HOMOSEXUALITY

1 If a man also lie with mankind, as he lieth with a woman, both of them have committed an abomination: they shall surely be put to death.
Leviticus, 20, 13

2 There are some eunuchs, which were so born from their mother's womb.
Matthew, 19, 12

3 Those of your women who commit indecency — call four witnesses against them, and if they testify — confine to their houses until death complete their term, or God appoint a way for them. The couples among you who commit it, revile, and if they repent and reform, turn from them.
Koran, 4, 19–20

4 A woman who pollutes a damsel shall instantly have her head shaved, or two fingers cut off, and be made to ride through the town on a donkey . . . A twice-born man who commits an unnatural offence with a male . . . shall bathe, dressed in his clothes.
Laws of Manu, VIII, 370; XI, 175

5 The woman who is a slice of the original female is attracted by women rather than by men — in fact she is a Lesbian — while men who are slices of the male are followers of the male, and show their masculinity throughout their boyhood by the way they make friends with men, and the delight they take in lying beside them and being taken in their arms.
Plato, *Symposium*, 191

6 The law of continence enjoined on priests, which was first ordained to the prejudice of

women, brings sodomy into all the Holy
Church.
The Lollard Conclusions, 3 (1394)

7 The legend of the 'persecution' of the
homosexual by the church is a gross and
unwarranted exaggeration . . . Indeed, there
is much to indicate that by retaining in its
hands the spiritual punishment of the
sodomist, the Church actually shielded him

from the penalties of the secular power.
D.S. Bailey, *Homosexuality and the
Western Christian Tradition* (1955)

8 A sexual theology . . . the need not only to
understand those whose sexuality is
expressed differently from that of the
majority, but also to learn from them.
J.B. Nelson, *Embodiment* (1978)

XVII
SOCIETY

152 SOCIAL BEHAVIOUR
See also 127. INDIVIDUAL BEHAVIOUR

1 I put on righteousness, and it clothed me: my judgment was as a robe and a diadem. I was eyes to the blind, and feet was I to the lame.
Job, 29, 14–15

2 Be kindly affectioned one to another with brotherly love; in honour preferring one another.
Romans, 12, 10

3 Let there be community of you inviting to what is good, urging what is reputable and restraining from what is disreputable.
Koran, 3, 100

4 In this world a twofold basis of religion has been declared by me: the discipline of knowledge for the followers of the method of reasoning, and the discipline of action for the followers of the method of discipline.
Bhagavad Gita 3, 3

5 The Sage relies on actionless activity, carries on wordless teaching, but the myriad creatures are worked upon by him.
He does not disown them, he rears them but does not lay claim to them; controls them but does not lean upon them.
Tao Te Ching, II

6 You are a citizen of the world, and a part of it; not a subservient but a principal part. You are capable of comprehending the divine order, and of considering the connections of things. What then does the character of a citizen promise? To hold no private interest, to deliberate about nothing as a separate individual but, like the hand and foot, which, if they had reason and understood the constitution of nature, would never pursue or desire anything without reference to the whole being.
Epictetus, *Discourses,* 2, 10 (2nd century)

7 Friendship may be shortly defined, 'a perfect conformity of opinions upon all religious and civil subjects, united with the highest degree of mutual esteem and affection.'
Cicero, *On Friendship* (1st century BCE)

8 Christians are not distinguished from the rest of mankind either in locality or in speech or in customs . . . They obey the established laws, and they surpass the laws in their own lives. They love all men, and they are persecuted by all . . . In a word, what the soul is in the body, this the Christians are in the world.
To Diognetus, 5–7 (2nd century)

9 The primitive Christian demonstrated his faith by his Virtues; and it was very justly supposed that the divine persuasion, which enlightened or subdued the understanding, must at the same time purify the heart and direct the actions of the believer.
Edward Gibbon, *The History of the Decline and Fall of the Roman Empire,* 15 (1776)

10 Consider the wise and sensible arrangements of Utopia, where everything is well ordered with very few laws, virtue is held in praise and esteem, and yet every man has plenty since all things are in common.
Thomas More, *Utopia,* i (1516)

11 We must divide all the children of Adam
    into two classes; the first belong to the
    kingdom of God, the second to the
    kingdom of the world . . . The one to produce piety,
    the other to bring about external peace and
    prevent evil deeds; neither is sufficient in the
    world without the other.
    Martin Luther, *Secular Authority*, XI (1523)

12 The Orthodox doctrine of *sobornost*
    [all-togetherness] achieves a nice balance. It
    avoids the West's occasional overemphasis
    on the claim of individuality which may end
    by alienating the person from the mystical
    body of Christ. On the other hand, it also
    avoids an over-valuation of a collective that
    kills all individuality, such as has emerged
    from the Bolshevik social doctrine.
    Ernst Benz, *The Orthodox Church* (1963)

13 No Man is an *Island*, entire of it self; every
    man is a piece of the *Continent*, a part of the
    main.
    John Donne, *Devotions*, Meditation XVII,
    (1624)

14 The noblest motive is the public good.
    Richard Steele, *The Spectator*, 200 (1712)

15 There is an imperative which commands a
    certain conduct immediately, without
    having as its condition any other purpose to
    be attained by it. The imperative is
    Categorical . . . This imperative may be
    called that of morality.
    Immanuel Kant, *Groundwork to a
    Metaphysic of Morals*, II (1785)

16 It is the greatest happiness of the greatest
    number that is the measure of right and
    wrong.
    Jeremy Bentham, *Introduction to Principles
    of Morals and Legislation* (1789)

17 Absolute morality is the regulation of
    conduct in such a way that pain shall not be
    inflicted.
    Herbert Spencer, *Essays*, iii (1891)

18 All political economy founded on
    self-interest being but the fulfilment of that
    which once brought schism into the Policy
    of angels, and ruin into the Economy of
    Heaven.
    John Ruskin, *Unto This Last* (1860)

19 The more these conscious illusions of the
    ruling classes are shown to be false and the
    less they satisfy common sense, the more
    dogmatically they are asserted and the more

deceitful, moralizing and spiritual becomes
the language of established society.
Karl Marx, *German Ideology* (1846)

20 The immediate service of all human beings
    becomes a necessary part of the endeavour
    simply because *the only way to find God
    is to see him in his creation and to be one
    with it.*
    Bede Griffiths, *Christ in India* (1966)

---

153 THE STATE AND RULERS

---

1 Hear therefore, ye kings, and understand;
   Learn, ye judges of the ends of the earth . . .
   Because your dominion was given you from
       the Lord,
   And your sovereignty from the Most High.
   Wisdom, 6, 1–3

2 Let every soul be subject unto the higher
   powers. For there is no power but of God:
   the powers that be are ordained of God.
   Romans, 13, 1

3 Lo, we have made thee a vice-gerent [caliph]
   in the earth, so judge between men in truth.
   Koran, 38, 25

4 Of a king, the religious vow is his readiness
   to action . . . In the happiness of his subjects
   lies his happiness; in their welfare his
   welfare; whatever pleases him he shall not
   consider as good, but whatever pleases his
   subjects he shall consider as good.
   Kautilya, *Artha-shastra*, 1, 19 (3rd century
   BCE)

5 The enlightened and worthy ruler . . .
   personally grasps the plough handle and
   ploughs a furrow, plucks the mulberry
   himself and feeds the silkworms, breaks new
   ground to increase the grain supply and
   opens the way for a sufficiency of clothing
   and food. In this way he serves the basis of
   earth. He sets up schools for the nobles and
   in the towns and villages to teach filial piety
   and brotherly affection, reverence and
   humility. He enlightens the people with
   education and moves them with rites and
   music. Thus he serves the basis of man.
   Tung Chung-shu, *Deep Significance of the
   Spring and Autumn Annals* (2nd century
   BCE)

6 When Marduk commanded me to guide the

people rightly and to direct the land, I established law and justice in the language of the land in order to promote the welfare of the people.
Code of Hammurabi (17th century BCE)

7 We must select from the whole body of guardians those individuals who appear to us, after due observation, to be remarkable above others for the zeal with which, through their whole life, they have done what they have thought advantageous to the state, and inflexibly refused to do what they thought the reverse.
Plato, *Republic*, III, 412

8 There is no vice more detestable than avarice, more especially in great men, and such as bear sway in the government of a state. For it is not only mean for a man to make a prey and advantage of the commonwealth, but even impious and abominable.
Cicero, *Offices*, 2, 22 (1st century BCE)

9 We pray also for emperors, for their ministers and for them that are in power, for the welfare of the world, for peace therein, for the delay of the end.
Tertullian, *Apology*, 39 (3rd century)

10 He said that about noon, when the day was already beginning to decline, he saw with his own eyes the trophy of a cross of light in the heavens, above the sun, and bearing the inscription, CONQUER BY THIS. At this sight he himself was struck with amazement, and his whole army also, which followed him on this expedition, and witnessed the miracle.
Eusebius, *Life of Constantine*, i, 29 (4th century)

11 Cuius regio, eius religio [In a prince's country, the prince's religion].
Peace of Augsburg (1555)

12 Had I but served God as diligently as I have served the King, he would not have given me over in my gray hairs.
Thomas Wolsey, quoted by G. Cavendish, *Negotiations of Thomas Woolsey* (1641)

13 We give not to our Princes the ministering either of God's Word, or of the Sacraments, . . . but that only prerogative, which we see to have been given always to all godly Princes in Holy Scriptures by God himself; that is, that they should rule all estates and degrees committed to their charge by God,

whether they be Ecclesiastical or Temporal, and restrain with the civil sword the stubborn and evildoers.
Book of Common Prayer, Articles of Religion XXXVII

14 That famous saying of Plato's is always quoted: 'Happy the states where either philosophers are kings or kings are philosophers!' But if you look at history you will find that no state has been so plagued by its rulers as when power has fallen into the hands of some dabbler in philosophy or literary addict.
Desiderius Erasmus, in *In Praise of Folly* (1511)

15 Men have dreamed up republics and principalities which in truth have never been known to exist. The gulf between how one does live and how one should is so wide that a man who neglects what is actually done for what should be done finds the way to self-destruction rather than self-preservation . . . Therefore if a prince wants to maintain his rule he must learn how not to be virtuous, and to make use of this or not according to his needs.
Niccolo Machiavelli, *The Prince*, 15 (1532)

16 Government even in its best state is but a necessary evil; in its worst state an intolerable one; for when we suffer, or are exposed to the same miseries *by a government*, which we might expect in a country *without government*, our calamity is heightened by reflecting that we furnish the means by which we suffer. Government, like dress, is the badge of lost innocence.
Thomas Paine, *Common Sense* (1776)

17 We hold these truths to be sacred and undeniable, that all men are created equal and independent, that from that equal creation they derive rights inherent and inalienable, among which are the preservation of life, and liberty, and the pursuit of happiness; that to secure these ends, governments are instituted among men.
Thomas Jefferson, Original Draft for the Declaration of Independence (1776)

18 The third and most cogent reason for restricting the interference of government is the great evil of adding unnecessarily to its power . . . A State which dwarfs its men, in order that they may be more docile instruments in its hands even for beneficial

purposes — will find that with small men no great thing can really be accomplished.
John Stuart Mill, *On Liberty* (1859)

19 Christianity popularized an important opinion, already implicit in the teaching of the Stoics, but foreign to the general spirit of antiquity — I mean, the opinion that a man's duty to God is more imperative than his duty to the State.
Bertrand Russell, *History of Western Philosophy* (1946)

20 Every actual state is corrupt. Good men must not obey the laws too well.
R.W. Emerson, *Essays*, Second Series, 'Politics' (1844)

21 The unselfish and intelligent may begin a movement — but it passes away from them. They are not the leaders of a revolution. They are its victims . . . There have been in every revolution hearts broken by such successes.
Joseph Conrad, *Under Western Eyes* (1911)

22 It was a mistake in the system; perhaps it lay in the precept which until now he had held to be incontestable, in whose name he had sacrificed others and was himself being sacrificed: in the precept, that the end justifies the means. It was this sentence which had killed the great fraternity of the Revolution and made them all run amuck.
Arthur Koestler, *Darkness at Noon* (1940)

23 The ties between Us and Our people have always stood upon mutual trust and affection. They do not depend upon mere legends and myths. They are not predicated upon the false conception that the Emperor is divine and that the Japanese people are superior to other races and are fated to rule the world.
Japanese Imperial Rescript, 1 January 1946

---

154 CAPITAL PUNISHMENT

1 Whoso sheddeth man's blood, by man shall his blood be shed.
Genesis, 9, 6

2 Ye have heard that it hath been said, An eye for an eye, and a tooth for a tooth; But I say unto you, That ye resist not evil: but

whosoever shall smite thee on thy right cheek, turn to him the other also.
Matthew, 5, 38–9

3 A Sanhedrin which executed a person once in seven years was called destructive. Rabbi Eleazer ben Azariah said, Once in seventy years.
Mishnah, *Makkoth*, 1, 10

4 The recompense of those who make war on God and his messenger, and exert themselves to cause corruption in the land, is that they should be killed or crucified . . . or that they should be banished from the land.
Koran, 5, 37

5 A just king shall not cause a thief to be put to death, unless taken with the stolen goods in his possession.
Laws of Manu, LX, 270

6 The man — he was the same one who had administered the poison — kept his hand upon Socrates, and after a little while examined his feet and legs, then pinched his foot hard and asked if he felt it. Socrates said no. Then he did the same to his legs, and moving gradually upward in this way let us see that he was getting cold and numb. Presently he felt him again and said that when it reached the heart, Socrates would be gone.
Plato, *Phaedo*, 117–18

7 Whenever Diocletian . . . saw a field more carefully tilled or a house more elegantly adorned than usual, straightway an accusation and capital sentence was prepared for the owner, as though he could not spoil his neighbour's goods without shedding of blood.
Lactantius, *De mortibus persecutorum*, 7 (4th century)

8 Manslaughter in war, or by pretended law of justice for a temporal cause, without spiritual revelation, is expressly contrary to the New Testament, which indeed is the law of grace and full of mercies.
Lollard Conclusions, 10 (1394)

9 The Laws of the Realm may punish Christian men with death, for heinous and grievous offences.
Book of Common Prayer, Articles of Religion XXXVII

10 Provided always, that no man, under the

pretence of conscience, prejudice his neighbour in his life or estate.
The Chief Principles of the Christian Religion, as Professed by the People Called the Quakers, XIV (1678)

11 What can we think of that is more frightful, when one looks at it with an unprejudiced eye, than the thought of a human being who is condemned to the flames because he is unwilling to break the faith that he has sworn to keep with the true God?
P. Bayle, *Dictionnaire historique et critique*, i (1702)

12 THE INQUISITOR. One gets used to it. Habit is everything. I am accustomed to the fire: it is soon over. But it is a terrible thing to see a young and innocent creature crushed between these mighty forces, the Church and the Law.
George Bernard Shaw, *Saint Joan*, vi (1923)

13 Upon these human shambles, I, who never raised this hand in prayer till now, call down the wrath of God! On that black tree, of which I am the ripened fruit, I do invoke the curse of all its victims, past, and present, and to come.
Charles Dickens, *Barnaby Rudge*, 77 (1841)

14 The Government . . . decided to bring forward to December 1969 the decision to make the abolition permanent . . . It was an overwhelming and decisive result which finally ended capital punishment for murder in Britain.
Annual Register, 4 (1969)

15 We never remember a capital verdict upon such insufficient evidence.
The Spectator (1868)

16 The Governor was strong upon
The Regulation Act:
The Doctor said that Death was but
A scientific fact:
And twice a day the Chaplain called,
And left a little tract.
Oscar Wilde, *The Ballad of Reading Gaol*, III, iii (1898)

17 The scaffold is a sort of monster created by the judge and the workman, a spectre which seems to live with a kind of unspeakable life, drawn from all the death which it has wrought.
Victor Hugo, *Les Misérables*, i, 4 (1862)

18 When a man knows he is to be hanged in a

fortnight, it concentrates his mind wonderfully.
Samuel Johnson, in Boswell, *Life of Samuel Johnson* (19 September 1777)

19 It is far more ignominious to die by justice than by an unjust sedition.
Blaise Pascal, *Pensées*, 789 (1670)

20 It is fairly obvious that those who are in favour of the death penalty have more affinity with assassins than those who are not.
Rémy de Goncourt, *Pensées inédites* (1924)

21 There is no great difficulty in separating the soul from the body, but it is not so easy to restore life to the dead.
Sa'di, *Gulistan* (1258)

---

155 WAR

1 They shall beat their swords into plowshares, and their spears into pruninghooks: nation shall not lift up sword against nation, neither shall they learn war any more.
Isaiah, 2, 4

2 Whence come wars and fightings among you? come they not hence, even of your lusts that war in your members?
James, 4, 1

3 A voluntary war can only be entered upon if so decided by a Court of seventy-one.
Mishnah, *Sanhedrin*, 1, 5

4 Fight in the way of God those who fight you, but do not provoke hostility.
Koran, 2, 186

5 When he fights with his foes in battle, let him not strike with weapons concealed in wood, nor with such as are barbed, poisoned, or the points of which are blazing with fire.
Laws of Manu, VII, 90

6 On conquering Kalinga the Beloved of the Gods felt remorse, for, when an independent country is conquered the slaughter, death and deportation of the people is extremely grievous to the Beloved of the Gods and weighs heavily on his mind . . . This inscription of Dhamma has been engraved so that any sons or great grandsons that I

may have should not think of gaining new conquests.
Ashoka, *Major Rock Edict,* XIII (3rd century BCE)

7 Victory breeds hatred; the conquered dwells in sorrow. He who has given up victory and defeat, he is calm and lives happily.
Dhammapada, 201

8 When men rise up in enmity and wish to fight,
It is not cowardice, say the wise, to refuse the challenge,
Even when your enemies do the utmost evil,
It is right to do no evil in return.
Tamil Quatrains, 67 (6th century)

9 He who by Tao purposes to help a ruler of men
Will oppose all conquest by force of arms;
For such things are wont to rebound.
Where armies are, thorns and brambles grow.
The raising of a great host
Is followed by a year of dearth.
Tao Te Ching, XXX

10 Fine weapons are none the less ill-omened things . . .
For to think them lovely means to delight in them, and to delight in them means to delight in the slaughter of men.
And he who delights in the slaughter of men will never get what he looks for out of those that dwell under heaven.
A host that has slain men is received with grief and mourning; he that has conquered in battle is received with rites of mourning.
Tao Te Ching, XXXI

11 What is it like when righteousness is the standard of conduct? The great do not attack the small, the strong do not attack the weak . . . Now what is it like when force becomes the standard of conduct? The great attack the small, the strong plunder the weak, the many oppress the few, the cunning deceive the simple, the noble disdain the humble. The rich mock the poor, the young take from the old, and the states in the empire ruin each other.
Mo Tzu, 28, 3 (5th century BCE)

12 The origin of all wars is the pursuit of wealth, and we are forced to pursue wealth because we live in slavery to the cares of the body.
Plato, *Phaedo,* 66

13 A prince should have no other object or thought, nor acquire skill in anything, except war, its organization and its discipline. The art of war is all that is expected of a ruler.
Niccolo Machiavelli, *The Prince,* 14 (1532)

14 They detest and abhor war and fighting as a very beastly thing, and yet not practised by any beasts as by men. And contrary to the custom of almost all other nations, they see nothing glorious in war but the contrary.
Thomas More, *Utopia,* 2 (1516)

15 St Thomas Aquinas laid down three conditions for a just resort to arms; legitimate authority (*legitima auctoritas*), just cause (*justa causa*), and right intention (*recta intentio*). To these was added, by Suarez (d. 1617) and Bellarmine (d. 1621), a fourth condition — the right way of conducting a war (*debitus modus*). A fifth condition, that there must be a moral certainty that the just cause will win, came from Cajetan (d. 1534).
Roger Smith, in *Nuclear Weapons and Christian Conscience* (1961)

16 It is lawful for Christian men, at the commandment of the Magistrate, to wear weapons, and serve in the wars.
Book of Common Prayer, Articles of Religion XXXVII

17 There is such a thing as legitimate warfare: war has its laws; there are things which may fairly be done, and things which may not be done.
John Henry Newman, *Apologia pro vita sua* (1864)

18 Manslaughter in war, or by pretended law of justice for a temporal cause, without spiritual revelation, is expressly contrary to the New Testament.
Lollard Conclusions, 10 (1394)

19 Christ could not imagine people believing in his teaching of humility, love and universal brotherhood, quietly and deliberately organizing the murder of their brother men.
Leo Tolstoy, *What I Believe* (1884)

20 Force, and fraud, are in war the two cardinal virtues.
Thomas Hobbes, *Leviathan,* 13 (1651)

21 Blood is the god of war's rich livery.
Christopher Marlowe, *Tamburlaine the Great,* 2, 3, 2 (1587)

22 It is said that God is always on the side of
the heaviest battalions.
Voltaire, letter, 6 February 1770

23 As peace is of all goodness, so war is an
emblem, a hieroglyphic, of all misery.
John Donne, *Sermons*, 12 (1622)

24 We used to wonder where war lived, what it
was that made it so vile. And now we realize
that we know where it lives, that it is inside
ourselves.
Albert Camus, *Notebooks*, 3 (1962)

25 Should the evil consequences of adopting
this method of warfare ever become so
extensive as to pass utterly beyond the
control of man, then indeed its use must be
rejected as immoral. In that event, it would
no longer be a question of 'defence' against
injustice and necessary 'protection' of
legitimate possessions, but of the
annihilation, pure and simple, of all human
life within the affected area. That is not
lawful on any title.
Pope Pius XII, address to the World
Medical Association (1954)

156 PEACE
See also 155. WAR

1 The Prince of Peace. Of the increase of his
government and peace there shall be no end.
Isaiah, 9, 6–7

2 Peace I leave with you, my peace I give unto
you: not as the world giveth, give I unto
you.
John, 14, 27

3 We are merrymakers; when we see men
troubled in mind we cheer them, and when
we see two men quarelling we make peace
between them.
Mishnah, *Taanith*, 22

4 It is peace until the rising of the dawn.
Koran, 97, 5

5 O God, thou art peace. From thee is peace
and unto thee is peace. Let us love, our
Lord, in peace and receive us in thy
paradise, the abode of peace.
Prayer, at close of formal Islamic Prayers,
trans. Kenneth Cragg, *Alive to God* (1970)

6 With gentleness one defeats the gentle as

well as the hard; there is nothing impossible
to the gentle: therefore the gentle is the
more severe. One should take action after
considering the place and time and one's
own strengths and weaknesses; at the wrong
place and time it fails, therefore wait till
both are right.
Mahabharata, 3, 30

7 The unreflecting man can know no peace,
and lacking peace how can there be bliss?
Bhagavad Gita, 2, 66

8 Better than a thousand utterances composed
of meaningless words is one sensible word,
on hearing which one becomes peaceful.
Dhammapada, 100

9 In words, truth; in government, good order;
In deeds, effectiveness; in actions,
        timeliness —
In each case it is because they prefer what
            does not lead to strife,
And therefore does not go amiss.
Tao Te Ching, VIII

10 Peace is liberty in tranquillity.
Cicero, *Philippics*, 2, 44 (1st century BCE)

11 In His will is our peace.
Dante Alighieri, *Paradiso*, iii, 85 (1320)

12 Keep thyself first in peace, and then shalt
thou be able to pacify others. A peaceable
man doth more good than he that is well
learned.
Thomas Kempis, *Of the Imitation of Christ*,
II, 3 (1418)

13 A peace is of the nature of a conquest;
For then both parties nobly are subdued,
And neither party loser.
William Shakespeare, *Henry IV, Part 2*, IV,
ii, 89–91 (*c.* 1597)

14 Peace hath her victories
No less renowned than war.
John Milton, *Sonnet XVI* (1652)

15 Mark! where his carnage and his conquests
            cease!
He makes a solitude and calls it — peace!
Lord Byron, *The Bride of Abydos*, II, 20
(1813)

16 'Peace upon earth!' was said. We sing it,
And pay a million priests to bring it.
After two thousand years of mass
We've got as far as poison-gas.
Thomas Hardy, *Christmas: 1924*

17 I take it that what all men are really after is some form or perhaps only some formula of peace.
Joseph Conrad, *Under Western Eyes* (1911)

18 Mutual cowardice keeps us in peace.
Samuel Johnson, in Boswell, *Life of Samuel Johnson*, 28 April 1778

19 To Mercy, Pity, Peace, and Love
All pray in their distress;
And to these virtues of delight
Return their thankfulness.
William Blake, *Songs of Innocence*, 'The Divine Image' (1789)

---

157 PROPERTY

---

1 They shall sit every man under his vine and under his fig tree; and none shall make them afraid.
Micah, 4, 4

2 I will say to my soul, Soul, thou hast much goods laid up for many years; take thine ease, eat, drink, and be merry. But God said unto him, Thou fool, this night thy soul shall be required of thee: then whose shall those things be, which thou hast provided?
Luke, 12, 19–20

3 Do not consume your property amongst you in vanity, and do not proffer it to the judges, that you may sinfully consume a portion of other men's goods, and that knowingly.
Koran, 2, 184

4 For the purpose of gaining bare subsistence, let him accumulate property by following those irreproachable occupations which are prescribed for his caste.
Laws of Manu, IV, 3

5 Not property of ancient glory makes a man noble, but self-denial, wisdom and energy.
Tamil Quatrains, 195 (6th century)

6 No one should possess any private property, if it can possibly be avoided: secondly, no one should have a dwelling or storehouse into which all who please may not enter.
Plato, *Republic*, III, 416

7 It is not the possessions but the desires of mankind which require to be equalized.
Aristotle, *Politics*, 2, 7

8 For Property itself was mine,
And Hedges, Ornaments:
Walls, Houses, Coffers, & their rich
    Contents,
To make me rich combine.
Clothes, costly Jewels, Laces, I esteemed
My Wealth by others worn,
For me they all to wear them seemed,
When I was born.
Thomas Traherne, *Poems of Felicity* (17th century)

9 It should be remembered that the foundation of the social contract is property; and its first condition, that everyone should be maintained in the peaceful possession of what belongs to him.
Jean-Jacques Rousseau, *A Discourse on Political Economy* (1758)

10 There is a desire of property in the sanest and best men, which Nature seems to have implanted as conservative of her works, and which is necessary to encourage and keep alive the arts.
W.S. Landor, *Imaginary Conversations* (1853)

11 Where there is no property there is no injustice.
John Locke, *An Essay Concerning Human Understanding* (1690)

12 Property is theft.
P.-J. Proudhon, *Qu'est-ce que la propriété?* (1840)

13 If a man own land, the land owns him. Now let him leave home, if he dare.
R.W. Emerson, *The Conduct of Life* (1860)

14 An acre in Middlesex is better than a principality in Utopia.
T.B. Macaulay, *Francis Bacon* (1837)

15 The newer people, of this modern age, are more eager to amass than to realize.
Rabindranath Tagore, *The Cycle of Spring* (1915)

---

158 RICHES

---

1 If riches increase, set not your heart upon them.
Psalm, 62, 10

2 How hard it is for them that trust in riches to enter into the kingdom of God!
Mark 10, 24

3 Those who contribute their wealth in the way of God are like a grain which produces seven ears in each of which are a hundred grains. God gives double to whom he wills.
Koran, 2, 263

4 Whether he be rich, or even in distress, let him not seek wealth through pursuits to which men cleave, nor by forbidden occupations.
Laws of Manu, IV, 15

5 Of the first three ends of human life, Kautilya holds that material gain is the most important, because right and love depend upon wealth for their realization.
Kautilya, *Artha-shastra*, 1, 7 (4th century)

6 The fool is tormented thinking 'these sons belong to me', 'this wealth belongs to me.' He himself does not belong to himself. How then can sons be his? How can wealth be his?
Dhammapada, 62

7 Only those rich men are truly wealthy who relieve the need of their neighbours.
Tamil Quatrains, 170 (6th century)

8 The Pharisees live modestly and despise luxuries in food. They follow reason, and do what it prescribes as good for them, and they think that they ought to strive earnestly to observe the dictates of reason in practice.
Josephus, *Antiquities*, 18, 1 (1st century)

9 The love of money is the metropolis of all evils . . . May the sons of your enemies live in luxury, said Diogenes.
Diogenes Laerti' i, 50 and 8 (3rd century)

10 The love of money is the root of all evil.
1 Timothy, 6, 10

11 What about those people who accumulate superfluous wealth, for no better purpose than to enjoy looking at it? Is their pleasure a real one, or merely a form of delusion? The opposite type of psychopath buries his gold, so that he will never be able to use it, and may never see it again. In fact, he deliberately loses it in his anxiety not to lose it.
Thomas More, *Utopia*, ii (1516)

12   Let none admire
That riches grow in Hell; that soil may best
Deserve the precious bane.
John Milton, *Paradise Lost*, 1, 690–2 (1667)

13 O, what a world of vile ill-favoured faults Looks handsome in three hundred pounds a year!
William Shakespeare, *The Merry Wives of Windsor*, III, iv, 32-3 (1597)

14 Money is like muck, not good except it be spread.
Francis Bacon, *Essays* (1625)

15 I bless God I do find that I am worth more than ever yet I was, which is £6,200, for which the Holy Name of God be praised!
Samuel Pepys, *Diary*, 31 October 1666

16 He gave it for his opinion, that whoever could make two ears of corn or two blades of grass to grow upon a spot of ground where only one grew before, would deserve better of mankind, and do more essential service to his country than the whole race of politicians together.
Jonathan Swift, *Gulliver's Travels*, 'Voyage to Brobdingnag' (1726)

17 Where the heart was set on greatness, success in business did not satisfy the craving; but that commonly with an increase of wealth the desire of wealth increased.
John Woolman, *Journal* (1774)

18 Wherever there is excessive wealth, there is also in the train of it excessive poverty; as, where the sun is brightest, the shade is deepest.
W.S. Landor, *Imaginary Conversations* (1853)

19 I know no previous instance in history of a nation's establishing a systematic disobedience to the first principles of its professed religion. The writings which we (verbally) esteem as divine, not only denounce the love of money as the source of all evil, and as an idolatry abhorred of the Deity, but declare mammon service to be the accurate and irreconcileable opposite of God's service.
John Ruskin, *Unto This Last* (1860)

20 There is a time when a man distinguishes the idea of felicity from the idea of wealth; it is the beginning of wisdom.
R.W. Emerson, *Journals* (1830)

21 I am a Millionaire. That is my religion.
George Bernard Shaw, *Major Barbara* (1907)

22 When the rich wage war it is the poor who
die.
Jean-Paul Sartre, *The Devil and the Good
Lord* (1951)

23 What has the lust of grabbing and of laying
up treasure in common with the joy in the
presence of the Present One? Can the
servant of Mammon say *Thou* to his money?
And how is he to behave towards God when
he does not understand how to say *Thou*?
He cannot serve two masters — not even
one after the other: he must first learn to
serve in a *different way*.
Martin Buber, *I and Thou* (1937)

---

159 POVERTY
See also 163. ALMSGIVING

---

1 Two things have I required of thee; deny me
them not before I die: Remove far from me
vanity and lies: give me neither poverty nor
riches; feed me with food convenient for
me: Lest I be full, and deny thee, and say,
Who is the LORD? or lest I be poor, and
steal, and take the name of my God in vain.
Proverbs, 30, 7–9

2 I have learned, in whatsoever state I am,
therewith to be content. I know both how to
be abased, and I know how to abound:
every where and in all things I am instructed
both to be full and to be hungry, both to
abound and to suffer need.
Philippians, 4, 11–12

3 I am an elementary teacher, and I instruct
the children of the poor exactly the same as I
teach the children of the rich. If any one is
unable to pay me a fee I forgo it.
Mishnah, *Taanith,* 24

4 When God tries him, and stints for him his
provision, man says: 'My Lord has scorned
me.'
Nay, but you do not honour the orphan, nor
urge to feed the destitute. You devour the
inheritance indiscriminately, and you love
wealth exceedingly.
Koran, 89, 16–21

5 Among the poor and aged, the officers of
Dhamma are working for the welfare and
happiness of those devoted to Dhamma and
for the removal of their troubles. They are
busy in promoting the welfare of prisoners

should they have behaved irresponsibly, or
releasing those that have children, are
afflicted, or are aged.
Ashoka, *Major Rock Edict,* V (3rd century
BCE)

6 The Master said, If any means of escaping
poverty presented itself that did not involve
doing wrong, I would adopt it, even though
my employment were only that of the
gentleman who holds the whip.
Confucius, *Analects,* VII, 11

7 The Riches and Goods of Christians are not
common, as touching the right, title, and
possession of the same, as certain
Anabaptists do falsely boast.
Notwithstanding, every man ought, of such
things as he possesseth, liberally to give alms
to the poor, according to his ability.
Book of Common Prayer, Articles of
Religion *XXXVIII*

8 The brothers shall possess nothing ...
This is the highest degree of that sublime
poverty, which has made you, my dearly
beloved brethren, heirs and kings of the
Kingdom of Heaven, which has made you
poor in goods but exalted in virtues.
Rule of St Francis, (1223)

9 Man's welfare then lies not in obtaining or
multiplying any external thing, but rather in
despising it, and utterly rooting it out from
the heart. And this you must understand not
only of income or money and riches, but of
seeking after honour also, and the desire of
vain praise, all which pass away with this
world.
Thomas Kempis, *Of the Imitation of Christ,*
III, 27 (*c.* 1418)

10 One will boast that for sixty years he has
never touched money without protecting his
fingers with two pairs of gloves, while
another wears a cowl so thick with dirt that
not even a sailor would want it near his
person . . . They never think of the time to
come when Christ will scorn all this and
enforce his own rule, that of charity.
Desiderius Erasmus, *In Praise of Folly* (1511)

11 Prosperity is the blessing of the Old
Testament, adversity is the blessing of the
New.
Francis Bacon, *Essays* (1625)

12 Poverty is no disgrace to a man, but it is
confoundedly inconvenient.
Sydney Smith, *His Wit and Wisdom* (1900)

13 Poverty is a great enemy to human happiness; it certainly destroys liberty, and it makes some virtues impracticable and others extremely difficult.
Samuel Johnson, in Boswell, *Life of Samuel Johnson* (7 December 1782)

14 Luxury at present can only be enjoyed by the ignorant; the cruellest man living could not sit at his feast, unless he sat blindfold. Raise the veil boldly, face the light . . . until the time come, and the kingdom, when Christ's gift of bread, and bequest of peace, shall be 'Unto this last as unto thee.'
John Ruskin, *Unto This Last* (1860)

15 Here is thy footstool and there rest thy feet where live the poorest, the lowliest, and lost . . . My heart can never find its way to where thou keepest company with the companionless among the poorest, the lowliest, and the lost.
Rabindranath Tagore, *Gitanjali*, 10 (1913)

16 Mother Teresa of Calcutta relates a story about her sisters . . . Just as we arrived the sister brought in a man covered with maggots. He had been picked up from a drain. 'I have been taking care of him. I have been touching Christ. I knew it was him', she said.
William Johnston, *The Inner Eye of Love* (1978)

17 Poverty — the poverty of spirit of the Sermon on the Mount — is a total detachment from the material world. It is to recognize that everything comes from God — our bodies, our breath, our very existence.
Bede Griffiths, *Return to the Centre* (1976)

18 The spirit of poverty is to live in the gladness of today.
Rule of Taizé (1961)

---

160 USURY AND TRADE

---

1 If thou lend money to any of my people that is poor by thee, thou shalt not be to him as an usurer, neither shalt thou lay upon him usury.
Exodus, 22, 25

2 Wherefore then gavest not thou my money into the bank, that at my coming I might have required mine own with usury?
Luke, 19, 23

3 Come and see the blindness of usurers . . . Usurers take witnesses, scribe, pen and ink, and write and seal a document to the effect, So-and-so denies the God of Israel.
Mishnah, *Baba Metzia*, 71

4 God has permitted bargaining, and forbidden usury.
Koran, 2, 276

5 Cursed be the taker of usury, the giver of usury, the writer of usury, and the witness of usury, for they are all equal.
Sahihu, *Tradition* (9th century)

6 The gods, having considered the respective merits of a niggardly Brahmin and of a liberal usurer, declared the food of both to be equal in quality.
The Lord of created beings came and spoke to them, 'Do not make that equal, which is unequal. The food of that liberal usurer is purified by faith; that of the other man is defiled by a want of faith.'
Laws of Manu, IV, 224–5

7 The wise and moral man shines like a fire on a hilltop, making money like the bee which does not hurt the flower. Such a man makes his pile as an anthill, gradually. The man grown wealthy thus can help his family and firmly bind his friends to himself.
Digha Nikaya, iii (3rd century BCE)

8 No depositing of money with one who is not trusted, and no lending on usury.
Plato, *Laws*, V, 742

9 The crime of usury, before the Reformation, consisted in the taking of *any* interest for the use of money; and now in taking an higher rate of interest than is authorised by law.
J. Erskine, *Principles of the Law of Scotland* (1754)

10 I know of but two definitions that can possibly be given of usury: one is, the taking of a greater interest than the law allows of . . . The other is the taking of a greater interest than it is usual for men to give and take.
J. Bentham, *Defence of Usury*, ii, 7 (1787)

11 He lends out money gratis, and brings down The rate of usance here with us in Venice. If I can catch him once upon the hip, I will feed fat the ancient grudge I bear him.
William Shakespeare, *The Merchant of Venice*, I, iii, 39–42 (*c.* 1596–8)

12 A man in business must put up many

affronts if he loves his own quiet.
William Penn, *Some Fruits of Solitude* (1693)

13 The human species, according to the best theory I can form of it, is composed of two distinct races, *the men who borrow*, and *the men who lend*.
Charles Lamb, *Essays of Elia* (1823)

14 The world is too much with us; late and soon,
Getting and spending, we lay waste our powers:
Little we see in Nature that is ours;
We have given our hearts away, a sordid boon!
William Wordsworth, *The World is Too Much with Us* (1807)

15 Honour sinks where commerce long prevails. prevails.
Oliver Goldsmith, *The Traveller* (1765)

16 Perpetual devotion to what a man calls his business, is only to be sustained by perpetual neglect of many other things.
R.L. Stevenson, *Virginibus Puerisque* (1881)

17 People of the same trade seldom meet together, even for merriment and diversion, but the conversation ends in a conspiracy against the public, or in some contrivance to raise prices.
Adam Smith, *The Wealth of Nations*, i, 10 (1776)

18 For the merchant, even honesty is a financial speculation.
Charles Baudelaire, *Intimate Journals* (1887)

19 Your honesty is *not* to be based either on religion or policy. Both your religion and policy must based on *it*. Your honesty must be based, as the sun is, in vacant heaven; poised, as the lights in the firmament, which have rule over the day and over the night.
John Ruskin, *Time and Tide*, viii (1867)

20 The reward of labour is *life* . . . The reward of creation. The wages which God gets, as people might have said time agone.
William Morris, *News From Nowhere* (1891)

21 It is difficult but not impossible to conduct strictly honest business. What is true is that honesty is incompatible with the amassing of a large fortune.
M.K. Gandhi, *Non-Violence in Peace and War* (1948)

161 SLAVERY

1 If thy brother, an Hebrew man, or an Hebrew woman, be sold unto thee, and serve thee six years; then in the seventh year thou shalt let him go free from thee. And when thou sendest him out free from thee, thou shalt not let him go away empty: thou shalt furnish him liberally out of thy flock, and out of thy floor, and out of thy winepress.
Deuteronomy, 15, 12–14

2 He was parted from you for a while, that you might have him back for ever, no longer as a slave but more than a slave, as a beloved brother.
Philemon, 15–16 (RSV)

3 Settle the unmarried among you in marriage, also the upright among your male and female slaves. . . and for those in your possession who desire the writing (of manumission) write it if you know any good in them, and give them of the wealth of God which He has given you.
Koran, 24, 32–3

4 There are slaves of seven kinds: he who is made a captive under a standard, he who serves for his daily food, he who is born in the house, he who is bought, and he who is given, he who is inherited from ancestors, and he who is enslaved by way of punishment.
Laws of Manu, VIII, 415

5 Villainous and tyrannical men, with profit as their sole concern, went so far as to kidnap and sell men and their wives and children, profaning the will of Heaven, destroying human relationships, and perverting the principle that man is the noblest creation of Heaven and earth.
Han Shu, *History of the Former Han Dynasty* (92 CE)

6 It is thus clear that just as some are by nature free, so others are by nature slaves, and for these latter the condition of slavery is both beneficial and just.
Aristotle, *Politics*, 1255

7 A slave is at last made free, and presently having nowhere to eat, he seeks one whom he may flatter and with whom he may sup. He then submits to the basest and most

infamous prostitution, and if he can gain admission to some great man's table he falls into a much worse slavery than the former.
Epictetus, *Discourses*, 4, 1 (2nd century)

8 Please reflect that the man you call your slave was born of the same seed, has the same good sky above him, breathes as you do, lives as you do, dies as you do! You may see him free, he may see you a slave — the odds are level.
Seneca, *Epistulae Morales*, Letter 47 (1st century)

9 'I acquired slaves and slave girls.' Tell me, what price did you pay for them? What did you find among your possessions that you could trade for human beings? . . . Who can buy a man, who can sell him, when he is made in the likeness of God? when he is ruler over the whole earth, when he has been given as his inheritance by God authority over all that is on the earth?
Gregory of Nyssa, *Homily on Ecclesiastes*, 4 (4th century)

10 The slaves that I have occasionally referred to are not, as you might imagine, non-combatant prisoners of war, slaves by birth, or purchases from foreign slave markets. They are either Utopian convicts or, much more often condemned criminals from other countries.
Thomas More, *Utopia*, ii (1516)

11 The love of ease and gain are the motives in general of keeping slaves, and men are wont to take hold of weak arguments to support a cause which is unreasonable. I have no interest on either side, save only the interest which I desire to have in the truth. I believe liberty is their right.
John Woolman, *Journal* (1774)

12 It will always be a subject of humiliating reflection to me, that I was once an active instrument in a business at which my heart now shudders . . . What I did I did ignorantly; considering it as the line of life which Divine Providence had allotted me, and having no concern, in point of conscience, but to treat the slaves, while under my care, with as much humanity as a regard for my own safety would admit.
John Newton, *Thoughts upon the African Slave Trade* (1788)

13 In giving freedom to the slave, we assure freedom to the free, — honourable alike in what we give and what we preserve.
Abraham Lincoln, message to Congress, 1 December 1862

14   The wretched slave,
Who with a body fill'd and vacant mind
Gets him to rest, cramm'd with distressful bread;
Never sees horrid night, the child of hell,
But, like a lackey, from the rise to set
Sweats in the eye of Phoebus, and all night
Sleeps in Elysium.
William Shakespeare, *Henry V*, IV, i, 264–70 (1599)

15 I was a King in Babylon
And you were a Christian Slave.
W.E. Henley, *Echoes* (1888)

16 Man is born free; and everywhere he is in chains. One man thinks he is the master of others, and yet he remains a greater slave than they are.
Jean-Jacques Rousseau, *The Social Contract* (1762)

17 All spirits are enslaved which serve things evil.
Percy Bysshe Shelley, *Prometheus Unbound* (1819)

18 That state is a state of Slavery in which a man does what he likes to do in his spare time and in his working time that which is required of him.
Eric Gill, *Slavery and Freedom* (1918)

19 The only purpose for which power can rightfully be exercised over any member of a civilized community, against his will, is to prevent harm to others. His own good, either physical or moral, is not a sufficient warrant.
John Stuart Mill, *On Liberty* (1859)

20 No one shall be held in slavery or servitude; slavery and the slave trade shall be prohibited in all their forms.
Universal Declaration of Human Rights, General Assembly of the United Nations, Article 4 (1948)

162 CLASS AND RACE

1 Blessed be Egypt my people, and Assyria the work of my hands, and Israel mine inheritance.
Isaiah, 19, 25

2 By one Spirit are we all baptized into one body, whether we be Jews or Gentiles, whether we be bond or free.
1 Corinthians, 12, 13

3 O mankind, we have created you male and female, and made you races and tribes, that you may show mutual recognition.
Koran, 49, 13

4 When they divided cosmic man, into how many parts did they separate him? . . . The priestly caste was his mouth, his two arms became the warriors, his two thighs are the artisans, and from his two feet the serfs were produced.
Rig Veda, 10, 90

5 Those who come to me for refuge,
even if their birth is low:
women, artisans, and serfs.
to the highest goal shall go.
Bhagavad Gita, 9, 32

6 People speak of high birth and low —
Mere words, with no real meaning!
Not property or ancient glory makes a man
        noble,
But self-denial, wisdom and energy.
Tamil Quatrains, 195 (6th century)

7 Not by matted hair, not by lineage, not by caste does one become a Brahmin. He is a Brahmin in whom there is truth and righteousness.
Dhammapada, 393

8 Though they say there are four castes
One God created all men:
All men were moulded out of the same clay,
The Great Potter has merely varied their
        shapes.
Hymns of Guru Amar Das, *jat ka* (16th century)

9 All the members of the Greek race are brethren and kinsmen to one another, but aliens and foreigners to the barbarian world . . . Then being Greeks, they will not devastate Greece, nor burn houses, nor admit that all the men, women, and children in a city are their foes.
Plato, *Republic*, V, 470–1

10 If what philosophers say of the kinship between God and man is true, what has anyone to do but, like Socrates, when he is asked of what country he is, never to say that he is a citizen of Athens or of Corinth, but of the world?
Epictetus, *Discourses* 1, 9 (2nd century)

11 Not because Socrates said it, but because this really is my feeling, and perhaps not without some excuse, I consider all men to be my countrymen. I embrace a Pole as kindly as a Frenchman, extending natural bonds to universal and common ones.
Michel de Montaigne, *Essays*, 1, 26 (1580)

12 Neither Pagan nor Mahometan nor Jew ought to be excluded from the civil rights of the commonwealth because of his religion.
John Locke, *A Letter Concerning Toleration* (1689)

13 The points of difference between Christianity and Judaism have very much to do with a man's fitness to be a bishop or a rabbi. But they have no more to do with his fitness to be a magistrate, a legislator, or a minister of finance, than with his fitness to be a cobbler . . . Why a man should be less fit to exercise those powers because he wears a beard, because he does not eat ham, because he goes to the synagogue on Saturdays instead of going to the church on Sundays, we cannot conceive.
T.B. Macaulay, *Civil Disabilities of the Jews* (1831)

14 How odd
Of God
To choose
The Jews.
W.N. Ewer, *How Odd* (1917)

15 But not so odd
As those who choose
A Jewish God,
But spurn the Jews.
Cecil Browne, reply to above

16 The idea of race is a powerful social force; around it cluster all kinds of prejudices, and it is made the basis of political action, which discriminates against whole groups of people . . . The colour bar is set up in defence of vested interests. Where these

interests are not thought to be threatened, where previous historical relations have tended to promote co-operation, where the dark-skinned population is small in comparison with the white population, where there is an honest attempt to apply the principles of social equality and forgo the advantages of exploitation, the colour bar is lowered, or may never have been set up.
Raymond Firth, *Human Types* (1938)

17 If I have to be reborn I should wish to be born as an 'untouchable', so that I may share their sorrows, sufferings and the affronts levelled at them, in order that I may free myself and them from that miserable condition.
M.K. Gandhi, speech quoted in C.F. Andrews, *Mahatma Gandhi's Ideas* (1929)

18 Everyone is entitled to all the rights and freedoms set forth in this Declaration, without distinction of any kind, such as race, colour, sex, language, religion, political or other opinion, national or social origin, property, birth or other status.
Universal Declaration of Human Rights, General Assembly of the United Nations, Article 2 (1948)

5 Works of sacrifice, almsgiving, and austerity should not be abandoned, but surely should be done; sacrifice, almsgiving, and austerity purify thoughtful men.
But even these works should be done with detachment and abandonment of rewards.
Bhagavad Gita, 18, 5–6

6 Giving alms, following the teaching, cherishing one's relatives, blameless actions: that is a supreme blessing.
Sutta Nipata, II, 4 (3rd century BCE)

7 Time hath, my Lord, a wallet at his back, Wherein he puts alms for oblivion.
William Shakespeare, *Troilus and Cressida,* III, iii, 145–6 (?1602)

8 I give no alms. For that I am not poor enough.
Friedrich Nietzsche, *Thus Spake Zarathustra* (1883)

9 The mistake of the best men through generation after generation, has been that great one of thinking to help the poor by almsgiving, and by preaching of patience or of hope, and by every other means, emollient or consolatory, except the one thing which God orders for them, justice.
John Ruskin, *Unto This Last* (1860)

163 ALMSGIVING
See also 159. POVERTY, 121. CHARITY

1 I was a father to the poor: and the cause which I knew not I searched out.
Job, 29, 16

2 When thou doest alms, let not thy left hand know what thy right hand doeth: that thine alms may be in secret.
Matthew, 6, 3–4

3 He who prolongs his stay at table prolongs his life; perhaps a poor man will come and he will give him some food.
Mishnah, *Berachoth,* 55

4 Whatever contribution you make, and whatever vow you vow, God knows it . . . If you give alms publicly it is well, but if you conceal it and give to the poor, it is better for you.
Koran, 2, 273

164 STRANGERS

1 If a stranger sojourn with thee in your land, ye shall not vex him. But the stranger that dwelleth with you shall be unto you as one born among you, and thou shalt love him as thyself; for ye were strangers in the land of Egypt.
Leviticus, 19, 33–4

2 I was a stranger, and ye took me in: naked, and ye clothed me.
Matthew, 25, 35–6

3 Show to parents kindness; also to relatives, orphans, and the poor, to the person under your protection be he relative or not, to the companion by your side, to the follower of the way.
Koran, 4, 40

4 He will deal harshly by a stranger who has not been himself often a traveller and stranger.
Sa'di, *Gulistan,* 3, 28 (1258)

5 If a man be gracious and courteous to
strangers, it shows he is a citizen of the
world.
Francis Bacon, *Essays* 'Goodness' (1625)

6 Poor World (said I) what wilt thou do
To entertain this starry Stranger?
Is this the best thou canst bestow?
A cold, and not too cleanly, manger?
Richard Crashaw, *A Hymn of the Nativity*
(1652)

7 I, a stranger and afraid
In a world I never made.
A.E. Housman, *Last Poems* (1922)

8 Admiration for ourselves and our
institutions is too often measured by our
contempt and dislike for foreigners.
W.R. Inge, *Outspoken Essays*, 'Patriotism'
(1919)

165 ANIMALS

1 Thou shalt not muzzle the ox when he
treadeth out the corn.
Deuteronomy, 25, 4

2 Are not five sparrows sold for two farthings,
and not one of them is forgotten before
God?
Luke, 12, 6

3 Preventing pain to an animal is a command
of the Torah.
Mishnah, *Shabbath*, 128

4 Herod revolted from the laws of his country,
and corrupted their ancient constitution, by
the introduction of foreign practices . . . He
made a great preparation of wild beasts, and
of lions themselves in great abundance, and
other animals such as were of unusual
strength or of a sort rarely seen. These were
prepared either to fight one with another, or
men who were condemned to death were to
fight with them. And truly foreigners were
greatly surprised and delighted at the
vastness of the expense shown here, and at
the great dangers that were seen. But to Jews
this was no better than a dissolution of those
customs for which they had a great
veneration. It appeared also no better than
an instance of barefaced impiety to throw
men to wild beasts, for the delight of the
spectators.
Josephus, *Antiquities*, xv, 8, 1 (1st century)

5 There is not a beast in the earth but God is
responsible for its sustenance. He knows its
lair and its resting-place.
Koran, 11, 8

6 *Indra*: In paradise there is no place for dogs
. . . Renounce the dog, there is nothing cruel
in that.
Yudhishthira: It has been said that to
renounce one who is loyal to you is an
infinite evil, as evil as the slaying of a
Brahmin. Hence I will by no means
whatever, seeking my own pleasure,
renounce this dog today.
Mahabharata, xv, 38

7 Formerly in the kitchens of the Beloved of
the Gods, the king Piyadassi, many
hundreds of thousands of living animals
were killed daily for meat. But now, at the
time of writing this inscription on Dhamma,
only three animals are killed . . . even these
three animals will not be killed in future.
Medicinal herbs whether useful to man or to
beast, have been brought and planted
wherever they did not grow.
Ashoka, *Major Rock Edicts*, I and II (3rd
century BCE)

8 Some kill animals for sacrificial purposes,
some kill for the sake of their skin, some kill
for the sake of their flesh, some kill them for
the sake of their blood . . . He who injures
these animals does not comprehend and
renounced the sinful acts; he who does not
injure these, comprehends and renounces
the sinful acts. Knowing them, a wise man
should not act sinfully towards animals, nor
cause others to act so, nor allow others to
act so.
Acharanga Sutra, I, i, 6 (3rd-1st centuries
BCE)

9 The higher type of man treats animals with
kindness, but not with the same sort of
benevolence that he shows to people; which,
again, is different from the personal
affection that he shows to his parents. He is
loving to his parents and benevolent to the
people; benevolent to people and kind to
animals.
Mencius, VII (4th century BCE)

10 A dog will never forget the crumb thou
gavest him, though thou mayest afterwards
throw a hundred stones at his head.
Sa'di, *Gulistan*, 8, 99 (1258)

11 There is this special difference between men and animals, that the latter are governed by nothing but their senses, never look any farther than just to what strikes and affects them at present, and have very little, or hardly any, concern for what is past or to come. But the former are creatures endowed with reason, which gives them a power to carry their thoughts to the consequences of things.
Cicero, *Offices*, 1, 4 (1st century BCE)

12 Each of the animals is constituted either for food, or husbandry, or to produce milk, and the rest of them for some similar use. And for these purposes what need is there to understand the appearances of things or to make distinctions about them? But God has introduced man as a spectator of himself and his works.
Epictetus, *Discourses*, 1, 6 (2nd century)

13 God's first blunder: Man did not find the animals amusing, — he dominated them, and did not even want to be an 'animal.'
Friedrich Nietzsche, *The Antichrist* (1888)

14 A Robin Redbreast in a cage
Puts all Heaven in a Rage.
William Blake, *Auguries of Innocence* (1803)

15 For I will consider my Cat Jeoffry.
For he is the servant of the Living God, duly and daily serving Him.
Christopher Smart, *Jubilate Agno* (1763)

16 There is no faith which has never yet been broken, except that of a truly faithful dog.
Konrad Lorenz, *King Solomon's Ring* (1952)

17 We have enslaved the rest of the animal creation, and have treated our distant cousins in fur and feathers so badly that beyond doubt, if they were able to formulate a religion, they would depict the Devil in human form.
W.R. Inge, *Outspoken Essays*, Second Series (1922)

18 'Hurt not the animal', said he, 'for within it is the soul of your own sister.'
George Borrow, *The Bible in Spain* (1834)

19 I think I could turn and live with animals,
they are so placid and
self-contain'd,
I stand and look at them long and long.
They do not sweat and whine about their
condition,
They do not lie awake in the dark and weep
for their sins,
They do not make me sick discussing their
duty to God.
Walt Whitman, *Leaves of Grass*, 'Song of Myself' (1855)

20 'God's humblest, they!' I muse. Yet why?
They know Earth-secrets that know not I.
Thomas Hardy, *An August Midnight* (1899)

XVIII
LAST THINGS

166 DEATH

1 Then shall the dust return to the earth as it was: and the spirit shall return unto God who gave it.
Ecclesiastes, 12, 7

2 It is appointed unto men once to die, but after this the judgment.
Hebrews, 9, 27

3 The ministering angels spoke before the Holy One, blessed be he, 'Why didst Thou inflict the penalty of death upon Adam?' He replied, 'I imposed a light precept upon him but he transgressed it.'
Mishnah, *Shabbath*, 55

4 God calls in the souls at the time of their death, and those which have not died, in their sleep; those upon whom he has decreed death he retains, the others he sends back until a stated term.
Koran, 39, 43

5 As a heavily loaded cart goes creaking, just so this bodily self, mounted by the intelligent Self, goes groaning when one is breathing one's last . . . As noblemen, policemen, chariot-drivers and village-heads gather around a king who is about to depart, just so do all the breaths gather around the soul at the end, when one is breathing one's last.
Brihad-aranyaka Upanishad, 4, 3

6 Put not your trust in life, for at the last death must overtake you; and dog and bird will rend your corpse and your bones will be tumbled on the earth. For three days and nights the soul sits beside the pillow of the body. And on the fourth day at dawn (the soul) . . . (will reach) the lofty and awful Bridge of the Requiter to which every man whose soul is saved and every man whose soul is damned must come.
Menok i Khrat, i, 71–4 (9th century)

7 When the breath has ceased, the vital force will have sunk into the nerve centre of Wisdom, and the Knower will be experiencing the Clear Light of the natural condition. Then the vital force, being thrown backwards and flying downwards through the right and left nerves, the Intermediate State momentarily dawns.
Tibetan Book of the Dead, i (8th century)

8 When Chuang Tzu's wife died, the logician Hui Tzu came to the house to join in the rites of mourning. To his astonishment he found Chuang Tzu sitting with an inverted bowl on his knees, drumming upon it and singing a song. 'After all' said Hui Tzu, 'she lived with you, brought up your children, grew old along with you. That you should not mourn for her is bad enough; but to let your friends find you drumming and singing — that is really going too far!' 'You misjudge me', said Chuang Tzu. 'When she died I was in despair, as any man well might be. But soon, pondering on what had happened, I told myself that in death no strange new fate befalls us . . . She whom I have lost has lain down to sleep for a while in the Great Inner Room. To break in upon her rest with the noise of lamentation would but show that I knew nothing of nature's Sovereign Law.'
Chuang Tzu, XVIII, 2 (3rd century BCE)

9 The state of death is one of two things: either the dead man wholly ceases to be, and loses all sensation; or, according to the common belief, it is a change and a migration of the soul to another place . . . But now the time has come, and we must go hence; I to die, and you to live. Whether life or death is better is known to God, and to God only.
Plato, *Apology*, 40–1

10 To stir a man up to the contempt of death, this is of such power and efficacy that even those who considered pleasure to be happiness and pain misery, nevertheless many of them despised death as much as any. And can death be terrible to him to whom only that seems good, which in the ordinary course of nature is seasonable?
Marcus Aurelius, *Meditations*, 12, 27 (2nd century)

11 So shalt thou feed on Death, that feeds on men,
And Death once dead, there's no more dying then.
William Shakespeare, *Sonnet*, 146

12 Men fear death as children fear to go in the dark;
and as that natural fear in children is increased with
tales, so is the other.
Francis Bacon, *Essays*, 'Of Death' (1625)

13 Any man's *death* diminishes *me*, because I am involved in *Mankind*. And therefore never send to know for whom the *bell* tolls; It tolls for *thee*.
John Donne, *Meditation*, XVII (1624)

14 But the fair guerdon when we hope to find, And think to burst out into sudden blaze, Comes the blind Fury with th'abhorred shears
And slits the thin-spun life.
John Milton, *Lycidas* (1637)

15 Life itself is but the shadow of death, and souls departed but the shadows of the living. All things fall under this name. The sun itself is but the dark *simulacrum*, and light but the shadow of God.
Thomas Browne, *The Garden of Cyrus*, 4 (1658)

16 The grave's a fine and private place, But none I think do there embrace.
Andrew Marvell, *To his Coy Mistress* (1681)

17 Peace, peace! he is not dead, he doth not sleep —
He hath awakened from the dream of life —
'Tis we, who lost in stormy visions, keep With phantoms an unprofitable strife.
Percy Bysshe Shelley, *Adonais*, XXXIX (1821)

18 It hath often been said, that it is not death, but dying, which is terrible.
Henry Fielding, *Amelia* (1751)

19 We dread life's termination as the close, not of enjoyment, but of hope.
William Hazlitt, *The Round Table* (1817)

20 Thou madest man, he knows not why, He thinks he was not made to die; And thou hast made him: thou art just.
Alfred Tennyson, *In Memoriam*, prologue (1850)

21   I love thee with the breath, Smiles, tears, of all my life! — and, if God choose,
I shall but love thee better after death.
E.B. Browning, *Sonnets from the Portuguese*, 43 (1850)

22 Pontifical Death, that doth the crevasse bridge
To the steep and trifid God.
Francis Thompson, *An Anthem of Earth* (1897)

23 And thus for ever with a wider span Humanity o'erarches time and death; Man can elect the universal man, And live in life that ends not with his breath,
And gather glory that increaseth still Till Time his glass with Death's last dust shall fill.
R.W. Dixon, *Humanity* (1864)

24 To die completely, a person must not only forget, but be forgotten, and he who is not forgotten is not dead.
Samuel Butler, *Note-books* (1912)

25 And death shall have no dominion, Dead men naked they shall be one With the man in the wind and the west moon, . . .
Though lovers be lost love shall not; And death shall have no dominion.
Dylan Thomas, *Collected Poems* (1952)

26 Death is the supreme festival on the road to freedom.
Dietrich Bonhoeffer, *Letters and Papers from Prison* (1953)

27 There is no such thing as a natural death; nothing that ever happens to a man is ever natural, since his presence calls the world into question. All men must die: but for every man his death is an accident and, even if he knows it and consents to it, an unjustifiable violation.
Simone de Beauvoir, *A Very Easy Death* (1964)

28 With living creatures, death is the regular, indispensable condition of the replacement of one individual by another along a phyletic stem. Death — the essential lever in the mechanism and upsurge of life.
Teilhard de Chardin, *The Phenomenon of Man* (1955)

29 Man is the only animal that contemplates death, and also the only animal that shows any sign of doubt of its finality.
W.E. Hocking, *The Meaning of Immortality in Human Experience* (1957)

30 Men are convinced of your arguments, your sincerity, and the seriousness of your efforts only by your death.
Albert Camus, *The Fall* (1956)

31 Do not seek death. Death will find you, But seek the road which makes death a fulfilment.
Dag Hammarskjöld, *Markings* (1964)

---

167 JUDGEMENT
See also 49. NEW WORLDS

---

1 For he cometh, for he cometh to judge the earth.
Psalm, 96, 13

2 The time is come that judgment must begin at the house of God: and if it first begin at us, what shall the end be of them that obey not the gospel of God?
1 Peter, 4, 17

3 At the time of a man's departure from the world, all his actions are detailed before him, and he is told, 'So and so have you done in such a place on such a day.' He assents and then is ordered to sign the record, which he does. Not only that, but he admits the justice of the verdict and says, 'Rightly hast thou judged me.'
Mishnah, *Taanith,* 11

4 The heaven shall be rent asunder, for then it will be weak.
The angels will be on its borders, and above them eight shall then bear the throne of thy Lord.
That day ye shall be mustered, not one of you concealed;
As for you who is given his book in his right hand, he will say: 'Here, read my book. Verily I thought I should read my account.'
Koran, 69, 16–19

5 God will stop creatures at the Station, and will settle accounts with the believers.
Al-Ash'ari, *Ibāna,* 30 (10th century)

6 Here (the soul . . . needs submit) to the weighing (of his deeds) by the righteous Rashn who lets the scales of the spiritual gods incline to neither side, neither for the saved nor yet for the damned, nor yet for kings and princes: not so much as a hair's breadth does he allow (the scales) to tip, and he is no respecter (of persons).
Menok i Khrat, 1, 75–7 (6th century)

7 Whether they perform the cremation obsequies in the case of such a person or not, the dead pass over into a flame . . .
Then there is a Person who is non-human. He leads them on to Brahma. This is the way to the gods, the way to Brahma. They who proceed by it return not to the human condition.
Chandogya Upanishad, 4, 15, 5–6

8 You are now before Yama, King of the Dead. In vain will you try to lie, and to deny or conceal the evil deeds you have done. The Judge holds up before you the shining mirror of Karma, wherein all your deeds are reflected.
Tibetan Book of the Dead, III (8th century)

9 At equal distances around sit three other personages, each on a throne. These are the daughters of Necessity, the Fates, Lachesis, Clotho, and Atropos . . . The souls, immediately on their arrival, were required to go to Lachesis. An interpreter first of all marshalled them in order, and took from the lap of Lachesis a number of lots and plans of life.
Plato, *Republic,* X

10 Many cry 'Christ, Christ', who at the judgment shall be far less near to him than he who knows not Christ; and such

Christians the Ethiopian shall condemn.
Dante Alighieri, *Paradiso*, XIX, 106–9
(1320)

11 There is no translating of souls into a new
estate before the great trial of the general
judgement. In the meantime, then, what
hinders them to receive comfort and
refreshment, rest and peace and light?
Herbert Thorndike, *Just Weights and
Measures* (1662)

12 All is, if I have grace to use it so,
As ever in my great task-Master's eye.
John Milton, *Sonnet* (1645)

13 Mine eyes have seen the glory of the coming
of the Lord;
He is trampling out the vintage where the
grapes of wrath are stored.
Julia Ward Howe, *Battle Hymn of the
American Republic* (1861)

14 The Last Judgment when all those are Cast
away who trouble Religion with Questions
concerning Good & Evil or Eating of the
Tree of those Knowledges or Reasonings
which hinder the Vision of God, turning all
into a Consuming Fire.
William Blake, *A Vision of the Last
Judgment* (1810)

15 What we call the beginning is often the end
And to make an end is to make a beginning.
The end is where we start from.
T.S. Eliot, *Little Gidding*, V (1942)

168 PURGATORY
See also 86. PRAYER FOR THE DEAD

1 If I make my bed in Sheol, behold, thou art
there.
Psalm, 139, 8 (RV)

2 He went and preached to the spirits in
prison; which sometime were disobedient.
1 Peter, 3, 19–20

3 'Passing through the valley of weeping', they
are sentenced for a time in Gehinnom; and
Abraham our father comes and takes them
out and receives them.
Mishnah, *Erubin*, 19

4 Until the Resurrection and the Final Body he
must remain in Hell, suffering much
torment and many kinds of chastisement.
Menok i Khrat, i, 121 (6th century)

5 Thou art about to experience its Reality in
the Bardo [intermediate] state, wherein all
things are like the void and cloudless sky,
and the naked, spotless intellect is like unto
a transparent vacuum without
circumference or centre.
Tibetan Book of the Dead (8th century)

6 I will sing of that second realm, where the
human spirit is purged and becomes worthy
to ascend to heaven.
Dante Alighieri, *Purgatorio*, i, 4–6 (1320)

7 The difference between Hell, Purgatory, and
Heaven seems to be the same as that
between despair, almost despair and
confidence . . . Those who assert that a soul
straightway flies out (of purgatory) as a coin
tinkles in the collection-box are preaching
an invention of man.
Martin Luther, *The Ninety-Five Theses*, 16
and 27 (1517)

8 The Romish Doctrine concerning Purgatory,
Pardons, Worshipping and Adoration, as
well of Images as of Reliques, and also
invocation of Saints, is a fond thing, vainly
invented, and grounded upon no warranty
of Scripture, but rather repugnant to the
Word of God.
Book of Common Prayer, Articles of
Religion XXII

9 By 'the Romish Doctrine' is not meant the
Tridentine, because this article was drawn
up before the decree of the Council of Trent.
What is opposed is the *received doctrine* of
the day, and unhappily of this day too, or
the doctrine of the *Roman schools*.
John Henry Newman, *Tract XC*, 6 (1841)

10 The sacred Synod instructs bishops to take
earnest care that the sound doctrine
concerning purgatory handed down by the
holy Fathers and sacred Councils be by
Christ's faithful believed, held, taught, and
everywhere preached.
Council of Trent, Session XXV (1563)

11 Why, Sir, it is a very harmless doctrine. They
are of opinion that the generality of
mankind are neither so obstinately wicked
as to deserve everlasting punishment, nor so
good as to merit being admitted into the
society of blessed spirits; and therefore that
GOD is graciously pleased to allow of a
middle state, where they may be purified by

certain degrees of suffering. You see, Sir, there is nothing unreasonable in this.
Samuel Johnson, in Boswell, *Life of Samuel Johnson* (1769)

169 HEAVEN

1 If I ascend up into heaven, thou art there.
Psalm, 139, 8

2 I heard a great voice out of heaven saying, Behold, the tabernacle of God is with men.
Revelation, 21, 3

3 In the world to come there is no eating or drinking or procreation or trading or jealousy or hatred or competition, but the righteous sit with crowns on their heads, feasting on the radiance of the Shechinah.
Mishnah, *Berachoth*, 17

4 God has promised the believers, male and female, Gardens through which the rivers flow in which to abide, and good dwellings in the Gardens of Eden.
Koran, 9, 73

5 Rābiʾa used to pray: O my Lord, if I worship Thee from fear of Hell, burn me in Hell, and if I worship Thee from hope of Paradise, exclude me thence, but if I worship Thee for Thine own sake then withhold not from me Thine Eternal Beauty.
Margaret Smith, *Rābiʾa the Mystic* (1928)

6 Verily, when a person departs from this world he goes to the wind . . . He goes to the world that is without heat, without cold. Therein he dwells eternal years.
Brihad-aranyaka Upanishad, 5, 12

7 The world called the Happy Land, belonging to the Lord Amitabha, is rich and prosperous, comfortable, fertile, and crowded with many gods and men.
Sukhavati-vyuha, 15 (4th century)

8 Heaven is eternal, the Earth everlasting. How come they to be so?
It is because they do not foster their own lives.
Tao Te Ching, VII

9 Those who have sufficiently purified themselves with philosophy, live thenceforth without bodies, and proceed to dwellings still fairer than these, which are not easily described, and of which I have not time to speak now.
Plato, *Phaedo*, LXII

10 All is heaven there; earth is heaven, and the sea is heaven, and so are animals, plants and men, all heavenly things in that heaven . . . Life is easy yonder, and truth is their parent and nurse, their substance and sustenance. They see all things, not such as are in flux but as have true being, and they see themselves in others.
Plotinus, *Enneads*, 5, 8, 3 (3rd century)

11 O how great and glorious are those sabbaths which the heavenly court for ever celebrates!
Peter Abelard, *Hymnus Paraclitensis* (12th century)

12 Paradise is a safe dwelling-place, the Word a sweet nourishment, eternity abundance without limit.
Bernard of Clairvaux, *Sermons on the Song of Songs*, 33 (12th century)

13 In the heaven which receives most of His light, have I been; and have seen things which whoso descends from there has neither knowledge nor power to recount.
Dante Alighieri, *Paradiso*, I, 4–6 (1320)

14 He's in Arthur's bosom, if ever man went to Arthur's bosom. A' made a finer end, and went away an it had been any christom child . . . and a' babbled of green fields.
William Shakespeare, *Henry V*, II, iii, 9–17 (1599)

15 He did not mind where he eventually died, for he had two favourite quotations, 'The unburied dead are covered by the sky' and 'You can get to heaven from anywhere' — an attitude which, but for the grace of God, might have led to serious trouble.
Thomas More, *Utopia*, i (1516)

16 The city seemed to stand in Eden, or to be built in Heaven. The streets were mine, the temple was mine, the people were mine . . . and all the World was mine; and I the only spectator and enjoyer of it.
Thomas Traherne, *Centuries of Meditations*, 3, 3 (17th century)

17 I give you the end of a golden string, Only wind it into a ball, It will lead you in at Heaven's gate Built in Jerusalem's wall.
William Blake, *Jerusalem*, Plate 77 (1804)

18 We know not when, we know not where,
We know not what that world will be;
But this we know: it will be fair
To see.
Christina Rossetti, *Verses* (1893)

19 Into that gate they shall enter, and in that
house they shall dwell, where there shall be
no Cloud nor Sun, no darkness nor dazzling,
but one equal light, no noise nor silence, but
one equal music, no fears nor hopes, but one
equal possession, no foes nor friends, but
one equal communion and Identity, no ends
nor beginnings, but one equal eternity.
John Donne, *Sermons*, XXVI (1660)

20 My God, I love Thee; not because
I hope for heaven thereby.
Edward Caswall, *Lyra Catholica* (1849)

21 In that prayer which they had straight from
the lips of the Light of the world, and which
He apparently thought sufficient prayer for
them, there is not anything about going to
another world; only something of another
government coming into this; or rather, not
another, but the only government, — that
government which will constitute it a world
indeed. New heavens and new earth.
John Ruskin, *Modern Painters*, IX, xii
(1860)

22 The heaven of faith is not the heaven of the
astronauts, even though the astronauts
themselves expressed it that way when they
recited in outer space the biblical account of
creation. The heaven of faith is the hidden
invisible-incomprehensible sphere of God
which no journey into space ever reaches. It
is not a place, but a mode of being.
Hans Küng, *On Being a Christian* (1974)

---

170 HELL

---

1 Hell from beneath is moved for thee to meet
thee at thy coming: it stirreth up the dead
for thee, even all the chief ones of the earth.
Isaiah, 14, 9

2 I looked, and behold a pale horse: and his
name that sat on him was Death, and Hell
followed with him.
Revelation, 6, 8

3 The King of kings, the Holy One, blessed be
He, Who lives and endures for all eternity,
Who if He be wrathful against me His anger

is eternal, Who if He imprisoned me the
imprisonment would be everlasting.
Mishnah, *Berachoth*, 28

4 Verily Gehenna is the place appointed for
them all. It has seven gates, to each gate a
portion of them is assigned.
Koran, 15, 43–4

5 We hope for the Garden for those guilty of
crimes, while fearing that they will be
punished by the Fire.
Al-Ash'ari, *Ibāna*, 28 (10th century)

6 One day a number of saints saw that Rābi'a
had taken fire in one hand and water in the
other and was running with speed. They
said to her, 'O lady of the next world, where
are you going and what is the meaning of
this?'
She said: I am going to light fire in Paradise
and to pour water on to Hell so that both
veils (i.e. hindrances to the true vision of
God) may completely disappear.
Margaret Smith, *Rābi'a the Mystic* (1928)

7 They will separate the saved from the
damned and carry off the saved to Paradise
and hurl the damned back to Hell; and for
three days and nights these denizens of Hell
will endure punishment in Hell, in their
bodies and in their souls.
Bundahishn (9th century), E.T.D.
Anklesaria (ed.), 220f.

8 This ruins the soul and is the threefold gate
of hell: desire, wrath, and greed.
Bhagavad Gita, 16, 21

9 He who speaks what is not real goes to hell;
he also, who having done a thing says 'I do
not do it.' After death both become equal,
being men with evil deeds in the next
existence.
Dhammapada, 22, 1

10 All who appear to be incurable from the
enormity of their sins — those who have
committed many and great sacrileges, and
foul and lawless murders, or other crimes
like these — are hurled down to Tartarus by
the fate which is their due, whence they
never come forth again.
Plato, *Phaedo*, LXII

11 Woe to you, depraved spirits! Hope not ever
to see Heaven:
I come to lead you to the other shore; into
eternal darkness.
Dante Alighieri, *Inferno*, III, 84–7 (1320)

12 Christ's soul must needs descend into hell,
before it ascended into heaven. So must also
the soul of man.
Theologia Germanica, XI (14th century)

13 They are happy too while they are depicting
everything in hell down to the last detail, as
if they had spent several years there, or
giving free rein to their fancy in fabricating
new spheres.
Desiderius Erasmus, *In Praise of Folly*
(1511)

14 Hell hath no limits, nor is circumscribed,
In one self place, but where we are is hell,
And where hell is, there must we ever be.
Christopher Marlowe, *Doctor Faustus*, 2, 2
(1588)

15 Which way I fly is Hell; my self am Hell;
And in the lowest deep a lower deep
Still threatening to devour me opens wide,
To which the Hell I suffer seems a Heaven.
John Milton, *Paradise Lost*, IV, 75–8
(1667)

16 Hell is a city much like London —
A populous and smoky city.
Percy Bysshe Shelley, *Peter Bell the Third*, 3,
1 (1819)

17 Hell is full of musical amateurs: music is the
brandy of the damned.
George Bernard Shaw, *Man and Superman*,
III (1903)

18 A belief in hell and the knowledge that every
ambition is doomed to frustration at the
hands of a skeleton have never prevented the
majority of human beings from behaving as
though death were no more than an
unfounded rumour, and survival a thing
beyond the bounds of possibility.
Aldous Huxley, *Themes and Variations*
(1950)

19 Hell is neither here nor there
Hell is not anywhere
Hell is hard to bear.
W.H. Auden, *Collected Shorter Poems*,
'Hell' (1930–44)

20 What is hell? Hell is oneself.
Hell is alone, the other figures in it
Merely projections
T.S. Eliot, *The Cocktail Party*, 1, 3 (1949)

21 So that's what Hell is. I'd never have
believed it . . . Do you remember,
brimstone, the stake, the gridiron? . . . What

a joke! No need of a gridiron. Hell, it's other
people.
Jean-Paul Sartre, *Huis Clos*, v (1944)

22 Is it not interesting to see
How the Christians continually
Try to separate themselves in vain
From the doctrine of eternal pain.
Stevie Smith, *Selected Poems* (1962)

23 The doctrine of the Church has traditionally
appeared to be that non-Christians are
going to Hell. Not many modern Christians
really believe this any more, but no clear
alternative has been formulated.
W.C. Smith, *The Christian and the Religions
of Asia* (1959)

171 THE DEAD
See also 86. PRAYER FOR THE DEAD

1 Moses took the bones of Joseph with him:
for he had straitly sworn the children of
Israel, saying, God will surely visit you; and
ye shall carry up my bones away hence with
you.
Exodus, 13, 19

2 Have ye not read in the book of Moses, how
in the bush God spake unto him, saying, I
am the God of Abraham, and the God of
Isaac, and the God of Jacob? He is not the
God of the dead, but the God of the living.
Mark, 12, 26–7

3 As for those who are happy, they are in the
Garden, therein to abide as long as the
heavens and the earth remain.
Koran, 11, 110

4 The ancestors fall degraded when the ritual
offerings of rice and water are interrupted.
Bhagavad Gita, 1, 42

5 The dead is regarded as still living in a sense.
The efforts of the survivors are to provide
him with food and guide his footsteps to the
paramount abode of the dead.
R.B. Pandey, *Hindu Samskāras* (1969)

6 The sweetest of all foods offered by the
spiritual gods to man or woman after the
parting of consciousness and body is always
the butter of early spring.
Menok i Khrat, 99 (6th century)

7 Benefactors on giving a gift assign it to

former ancestors now departed, thinking: 'Let the profit from this accrue to them.'
Milinda's Questions, 294 (1st century)

8 You choose an auspicious day, and having made the prescribed purifications you prepare the sacrifices to be made to your ancestors . . . The spirits of your ancestors are present, and obtain for you many blessings.
Book of Odes, 2, 1, 6 (9th–8th centuries BCE)

9 Tzu-lu asked how one should serve ghosts and spirits.
The Master said, How can there be any proper service of spirits until living men have been properly served?
Tzu-lu then ventured upon a question about the dead [whether they are conscious].
The Master said, Until a man knows about the living, how can he know about the dead?
Confucius, *Analects*, XI, 11

10 The mirror stands first in importance among the regalia, and is revered as the true substance of ancestor-worship. The mirror has brightness as its form: the enlightened mind possesses both compassion and decision. As it also gives a true reflection of the Great Goddess, she must have given her profound care to the mirror.
Records of the Legitimate Succession, 22 (14th century)

11 Japanese Buddhists even nowadays observe strictly the periodical services in memory of the deceased members of the family. This is a family cult and ancestor-worship.
Mahasaru Anesaki, *History of Japanese Religion* (1930)

12 Past Ocean Stream, past the White Rock, past the Gates of the Sun and the region of dreams they went, and before long they reached the meadow of asphodel, which is the dwelling-place of souls, the disembodied wraiths of men.
Homer, *Odyssey*, XXIV

13 I inquired of Africanus whether he himself was still alive, and also whether my father Paulus was, and also the others whom we think of as having ceased to be. 'Of course they are alive', he replied. 'They have taken their flight from the bonds of the body as from a prison.'
Cicero, *On the Republic*, VI, 14 (1st century BCE)

14 O good and innocent dead, hear us; hear us, thou guiding all-knowing ancestors: thou art neither blind nor deaf to this life we live: thou didst thyself once share it.
F.W. Butt-Thompson, *West African Secret Societies* (1929)

15 My spirit grandfathers, today is the Wednesday *Adae*, come and receive this mashed plantain and eat; let this town prosper; and permit the bearers of children to bear children; and may all the people who are in this town get riches.
R.S. Rattray, *Ashanti* (1923)

16 Ancestor-worship is the root of every religion.
Herbert Spencer, *The Principles of Sociology* (1882)

17 It does not seem to have occurred to [Spencer] to ask himself how, if the ideas of soul and ghost arose from such fallacious reasoning about clouds and butterflies and dreams and trances, the beliefs could have persisted throughout millenia and could still be held by millions of civilized people in his day and ours.
E.E. Evans-Pritchard, *Theories of Primitive Religion* (1965)

18 Our ancestors are very good kind of folks; but they are the last people I should choose to have a visiting acquaintance with.
R.B. Sheridan, *The Rivals*, IV, i (1775)

19 People will not look forward to posterity, who never look backward to their ancestors.
Edmund Burke, *Reflections on the Revolution in France* (1790)

20 And 'mid this tumult Kubla heard from far Ancestral voices prophesying war.
S.T. Coleridge, *Kubla Khan* (1816)

21 That friend of mine who lives in God.
Alfred Tennyson, *In Memoriam*, cxxx (1850)

22 The dead are all holy, even they that were base and wicked while alive. Their baseness and wickedness was not they, was but the heavy and unmanageable environment that lay round them.
Thomas Carlyle, *Biography* (1832)

23 The distance that the dead have gone
Does not at first appear —
Their coming back seems possible
For many an ardent year.
Emily Dickinson, *Poems* (1862–86)

24 Do you know why we are more fair and just
toward the dead? . . . We are not obliged to
them, we can take our time, fit in the paying
of respects between a cocktail party and an
affectionate mistress, in our spare time.
Albert Camus, *The Fall* (1956)

---

172 GHOSTS AND APPARITIONS
See also 52. SOUL AND SPIRIT

---

1 Haunted by monstrous apparitions, and
now were paralysed by their soul's
surrendering; for fear sudden and unlooked
for came upon them.
Wisdom, 17, 15

2 They thought it was a ghost, and cried out.
Mark, 6, 49 (RSV)

3 As to ordinary dead people I have been
assured over and over again that the dead
do not walk, and I remember how heartily
my friends in the tribe of Jbel Hbib laughed
when I told them that many Christians
believe in ghosts.
E. Westermarck, *Ritual and Belief in
Morocco* (1926)

4 They who pay their vows to the Fathers go
to the Fathers, and they who offer to the
Ghosts go to the Ghosts.
Bhagavad Gita, 9, 25

5 Being a mighty ghost (in the guise) of a
recluse (belonging to the class of those)
consumed by craving, wandering over the
earth.
Milinda's Questions, 357 (1st century)

6 Of these malevolent ghosts, several different
kinds are recognised. There are those in the
first place who . . . suffer neglect from their
descendants . . . A second class of
discontented ghost may be seen in the . . .
spirits of no affinity . . . Most dangerous of
all, however, are those ghosts whose manner
of death was violent, lonely or untoward.
Carmen Blacker, *The Catalpa Bow* (1975)

7 The widow remains in the hut, armed with a
good stout stick, as a precaution against the
ghost of her husband.
Mary Kingsley, *Travels in West Africa*
(1897)

8 This night my father's ghost, Hath in my
sleep so sore me tormented.
Geoffrey Chaucer, *The Legend of Good
Women*, 'Dido', 1295 (1385)

9 *Ghost*. I am thy father's spirit;
Doom'd for a certain term to walk the night,
And for the day confin'd to fast in fires,
Till the foul crimes done in my days of
                    nature
Are burnt and purg'd away.
William Shakespeare, *Hamlet*, I, v, 9–13
(*c.* 1603)

10 Methought I saw my late espoused Saint
Brought to me like Alcestis from the
                    grave . . .
But O as to embrace me she enclin'd,
I wak'd, she fled, and day brought back my
                    night.
John Milton, *Sonnets* (1645)

11 For love of Admetus, Alcestis took poison
and her ghost descended to Tartarus; but
Persephone considered it an evil thing that a
wife should die instead of a husband. 'Back
with you to the upper air!' she cried.
Robert Graves, *The Greek Myths* (1955)

12 I asked him what he knew of Parson Ford
. . . Was there not a story of his ghost
having appeared?
Johnson. 'Sir, it was believed. A waiter at
the Hummums, in which house Ford died,
had been absent for some time, and
returned, not knowing that Ford was dead.
Going down to the cellar, according to the
story, he met him; going down again he met
him a second time. When he came up, he
asked some of the people of the house what
Ford could be doing there. They told him
Ford was dead.'
Samuel Johnson, in Boswell, *Life of Samuel
Johnson* (1778)

13 I long to talk with some old lover's ghost.
Who died before the god of love was born.
John Donne, *Love's Deity* (1590–1615)

14 What beck'ning ghost, along the moonlight
                    shade
Invites my step, and points to yonder glade?
Alexander Pope, *Elegy to the Memory of an
Unfortunate Lady* (1717)

15 Your ghost will walk, you lover of trees,
(If our loves remain)
In an English lane.
Robert Browning, *De Gustibus* (1842)

16 There's the ghost of a crazy younger son
Who murder'd in Thirteen Fifty-One.
Noel Coward, *The Stately Homes of
England* (1938)

17 We saw the ghost of Captain Webb,
Webb in a water sheeting,
Come dripping along in a bathing dress
to the Saturday evening meeting.
John Betjeman, *A Shropshire Lad* (1940)

18 The ghost of Roger Casement
Is beating on the door.
W.B Yeats, *The Ghost of Roger Casement*
(1939)

19 That she, the said Ghostess, or Ghost, as the
matter may be,
From 'impediment', 'hindrance', and 'let'
shall be free,
To sleep in her grave.
R.H. Barham, *The Ingoldsby Legends*
(1842)

20 Descend, and touch, and enter; hear
The wish too strong for words to name;
That in this blindness of the frame
My Ghost may feel that thine is near.
Alfred Tennyson, *In Memoriam,* xcii (1850)

21 While yet a boy I sought for ghosts, and
sped
Through many a listening chamber, cave
and ruin,
And starlight wood, with fearful steps
pursuing
Hopes of high talk with the departed dead.
Percy Bysshe Shelley, *Hymn to Intellectual
Beauty* (1816)

22 In the Highlands there is an old legend that
at death the souls of fighting men are
gathered up into the air, where for years
they are cast backwards and forwards, over
the hills like migratory birds, unable to gain
peace until they make expiation for their
sins on earth. Sometimes on windy nights
they can be heard fighting high up in the
scudding clouds, and in the morning the
rocks are spotted with blood.
John Hillaby, *Journey through Britain*
(1968)

23 I'm inclined to think we are all ghosts —
every one of us. It's not just what we inherit
from our mothers and fathers that haunts
us. It's all kinds of old defunct theories, all
sorts of old defunct beliefs, and things like
that. It's not that they actually *live* on in us;
they are simply lodged there, and we cannot

get rid of them. I've only to pick up a
newspaper and I seem to see ghosts gliding
between the lines.
Henrik Ibsen, *Ghosts,* 2 (1881)

24 The dogma of the Ghost in the machine . . .
maintains that there exist both bodies and
minds; that there are mechanical causes of
corporeal movements and mental causes of
corporeal movements.
Gilbert Ryle, *The Concept of Mind,* i (1949)

173 LIFE AFTER DEATH AND IMMORTALITY

1 The souls of the righteous are in the hands
of God, and no torment shall touch them. In
the eyes of the foolish they seemed to have
died; and their departure was accounted to
be their hurt, and their journeying away
from us to be their ruin; but they are in
peace.
Wisdom, 3, 1–3

2 That which thou sowest, thou sowest not
that body that shall be, but bare grain, it
may chance of wheat, or of some other
grain: but God giveth it a body as it hath
pleased him, and to every seed his own
body.
1 Corinthians, 15, 37–8

3 On the day when people in general are dead
you will live, and as you are alive this day so
will you all live in the world to come.
Mishnah, *Sanhedrin,* 90

4 God brings forth the living from the dead,
and he brings forth the dead from the living.
He quickens the earth after it is dead, so will
you be caused to come forth.
Koran, 33, 17

5 The wise one is not born or dies,
This one has not come from anywhere, has
not become anyone;
Unborn, constant, eternal, primeval, this
one
Is not slain when the body is slain.

If the slayer think to slay,
If the slain think himself slain,
Both these understand not.
This one slays not, is not slain.
Katha Upanishad, 2, 18–19; **Bhagavad
Gita,** 2, 19–20

6 The Wise Lord, as the Holy Spirit, shall give
us
For Best Mind and deed and word true to
Righteousness,
Through Dominion and Devotion, Salvation
and Immortality.
Gathas, *Yasna*, 47

7 Since a Buddha, even when actually present,
is incomprehensible, it is inept to say of him
— of the Uttermost Person, the Supernal
Person, the Attainer of the Supernal — that
after dying the Buddha is, or is not, or both
is and is not, or neither is nor is not.
Samyutta Nikaya, III, 118 (3rd century BCE)

8 *Socrates*: They say that the soul of man is
immortal, At one time it comes to an end —
that which is called death — and at another
is born again, but is never finally
exterminated. On these grounds a man must
live all his days as righteously as possible.
Plato, *Meno*, 81

9 Should this my firm persuasion of the soul's
Immortality prove to be a mere delusion, it
is at least a pleasing delusion, and I will
cherish it to my latest breath.
Cicero, *De Senectute* (1st century BCE)

10 The human mind cannot be absolutely
destroyed with the body, but there remains
something of it which is eternal.
Baruch Spinoza, *Ethics*, V, 23 (1677)

11   Who would fardels bear,
To grunt and sweat under a weary life,
But that the dread of something after death,
The undiscover'd country from whose
bourn
No traveller returns, puzzles the will,
And makes us rather bear those ills we have,
Than fly to others that we know not of?
William Shakespeare, *Hamlet*, III, i, 76–82
(c. 1603)

12 Death be not proud, though some have
called thee
Mighty and dreadful, for, thou art not so,
For, those, whom thou think'st, thou dost
overthrow,
Die not, poor death, nor yet canst thou kill
me.
John Donne, *Holy Sonnets* (1633)

13 Death cannot kill what never dies. Nor can
Spirits ever be divided that love and live in
the same Divine Principle; the Root and
Record of their Friendship.
If Absence be not Death, neither is it theirs.

Death is but crossing the World, as Friends
do the Seas; they live in one another still.
William Penn, *Some Fruits of Solitude*
(1693)

14 Endless progress is only possible on the
supposition of an *endless* duration of the
existence and personality of the same
rational being (which is called the
immortality of the soul).
Immanuel Kant, *Critique of Practical
Reason*, II, 3 (1788)

15 Hence, in a season of calm weather,
        Though inland far we be,
Our Souls have sight of that immortal sea
        Which brought us hither,
        Can in a moment travel thither.
William Wordsworth, *Intimations of
Immortality* (1807)

16 He has outsoared the shadow of our night;
Envy and calumny and hate and pain,
And that unrest which men miscall delight,
Can touch him not and torture not again.
Percy Bysshe Shelley, *Adonais*, XI (1821)

17 I long to believe in immortality . . . If I am
destined to be happy with you here — how
short is the longest life. I wish to believe in
immortality — I wish to live with you for
ever.
John Keats, letter to Fanny Brawne (1820)

18 Ah Christ, that it were possible
For one short hour to see
The souls we loved, that they might tell us
What and where they be.
Alfred Tennyson, *Maud* (1855)

19 Oh may I join the choir invisible
Of those immortal dead who live again
In minds made better by their presence.
George Eliot, *Poems* (1867)

20 If you were to destroy the belief in
immortality in mankind, not only love but
every living force on which the continuation
of all life in the world depended, would dry
up at once. Moreover, there would be
nothing immoral then, everything would be
permitted.
Fyodor Dostoyevsky, *The Brothers
Karamazov*, I, 2, 6 (1880)

21 Do you believe in a future life? asked Pierre
. . . If I see, and see clearly, the ladder rising
from plant to man, why should I suppose
that it breaks off with me, and does not lead
further and further? I feel not only that I

cannot perish, since nothing in the universe is annihilated, but that I always shall exist and always have existed.
Leo Tolstoy, *War and Peace*, 2, 12 (1869)

22 Men are not morally good if they do their duty only for the sake of future reward; but it is hard to see why they should abandon the hope of immortality if their assumption of human freedom has led them to a belief in the goodness of God.
H.J. Paton, *The Modern Predicament* (1955)

23 It's true that Christianity has always been regarded as a religion of redemption. But isn't this a cardinal error, which separates Christ from the Old Testament and interprets him on the lines of the myths about redemption? . . . The redemption myths try unhistorically to find an eternity after death . . . The difference between the Christian hope of resurrection and the mythological hope is that the former sends a man back to his life on earth in a wholly new way.
Dietrich Bonhoeffer, *Letters and Papers from Prison* (1953)

---

174 REBIRTH, REINCARNATION AND TRANSMIGRATION

---

1 Who did sin, this man, or his parents, that he was born blind?
John, 9, 2

2 The Pharisees (hold that) . . . every soul is imperishable, but only the souls of good men pass into other bodies, the souls of bad men being subjected to eternal punishment.
Josephus, *The Jewish War*, ii, 165 (1st century)

3 I died as mineral and became a plant,
I died as plant and rose as animal,
I died as animal and I was Man . . .
Yet once more I shall die as Man, to soar
With angels blest; but even from angelhood
I must pass on: *all except God doth perish.*
Jalalu'l-Din Rumi, *Mathnawi*, III, 3901 (13th century)

4 Thou shalt change into a living Ba [animation] and surely he will have power to obtain bread and water and air; and thou shalt take shape as a heron or swallow, as a falcon or a bittern, whichever thou pleasest.
Egyptian Cenotaph Text of Seti I, (12th century BCE)

5 Whenever one of those demi-gods, whose lot is long-lasting life, has sinfully defiled his limbs with bloodshed, or following strife has sworn a false oath, thrice ten thousand seasons does he wander far from the blessed, being born throughout that time in the forms of all manner of mortal things.
Empedocles, *Fragments*, 115 (5th century BCE)

6 The soul, since it is immortal and has been born many times, and has seen all things both here and in the other world, has learned everything that is. So we need not be surprised if it can recall the knowledge of virtue or anything else which, as we see, it once possessed.
Plato, *Meno*, 81

7 Souls, peering out of the intelligible realm, descend first into the heavens and there assume body . . . Some pass from the heavens to lower bodies. Others go from one base body into another because they have not the strength to raise themselves up from the earth.
Plotinus, *Enneads*, IV, 3 (3rd century)

8 Those who are of pleasant conduct here — the prospect is, indeed, that they will enter a pleasant womb, either the womb of a priest's wife, or the womb of a noble's, or the womb of a merchant's. But those who are of stinking conduct here — the prospect is, indeed, that they will enter a stinking womb, either the womb of a bitch, or the womb of a sow, or the womb of an outcast's woman.
Chandogya Upanishad, 5, 10, 7

9 Many births have passed for Me, and for thee. I know them all; but thou knowest not.
Bhagavad Gita, 4, 5

10 Having obtained a human birth, if you miss your chance.
You'll fall back into the whirlpool of Existence, to receive blow after blow.
Sākhi, 15, 6 in Charlotte Vaudeville, *Kabir* (1974)

11 I have run through a course of many births looking for the maker of this dwelling and

not finding him; birth again and again is
painful.
Dhammapada, 153

12 The king asked: 'When someone is reborn,
is he the same as the one who has just died,
or is he another?'
The Elder replied: 'He is neither the same
nor another.'
— 'Give me an illustration.'
'What do you think, great king; when you
were a tiny infant, newly born and quite
soft, were you then the same as the one who
is now grown up?'
— 'No, that infant was one, I now grown up
am another.'
— 'If that is so then, great king, you have
had no mother, no father, no teaching, and
no schooling! . . . We must understand it as
the collocation of a series of successive
conditions. At rebirth one condition arises,
while another stops.'
Milinda's Questions, 40 (1st century)

13 The saint who has crossed the stream of
transmigration, doing away with all
hesitation, knowing all things but himself
unknown, leaves his frail body. Overcoming
manifold hardships and troubles, with trust
in his religion he performs this terrible
penance. Thus in due time he puts an end to
his existence.
Acharanga Sutra, 1, 7, 6 (3rd century BCE)

14 *Clown*: What is the opinion of Pythagoras
concerning wild fowl?
Malvolio: That the soul of our grandam
might haply inhabit a bird.
Clown: What thinkest thou of his opinion?
Malvolio: I think nobly of the soul, and no
way approve his opinion.
William Shakespeare, *Twelfth Night*, IV, ii,
48–54 (1601)

15 Our birth is but a sleep and a forgetting;
The Soul that rises with us, our life's Star,
Hath had elsewhere its setting.
And cometh from afar.
William Wordsworth, *Ode, Intimations of
Immortality* (1807)

16 He is made one with Nature: there is heard
His voice in all her music, from the moan
Of thunder, to the song of night's sweet
bird.
Percy Bysshe Shelley, *Adonais*, XLII (1821)

17 I believe the souls of the dead in some way
re-enter and pervade the souls of the living;

so that life is always the life of living
creatures, and death is always our affair.
D.H. Lawrence, *Fantasia of the Unconscious*
(1923)

18 According to the Eastern view, karma
implies a sort of psychic theory of heredity
based on the hypothesis of reincarnation,
which in the last resort is an hypothesis of
the supratemporality of the soul. Neither
our scientific knowledge nor our reason can
keep in step with this idea. There are too
many if's and but's.
C.G. Jung, *Psychology and Religion* (1958)

---

175 RESURRECTION

---

1 Many of them that sleep in the dust of the
earth shall awake, some to everlasting life,
and some to shame and everlasting
contempt.
Daniel, 12, 2

2 So also is the resurrection of the dead. It is
sown in corruption; it is raised in
incorruption . . . It is sown a natural body;
it is raised a spiritual body.
1 Corinthians, 15, 42–4

3 Queen Cleopatra asked Rabbi Meir, 'I know
that the dead will revive, for it is written,
"They of the city shall flourish like grass of
the earth." But when they arise will they
stand up naked or clothed?' He replied, 'An
argument may be based on the analogy of
wheat: As wheat is buried in the soil naked
and comes forth with various garbs, how
much more so with the righteous who are
buried in their garments.'
Mishnah, *Sanhedrin*, 90

4 There will be a blast upon the trumpet, and
there they will be sliding down from their
tombs to their Lord. They say: 'Alas for us!
Who has raised us up from our
resting-place?' This is what the Merciful
promised and the Envoys spoke truly.
Koran, 36, 51–2

5 We hold that God will come on the Day of
the Resurrection, as he said: 'And thy Lord
will come, and the angels, rank on rank.'
Al-Ash'ari, *Ibāna*, 39 (10th century)

6 All men will be resurrected, both those who
were saved and those who were damned.

And each man will arise in the place where his spirit left him or where he first fell to the ground.
Bundahishn (9th century) E.T.D. Anklesaria (ed.)

7 So Lycidas sunk low, but mounted high,
Through the dear might of Him that walked
the waves.
John Milton, *Lycidas* (1637)

8 The soul of Adonais, like a star,
Beacons from the abode where the Eternal
are.
Percy Bysshe Shelley, *Adonais,* LV (1821)

9 With some gleams, it is true, of more than mock solace, *Adonais* is lighted; but they are obtained by implicitly assuming the personal immortality which the poem explicitly denies . . . The soul of Adonais? —
Adonais, who is but
A portion of that loveliness
Which once he made more lovely.
Francis Thompson, *Shelley* (1893)

10 His books arranged three by three kept watch like angels with outspread wings and seemed, for him who was no more, the symbol of his resurrection.
Marcel Proust, *La Prisonnière,* i, 1 (1923)

11 Faith in the resurrection is really the same as faith in the saving efficacy of the cross.
Rudolf Bultmann, *Kerygma and Myth* (1961)

12 It is only when one loves life and the earth so much that one may believe in the resurrection and a new world.
Dietrich Bonhoeffer, *Letters and Papers from Prison* (1953)

---

176 NIRVANA, NEGATION

1 I sought after the consummate peace of Nirvana, which knows neither sorrow nor decay, neither disease nor death, neither sorrow nor impurity: — this I pursued and this I won; and there arose within me the conviction, the insight, that now my deliverance was assured, that this was my last birth, nor should I ever be reborn again.
Majjhima Nikaya, 26 (3rd century BCE)

2 Now are you seen, O builder of the house, you will not build the house again. All your rafters are broken, your ridge-pole is destroyed, your mind, set on the attainment of Nirvana, has attained the extinction of desires.
Dhammapada, 154

3 It is called Nirvana, because of the getting rid of craving . . . The stopping of becoming is Nirvana.
Samyutta Nikaya, 1, 39; 2, 117 (3rd century BCE)

4 Thou dost not vanish in Nirvana, nor is Nirvana abiding in thee; for it transcends the duality of knowing and known, and of being and non-being.
Lankavatara Sutra, 23 (3rd–5th centuries)

5 Nirvana is absolute ease, and nevertheless one cannot point to its form or shape, its duration or size, either by simile or explanation, by reason or by argument . . . As a mountain peak is unshakable, so is Nirvana. As a mountain peak is inaccessible, so is Nirvana inaccessible to the passions.
Milinda's Questions, 322 (1st century)

6 Avalokita, the Holy Lord and Bodhisattva, was moving in the deep course of the Wisdom that has gone beyond. He looked down from on high, he beheld but five heaps, and he saw that in their own-being they were empty.
Heart Sutra, II (4th century)

7 Gone, gone, gone beyond, gone altogether beyond, O what an awakening, all-hail!
Heart Sutra, VIII (4th century)

8 All worldly ideas are stopped without exception in emptiness, where there is a vision of the emptiness of the own-being of all existents.
Prasannapada, 18 (7th century)

9 Because there is an unborn, not become, not made, uncompounded, therefore an escape can be shown for what is born, has become, is made, is compounded.
Udana, 81 (3rd century BCE)

10 To enter Nirvana is to become one's self, to become what one really is. It is to behold the Self in all things and all things in the Self. In this sense Nirvana is the most personal of all experiences. That is why at the heart of Buddhism, in spite of its negative doctrine,

there is found a person of infinite compassion, the person of the Buddha.
Bede Griffiths, *Return to the Centre* (1976)

11 Thus ever disciplining himself, the man of Yoga, with controlled mind, attains to peace that culminates in Nirvana and rests in Me.
Bhagavad Gita, 6, 15

12 Push far enough towards the Void,
Hold fast to Quietness,
And of the ten thousand things none but can
        be worked on by you.
Tao Te Ching, XVI

13 When a hundred thousand generations had passed, the mortal birds surrendered themselves spontaneously to total annihilation. No man, neither young nor old, can speak fittingly of death or immortality.
Attar, *The Conference of the Birds* (12th century)

14 I became a bird whose body was of oneness, and whose wings were of everlastingness. I flew continuously in an atmosphere of relativity. When I had vanished from created things, I said: 'I have reached the Creator.'
Abu Yazid, *Miraj* (9th century)

15 You exist only in the existence of God because you have been obliterated. Your physical being continues but your individuality has departed.
Al-Junayd, *Risala* (9th century)

16 I play the tune of negation: when you die death will disclose the mystery.
Jalalu'l-Din Rumi, *Mathnawi*, VI, 703 (13th century)

17 The soul lays hold of the Godhead where it is pure, where there is nothing beside it, nothing else to consider. The One is a negation of negations.
Meister Eckhart,, *Fragments* (13th–14th centuries)

18 This nothingness, and this acknowledged abasement, is the means by which the Lord works wonders in the soul. Clothe thyself with this Nothingness.
Miguel de Molinos, *The Spiritual Guide*, III, 20 (17th century)

19 The mystics heap up terms of negation — darkness, void, nothingness — in endeavouring to describe the Absolute which they have apprehended. It may be, of course, that their apprehension had such a fullness and richness of content that in human language it could only be described negatively.
Cuthbert Butler, *Western Mysticism* (1923)

20 If one waits in emptiness one comes to realize that the void is God: it is not a preparatory stage but the experience of God Himself.
William Johnston, *The Inner Eye of Love* (1978)

21 The Dew is on the lotus! — Rise, Great Sun!
And lift my leaf, and mix me with the wave.
OM MANI PADME HUM, the Sunrise
        comes!
The Dewdrop slips into the shining Sea.
Edwin Arnold, *The Light of Asia* (1879)

22 That which is not is that which is actual only in the negativity allotted to it by the divine decision, only in its exclusion from creation, only, if we may put it thus, at the left hand of God.
Karl Barth, *Church Dogmatics*, III, iii (1936)

23 There is a logical paradox even in saying that one knows that there exists something about which no one can know anything . . . The logical difficulty was that one was saying important things about the unsayable. The epistemological difficulty is that there is no way of being sure that an object of experience has the qualities one thinks it to have.
Keith Ward, *Images of Eternity* (1987)

---

177 ETERNITY

---

1 The sand of the seas, and the drops of rain, and the days of eternity, who shall number?
Ecclesiasticus, 1, 2

2 This is life eternal, that they might know thee the only true God, and Jesus Christ, whom thou hast sent.
John, 17, 3

3 The Garden of Eternity, which is promised to those who show piety.
Koran, 25, 16

4 Unborn, eternal, everlasting, this ancient
        one
Is not slain when the body is slain.
Bhagavad Gita, 2, 20

5 Eternity may be properly denominated a
God unfolding himself into light, and
shining forth, such as he essentially is,
namely, as immutable and the same.
Plotinus, *Enneads*, III, vii (3rd century)

6 I saw Eternity the other night,
Like a great ring of pure and endless light,
    All calm, as it was bright;
And round beneath it, Time in hours, days,
    years,
        Driv'n by the spheres
Like a vast shadow mov'd; in which the
    world
        And all her train were hurl'd.
Henry Vaughan, *Silex Scintillans*, 'The
World' (1650)

7 But at my back I always hear
Time's winged chariot hurrying near,
And yonder all before us lie
Deserts of vast eternity.
Andrew Marvell, *To his Coy Mistress*
(1681)

8 But souls that of His own good life partake
He loves as His own self: dear as His eye
They are to Him; He'll never them forsake:
When they shall die, then God Himself shall
    die:
They live, they live in blest eternity.
Henry More, *Philosophical Poems* (1647)

9 All things abided eternally in their proper
places as they were. Eternity was manifest in
the Light of the Day, and something infinite
behind everything appeared.
Thomas Traherne, *Centuries of
Meditations*, 3, 3 (17th century)

10 To see a World in a Grain of Sand,
And a Heaven in a Wild Flower,
Hold Infinity in the palm of your hand,
And Eternity in an hour.
William Blake, *Auguries of Innocence*, 1
(1803)

11 Through all Eternity to Thee
A joyful Song I'll raise,
For oh! Eternity's too short
To utter all thy Praise.
Joseph Addison, *The Spectator*
(1712)

12 Yet ever and anon a trumpet sounds
From the hid battlements of Eternity.
Francis Thompson, *The Hound of Heaven*
(1893)

13 God will not be alone in eternity, but with
the creature. He will allow it to partake of
His own eternal life. And in this way the
creature will continue to be, in its limitation.
Karl Barth, *Church Dogmatics*, III, iii
(1936)

14 The unfettered clouds and region of the
    Heavens,
Tumult and peace, the darkness and the
    light —
Were all like workings of one mind, the
    features
Of the same face, blossoms upon one tree:
Characters of the great Apocalypse,
The types and symbols of Eternity,
Of first, and last, and midst, and without
    end.
William Wordsworth, *The Prelude*, 6,
634–40

TEXT AND AUTHOR INDEX

Numbers refer to sections and items

SUBJECT INDEX

The subject index provides keywords, both to help in
finding quotations and to supplement the topic
headings that appear in the list of contents. The
order is alphabetical, singular and plural nouns being
grouped separately. Definite and indefinite articles
are omitted from most entries. The numbers
following each entry refer to the section number
and item.

voice: v. within you 126,21;
  indignation is v. of God 83,18
Void: V. came into being 43,9; push
  towards V. 176,12
votive: v. offerings on walls 63,15
Vows: Four Great V. 112,7

wager: Pascal's w. 111,20
wages: w. which God gets 160,20
wanted: w. like a God 32,11
war 155,1–25: w. emblem of misery
  155,23; w. has laws 155,17; w.
  inside ourselves 155,24; w. in
  your members 155,2; w. is
  pursuit of wealth 155,12; abhor
  w. and fighting 155,14; art of w.
  155,13; conditions for just w.
  155,15; god of w. 155,21; learn
  w. no more 155,1; manslaughter
  in w. 154,8; 155,18; voluntary
  w. 155,3
warn: rise and w. 66,3
wars: serve in w. 155,16
was: w.I, w. I not 110,5
water: make use of w. 47,12
waves: walked the w. 175,7
way: w. like empty vessel 123,9; w.
  to hell 123,16; w. to perfection
  123,17; w. out or w. in 135,11;
  any of this w. 123,2; Middle W.
  123,5; Great W. practised
  123,8; pursuit of w. 123,6; set
  heart on w. 123,7; system of w.
  123,10; undefiled in w. 123,1;
ways: w. of God to man 41,12; God
  proved in five w. 111,10
wealth: w. belongs to me 158,6;
  contribute w. 158,3; depend on
  w. 158,5; desire of w. 158,17;
  excessive w. 158,18; idea of w.
  158,20; not seek w. 158,4;
  superfluous w. 158,11
wealthy: only truly w. 121,7; 58,7
weapons: fine w. ill-omened 155,10
whisky: w. bottle by roadside 3,8
white: whiteness most w. 136,8
whore: large sums to w. 149,9
wicked: all world equally w. 129,16;
  never wonder to see w. 129,15
widow: care for w. 140,9; if w. have
  children 140,2; oppress not w.
  140,6; some undone w. 140,7;
  w.'s heart sings 140,1
widows: w. abide even as I 150,2; w.
  faithful to lords 140,5; visit the
  w. 1,1
wife: w. cannot leave husband
  145,7; w. no power over body
  146,2; cleave to w. 143,1;
  husband of one w. 144,2; liaison
  with another's w. 148,6; love his
  w. 143,19; not w. but 'home'
  143,3; please his w. 143,2; put
  away w. 145,2; take no w. 150,1
will: act against your w. 109,6
willed: had God so w. 95,3
wine: w. and wicked practices 133,7;

w. a mocker 133,1; doesn't get
  into w. 133,13; drink no w.
  67,1; not drink w. 133,8; too
  little w. 133,10; use a little w.
  133,2
wisdom: w. care so little 108,14; w.
  chief mental state 105,5; w. from
  instruction 104,8; w. in theory
  123,4; w. of God 37,2; w.
  requires no form 37,17; banish
  w. 62,10; eternal w. 37,10;
  115,9; good religion innate w.
  1,4; highest w. 37,13; much w.,
  much grief 110,1; Perfection of
  W. 22,8; teach book and w.
  37,14; 104,4; secularisation of
  w. 115,11; Spirit of w. 112,1;
  supreme w. 37,12; understand
  w. 105,1; where shall w. be
  found? 104,1
witch: w. animals of Japan 13,19; w.
  doctors were bribed 13,22; w.
  laws beguiled world 13,14; w.
  no real existence 13,21; w.
  performs no rite 13,18; w. still
  lived at Endor 13,5; condemned
  w. to die 13,15; first w. 13,9;
  not suffer w. to live 13,1; spirit
  of w. leaves body 13,20
witchcraft: w. and sorcery 13,21; w.
  not any real power 13,11;
  aggression of w. beliefs 13,23;
  idolatry, w., hatred 13,2; name
  of w. 13,12; possibility of w. 13,13
witches: w. deny baptism 13,8; if a
  man meets w. 13,3; medieval w.
  13,16
wives: w. common to all 143,7; w. of
  equal caste 143,5; w. turned
  away heart 144,1; have w. as
  though none 147,2; marry as
  many w. 144,3; system of w. in
  common 143,8
woe: feel another's w. 118,16
woman: w. dish for gods 142,12; w.
  God's second blunder 142,13;
  w. like snake 142,9; w. who
  pollutes damsel 151,4; dignity of
  w. 146,18; in every w.'s heart
  142,16; nakedness of w. 142,14;
  not made me w. 141,3; that w.
  thou 146,4; virtuous w. 142,1
womankind: in regard to w. 142,7
womb: enter pleasant w. 174,8
women: w., artisans and serfs 162,5;
  w. as furrows 146,3; w. full of
  deceit 142,8; w. to share labours
  142,11; blessed among w.
  142,2; gossip with w. 148,3;
  indecent w. 151,3; men and w.
  on equality 142,3; no talk with
  w. 150,6; self-surrendering w.
  142,4
wonder: full mind with w. 111,17;
  philosophy because of w.
  104,11; 104,26; w. God has
  wrought 78,13

wonders: w. between heaven and
  earth 83,4
word: w. made flesh 30,1; w. united
  to flesh 30,11; good w. like good
  tree 102,4
work: cunning w. 116,1; our daily w.
  49,12
world: w. a vestibule 49,3; w. is not
  Divinity 45,7; w. of faults
  158,13; w. to come 49,3; w. too
  much with us 160,14; w.
  without heat 169,6; w. without
  truth 15,4; 95,8; Berkeley
  destroyed w. 45,29; enjoy w.
  aright 45,17; happy w. after all
  45,24; love not w. 89,2; who
  made w. 44,16; wicked w. 45,37
worlds: he wanted w. 32,11
worse: it might be w. 108,8
worship: 73,1-24; w. Father in spirit
  73,2; w. God who knows 73,12;
  w. of darkness 53,7; 74,5; w. of
  New Testament 73,14; w. not
  rule of safety 73,23; w.
  transcendent wonder 73,19;
  come let us w. 73,1; freedom of
  w. 73,24; indifferent in w.
  73,16; manner of w. 73,17;
  place of w. on piety 73,4; public
  w. better 73,5; recipient of w.
  73,8; requirement of w. 73,6;
  supposed to be w. 73,22; world
  based on w. 73,3
worshipper: w. offers water 73,9
worshipping: no time to waste in w.
  142,6; w. with single flower
  73,10
worth: w. more than I was 158,15
wraith: disembodied w. 171,12
wrath: w. eternal 170,3; w. of lion
  37,16; grapes of w. 167,13
written: what God has w. 42,3
wrong: not repay w. with w. 124,7

Yahweh: Y. could teach him 36,9
Yang: Y. union with Yin 45,10;
  blending of Yin and Y. 146,7;
  essences of Yin and Y. 7,8;
  Ultimate generates Y. 7,9; Yin
  can diminish Y. 147,5
yoga: 88,1-9; y. is eternal 4,6; y. of
  action 127,4; consider as Y.
  88,1; eight parts of y. 88,2;
  112,5; goal of Christian y. 88,8;
  parts of y. practice 88,7; practise
  y. to purify 88,4
yogi: y. higher than ascetics 59,9

Zarathustra: best possession of Z.
  4,5
zeal: bigot z. 96,18; proselytizing z.
  98,22
Zen: Z. masters of one type 70,10;
  Z. mysticism? 78,15; Koan or Z.
  problem 88,5; Sermon compared
  to Z. 88,9
Zion: come to Z. 101,1